The Mead Hall
The Feasting Tradition in Anglo-Saxon England

Stephen Pollington

Anglo-Saxon Books

BY THE SAME AUTHOR

Wordcraft
First Steps in Old English
An Introduction to the Old English Language & its Literature
Rudiments of Runelore
The English Warrior
The Warrior's Way
Leechcraft

Published 2003 by
Anglo-Saxon Books
Frithgarth
Thetford Forest Park
Hockwold-cum-Wilton
Norfolk   England

© Copyright Stephen Pollington

Illustrations by Lindsay Kerr
© Copyright Anglo-Saxon Books

All rights reserved. No part of this publication may be reproduced or transmitted in any form or by any means, electronic or mechanical including photo-copying, recording, or any information storage or retrieval system, without prior permission in writing from the publisher, except for the quotation of brief passages in connection with a review written for inclusion in a magazine or newspaper.

This book may not be lent, resold, hired out or otherwise disposed of by way of trade in any form of binding or cover other than that in which it is published, without the prior consent of the publishers.

British Library Cataloguing-in-Publication Data. A catalogue record for this book is available from the British Library.

ISBN 1–898281–30–0

Contents

FOREWORD 9

ABBREVIATIONS & GLOSSARY 12
   Notes on conventions. 14

INTRODUCTION 15

1 FEASTING AND SOCIETY 19
   A Window on Early English Society 19
   Feasting in the Hall 31
   Meals and Mealtimes 36
   Symbel 38
   Organisation of the Symbel 42
   Ritual Background To The Symbel 47
      The Lord As Ring-Giver 51
   Oaths And Boasts 54
   Gebeorscipe 55
   Feasts, Marriages and Alliances 60

2 LIVING SPACE: THE HALL IN REALITY 65
   The Hall and its Settlement 65
   Construction & Layout 68
   Building Techniques 71
   Measuring and Laying-Out 73
   Woodworking techniques 75
   Hearth 78
   Seating 80
   Chairs & Stools 80
   Frithstool 81
   Gift-Stool (Giefstol) 81
   Mead-benches 84
   Boards & Tables 85
   Flooring 86
   Hall Development in Anglo-Saxon England 88
      Early -Saxon Period – 5th to 7th centuries 88
      Mid-Saxon Period - 8th & 9th centuries 93
      Lare-Saxon Period – 10th & 11th centuries 95
      The British tradition 97

3 RITUAL SPACE: THE HALL IN IDEOLOGY 99
    The Hall as the Ideal Dwelling 99
    Heorot 101
    Mead-hall and Men's Hall 105
    The Hall as 'Central Place' 111
    The Hall Of Dreams 114
    The Joys Of The Hall 116

4 FOOD AND FEASTING EQUIPMENT 119
    Consumables 121
    Food 123
    Drink 128
    Tableware 130
    Wood 130
    Horn 131
    Metal 132
    Ceramic 133
    Glass 134
    Bone, Ivory and Antler 137
    Leather 138
    Cutlery 139
    Plates, Bowls & Dishes 141
        Dishes 141
        Bowls 141
    Drinking Vessels 143
        Cups & Bottles 143
        Drinking Horns 146
    Buckets & Tubs 151
    Strainers 154
    Clawbeakers 157
    Conebeakers 161
    Cauldrons & Hanging Bowls 162
        Hanging Bowls 162
        Cauldrons 166
    Textiles & Clothing 167
        Textiles 167
    Clothing 171
    Female Dress 174
    Male Dress 175
    Table Linen, Tapestry & Embroidery 176

5 POSITIONS OF POWER ... 181

Lord (Hlaford) ... 182
Lady (Hlafdige) ... 183
Household (Hlafætan) ... 187
Þyle ... 188
Flyting and Verbal Duelling ... 188
Unferþ and The Role of the Þyle ... 189
Poet (Scop) ... 190
Hall Attendants ... 195
- *Meteðegn* ... 195
- *Discþegn* ... 196
- *Byrele* ... 196
- *Burþegn* ... 197
- Doorkeeper (*Duruþegn*) ... 198

6 ENTERTAINMENT ... 199

Storytelling & Poetry ... 199
Music ... 202
Harp or Lyre ... 204
Riddles ... 208
- *Riddle 45* ... 214
- *Riddle 33* ... 214
- *Riddle 23* ... 215
Board games ... 215

APPENDICES ... 221

1 Hall- and Feasting-Themes in Old English Verse ... 221
2 Some Old English Sources ... 226
- *The Poet Cædmon* ... 226
- *From the Old English version of* ... 226
- Bede's *Historia Ecclesiastica Gentis Anglorum* ... 226
- *Beowulf (extract) - Heorot's Feasting* ... 232
- *Beowulf (extract) – Unferþ's Flyting* ... 234
- *The Fortunes Of Men (extracts)* ... 240
- *The Seafarer (extract)* ... 240
- *Vainglory (extract)* ... 240
- *The Battle of Maldon (Extract)* ... 242
- *The Wanderer* ... 244
- *Widsiþ* ... 250

3 The Structure and Origins of the Warband ... 259

BIBLIOGRAPHY ... 267

List of Illustrations   Drawings by Lindsay Kerr

page

38 *1* Spoon carved from a single piece of bone, decorated with ribbing on the shaft and animal head detail where the shaft joins the bowl. A leaf-shaped finial completes the piece. 8th-9th century.

40 *2* Harold and his men dine in his residence at Bosham, Sussex. The fellow on the right is draining his drinking horn, while talking to the man to his left. Harold is the central figure with the palm-cup. The drinker on the right, and the man ascending the steps are pointing to Harold's ship (in the next scene) which is prepared for sailing. . The house is clearly meant to be two-storeyed, with the dining area on the upper floor. Redrawn scene from the Bayeux Tapestry.

49 *3* Drinking horn from Sutton Hoo, Mound 1 One of a pair of magnificent feasting vessels, made from the horns of an aurochs.

58 *4* Feasting scene. The lack of drinking horns among these Norman diners is noticeable, as is the rather aggressive posture of the bearded figure on the left who is crowding out his neighbour. Redrawn scene from the Bayeux Tapestry.

64 *5* Fragment of a silver spoon with waisting on the shaft and opposed animal heads on the finial. Found at Desborough, Northamptonshire. Possibly early 7th century.

67 *6* Schematic plan of an Anglo-Saxon hall. S. Pollington

78 *7* Wooden 'bottle' or serving vessel from Sutton Hoo, Mound 1. The bottle was turned on a pole-lathe from a block of dried timber.

107 *8* The traditional Germanic military structure. S. Pollington

109 *9* The Germanic military structure with Warbands. S. Pollington

125 *10* Preparing food in the open air. To the left a cauldron is boiling over an open fire, attended by two servants who have impaled some pieces of food on spikes. Centre, a bearded cook uses a "meat-hook" to take what appears to be bread from an oven and place it on a platter. Right, a table-servant takes the spitted meat to the table. Redrawn scene from the Bayeux Tapestry.

131 *11* Two vessels from the ship burial at Sutton Hoo, Mound 1. They are of burrwood, with decorative mounts. The grave contained matched sets of cups, one with silver fluted collars, the other with silver-gilt cast panels.

135 *12* Ceramic bottle from Winchester, Hampshire. Vessels of this type are known as 'Winchester ware'. The simulated stitching and semi-circular extensions at the shoulders replicate the appearance of a leather flask. 10th century.

List of Illustrations

139   *13* A double-ended spoon and combined spoon-and-fork from Sevington, Lincolnshire. An elegant solution to the problem of dealing with solid and liquid foods with one utensil. The decoration is very lightly incised. Late 9th century.

145   *14* A bronze Coptic bowl excavated from a grave at Chilton Hall, Sudbury, Suffolk. Height: 11.5cm, diameter: 34.5cm.

145   *15* The remarkable bronze Coptic bowl with its pedestal, from the burial mound at Taplow, Buckinghamshire. It is unusual in having twelve knobs or lugs around the rim, and a large pair of drop-handles. The base was packed with a lead alloy to maintain a low centre of gravity, since otherwise it would have been unstable when filled with drink. Height: 20.5cm, diameter 40.6cm.

155   *16* Three richly decorated strainers from pagan period graves at Bifrons, Kent. Redrawn by Lindsay Kerr, after C. Praetorius.

157   *17* Three strainers from pagan period graves at Bifrons, Kent. Redrawn by Lindsay Kerr, after C. Praetorius.

158   *18* Clawbeaker from Taplow, Berkshire. The extruded claws with their shaped decorative trails make these vessels very distinctive. Early 7th century.

163   *19* Conebeaker from Kempston, Bedforshire. The clean lines and gentle twist of the barrelling are typical of this kind of glassware. 6th century.

165   *20* Hanging bowl from the 6th century cremation cemetery at Sutton Hoo. Inset: detail of the enamelled escutcheon on the rim, with typical La Tene style ornament, and suspension ring. The vessel had been repaired before use as the container for the cremation.

169   *21 Tabby* and *Twill* weave patterns. S.Pollington

177   *22* Norman servants preparing a meal and serving it on a makeshift sideboard formed from shields. The Normans have just landed at Pevensey Bay, Sussex, and their cooks have prepared a meal. The servant, left, is carrying a spitted fowl to a trestle. The man second from right is summoning the diners with his horn. Scene from the Bayeux Tapestry, redrawn by Lindsay Kerr.

203   *23* Lyre From Bergh Apton, Norfolk. A less regal instrument than that from Sutton Hoo, it is one of only four found in England. It is likely that an instrument such as this would have been familiar to most *scopas* working in the English verse tradition.

205   *24* Lyre from Sutton Hoo, Mound 1. The inclusion of the lyre in its pouch at the head end of the funerary chamber, along with the whetstone, iron stand and gaming equipment, suggests that music and song were important accomplishments for the king.

Foreword

In the house where I grew up, the part we called 'the hall' was nothing more than a corridor running between the doorways into the various rooms. Yet 'a hall' was understood to be a large and rather grand dwelling, or a building used for meetings (the village hall, the town hall, the Salvation Army hall). The story of the hall is the story of the English house: originally a large, freestanding structure, it was surrounded by outbuildings in which various activities took place - cooking, washing, working, dining; these eventually became rooms under the same roof, and the hall itself dwindled to a central space affording access to the other areas. The journey from 'important building' to 'passageway' is a complex one; the fact that the older meaning still exists alongside the humbler modern one means that the original idea has not quite been lost.

Indeed, the idea of the "hall" has been revived. One of the most memorable and dramatic scenes in Tolkien's *Lord of the Rings* takes place in the great hall *Meduseld* where King Theoden of the Mark holds court. Tolkien, being nothing if not an enthusiast for the culture and traditions of the Anglo-Saxons and their relatives, chose the name well: *Meduseld* is an Old English term meaning "mead-hall" and this word was one of the most emotionally charged items in their vocabulary.

In this study, we will be looking at the subject of halls and feasting in Anglo-Saxon England and neighbouring territories from a variety of angles. The idea of the communal meal was very important in the period, among nobles and yeomen, churchmen and laity, warriors and farmers. One of the aims of the book is to demonstrate that there is not just one 'feast' but several, divisible into two main types: the informal social gathering (*gebeorscipe*) and the formal, ritual occasion (*symbel*). Almost all the evidence we have for 'feasts' falls into one of these two groups.

Some of the most important evidence comes from Old English verse. There are about 30,000 lines of poetry from before the Norman invasion, surviving in five main manuscripts and more than a hundred separate works. With a handful of exceptions, almost *every one* of these poems refers in some way to the hall- and feast-centred social life of the Anglo-Saxon period. The notions of 'hall' and 'communal meal' were a major part of the ideology and social structure even when the entities themselves (the hall as a building, the feast as an event) had lost their original importance and purpose. Old English verse was intended for recitation in the hall - at the feast and the gift-giving – and that element of its background continued with it throughout its history. The death of the early

Foreword

English verse tradition came about only with the replacement of the communal hall as the central structure of society.

I have tried to include as wide a range of evidence as I could find for aspects of the 'feast' or social gathering for the consumption of a communal meal and drink. In this book, we will look at the 'consumables': the range of food and drink available to the Anglo-Saxons, how they produced, cooked and served it. We will also look at the 'hardware' of feasting: the buildings where it took place; the tableware, cutlery, cooking and serving vessels; the furniture and surroundings. We will look at the feast as an event - a social ritual with fixed roles filled by members of a social group. We will also review the other activities which took place in the hall – pastimes and entertainments.

The mead-hall held a place in Anglo-Saxon culture which has no exact counterpart in ours; it was a theatre, a church, a court, a town-hall, a community centre and a pub.

Much has been written about the role of kings, warriors, clergymen and how these groups overlap and interact in Anglo-Saxon times. An attempt at a comprehensive review of early English social customs, focussing on an aspect of their lives which was central to their social identities, has not been made so far although aspects of this have been presented in other works. This book is intended to lay the groundwork for such a treatment.

— ᚲ —

I have consulted many people for advice and assistance in researching this subject, which touches on so many aspects of early English social and cultural life.

A personal thank-you goes to two friends who both inspired me to take on this challenge in the first place: Octavia Porter-Randolph and Georgina Ryall, who each suggested that the one thing missing from *The English Warrior* was a carefully-researched and meaty section on feasting and rewards. That provided the impetus to start work on this project.

I would like to record my thanks to Melanie Wilson, whose friendly advice in the areas of glass, textile production and clothing was of great assistance to me in dealing with some highly technical data. I hope I have not entirely misrepresented all the information passed to me.

Without the impetus of many long conversations with Alan Haymes, and access to his store of sources, this book would be much the poorer. I would like to acknowledge also the help and encouragement provided by John Osborne and Paul Mortimer, especially in matters relating to Sutton Hoo. Thanks once again to Lindsay Kerr, who tracked down a lot of Taplow-related material, and

Foreword

encouraged me to believe that the subject could be tackled in one book-length treatment.

My special thanks go to Tony Linsell of Anglo-Saxon Books for his continued support and encouragement with this project.

Naturally, not every piece of information gathered from friends and contacts was used, and I apologise if I have omitted to mention some others whose ideas and sources were instrumental in completing the project.

Steve Pollington

Essex 2002

Abbreviations & Glossary

ASC	The *Anglo-Saxon Chronicle*, a series of six manuscripts recording the history of Britain and the English nation
barrow	tumulus or burial mound
burh	(pronounced 'boor-kh' where 'kh' is the sound in Scottish 'loch') OE, a borough, a defensive site which later grew into an administrative centre
clawbeaker	type of high-status glass drinking vessel with rows of extrusions around the body and a small foot
comitatus	(Latin) a group of warriors having sworn personal loyalty to an individual leader
conebeaker	type of high-status glass drinking vessel, funnel-shaped with no foot
cyn	(pronounced 'keen') OE, kindred, family, clan
(ge)driht	(pronounced 'ye-drikht') OE, band of warriors, household troop, *comitatus*
duguð	(pronounced 'doo-guth') OE, doughty warriors, veterans
ealdormann	(pronounced 'elderman') OE, a regional governor, royal deputy
Exeter Book	a large book of Old English verse, compiled and written around 1000 AD and presented to Exeter Cathedral shortly after, where it has remained ever since
frumstol	(pronounced 'froom-stoal') OE, seat of authority
futhark	The earliest form of Germanic runic script
futhorc	The form of runic script used in England and Frisia, developed from the *futhark*
fyrd	(pronounced 'feerd') OE, defensive military force
geoguð	(pronounced 'yo-guth') OE, young men, young warriors, youths
giefstol	(pronounced 'yif-stol') OE, the gift-stool, the seat from which the lord distributes wealth as a reward to his followers

gleoman	(pronounced 'glay-man') OE, a poet or musician
grið	(pronounced 'grith') OE, an area where violence and threats were forbidden
Grubenhaus	(German) 'pit-house', an alternative name for an SFB
handseax	(pronounced 'handsax') OE, a small, general purpose knife
HE	*Historia Ecclesiastica Gentis Anglorum*, a work by Bede covering the conversion and early history of the English nation
hide	family unit, and the land occupied by that unit
hlafdige	(pronounced 'lahf-deeye') OE, 'lady', principal female of the household
hlaford	(pronounced 'lah-vord') OE 'lord', provider of food at a feast
OE	Old English (language)
OHG	Old High German
ON	Old Norse
ombeht	(pronounced "ombekht") OE, king's man, royal official
Saxo-Norman	architectural period immediately after the Norman invasion when Anglo-Saxon craftsmen worked to Norman designs (c.1066-1100)
scop	(pronounced 'shop') OE, a poet; plural *scopas*
SFB	Sunken-Featured Building – a smallish building constructed over a shallow pit, often used as a workshop or for storage
symbel	(pronounced 'seembel') OE, a ritual gathering and meal
þegn	(pronounced 'thane') OE, a 'thane' or local minor nobleman, a knight
þing	(pronounced 'thing') OE, a meeting of freemen held to discuss policy
þyle	(pronounced 'thee –le') OE, spokesman, challenger
werod	(pronounced 'werrod') OE, warband, *comitatus*
wyrd	(pronounced 'weerd') OE, course of events, fate, history

Notes on conventions.

In epigraphic quotations, lower case **bold type** indicates transcribed runic texts.

In Old English words, the letters Ð, ð and Þ, þ represent the two sounds we now write as 'th' (as in 'this', 'thin'); they are used interchangeably, so that spellings such as *Widsið* or *Widsiþ* may be found for the same word. The letter Æ, æ represents the vowel heard in 'cat'.

In Old Norse Ð, ð can only have the sound in 'this', and Þ, þ can only have the 'thin' sound.

I have generally retained original Old English spellings (e.g. Æþelberht) but where a modern form is well established I have used this in preference (e.g. Ethelbert).

All translations are my own unless otherwise stated.

* before a word indicates a reconstructed form not actually found in any texts.

Introduction

This book is an attempt to bring together some of the material relating to Anglo-Saxon feasting – in its various senses – and the 'mead-hall' culture in which such feasting took place. The central place of these ideas in Anglo-Saxon society is evident from the high incidence of related words in the formal vocabulary of the language, and from the high status accorded to feasting paraphernalia in material culture.

In investigating a topic such as the mead-hall one quickly comes face-to-face with the difficulties of interpreting evidence. Archaeological material holds many problems; in Anglo-Saxon contexts it is usually totally lacking any inscriptions or other textual evidence that would offer assistance with origin and dating. Most of the material from pagan graves survives in a historical vacuum, where almost nothing can be said for certain about the users and owners of the items; even sexing the skeletal remains has proven problematic. Literary texts are deceptive: while they may appear to be very helpful, explaining motives and offering names and dates, we have to bear in mind that we are not the intended audience for these works and we do not share the same cultural assumptions. Words are slippery things within a language – after some centuries, they are often impossible to pin down.

Other evidence comes from representations of feasts, halls and tableware in manuscript illustrations and other artwork. These are not all original pieces, and have to be studied carefully to allow for copying conventions and misunderstanding.

All these sources of evidence can only be treated properly within their appropriate contexts – something we cannot always identify. However, the oft-repeated themes of literary convention and the common finds of grave-goods do at least allow us to make some reasonable assumptions about context, in the absence of direct knowledge.

When reviewing the physical evidence for feasting equipment, two names recur at every point of the discussion: Sutton Hoo and Taplow. These two remarkable burials contained a wealth of information for the enquirer after knowledge of the early Anglo-Saxon world.

The finds from Taplow, Buckinghamshire, were for a long time the nearest things to the fine feasting equipment we read of in the *Beowulf* story – until Sutton Hoo was discovered in 1938-9. The Taplow burial mound was excavated in the Victorian age and, although many of the treasures survive, most of the information was lost. A sketch of the objects' disposition in the grave and a few handwritten notes are all that we have to rely on. There were drinking horns, a gaming board, vessels, musical instruments and weapons – all deposited in a huge burial mound by the Thames.

Sutton Hoo is world-famous for being the single wealthiest treasure find in Great Britain. It deservedly ranks alongside Stonehenge as our most important World Heritage Site. The gravefield at Sutton Hoo, above the River Deben in Suffolk, contained some 19 mounds, mostly ploughed out or robbed in earlier centuries. The so-called Mound 1 burial comprised a truly staggering amount of precious materials collected in a burial chamber built into the hull of a ship that had been dragged to the top of a steep slope overlooking the river estuary. The contents of Mound 1 have been published in a monumental work by Rupert Bruce-Mitford. Subsequent excavations of the gravemounds and their immediate environment in the 1990s by Martin Carver await full publication. The construction of the Sutton Hoo visitors' centre in 2000, some half a mile from the gravefield, revealed a hitherto unsuspected further collection of burials. Sutton Hoo is important because it is is undeniably kingly, and is the earliest royal monument of the English nation.

Part of the tragedy is that these are just two of what may well have been scores of such interments, most now dug out by antiquarians in the 'Age of Enlightenment' or robbed in antiquity. Even well-intentioned 19th century excavations were totally destructive in nature; only with the remote-sensing techniques of the last third of the 20th century did there develop a reluctance to excavate on sites which were not threatened by the plough, tarmac and concrete, or bricks and mortar. If other sites of this kind still await discovery, it is to be hoped that the maximum care will be taken to extract every last scrap of information.

Literary investigations have advanced since their beginnings in the Renaissance, and their popularisation in Victorian times. The known corpus of Old English literature has been studied, catalogued and reviewed from every conceivable angle. A poem such as *Beowulf* can tell us more about the experience of the meadhall than any archaeological dig ever will. Yet it will never answer all the questions we should like to ask of it. Our own interests, preferences and preconceptions affect our reading of the texts to a larger extent than we may realise. For example, while the concepts of the 'hall', 'treasure' and 'lordship' are emphasised in most Old English verse, there have been attempts to re-interpret these motifs as devoutly Christian allegorical themes – the hall is really 'heaven', treasure is really 'salvation' and the leader is really 'Christ'. Whether the poems can be read in that way, or were so intended by their composers, I leave the reader to decide. But I would stress that the point of any such metaphors would be lost if the concepts were not in themselves highly significant and emotive.

The early English led much more 'public' lives than is usual in modern times, or in the classical world. Many ate and slept in communal buildings, whether farm-workers' cots or monastic refectories and dormitories, and even the wealthiest

Introduction

and most important were obliged to show themselves to their people, so that for them mealtimes were as much about display as about nourishment. The relationships shown in the hall were part of the public enactment of the social order and conventions, and the verse reflects this: Old English poetry does not deal well with the expression of personal, private, intimate relationships (although there are a few exceptions, the 'Frisian wife' in the poem *Maxims I* is one example, as are the domestic scenes in some of the riddles, and aspects of *The Husband's Message* or *The Wife's Lament*). By and large, early English verse is public verse for public occasions.

More than almost any other of his contemporaries in the academic world, Professor J.R.R. Tolkien loved the countryside of England and cared about the rich cultural heritage of the English, while the tastes of his academic colleagues were often more inclined to the Classical Latin and Greek culture of the Mediterranean, or to the excesses of the Ancient Egyptians. Yet even he felt the limitations of his subject: "What is the house of Eorl but a thatched barn where brigands drink in the reek, and their brats roll on the floor among the dogs?" This question is put by Saruman in *Lord of the Rings*, and it seems to have been one which bothered – or, at the very least, stimulated – Tolkien's imagination. What, indeed, is the worth of the fictive "Germanic" tribes measured against the power and majesty of the more rigidly organised societies to the south? *The Lord of the Rings* is, in part, an examination of the home-loving, earth-fast traditions of the Rohirrim as contrasted with the magic-wielding sophistry of the Numenorians.

The Rohan hall *Meduseld* reflects in its basic structure the Germanic feasting-hall. Yet it is not exactly like an Anglo-Saxon hall any more than the Rohirrim are exactly like early English folk; in their horse-riding they recall the Gothic nations more than the sailors of the North Sea. The point is not 'which historical folk are the Riders of the Mark meant to be?', but rather 'what is to be valued about these folk?' and Tolkien's answer is to put them at the centre of his book. Along with the hobbits – the inward-focussed, rural agriculturalists – and the nostalgic, otherworldly elves, they are among the best-loved characters from the tales. They inspire affection as well as admiration because they feel like northern Europeans, they have the same values, strengths and weaknesses. This is of course not accidental. Tolkien was a keen observer of people, and he saw courage in the quiet stolidity of the English working classes, as much as in the dashing valour of the warrior élite.

Meduseld – the 'house of Eorl' – was a 'thatched barn' in the same way and to the same extent that Anglo-Saxon halls were large, wooden buildings with a wide range of practical functions. These halls served as the focal points of the communities they served – all commercial business was witnessed there, all justice was enacted there, all judgements were spoken there, all contracts were made and dissolved there, all praiseworthy deeds began and ended there. The hall and its community were identified, one with the other.

The window of the hall is a window into early English society.

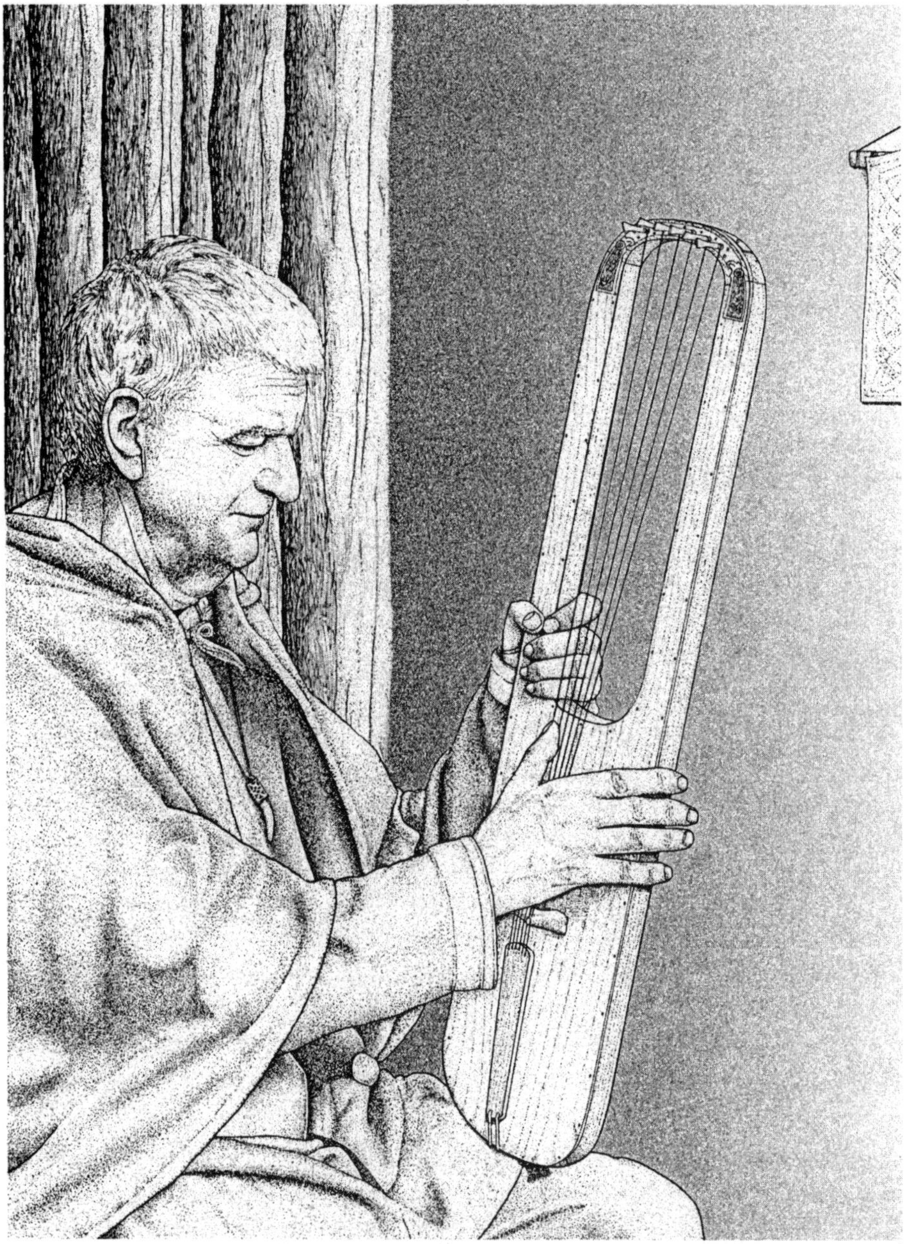

1 Feasting and Society

A Window on Early English Society

One of the strongest and most oft-repeated themes in Old English literature, whether secular or religious, prose or verse, is the image of the community, the structured human social group. Typically, in surviving Old English literary texts, this is conceived of and portayed as a variant of the idealised Germanic warrior society – the community of the *Beowulf* poem, in which every leader and every follower knows his place, his rights and his duties. The act of accepting the leader's food placed the follower under a strong social obligation to its provider. This is no less true of the early religious communities, where headmen and henchmen are distinguished as clearly as in any warband.

Anglo-Saxon literature – especially verse – employs a range of conventions which reinforce this idea of community among the readers and hearers of the poet's work.[1] Typically, the poet, or *scop*, may refer to personal experience and understanding in his narrative:

ne hyrde ic cymlicor ceol gegyrwan
I have not heard of a more comely ship being made ready
Beowulf l.38

mine gefræge
according to my information   *Beowulf* l.776

me wæs noma Deor
my name was Deor   *Deor* l.37

mæg ic be me selfum soðgied wrecan
I can make a song of truth about myself   *The Seafarer* l.1

At the same time the poet is implicating his audience in his own assumptions:

We Gardena in geardagum þeodcyninga þrym gefrunon
we have heard of the glory of kings of the Spear-Danes in olden days
Beowulf l.1-2

---

[1] Magennis, 1996

with his pre-emptive use of 'we'. That *scopas* were at times court poets and narrators of events from the community's life, interpreters of social history and mediators between the 'then' of story and the 'now' of performance, is undeniable. What is interesting is that poets continued to use these devices of inclusion and participation even when verse was becoming a literary rather than an oral activity, when the intended participants were more likely to be readers than listeners.[1]

Some of the most moving passages of OE verse - poems such as *The Seafarer*, *The Wanderer* or *The Wife's Lament* - point up very clearly the chasm of experience between inclusion in a communal life and exclusion from the society of men. These verses are no less *about* community, therefore, than the poems that celebrate and affirm the communal life of their subjects, such as *Beowulf* or *The Husband's Message*. Indeed, the ability to show both sides of the coin, life within and without a social group, demonstrates that the Anglo-Saxons had a clear appreciation of the value and limitations of community for their own society. Some poems – the so-called 'wisdom literature' in particular – underscore the communal values of secular and religious togetherness, the present joy of brotherhood on earth and the future joy of membership of the kingdom of heaven. Poets conveyed the religious community of the hereafter very much in terms of the material rewards of the here-and-now:

.... Þær is blis micel
dream on heofenum þær is drihtnes folc
geseted to symle, þær is singal blis

… there is great happiness,
joy in the heavens where the lord's group is
seated at a feast, where happiness is everlasting
Dream of the Rood, l.139-41

The central benefits of human community – sociability, warmth, security, sufficient provisions – are expressed and typified as being *geseted to symle* 'seated at a feast' for the Anglo-Saxon audience to whom such occasions were clearly very important and the highest expression of the positive values of their society. An English *gegadorwiste* was a group of people who assembled for the

---

[1] This does presuppose that written poems and stories were intended for private or public reading, but there is a good deal of evidence to suggest that written texts were intended for reading out loud to an audience, in which case the 'we' structure of the original poetic style may have continued to serve its purpose of 'inclusion'. The lack of definite information about the composition and intended audience or readership of OE verse is one of the more annoying unresolved questions in evaluating the body of work – in conjunction with the lack of any reliable details of authorship or date of composition for the majority of the poems.

purpose of consuming their food surplus in as agreeable a manner as possible.[1] The emphasis on shared values seems to have been very important in this event.

A particularly engaging example of the metaphorical relationship between human habitation and human life, is the so-called "sparrow episode" from Bede's *Historia Ecclesiastica Gentis Anglorum* in which King Edwin of Northumbria is taking counsel with his advisers one day about whether they should convert to the new Christian faith or stick with their traditional gods. In the story Edwin had himself already determined to convert, and his main priest likewise - giving as his reason that he had done most to serve the old gods but had not received correspondingly greater rewards. The text continues:

> *Þæs wordum oþer cyninges wita 7 ealdormann geþafunge sealde 7 to þære spræce feng 7 þus cwæð: "Þyslic me is gesewen, þu cyning, þis andwearde lif manna on eorðan to wiðmetenesse þære tide þe us uncuð is: swylc swa þu æt swæsendum sitte mid þinum ealdormannum 7 þegnum on wintertide 7 sie fyr onæled 7 þin heall gewyrmed 7 hit rine 7 sniwe 7 styrme ute; cume an spearwa 7 hrædlice þæt hus þurhfleo, cume þurh oþre duru in, þurh oþre ut gewite. Hwæt, he on þa tid þe he inne bið ne bið hrinen mid þy storme þæs winters; ac þæt bið an eagan bryhtm 7 þæt læsste fæc, ac he sona of wintra on þone winter eft cymeð. Swa ðonne þis monna lif to medmiclum fæce ætyweð, hwæt þær foregange oððe hwæt þæt æfterfylige we ne cunnun.*

To that one's words another of the king's advisers and eldermen gave consent, and took up the discussion and spoke thus: "It seems to me thus, O king, this present life of men on earth as measured against the time which is unknown to us: as if you were sitting at a banquet with your ealdormenn and thanes in wintertime, and a fire has been lit and your hall warmed, and outside there is rain and snow and storm; a sparrow comes and quickly flies through the house – he comes in through one door, and goes out through the other. Lo, for the time that he is inside he is not touched by the winter's storm, but that is one eye's blink and the least space of time, yet from the winter he straightaway comes back to the winter. So then, this life of men shows as a brief space of time: what precedes it, or what follows it, we do not know.

Whether this image is Bede's own, or whether it really was used by a 7th century Northumbrian leader in his deliberations on the possible advantages to be gained from the new faith, is unimportant. The central theme of the simile – the warmth

---

[1] Hagen, 1992; the point is taken that in OE Christian tradition, Christ feeding the multitude is described in similar terms.

and comfort of our time within these walls, the cold and discomfort of what lies outside – is one that recurs throughout Anglo-Saxon literature.

Indeed, the sparrow's origin and destination, the unknown, the unstructured wilderness, was to be feared. Where there is no feasting, in the dark gloomy caverns of the wasteland where goblins and trolls live, the antithetical imagery is introduced of alienation, isolation, exclusion: the misery of being an outcast. This is the home of the anti-social monster, Grendel:

> *[atol] æglæca ehtende wæs*
> *deorc deaþscua duguþe ond geogoþe*
> *seomade ond syrede, sinnihte heold*
> *mistige moras, men ne cunnon*
> *hwyder helrunan hwyrftum scriþað.*

> The terrible monster began to persecute
> Young men and old, the dark shade of death
> Waited and ensnared [them] during long nights he ruled
> The misty moors – men do not know
> Where hell-runers[1] stalk in their travels.
> *Beowulf*, 1.159-63

And of Grendel's kin it is said

> *... hie dygol land*
> *warigeað, wulfhleoþu, windige næssas*
> *frecne fengelad ðær fyrgenstream*
> *under næssa genipu niþer gewiteð*
> *flod under foldan ....*

> ... a gloomy land
> they inhabit, wolf-slopes, windy headlands
> perilous fen-paths where the mountain stream
> under mists of headlands flows downwards,
> the water beneath the earth ....
> *Beowulf*, 1.1357-61

In this merciless environment, mankind has no home; it is the wilderness surrendered to outcasts and monstrous ogres. Hearing of such inhospitable regions – confronting them in the imagination - serves to reinforce the audience's attachment to the familiar, homely places of their everyday experience.

---

[1] The exact nature of a *helruna* is undetermined, but the implication is clearly of witchcraft and ungodly practices

With a strong, emotional focus on the 'community' as a moral good and a social necessity, it is hardly surprising that literary treatments of those who destroy the community and the mutual trust on which it is founded – those who betray their fellows – are harsh. Inviting someone to a feast meant a legal duty of care and protection for the host, and a reciprocal bond for the guest. In story – and possibly in fact – this duty to protect one's invited guests could extend beyond the duty of vengeance.[1]

There are examples enough of treachery in Old English literature, both biblical and patristic models on the one hand, and secular, heroic ones on the other. The biblical story of the 'fall of the angels' was recounted very much in terms of the followers (angels) betraying the leader (God) whom it was their moral duty to support. For example, we read in the poem *Christ and Satan*, 1.81-96 Lucifer speaking thus to the angels who have followed him:

Ic wæs iu in heofnum halig ængel;
dryhtene deore; hefde me dream mid gode,
micelne for meotode, and ðeos menego swa some.
þa ic in mode minum hogade
þæt ic wolde towerpan wuldres leoman,
bearn helendes, agan me burga gewald
eall to æhte, and ðeos earme heap
þe ic hebbe to helle ham geledde.
Wene þæt tacen sutol þa ic aseald wes on wærgðu,
niðer under nessas in ðone neowlan grund.
Nu ic eow hebbe to hæftum ham gefærde
alle of earde. Nis her eadiges tir,
wloncra winsele, ne worulde dream,
ne ængla ðreat, ne we upheofon
agan moten. Is ðes atola ham
fyre onæled. Ic eom fah wið god.

---

[1] For example the story of King Finn of the Frisians who invited his sister Hildeburh and brother-in-law King Hnæf of the Danes to a midwinter feast; violence flared between the two retinues and both Hnæf and Finn's son were killed in the fighting. Far from taking vengeance on the strangers, Finn offered the Danes a temporary meadhall of their own, separate from the Frisians' main hall, for the rest of the winter until they could return home. (See Tolkien, 1982.) That this ideal was sometimes exploited by the ruthless is shown clearly by the story of King Þeoderic the Ostrogoth who invited his rival, Odoacer, to a feast and brutally slew him. (Todd, 2001) In 11th century England, there is the tale of the murderous connivance of King Cnut and Þurbrand, who invited Earl Uhtred, the most powerful man in the north, to a feast at *Wiheal*, and treacherously slew him (Fletcher, 2002).

Chapter One

> Before, I was a holy angel in the heavens
> dear to my lord, I had great joy with god,
> with the measurer, and this multitude together likewise,
> then I thought in my heart
> that I would throw down the light of glory,
> the healer's sons, have control of strongholds for myself
> – all my own property – and this poor troop
> which I have led home into hell.
> Remember that clear sign when I was driven into outlawry
> down beneath headlands into the deep ground.
> Now I have brought you all home as captives
> from your fatherland; here is no glory of the blessed one,
> wine-hall of the proud, nor joy of the world,
> nor company of angels, nor high heaven
> can we ever reach: this hateful dwelling is
> ablaze with fire. I am at odds with god.

Secular society was founded on personal loyalties. The legal position of traitors was unequivocal: Alfred's law-code allows no compensatory payment for acts of betrayal, based on biblical precedent:

> ... buton æt hlafordsearwe hie nane mildheortnesse ne dorston gecweðan for þam ðe god ælmihtig þam nane ne gedemde þe hine oferhogdon ....
>
> except that for betrayal of a lord they dared declare no mercy, because God Almighty deemed none for those who mocked him
> *(Laws of Alfred, Introduction)*

Most crimes could be atoned for by payments to the victims and their families and with a fine to the king. Even a murder could be set right with payment of the victim's *wergild* ('man-price'), which varied according to his rank, to the dead man's kindred. This principle enabled wrongdoing to be deterred, as the sums involved were large, and also limited the effects of the alternative, the feud, in which any member of the murderer's family might be attacked for vengeance. Alfred's premise, that human leaders are entitled to the unwavering loyalty and respect of their followers, is at the heart of the mediaeval notion of kingship and, it may be surmised, of the much older notions of leadership in the tribal warband.

The most telling and oft-cited example of this occurs in the *ASC* annal for 755, the famous episode of Cynewulf and Cyneheard, a situation where a king has been slain by a rival while paying a visit to his mistress, and the king's followers have arrived to avenge his murder, only to find that some in their group have kinsmen among the enemy force. Offered their freedom in exchange for changing sides and leaving their colleagues, the record says:

> *...Ond þa cuædon hie þæt him nænig mæg leofra nære þonne hiera hlaford, ond hie næfre his banan folgian noldon; ond þa budon hie hiera mægum þæt hie gesunde from eodon; ond hie cuædon þæt ilce hiera geferum geboden wære þe ær mid þam cyninge wærun. Þa cuædon hie þæt hie hie þæs ne onmunden...*

> ...And then they said that no kinsman was dearer to them than their lord, and they would never follow his killer; and then they offered their kinsmen that they might leave unharmed, and they said that the same [terms] should be offered to their companions who had previously been with the king. Then they said that they could not accept that...
>
> ASC s.a. 755

Loyalty to *geferan* 'companions, men with whom one travels' claimed first place for warriors, beyond the calls of family duty, even though for kinship's sake the offer of safe passage had been made.

There are many kings and nobles whose deaths are recorded in the early annals in possibly 'dubious' circumstances. Only rarely is treachery alluded to as a factor in these deaths. An unusual entry for the year 626 in *ASC* MS 'E' hints at a poignant story. It begins:

> *Her com Eomer fram Cwichelme West Seana cininge þohte þæt he wolde ofstingan Eadwine cininge ac he ofstang Lillan his ðegn 7 Forðhere 7 þone cining gewundode 7 þære ilcan nihte wes Eadwine dohter acenned, seo wæs gehaten Eanfled.*

> Here (in this year) Eomer came from Cwichelm, king of the West Saxons; he meant to stab King Eadwine [of Northumbria] but he stabbed Lilla his thane, and Forðhere, and wounded the king; and the same night a daughter was born to Eadwine, who was called Eanfled.

It seems that Eomer was received as a guest by King Edwin, and he treacherously tried to knife his host, on the instructions of the West Saxon King Cwichelm, but was overpowered, having first killed two of the king's nobles. The story was considered worth recording, which suggests that it must have been at least remarkable, possibly scandalous, because it was an abuse of hospitality.

A later example of the disgrace which stems from disloyalty is found in the poem *The Battle of Maldon*, which commemorates the defeat of an English army at Maldon, Essex, and which we know from the *ASC* took place in 991AD. The English faced a fleet of Scandinavian raiders who had devastated many coastal towns until they came to Maldon early in August of that year. The local *ealdormann*, Byrhtnoð by name, led his forces out to try to bring the Vikings to battle; in the fighting the English leader was cut down. Seeing this, one of his thanes seized Byrhtnoð's horse – the only one on the field – and rode off, followed by his two brothers.

> *Hi bugon þa fram beaduwe þe þær beon noldon;*
> *þær wearð Oddan bearn ærest on fleame,*
> *Godric fram guþe, and þone godan forlet*
> *þe him mænigne oft mear gesealde;*
> *he gehleop þone eoh þe ahte his hlaford,*
> *on þam gerædum þe hit riht ne wæs,*
> *and his broðru mid him begen ærndon,*
> *Godwine and Godwig, guþe ne gymdon,*
> *ac wendon fram þam wige and þone wudu sohton,*
> *flugon on þæt fæsten and hyra feore burgon,*
> *and manna ma þonne hit ænig mæð wære,*
> *gyf hi þa geearnunga ealle gemundon*
> *þe he him to duguþe gedon hæfde.*

Those who did not want to be there then turned from battle;
Odda's sons were first in flight there,
Godric went from the warfare and abandoned the good man
who often gave him many a horse,
he leapt onto the steed which his lord owned,
into the trappings, as it was not right to do
and with him his brothers both ran off,
Godwine and Godwig, they did not heed the fighting
but turned from the warfare and sought the woods,
fled to the fastness and protected their lives
and many more men than was at all fitting
if they had all taken thought for the rewards
which he had given them for their steadfastness.
Battle of Maldon, 1.185-97[1]

Interestingly, the poem specifically credits one of the English leaders, called Offa, with having predicted that not all who spoke bravely would match their words with deeds when they had previously assembled at the *mæðelstede*, the 'speaking-place', where they had boasted over their mead. This imagery immediately calls to mind the mead-halls of *Beowulf* and the simple lord-retainer bonds of the warband, even though the English society of the late tenth century had long before outgrown these structures of a simpler, bygone age. The invocation of this imagery is not accidental, but is meant to remind the audience of the homely values of their society.

---

[1] Scragg, 1981; Griffiths, 1991

Tacitus's statement about the 1st century AD Germanic folk (*Germania*, ch.14) is clear: *iam vero infame in omnem vitam ac probrosum superstitem principi suo ex acie recessisse* "furthermore to outlive the leader and withdraw from battle is lifelong shame and dishonour", yet there must have been many who – by design or chance – did not fall valiantly avenging their slain leader on the foe. Nevertheless, a strongly similar sentiment is found on the lips of an English warrior in 991 AD at Maldon:[1]

Hige sceal þe heardra, heorte þe cenre,
mod sceal þe mare, þe ure mægen lytlað.
 Her lið ure ealdor eall forheawen,
god on greote. A mæg gnornian
se ðe nu fram þis wigplegan wendan þenceð.
 Ic eom frod feores; fram ic ne wille,
ac ic me be healfe minum hlaforde,
be swa leofan men, licgan þence.

Thought shall be the harder, heart the keener
courage shall be the greater as our strength dwindles.
Here lies our leader, cut down,
the good man in the dirt – may he ever grieve
who now thinks to turn from this war-play.
I am old in life – I will not go from here
but rather at my lord's side,
by so dear a man, do I mean to lie dead.
The Battle of Maldon, l. 312-9

As noble and defiant as this sentiment is, reality was not often so simple. Political considerations and opportunities for advancement must at times have overridden the tradition of loyalty. A case in point would be the notorious Ealdormann of Mercia, Eadric Streona, whose rise to power involved the murder of Ealdormann Ælfhelm of Northumbria and the blinding of his two sons. Eadric ruled most of England – a king in all but name – for nearly a decade under Æðelræd (Ethelred the Unready) and he married the king's daughter. When the struggle with the Danes became bitter, in the early years of the 11th century, Eadric advised the payment of Danegeld[2] rather than using the money to raise an army. More than once he caused a military strategy to fail by holding his troops back. In 1015, when Cnut and Edmund Ironside were contending for the throne, Eadric changed sides and threw his men in with Cnut's forces; the next year, when Edmund seemed to be gaining the upper hand, he reverted to Edmund's cause. In a

---

[1] Woolf, 1976; Locherbie-Cameron, 1995; for text see Griffiths, 1991; Scragg, 1981.

[2] Danegeld was a payment made to the marauders to secure peace – a bribe to leave, in effect.

Chapter One

decisive encounter at Ashingdon, Essex, Eadric held his forces back and eventually fled the field, instigating a rout and dooming Edmund's party to failure. When Cnut became the all-out ruler, he retained Eadric in his position of power, but by the end of 1017 his doubts had been confirmed and he had the Mercian leader murdered. No English sources appear to criticise Cnut for this.[1]

Tenth and eleventh century English society was under threat in many ways – the political and military threat of the Danish armies; the political threat of collaborators and supporters of the Danish cause;[2] the religious threat of Christian despair at God's inactivity and of renewed heathenism; the threat to social cohesion caused by hatred and revenge (for example, runaway slaves joining Viking warbands and leading them to the homes of their former masters to exact vengeance). Concerns of these kinds were expressed in the homilies and sermons of the age, most notably the *Sermo Lupi ad Anglos* and other writings by Wulfstan, for example:

> *Ond la hu mæg mare scamu þurh godes yrre mannum gelimpan þonne us deð gelome for agenum gewyrhtum? Ðeah þræla hwylc hlaforde æthleape 7 of cristendome to wicinge weorðe 7 hit æfter þam eft geweorðe þæt wæpngewrixl weorðe gemæne þegene 7 þræle, gyf þræl þæne þegen fullice afylle licge ægylde ealre his mægðe, 7 gyf se þegen þæne þræl þe he ær ahte fullice afylle, gylde þegengylde.*
>
> And look – how can greater shame befall men through God's anger than happens to us continually through our own deeds? Yet, some servant may get away from his lord and from Christianity and become a viking, and after that it may happen again that an armed fight may come about between thane and thrall. If the thrall foully kills the thane, he will lie dead without his kindred having been recompensed. And if the thane should foully kill the thrall whom he had before, he must pay a thane's recompense.[3]

The need to bind the English nation together was taken up in a number of activities, including both the sermonising of the priesthood and the encouragement of the martial virtues among the leaders and warriors of the *fyrd*. It may be that this urgent need for cohesion among the Anglo-Saxons encouraged

---

[1] Fletcher, 1989; Stenton, 1971

[2] Areas of eastern England had been settled by Danes in the 9th century, and there may have been some pro-Danish sentiment among their descendants. Moreover, Anglo-Saxon kings did not have to win a mandate through elections and could afford to be unpopular as long as they were successful. Contenders who could present themselves as more effective and competent could always win support.

[3] Whitelock, 1976. Due to the shift in the balance of power, Englishmen had to make full man-price payments to their Viking persecutors if the latter were slain, while no reciprocal arrangements existed for English families with relatives slain by the Vikings.

the poets of that time to emphasise the spirit of community in their work - on the one hand to idolise their society's protectors and builders, and on the other to demonise its betrayers and destroyers. Even poems which praise people who turn their back on society – St. Guthlac in his fenland retreat, or the Seafarer alone in his boat – do so against a backdrop which shows 'clearly how comforting and important the community was, and therefore how courageous and determined these exceptional people were in forsaking it.

The secular view appears to have been that human life outside a community was devoid of purpose or meaning. This was accepted as part of the normal worldview of people of this time, and no-one (in the verse tradition at least) appears seriously to question it, even when the price of acceptance is a lifetime of misery - for example, the lady Hildeburh who loses both a son and a brother to the strife of competing communities (see p.23).

The religious dimension could have been difficult to incorporate, since the orthodox Christian view should be that the matters of this world are transitory and unimportant, and so in that sense the joy of feasting was ultimately illusory. Yet it was possible to portray the Anglo-Saxon mead-hall as a kind of re-branded Roman *civitas*, and the feast as a form of *convivium* where faith could be fortified. An appeal to traditional Anglo-Saxon and Christian values, as then understood, may lie behind this re-appraisal.

The comparatively large volume of Old English verse which survives from around the year 1000 gives us a sample which, though possibly not representative of the corpus as a whole, does nevertheless indicate this insistence on community as a recurrent theme. The consistent and omnipresent symbol for the life of the community is the hall, which is referred to in almost every Old English poem (other than the riddles).[1] Even where the presence of a Germanic mead-hall is unhistorical, as in some of the biblical and classical references, the social structure of the familiar communal buildings is superimposed on Judaic or Roman equivalents.[2] Keeping the exemplar texts relevant to the community using

---

[1] Magennis, 1996, ch.2. The riddles are in some ways a good 'control' corpus. Formally they are constructed as well as any other species of Old English verse, using as much skill and art as the commemorative, religious or didactic verse. Yet their subject matter is very diverse, and divergent from the rest of the tradition as we understand it. For every lofty biblical narrative work (*Judith*, *Andreas* and the like) there must have been many more earthy and well-crafted verses of types no longer present in the corpus. If we had access to Magennis's 'oral communities' no doubt we would have a better understanding of the social reality of the verse-makers, of the subjects they dealt with and the verbal traditions they preserved. Romance, love and sex must have played a considerably larger role in the lives of the men and women of the period than could ever be deduced from the verse or prose literature. The handful of rather rude riddles punctures the stifling air of sanctimony present in the religious verse.

[2] For example, the Israelites in *Exodus* (1.564) find *beorselas beorna* 'warriors' beer-halls' in Canaan.

them must have been the purpose of this policy;[1] this implies that the concept of the hall as the community's centre remained constant to the end of the Anglo-Saxon period, even though by the ninth century there were new social and economic forms of secular community – trading posts,[2] defensive strongholds, market towns. Likewise, the development of the ecclesiastical structure and network grew more complex throughout the period, yet still the hall is invoked as the ideal of human togetherness in religious as in secular verse.[3]

A parallel tradition from a common source is the Scandinavian.[4] Old Norse mythology is replete with references to halls and feasts and alcohol. As chief god, Óðinn's main hall in myth is *Válhöll* (Valhalla) in which the fallen heroes – the *Einherjar*, the *gedriht* of the god – feast and drink to their hearts' content; he has another dwelling called *Válaskjálf*. Válhöll is in a part of heaven called *Glaðsheimr* (land of happiness). Cooked meat is provided by a boar called *Sæhrimnir* in a pot called *Eldhrimnir* by a cook called *Audhrimnir*. There is no lack of anything desirable in this warriors' afterlife.

Many of the myths concerning Óðinn contain feasting or drinking references: the gaining of the gift of poetry by the god is in the form of mead brewed from the blood of a murdered divinity, Kvasir. Óðinn stole the mead from the giant Suttungr by deceiving and seducing the giant's daughter, whose task it was to guard it. This myth is known to have existed in two or three different versions from Icelandic tradition (in Snorri's *Skáldskaparmál*, and in different verses of *Hávamál*) and is of an ancient type concerning the winning of blessings in the form of strong drink.[5]

---

[1] Alternatively, one might see this as a lack of wider perspective, a pre-occupation with the familiar over the exotic. Yet the image is so central to almost all the surviving verse, and the real social situation must often have been so different from the ideal portrayed, that only a deeply traditional form of verse-making can explain this satisfactorily.

[2] The element *wic* found in many English place-names may have its origin in the Latin *vicus*, a civilian settlement attached to a military site. These areas were used for the relatively small-scale trade of the 5th and 6th centuries, where typically a trading vessel was hauled up on a suitable strand and goods were exchanged on the beach. By the 7th century a new range of facilities had been developed at selected locations with good marine access: London, Ipswich, York and *Hamwic* (Southampton) are the best known. In the ninth century Alfred developed a series of military structures (the *burh* system) across southern England, which his successors extended into the Midlands and north. By the tenth century, many of these *burh* sites had become administrative centres, the site of mints and other governmental functions. The rural economy had been transformed from barter to a fully-developed and well-managed coinage.

[3] Nevertheless, while the hall represents society, it is the way of the hero to step outside it: in defending the hall from monstrous attacks, Beowulf is seeking his own glory as much as the preservation of human social order. Significantly, the hero must prevail where the community has failed, in order to assert the value of the heroic in the verse tradition.

[4] Ellis Davidson, 1964; Branston, 1980; North, 1997.

[5] Simek, 1993

Another giant, Hrungnir, claimed the guest's right to safety when he got drunk and abusive at Óðinn's table and was challenged to fight by Þórr. The latter figures in a long tale about his visit to the realms of the giant Geirröðr, whom he overcomes, and in another about the theft of his hammer which involves him dressing up in bridal costume to trick the giant thief, Þrymr.

Óðinn's handmaidens at the feast are the *válkyrjar*, depicted as noble and beautiful young ladies who serve the heroes with mead and greet new arrivals from the land of the living with a stirrup-cup; they are present on the battlefield and choose the virtuous dead for Óðinn's troop.

Freyja is the youthful love-goddess of Norse myth, while her *alter ego* is Frigg, the noble, wise and matronly householder goddess. Loki, a devious trickster figure, appears at the hall of Ægir and his wife Ran, while the gods are seated to a feast and he proceeds to abuse them with ritual taunting (p. 188 below).

Hel, the name of both the underworld and its hideous female ruler, was conceived of as a land of cold and dark; her hall *Eljuðnir* "damp place" was the antithesis of the warm and friendly human mead-hall, and her table was set with an eating knife called 'famine' and a dish called 'hunger'. While the literary nature of the mediaeval Icelandic depiction is undoubted, and the allegorical symbolism in the naming of its main features is probably down to Snorri Sturluson, nevertheless the notion of Hel as the cold, dark room is ancient – it is an image of the grave.[1]

Feasting in the Hall

The central theme in hall-life in Old English verse (as also in its Norse counterpart) is that of the 'feast'. This word is used in Modern English to denote at least two separate concepts. The first of these is the formal, ritualised *symbel* with its gift-giving and opportunities for performance, speech-making, verse-recital, exchanging praise and honour. Another term designated as a 'feast' is *gebeorscipe* which may be a much less structured, informal event involving drinking, merry-making and conviviality. These two terms will be discussed separately below.

In Old English literature one of the essential elements in any 'feast' is the consumption of strong drink. This is mentioned in many of the texts, for example:

    ðæt healreced hatan wolde medoærn micel men gewyrcan
    that he would order men to make a great mead-building   *Beowulf*, l. 68-9

---

[1] The Gothic cognate *halja* refers to 'hell' in its theological sense; a further cognate is Old Irish *cuile* 'cellar, underground room'. Simek, 1993

Chapter One

> *meoduheall monig mondreama full*
> many a mead-hall filled with the joys of men *The Ruin*, l. 23

> *gemunað þara mæla þe we oft æt meodo spræcon*
> remember those speeches which we often spoke over the mead
> *The Battle of Maldon*, l.212

There are certain ideas repeatedly emphasised in these passages and many others of similar sort: togetherness, friendship, hospitality, fellowship, brightness and warmth. They represent the 'indoor' aspects of men's lives, the world of shelter and comradeship, contrasted with the 'outdoor' world of toil and danger, warfare and exile.[1]

The values of the community as a 'coming together', an aggregate of many individuals, are celebrated; equally, the individual community defines itself through separation and distinction from all others. Guests – people from outside the community given temporary, honorary membership – were traditionally welcomed. The more noble the guest, the more important he made the host look among his own people. The very fact that strangers thought it worthwhile to journey for many miles to visit the leader of a settlement underscored that leader's authority and prestige.

The independence of self-determination was apparently a highly-prized asset, and the security of the members of the group resided to some extent in the measures which all group members would take to protect their own. The dissolution of the community is expressed through the destruction of its hall, removing its social focus:

> *Oft Scyld Sceafing sceaþena þreatum monegum mægþum meodusetla ofteah*
>
> Often Scyld Sceafing, with troops of attackers, took away the mead-benches from many peoples *Beowulf*, l. 4-5

The *meduseld*, the mead-hall, was the symbol of power and independence and group identity. In all of *Beowulf* the only building given a name of its own is the hall of the Danish king:

> *healærna mæst, scop him heort naman*
>
> the greatest of hall-buildings – he made its name 'Heorot'
> *Beowulf*, l.78

---

[1] While it is certainly true that hunting was among the pastimes of Anglo-Saxon society, this seems to have been regarded as a pleasure only by the upper classes who could afford to treat it as a leisure activity. For the poorer folk, hunting was a means of gathering food from the wild and could contribute an important source of protein to their diet.

Hall Layout

It is assumed that the lower end of the hall, where the meadbenches were thronged with followers of the chieftain, was the scene of relatively free talk among the freemen; at the upper end of the hall, where the leader and his advisers sat, all speech was relatively formal and carried official weight[1] - feasting here was as much about discussing serious business as about entertaining the fellowship. Among the freemen, exchanges of boasts and vows took place to reinforce the solidarity of the assembly and these words are called to mind on the battlefield: *gemunað þara gemæla þe we oft æt meodo spræcon þonne we on bence beot ahofon* "remember those words which we often spoke over the mead when we raised a boast on the bench" (*Maldon*, 1.212-3). Similarly, before facing Grendel, Beowulf focuses his mind by recalling the words he spoke in the hall.

It may be the case that the lower end of the hall was open to all men who cared to participate, while in the upper end only the invited guest and the leader - or a representative such as his wife, *þyle* or *scop* – could take the floor to speak. The upper, official end of the hall acted as a kind of court where evidence was heard (in the form of speeches from participants) before the presiding authority could reach a decision. The process must have been open and visible to all, and therefore a public setting was the only proper scene for this process; the information presented may not actually be new or unknown, but the logic of the leader's decision, bound by the various aspects of tradition, must be transparent. This use of a top-down delivery structure translated itself successfully into Anglo-Saxon ecclesiastical usage, where sermonising and recitation of biblical lore took the place of formal decision-making in the hall.

It is sadly the case that poets expected their audiences to know broadly how a hall was built and laid out, what rituals were followed and how a 'feast' was conducted. No poems give us very much in the way of specific information on these points, and we are left to draw inferences by comparing details in different texts. Virtually nothing is said anywhere in Old English verse about the construction or disposition of the hall, beyond the very generalised account of the building of Heorot given early on in *Beowulf* (below, p. 101).

The poem *Beowulf*, which is still undated despite a century of scholarship,[2] tells us a great deal about an early English audience's expectations of a feast among the great and the good of their society. It is a poem about many ideas – the nature of heroism, the purpose of courage, the place of man in the world, maintenance of community and of identity. No less is *Beowulf* about the 'hall-life', the social structures and the dynamic relationships between lord and followers, lord and lady, warriors and guests. The hall and its functions form the backdrop to a large part of this exploration, mainly in the first section of the poem where Beowulf is

---

[1] Herschend, 1998

[2] See Chase, 1981 for a useful collection of essays arguing for various periods.

a young adventurer cleansing the hall for his Danish host. The images of the second section, where he is older and a king himself, are consonant with those presented in the first section. However, as king, he is a bestower rather than receiver of gifts and the poet shows less enthusiasm for the task of feast description. The Geatish hall of King Beowulf is *betlic* 'fine' (l. 1925) but it is doomed to fall to the attack of the dragon, which effectively destroys the Geats' kingdom. The safety and magnificence of the hall is therefore a measure and symbol of the power and prosperity of those who dwell in it. Likewise, the grim underwater lair of the monstrous Grendel-kin is a clear indication of the nature of its inhabitants. Grendel himself is filled with anger at the imposition of human values and communal structures on his wasteland:

> *Ða se ellengæst earfoðlice*
> *þrage geþolode se þe in þystrum bad*
> *þæt he dogora gehwæm dream gehyrde*
> *hlude in heale, swutol sang scopes ...*

> Then the mighty spirit with difficulty
> endured that time – he who lurked in darkness -
> that every day he heard the pleasure
> loud in the hall, the *scop*'s clear song ...
> *Beowulf*, l.86-9

In attacking the hall, Grendel attempts to drive out human society; he becomes a substitute for and travesty of the hall's inhabitants, a *healðegn* 'hall-thane' of a different, ironic kind.

The secular, Germanic imagery of the hall and its feasting was not always given whole-hearted ecclesiastical approval and some Christian poets use its themes to convey the sense of transitory, worldly pleasures as distinct from the everlasting joy awaiting the pious in heaven. The Hebrews were enticed to ungodly ways through such *seledreamas*:

> *Hie þæs wlenco onwod and wingedrinc*
> *þæt hie firendæda to frece wurdon*

> For that, pride maddened them - and the drinking of wine -
> so that they became too eager for evil deeds.
> *Genesis*, l.2581-2

The only closely comparable body of verse to the Old English is that from early Iceland, written in Old Norse, some of which dates from the tenth century. It sometimes shows remarkable agreement with the themes of Old English verse, due to its common origins in the stories and traditions of the Germanic Iron Age. The English corpus shows a great deal of Christian influence in its subject matter, even where we may suspect that the text is a reworking of something older.[1] The Scandinavian corpus is less overtly Christian and often seems to revel in its pagan past. This deep association with heathen lore may not always be helpful: it is difficult to allow for subtle, even subconscious, Christian influence in verse which was already several hundred years old in some cases when recorded.

We know that characters may occur in both English and Norse tradition: Ingeld and his bride, for example, or Hroþwulf in *Beowulf* who is identical with Hrólfr (Kraki) of Norse tradition. The Norse literature likewise stresses the ritual nature of the feast, and its great importance in cementing the bonds of the society. The Danish writer Saxo Grammaticus refers to the *sacra mense* 'sacred matters of the table'[2] which would be comprehensible in both traditions. A concomitant of this 'hallowed' tradition of feasting is the horror felt at treachery or bad faith – themes dealt with occasionally in both bodies of literature.

In the latter part of *Beowulf*, the hero has aged and come to great responsibility while being past the peak of his personal powers. The poet does not present us with graphic details of any feasts in this second part of *Beowulf*, but significantly he still retains the hall- and feast-imagery as symbols of community. In keeping with themes in many other Old English poems, these symbols are now demonstrated to be ultimately empty:

> *Hwær cwom mearg, hwær cwom mago, hwær cwom maþþumgyfa?*
> *Hwær cwom symbla gesetu? Hwær sindon seledreamas?*
> *Eala beorht bune, eala byrnwiga*
> *eala þeodnes þrym, hu seo þrag gewat*
> *genap under nihthelm swa heo no wære*

> Where is the horse? Where is the kinsman? Where is the treasure-giver?
> Where are the feast-benches? Where are the hall-joys?
> Lo, bright cup! Lo, byrnied warrior!
> Lo, lord's might! That time is past,
> dimmed beneath darkness as if it had never been.
> *The Wanderer, l.92-6*

> *Beorht wæron burgræced, burnsele monige*
> *heah horngestreon, heresweg micel,*
> *meodoheall monig mondreama full*
> *oþþæt þæt onwende wyrd seo swiþe*

---

[1] See, for example, Branston 1957 and North 1997. As an example, one might cite the poem *The Dream of the Rood* where the narrator is the tree, cut down to be used as a gallows, which fortuitously is then venerated as it is the cross on which Christ was killed. There are non-biblical details in the poem which may echo older myths of the World Tree supporting the Dying God, Baldur.

[2] Magennis, 1996.

> bright were the town buildings, many bath-houses
> high gables aplenty, a great noise of warriors,
> many a mead-hall full of men's pleasures
> until mighty fate changed all that
>
> *The Ruin*, l.21-4

Even the dragon, which has brought death to Beowulf and destruction to his land, has its own hoard of drinking vessels and feasting gear:

Him big stodan bunan 7 orcas	Beside him stood cups and vessels,
discas lagon 7 dyre swyrd	dishes lay around and precious swords
omige, þurhetone	rusty, eaten through ....

Beowulf, l. 3047-9

The harsh juxtaposition of bright hall-joys and empty, rusted, useless metalwork exposes the transitory nature of all human pleasures. This theme inspires a great deal of Old English verse, not only for its melancholy nostalgia for glories past and irrecoverable, but also because it underscores the absolute duty of men to value and enjoy the comradeship of their fellows while they are still able.[1]

Meals and Mealtimes

In relatively large communities where communal meals for tens of people were the norm, regular and regulated mealtimes were essential to ensure all received their share. Ecclesiastics' mealtimes were dictated by the requirements of the daily routine, fitting in around services and private prayer. Priests were expected to eat at midday and in the evening, according to one source.[2] On Sundays, the first meal was taken at dawn and the next in the evening.

For secular persons, the provision of two meals seems to have been a standard arrangement – one on rising and another in the afternoon or evening. For agricultural labourers working far off in the woods and fields, some meals may have had to be taken in the open air, made up from cold provisions such as bread, butter, cheese and hard boiled eggs.

---

[1] The various forms of disaster and downfall presented in the poem illustrate the complexity of the Anglo-Saxon mindset. While there is the clear-cut case of Grendel who attacks human community because it displeases him, as the poem progresses the motives of the characters become more complex. Grendel's mother attacks the Danes' hall not for greed but in pursuit of the absolute duty of the blood-feud; the dragon which finishes Beowulf has been disturbed by human greed. King Hygelac's death is brought about by his own restless search for fame. The fall of Hroðgar's line is due to internal quarrelling, as Ingeld's peace-treaty founders on bitter resentment among the rival warbands. Threats to a society may as often lie within the hearts of its members as in the halls of neighbours.

[2] *OE Rule of Chrodegang*, cited in Hagen, 1992.

Seasonal variation in the diet was unavoidable and caused severe hardship in some communities. Despite skilful preservation strategies, it was nevertheless always possible that the stocks of winter provisions – hard cheeses, salt meat, dried cereals and pulses – would be consumed before the spring crops and animals (lambs, calves, kids) became available.

The standard form of meal consisted of three courses: menus in ecclesiastical sources suggest the following possible combinations:

First course	soft cheese	meat pudding or sausage
Second course	meat pudding or sausage	cheese
Third course	fish or vegetables	vegetables or stewed meat

The monastic Benedictine Rule insisted that the midday meal should consist of two cooked courses and a third of fresh fruit and raw vegetables.

Nevertheless it seems likely that important occasions were marked with long-running feasts of several courses, interspersed with music and entertainment.

Hospitality was a major concern for leaders, both ecclesiastical and secular. Reputations were won or lost on the quantity and quality of the fare served at a man's table. Nevertheless it was considered very poor behaviour to encourage another to drink more than he could take, and monastic rules forbade *oferdrenc* 'excessive drinking'. Yet the tale is told of King Eadred who granted land for the establishment of a monastery at Abingdon, Oxfordshire, and was subsequently invited to a feast in the refectory there. Drink was served copiously all the day, but the level in the cask never fell below a span's depth, which was hailed as a miracle.[1]

There was a limit to the hospitality to be provided by the householder. It seems to have been the tradition that the guest should spend no more than two nights and three days with the host. This was intended to keep the duty of welcoming travellers within reasonable bounds for the provider, and to avoid the guest outstaying his welcome.

Due to the Anglo-Saxon liking for transformation and their emphasis on the transient nature of earthly splendour – they inhabited a landscape in which the faded glory of Rome was still to be seen – there is a recurrent theme in the literature dealing with the 'ups and downs' of life, which has been called the *wop æfter wiste* theme. This is a paraphrase of *Beowulf* line 128: *þa wæs æfter wiste wop up ahafen* "then after feasting was weeping arisen". Every scene of building or feasting or merriment in *Beowulf* is immediately – often abruptly – followed

---

[1] Hagen, 1995

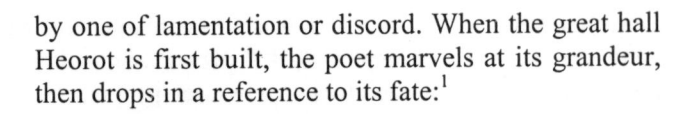

by one of lamentation or discord. When the great hall Heorot is first built, the poet marvels at its grandeur, then drops in a reference to its fate:[1]

...Sele hlifade,
heah ond horngeap,heaðowylma bad,
laðan liges; ne wæs hit lenge þa gen
þæt se ecghete aþumsweorum
æfter wælniðe wæcnan scolde.

...The hall towered
high and horn-gabled, it awaited the battle-flames
of hateful fire – it was not long after then
that the sword-hatred between father- and son-in-law
should awake after murderous deeds.

Beowulf, l. 81-5

Symbel

The *symbel*, as a formal rite with both a social and religious dimension, has been dealt with several times - most notably in Bauschatz's *The Well and the Tree*, a study on which most other modern works rely. Bauschatz rightly emphasises the fact that the *symbel* was an event characterised by both festivity and seriousness, a structured affair where order, orderliness and participation in a traditional joint activity were the whole point. It is perhaps worth stressing that for most ordinary people, living and working outdoors in the countryside, left to their own devices and under considerable pressure to produce enough food for the community, coming together indoors for an ordered, communal activity was a special occasion.

Fig.1 Spoon carved from a single piece of bone, decorated with ribbing on the shaft and animal head detail where the shaft joins the bowl. A leaf-shaped finial completes the piece. 8th-9th century.

---

[1] Heorot was burnt down by Ingeld in an abortive raid – see *Widsið* l.45-8.

Feasting and Society

The feast with strong drink, speech-making, gift-giving and ritual is in many ways the defining image of the warrior society presented in *Beowulf*.[1] The occasion is serious, but not glum; there is laughter and comradeship but not rowdiness or insolence. The strong drink[2] is taken in a strict schedule, accompanied by ritual acts of self-definition e.g. the making of vows, the acceptance of due rewards.

The descriptions and narrative content of these scenes revolve around certain key concepts which Magennis[3] identifies in the following themes:-

- Drinking
- The hall setting
- High status of the participants
- Attendance by stewards and servants
- Presence of music
- Gift-giving
- Presence of (noble) women
- Physical splendour of the scene and its setting
- Rejoicing and merrymaking
- Delivery of speeches

Not all these features are present in all of the many passages dealing with the subject, but taken together they summarise the total 'feast experience' for the poem's audience. A short section such as the following reflects aspects of most of them. It follows the king's invitation to Beowulf and his men to sit at the *symbel* (l.489 - *site nu to symle*) and is a fairly concise demonstration of what to expect:

> *Þa wæs Geatmæcgum geador ætsomne*
> *on beorsele benc gerymed*
> *þær swiðferhþe sittan eodon*
> *þryðum dealle, þegn nytte beheold*
> *se þe on handa bær hroden ealowæge*
> *scencte scirwered scop hwilum sang*
> *hador on Heorote, þær wæs hæleða dream*
> *duguð unlytel Dena 7 Wedera*
> *Unferð maþelode Ecglafes bearn*
> *Þe æt fotum sæt frean Scyldinga*

---

[1] Bauschatz, 1982

[2] One suggested etymology for *symbel* is *som 'together' + *alu 'strong drink, ale'. Bauschatz, 1982

[3] Magennis, 1996, 'The Feast Scenes'; I paraphrase some of the topics for clarity in the present work.

Chapter One

> Then for the Geat-men all together
> a bench was cleared off in the beer-hall
> where the strong-willed ones went to sit
> proud in their strength, the thane held to his duties,
> he who bore the fair ale-cup in his hand
> poured the bright liquid, a *scop* sang at times
> clearly in Heorot, there was joy for heroes
> no small war-troop of Danes and Wederas.
> Unferþ spoke up, the son of Ecglaf,
> who sat at the feet of the Scyldings' lord ...   *Beowulf* 1.491-500

The poet manages to work into these few lines the following themes: drinking (*beorsele* 'beerhall', *ealowæg* 'ale-cup'); the hall setting (*beorsele* 'beerhall', Heorot); high status (*hæleða* ' of heroes', *duguð unlytel* 'no small war-troop' *frean Scyldinga* 'of the Scyldings' lord'); attendance by servants (*þegn nytte beheold* 'the thane held to his duties' *þe æt fotum sæt frean Scyldinga* 'who sat at the feet of the Scyldings' lord'); presence of music (*scop hwilum sang* 'a *scop* sang at times'); physical splendour (*bær hroden ealowæge* 'bore the fair ale-cup'); rejoicing (*þær wæs hæleða dream* 'there was joy for heroes'). Gift-giving plays no part at this early stage in the story – there is as yet no reason to reward the Geats.

Fig.2. Harold and his men dine in his residence at Bosham, Sussex. The fellow on the left is draining his drinking horn, while talking to the man to his left. Harold is the central figure with the palm-cup. The drinker on the right, and the man ascending the steps are pointing to Harold's ship (in the next scene) which is prepared for sailing. The house is clearly meant to be two-storeyed, with the dining area on the upper floor. Scene from the Bayeux Tapestry, redrawn by Lindsay Kerr.

The presence of noblewomen is not an explicit feature of this scene either, yet Hroþgar's queen, Wealhþeow, is present as is the lady Freawaru, as we later learn when Beowulf tells of the feast to his own lord, Hygelac, on his return:

> .... *Ic ðær furðum cwom*
> *to ðam hringsele Hroðgar gretan*
> *sona me se mæra mago Healfdenes*
> *syððan he modsefan minne cuðe*
> *wið his selfes sunu setl getæhte.*
> *Werod wæs on wynne, ne seah ic widan feorh*
> *under heofones hwealf healsittendra*
> *meadudream maran, hwilum mæru cwen*
> *friðusibb folca flet eall geondhwearf*
> *bædde byre geonge, oft hio beahwriðan*
> *secge sealde ær hie to setle geong,*
> *hwilum for duguðe dohtor Hroðgares*
> *eorlum on ende ealuwæge bær*
> *þa ic Freware fletsittende*
> *nemnan hyrde þær hio nægledsinc*
> *hæleðum sealde, sio gehaten is*
> *geong goldhroden gladum suna Frodan*

> … Moreover I came there
> to the ring-hall to greet Hroþgar,
> straightaway the renowned kinsman of Healfdene
> – once he knew my mind –
> showed me a seat by his own son.
> The warband was merry-making, nor have I ever seen in all my life
> under the reach of the heavens, for hall-dwellers
> a greater mead-joy; at times the famed queen,
> the peace-pledge of nations, went about the floor,
> urged the young kinsmen; often, ring-wreathed,
> she passed to a man before she went to her seat,
> sometimes for the older men[1] Hroþgar's daughter
> bore the ale-vessel to the nobles in turn.
> 'Freawaru' a hall-dweller
> I heard name her when a studded gem
> she handed to the heroes; she is betrothed
> – young and gold-adorned – to the lucky son of Froda.
>   *Beowulf*, l.2009-25

---

[1] The *duguð* is the section of the king's warband who are older and more experienced, as contrasted with the *geoguð* 'youth' who supply the muscle and audacity.

The notion of community fostered by the feast imagery is not consistent with a flat social structure. Rather the purpose of the ritual feast – *symbel* – was to highlight and re-affirm the hierarchical structure of the group, the position of leader and the various grades of followers. The role of the richly-dressed female in this structure has been examined by Enright in his study of the figure of "the lady with the mead-cup"[1] while there are many treatments of the role of feasting for the male warbands.

Organisation of the Symbel

The formal sequence of events at the *symbel* appears to be as follows, based partly on the first feasting scene in *Beowulf* (1.607-41):[2] There is a clear distinction in treatment between those of 'guest' status and those of 'guest of honour'. The latter are seated opposite the lord and are assumed to be of equal rank to him, or at least to be similarly exalted. They are accorded privileged status. Ordinary visitors are seated among the ranks of the warriors and take their turn in the rounds of drinking. They stand to be challenged by the lady and the *þyle*,[3] and are assumed to be of lower rank than the lord.

A horn summons the guests to the hall
The Bayeux Tapestry, in a late scene, shows a group of men sitting down to an outdoor meal; one of them has a horn raised to his lips at the narrow end, indicating that he is blowing it (rather than drinking, which would be from the wide end). (See Fig.22 p.177)

The guests enter and wash their hands
Provision of water and a towel was a point of honour in later Norse sagas and some early Continental sources,[4] and may have been an integral part of the tradition of welcoming guests. The Norse *Hávamál* says: *Vatn og handkle og vennlige ord trenger mannen før måltid, gjestfritt sinn, vil han gjerne møte, tale og taushet igjen.* "Water and handcloth and friendly word, a chance to speak, guest-friendship will he gladly find, kindness and attention".

The company stands ready, until the lord enters the hall

---

[1] Enright, 1996

[2] Enright, 1996, Hagen, 1992; the procedure is depicted as the custom of *Heorot* – the greatest of halls – but is by implication to be found in all Anglo-Saxon lordly halls. See Appendix 2 for the OE text and translation.

[3] For more on the *þyle* - see page 174

[4] Enright, 1996 has much to say about the use of the hand-cloth as symbolic of the (female) household's well-being.

The lord directs each person to his or her place

Essentially, the hall-seating was divided between the lord's own circle, guests, tried veteran warriors (the *duguþ* or 'doughty men') who support and advise the lord, and the youngsters (*geoguð* or 'youth') who form the greater part of the armed forces. Rank, length of service, ancestry and other factors determined the hierarchical position of each man present; doubtless those with the best recent track record were accorded the highest honour, which would have involved proximity to the *giefstol*.

The company is seated at the lord's signal

Some men and women remain standing throughout, specifically those detailed to guard the hall and those with a special office or duty.[1] The seating arrangements are a matter of pride, and the seating of a guest reflects clearly the lord's estimation of his worth and status.[2]

The lady enters the hall with a special drinking vessel

She is dressed in fine garments, jewellery and wears a diadem (*gyldnum beage*) – all emphasising the importance and significance of the occasion. When she speaks, she uses carefully chosen words to express noble sentiments; nevertheless, she is entitled to ask direct questions and express views separate from those of the host. (It may be that the whole company of free women enters with the hostess, and that they collectively bear the ale to their menfolk. There is no suggestion that the free women are excluded from the *symbel*, yet *Beowulf* does not make it clear as to how they are involved.)

She greets the gathering and the warriors

As the hostess at the event, the lady is the binding force for the gathering. The warriors stand in a relationship of 'fictive kinship' whereby each of them is adopted into a family structure within the hall. The lady is the matriarchal figure in that scheme.

She offers the first drink to the lord, bidding him enjoy it

The lord stands before his special, prominent seat (*giefstol*) where he can see the whole gathering, and can be seen by them. His seat is the focus of attention, and may have had religious significance in heathen times. To approach the *giefstol* is to risk public exposure as well as to seek public reward. The words she uses are

---

[1] OE uses the word *ombeht* for an official of the hall, a person of rank who nevertheless does not join in the *symbel* rite. The term is borrowed from Gaulish *anda-bactos* 'one who goes around' and when used collectively 'those who walk round' refers to the servants who walk round the hall. Enright (1996, p147) further refers this to the Gaulish custom reported by Posidonius whereby the most important guest at a Celtic feast is seated next to the host, and others in order of distinction in a circle of seats; shield-bearers (=*andabacti*) stand behind their leaders at all times, while spearmen (=*soldurii*) form an inner circle and join in the feasting.

[2] Enright, 1996. Before his fight with Grendel, when he is an unproven quantity, Hroðgar assigns Beowulf a seat among the *geoguð* as the son of his old friend; on his return to Geatland as a valiant, proven hero, Beowulf's own king, Hygelac, seats the warrior at his own side.

not given here, but in a later scene (l.1169-75) a parallel, probably typical, speech is noted: *onfoh þissum fulle, freodrihten min, sinces brytta, þu on sælum wes, goldwine gumena, ond to Geatum spæc mildum wordum – swa sceal man don, beo wið Geatas glæd, geofena gemyndig nean ond feorran þu nu hafast* "Take this cup, my noble lord, sharer of treasure, gold-friend of men, be in good times, speak with kind words to the Geats as one ought to do, be cheerful towards the Geats, mindful of the gifts from near and far which you have now." The repetitive direct address of the lord with grandiloquent epithets – so typical of this poem – is probably based on actual practice, where the purpose of the *symbel* event for the host was to underscore and re-affirm his power and prestige as the leader.[1] The drink should be offered in a splendid drinking horn, rather than the normal cup or beaker; horns were a status symbol at public events.[2] (See Fig.3 p.49)

The lord takes the first drink

By what means was the start of proceedings signalled to the gathering? The following extract[3] from the *Gospel of St.Luke* in the Gothic bible of Bishop Wulfila may throw some light on this. It relates the story of the son who took his share of the inheritance and wasted it, then returned home to ask for forgiveness.

Qaþ þan sa atta du skalkam seinaim "Sprauto bringiþ wastya þo frumiston yah giwasyiþ ina, yah gibiþ figgragulþ in handu is, yah gaskohi ana fotuns is; yah briggandans stiur þana alidan, ufsneiþiþ, yah matyandans, wisam weila. Unte sa sunus meins dauþs was, yah gaqiunoda, yah fralusans was, yah bigitans warþ." Yah dugunnun wisan.

Then the father said to his servants "Quickly, bring the finest garment and clothe him, and put a finger-ring to his hand and shoes to his feet; and bring the fatted steer, kill it and, in eating, let us be merry. For my son was dead and came to life, and he was lost and became found."
And they began to be merry.

The interesting thing here is that the rejoicing father calls for a celebratory meal with the words *'wisam weila'* "let us be well", where 'be well' evidently means 'make merry, enjoy ourselves'; and at the feast they *dugunnun wisan* 'began to be' (sc. *weila* 'well, merry, glad'). It may be that traditionally a Germanic festivity was considered offically underway when the host declared 'let us be well' (OE: *wuton wesan wel*), perhaps accompanied by some gesture such as raising his drinking horn and taking the first drink. Having drunk, he sits.

---

[1] Enright, op.cit. offers parallel orders of service from other contemporary Germanic cultures in support. The opportunity for offence to be given through inappropriately relegating a high-ranker to a lowly position is explored in many Icelandic sagas and elsewhere. See also Hagen, 1995 p.240ff

[2] Hagen, 1995

[3] The text and transliteration used is that of Heather & Matthews, 1991, with 'y' for Gothic 'j'. See also Wright, 1910, p.276

The blessing is said

The grace is said, in Christian times. The guest of honour or highest-ranking person present then symbolically breaks the first loaf.[1] At a heathen feast, it may have been the tradition to toast the gods,[2] or invoke their protection and blessings on the gathering.[3]

The lady greets the guests with welcoming words

As important persons within the event, the guests are accorded special attention which introduces them to the gathering, sets out their lineage and past deeds of fame. Knowing their ancestry, the company have some idea of what can be expected from the guests.

The guest replies with a *beot* and words of thanks

The *beot* is an undertaking to perform some deed which will enhance his own worth and that of the person – the lord – for whom it is undertaken.

The *þyle* challenges the guest's *beot* and the guest responds

The *þyle* sits at the lord's feet and is in some respects his spokesman; the *þyle* has the duty to challenge any claims made by the guest, which it would be ungracious for the lord to do. Between the lady and the *þyle*, views can be aired which would appear respectively suspicious or hostile if presented by the host, whose words have the effect of representing the official view of the gathering. The two associates are thus able to help the lord govern his hall without directly entering into unseemly argument or excessive flattery. The guest must respond to the hard questioning and mocking of the *þyle*, and in so doing he can display either cool-headed reasoning or – it must be assumed – rise to the bait and descend into abuse or angry banter.

---

[1] Hagen, 2000, p.82

[2] King Hákon of Norway made the sign of the cross over his meal, while those about him invoked Þorr's hammer – see below p.48 While it appears that Hákon was present at a traditional celebratory meal – not necessarily a *symbel* – using religious symbols in such circumstances was probably customary.

[3] At a heathen feast, it was customary for the *blot* or animal sacrifice to have taken place; the vessel of blood stood ready and the meat was already cooked. All those who were to take part in the *symbel* had to eat the sacrificial meat – this was the difficulty King Hákon faced, since his Christian faith forbade him to do so. In OE 'to sacrifice to the gods' was *bletsian*, which is the root of our word 'bless'. The boiling of the meat of the slaughtered animal was an integral part of the rite: in Gothic *sauþs* means 'sacrifice', but is based on the verb **seuðan* 'seethe, boil'; cognate is Norse *sauðr* 'sheep'. An alternative term is OE *husl*, Gothic *hunsl*, used of the Christian sacrament but originally meaning 'an offering of food to the gods'. Gothic also recognised the *alabraunsts* 'burnt offering'. See Green, 1998. The great heathen temple at Uppsala, of which Adam of Bremen writes, was called by him both *templum* 'temple' and *triclinium* 'dining-hall' which suggests that he knew of the rites enacted there. See Brink, 1996

The lady moves in procession to the *duguþ* and *geoguþ*, offering a drink to each man in turn

As the lord has taken the first drink, the man closest to him – and therefore with the next highest status – is next to receive the honour of being served. The lady's procession through the hall entrenches and sanctifies the relative status of the various recipients. Each man rises to take the offered vessel, and stands to drink from it. On finishing his draught, he sits again and the lady proceeds to the next man. The last member having been served,[1] the ritual dispensation is over.

The lady returns to her seat beside the lord

As the highest-ranking woman present and the hostess, the representative of the host community, she is responsible for the success of the *symbel* as a social occasion. Her seat is perhaps less prominent than the *giefstol* but is nevertheless in full view of the company. Having served all those who are entitled to be served, she has created a symbolic bond of union for the occasion, a ritual congregation whose members are bound by oaths of brotherhood and, having accepted the lord's cup, have undertaken to show deference to customary good manners.

Although not directly described in *Beowulf* as part of the hall-scenes, there is a strong possibility that one of the further duties of the lady was to make formal announcements, to offer blessings and to utter prophesy.[2]

The guests greet each other

The initiating formalities having been concluded, the guests would now drink each others' health and greet each other. Drinking one's health probably involved raising the horn or cup to the addressee and uttering the formal greeting – more properly a blessing – *wes hal* 'be hale'.[3]

The horn circulates round the hall

The horn goes round in a clockwise – properly sun-wise – rotation, handed on from one man to the next. It is re-filled as necessary by *byrelas* 'cup-bearers' whose task is to ensure that the proper rites of drinking and honouring are

---

[1] While we may conclude that the last person to receive the ale might feel slighted, it may be that the fact of having been served was itself an honour and therefore the warrior or dependant so treated may still have felt himself more favoured than those who were not served at all. Moreover, it would be natural for the hostess to comfort and console those who were not accorded the highest honours, encouraging them to bide their time for the validation which might one day be theirs. Our literature generally focuses on success, and little is known of life at the bottom end of the hall; a great deal of it deals with changeability and the unpredictable nature of worldly fortune, which would be useful in such circumstances.

[2] See below p.184 on the lady's role and ritual background as a 'spaewife'.

[3] *Wes hal* is the origin of our word 'wassail', a formal greeting or benediction. Wishing that somebody be *hal* is more comprehensive than the word 'hale' implies: it survives as both 'hale' (in good health) and 'whole' (lacking nothing). The quality of being *hal* is *hælu* or *hælþu*, 'health, wholeness'. Hagen, 1995, p.244, notes that the monastic *Regularis Concordia* calls for the abbot to drink the health of each monk seated at dinner on Maundy Thursday.

observed. This circulation continues for the duration of the *symbel* and the event cannot end until the horn comes to rest. While individuals may excuse themselves and leave when they have had enough to drink, it is an act of great disrespect for any participant to lay down the drinking horn.[1]

The symbel closes

Quite how the symbel could be wound down, we are not shown. The horn must at some point have ceased to circulate. Possibly, when the lord wished to draw the event to an end he would use his opportunity to speak over the next draught of ale to declare a 'weapon-cup', a last round of drinking. As as the horn left the drinker's hand, he would be given back the weapons he could not have by him at the ceremony, and would then be granted permission to leave.

Head		LORD		
Spokesmen	Scop	LADY	Þyle	GUEST
Officers	Burþegn	Discþegn	Byrele	Duruþegn
Feasters	Geogoð	Duguð	Other Freemen & Guests	

Table 1. The mead-hall hierarchy

Ritual Background To The Symbel

The purpose of ritual is to affirm social values and cohesion; myth necessarily accompanies ritual, and myth likewise re-affirms the identity of the group and of the individuals within that group. The detail of ritual should be unchanging (or, at least, presented as such), but this does not entail that society itself should be unchanged; indeed, part of the importance of myth and ritual is to act as an immutable 'core' to the society and its structures. It is clear, then, that rituals can both be used to create new identities and to distort present social realities. New ideologies, new social structures, new groupings can all be created from the skilful use of ritual enactments, which gain added meaning with every recurrence.[2]

Old English uses the term *weddbroðer* 'pledge-brother' to describe two or more men bound to each other by the power of a voluntary oath, rather than by blood or kinship. These may be men held together in common service to a lord, the

---

[1] Under the Kentish laws of Eadric and Hloðere, a fine was payable for this act of frith-breach – 1 shilling to the lord, 6 shillings to the next man (who should have received the horn) and 12 shillings to the king. (Grönbech, 1931)
[2] Hedeager, 1992

members of the lord's *comitatus* – each a fictive brother through their relationship to their common fictive father. However, the word might also denote men brought into a relationship of mutual support due to their circumstances – members of a guild, for example.

Enright[1] stresses the ritual nature of the *symbel*, and the 'religious aura' which surrounds the key role of wife – lady – hostess in the process. At the first *symbel* in *Beowulf*, before the hero has performed any heroic acts, the lady Wealhþeow offers thanks to God for the help which has been sent at the same time as she offers the cup to Beowulf – a telling combination of religious invocation and symbolic act. In handing a ring to the hero she bids him: *bruc ðisses beages, Beowulf leofa ... ond geþeoh tela* (1.1216-8) 'enjoy this ring, dear Beowulf ... and thrive well' which may be a ritual benison. It appears from the context of the poem that the occasion demands that she make a formal speech at certain points in the proceedings. In this, her behavious verges on that of a 'priestess' but it is clear that her authority is not specifically religious. Wealhþeow is noted for her nobility – she is *ides Helminga* 'lady of the Helmings' – and her wisdom in speech; she may therefore be a 'spaewife', a prophetess, one who can see what is to come.[2] On those occasions where she offers the mead-cup to her guest, a formal speech is called for on acceptance.

Kings and leaders could and did change the detail and meaning of the ceremony.[3] We have scant information regarding Anglo-Saxon England, but we know that in the process of converting Norway to Christianity King Hakon the Good refused to take part in heathen rites at a midwinter meal and instead of making the sign of Þórr's hammer over his food he substituted the sign of the cross. The assembly did not take this divergence well, because it was customary for the whole company to eat the consecrated meat and to drink from the sacred horn. His guests disliked the break with tradition, yet they accepted the right of the leading man among them to set the ceremonial agenda.[4] Their aversion stemmed, it seems, from the communal nature of the gathering at which it was viewed as highly discourteous for the king to intrude his own personal preferences: this was anti-social behaviour in the literal sense.

---

[1] Enright, 1996, Ch.2 Warlords, *Hetzerinnen* and Sibyls

[2] There is an irony in this, for Wealhþeow tries to dissuade Beowulf from becoming the heir of King Hroðgar in favour of Hroþwulf; the latter would later murder her two sons on his way to the throne. Her oracular powers were apparently not infallible.

[3] Herschend, 1998

[4] In Iceland, the division between political and religious leadership was blurred: the 'chieftains' of Icelandic society (which recognised no king in the early years of its existence) were named *goði*, a word which elsewhere means 'priest' (Gothic *gudja*). There is little evidence for a professional priesthood in any Germanic society, and most priestly functions seem to have been fulfilled by leaders or householders. Bede's reference to King Edwin's 'priest' Coifi is very unusual for this reason, and may be the Christian writer's rationalisation of a situation he did not understand. See Brink, 1996 for other words for officials with religious authority: **vivil*, **lytir* and **þul*.

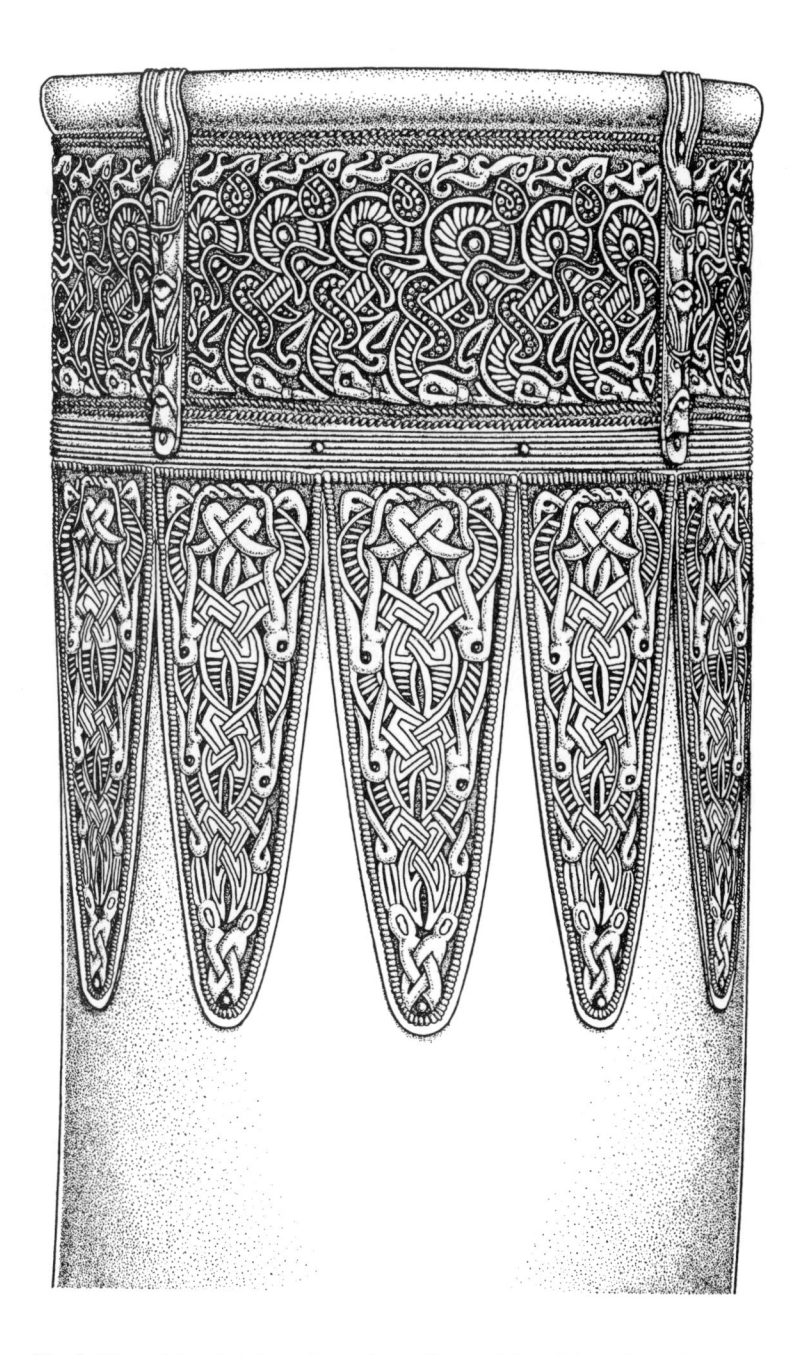

Fig.3 Rim of the drinking horn from Sutton Hoo, Mound 1. One of a pair of magnificent feasting vessels, made from the horns of an aurochs.

It is nevertheless important to recall that there was no single northern European pagan religion replaced by Christianity. For the Anglo-Saxons, we have only a handful of references to pagan belief and practice; though we believe that a range of deities were worshipped, we have little to base this belief on.[1] Place-names, days of the week and a handful of literary references must do service, along with earlier (Roman) and later (mediaeval Icelandic and Danish) sources. That the cults and rites of the various pagan societies were constantly evolving is hardly to be doubted; that Christianity was itself in the process of transformation is often overlooked. Practices such as blessing the plough or working charms for fruitfulness in Anglo-Saxon England are plausibly seen as pagan in origin, yet the instructions for their performance indicate that the Christian clergy were involved.[2] Competing forms of Christianity led to charges of heresy and paganism within and among Christian communities.

It is possible that, in heathen times, at certain festivals the noble vessel carried in by the lady of the household might have contained sacrificial blood from an animal offered to the gods.[3] The communal drinking of this blood – whether mixed into ale or otherwise kept liquid – served as an act of binding together the community in worship of the gods. Enright[4] mentions the tale from the *Vita Columbani* where a group of heathens are about to offer a libation to their god, Wodan, from a special vessel of beer, and the reluctance of pagans and Christians to share a common drink at a feast in the *Vita Vedastis*. It is significant that the ancient word for the act of sacrifice, evidenced in the *asvamedha* or 'horse-sacrifice' of the *Rig Veda*, is based on the same root *medh- as OE *medu* (NE 'mead') an alcoholic drink.[5]

The vessels themselves have been seen as emblematic of the mythical well which was the source of space-time; it was important that they should not be mundane but rather treasured heirlooms or imported exotic pieces, demonstrating the leader's mastery of both time (old vessels) and space (foreign vessels). An

---

[1] Wood, 1995

[2] Pollington, 2000

[3] Tacitus, *Germania*, chapter 9, mentions that the Germani of his day were wont to propitiate their gods with sacrifice of customary animals. Finds of sacrificed animals – especially horses, but also sheep, pigs and other livestock – have been made in many northern European contexts from the Iron Age, and it is noted that they often appear to have been butchered for cooking. (Rives, 1999, p.161-2)

[4] Enright, op.cit. p.16

[5] Puhvel, 1987 Like the early Irish rite of kingly ordination, involving copulation with a mare, then slaughtering the animal, bathing in its blood while drinking the broth and eating its flesh, the *asvamedha* was associated with the strengthening of royal power (Watkins, 1995). Whether sacrificial blood was ever involved or not in Germanic *symbel* rites, the drink at a heathen feast was clearly charged with great significance and could not be accepted by Christians; imbibing the liquid implied acceptance of a cultic bond which was tabu for followers of the new religion.

emphasis on heirlooms and imports is characteristic of Germanic high-status burials, such as Sutton Hoo[1] and Taplow.[2]

The Lord As Ring-Giver

Gift-giving was a central act in Germanic society, cementing the bonds among the free classes.[3] It was neither random, spontaneous, nor purely emotional, but rather was strictly controlled by rules of reciprocation. Warlords handed out weapons to their followers, but the weapons were not 'given away', they were held by the hearth-troop to be used in defence of the leader. The *Beowulf* poet spells out clearly the purpose of liberality (l.20-6):

Swa sceal geong guma gode gewyrcean,
fromum feohgiftum on fæder bearme,
þæt hine on ylde eft gewunigen
wilgesiþas, þonne wig cume,
leode gelæsten; lofdædum sceal
in mægþa gehwære man geþeon.

Thus shall a young warrior bring about good
with splendid[4] gift-giving in his father's embrace
so that in old age still remain with him
his willing companions, when war comes
they help their prince; with praiseworthy deeds shall
a man thrive in any nation.

Broadly speaking, when any man gave a gift he expected a return, a counter-gift. What form that return might take would depend on the relative social status of giver and recipient. A gift to a superior would be rewarded by favour; to an equal, by counter-gift; to an inferior, by service.[5] The concept survives into our own times. (See diagram next page)

---

[1] Sutton Hoo is a fascinating and unique location. There were probably two ship burials there, as well as cremations, mound burials and one young man buried with his horse. If burying a man with his steed was intended to display his worth – some Thuringians were buried with many horses, and Childerich of the Franks was accompanied by twenty-one – then how much greater was the worth of the man who took an entire ship to his grave!

[2] Bauschatz, 1982

[3] This extends to reciprocation in other areas – for as much as a gift had to be repaid, so did an act of aggression have to be met with revenge. Balance was the aim throughout.

[4] Hill, 1995, notes that *from* in this context may be deliberately ambiguous, meaning either 'splendid' to emphasise the richness of the gifts, or 'warlike, bold' to stress the martial qualities which the gifts are supposed to enhance.

[5] Hedeager, 1992

Chapter One

Higher Status Receiver

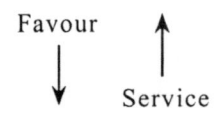

Favour ↓   ↑ Service

Lower Status Receiver

Gifts tend to move down the social scale, because in so doing they create bonds of loyalty and gratitude, or political dependency. Gifts among equals, unless of similar worth, will similarly reflect degrees of hierarchy within a social stratum; the wealthier man can give more lavish presents to his less affluent peers.

Gifts are badges of friendship in Anglo-Saxon society: friends are people who exchange gifts. Gifts are also rewards for good service in the past and in earnest of goodwill – in that sense, they are a mark of trust by the leader in the follower's continued allegiance. As John M. Hill remarks: "the rightful possession of treasure marks honor".[1] The crucial word here is "rightful", since theft or deception are not honourable.

Beowulf can be read as an exploration of the heroic ideal, but it seems an uneasy peace that the hero wins for his people. The poem is perhaps more about the ethics of reciprocal social bonds, and how to survive in a changeable world.

In the Roman Iron Age, lavish Mediterranean imports took on a symbolic function among the Germanic kingly classes as prestige goods which circulated among the high-status group only. These goods included gold jewelry, glassware and sets of feasting equipment such as bronze dishes, vats, wine-strainers, flagons and cups which symbolised for the users both the exotic, abundant eating habits of the Roman Empire and exclusive, unattainable material wealth.[2] These Roman goods were never copied by local craftsmen: their value lay in their foreign origins and unusual forms, and in the fact that only the elite had access to them. Possession of these prestige goods signified membership of the elite, and thereby conferred status on the owner. They were evidently exchanged over long distances in northern and eastern Europe, probably as part of the network of alliances which bound tribal leaders together. They were also used on a smaller scale in regional exchange networks, where kings bound local chiefs to their political structures. Some ended up as grave-goods, in rituals which reinforced

---

[1] Hill, 1997

[2] In the preceding pre-Roman Iron Age, Central European goods such as neck-rings, bronze cauldrons and weapons decorated with La Tene art-styles fulfil a similar function.

the position of the deceased's kindred in its society.[1] Notably, weapons began to be deposited in inhumation graves from this time onwards in a break with the previous cremation tradition. Weapons in graves probably signified membership of the weapon-bearing classes, the freemen; the possession of weapons became to some extent a badge denoting status. Warriors, who did not themselves have access to prestige goods, must have bound themselves to leaders who were connected to the long-range exchange network; in this way a new relationship between leaders and followers was developed, based on the handing out of costly items with considerable display value.

Beyond mere portable wealth (OE *feoh*) there was the added advantage, for those who lasted long enough to earn it, of land and property (OE *ebel*). Land sustained the lifestyle aspirations of the *duguð*, providing them with material comfort, marriage, family and an elevated status; they became lords of their own lands, with their own followers and halls. A grant of land was normally only made to the individual, however, and each succeeding generation of the family had to earn the right to inherit in turn. The poet Deor bemoans the fact that the estate he had long enjoyed had recently been allocated to another (l. 38-41) *ahte ic fela wintra folgaþ tilne, holdne hlaford oþþæt Heorrenda nu, leoðcræftig monn, londryht geþah þæt me eorla hleo ær gesealde* ('for many years I had a good following, a trusty lord, until now that Heorrenda, the song-skilled man, received that land-right which the heroes' protector gave to me before') while another, Widsið, tells how he used a valuable armring, given to him as a reward, to buy the estates which had belonged to his father from Eadgils, King of the Myrgingas *þæs þe he me lond forgeaf mines fæder eþel frea Myrginga* (1.95-6) 'so that he, the Myrgings' lord, should give me the land, my father's estate'. It is evident, then, that an estate was not an inheritable possession in the modern sense: all the sons of a land-holder could expect was the right to earn the land anew. That this arrangement must have created enormous family tensions is undoubted; likewise, it must have created intense rivalries in political units where successes were not plentiful, and there was less and less land to award for faithful service.

The gifts offered by the leader at the *symbel* were tokens of esteem (OE *weorþ* 'honour, worthiness'[2]) and they were symbolically charged, as with the ring-hilted swords whose decorative feature marked the contract between leader and honoured follower. Acceptance of these gifts was accompanied by formal gestures. The lord offered the gift and his right hand which the follower took and kissed, placing his head on the lord's knee.

---

[1] Hedeager, 1992. It is fair to remark that we still have no accurate idea as to what grave-goods meant to those who deposited them.

[2] Bazelmans, 1999

þinceð him on mode þæt he his mondryhten
clyppe ond cysse, ond on cneo lecge
honda ond heafod, swa he hwilum ær
in geardagum giefstolas breac.

It seems to him in his mind that his lord
He calls and kisses, and onto his knee lays
Hands and head, as he sometimes before
Enjoyed the gift-stools in former times.   *The Wanderer*, l.41-4[1]

The elevated seating of the lord on a dais – the 'high-seat' – would allow the recipient to perform this act without undue abasement. The ceremonial act was closed with the taking of strong drink by the recipient, served by a female.[2]

Each reward looked to its return, and any gift was but one move in an ongoing social ritual in which nobility defined itself through openhandedness. Whether the gift bought the favour of mighty leaders, or firm friendship in times of need, or the esteem of peers, it was nevertheless important that it be used wisely. Warlords handed out weapons to be used in their own defence, and honours which would reflect well on giver and receiver alike.[3] The cycle of 'reward for service – service for reward' was central to the ethic of hall-life.

Oaths And Boasts

There are a number of terms used to describe the formal speech of the warriors, including *gilp*, *gilpspæc* and *gilpcwide*. Although often translated as 'vow' or 'boast', none of these terms quite capture the significance of the act of speaking ritual words: the *beot* is closer to 'incantation' than any kind of boasting. It is intended to fill the speaker and the audience with confidence, to strengthen his resolve to accomplish the task he has set himself and to re-affirm the communal value of courage, facing danger on behalf of the host community.

The word *beot* is derived from *bi-hat* 'calling' (*hatan* 'to call, to name') and is involved with the Germanic notion of single-combat and duelling. A warrior who challenges another to fight is called an *oretta* or *oretmecg* 'challenger'.[4] The same verb *hatan* is used for promises (*Beowulf* l.1392 *ic hit þe gehate* 'I promise it to you') in Old English; the related Gothic form *ushaitan* is 'to provoke, to challenge' and the Norse form *heita* can mean 'to threaten'. The ideas of 'naming' and 'calling' imply an open challenge or offer, publicly made, on which one's reputation will rest.

---

[1] Leslie, 1985

[2] Enright, 1996 p.85 stresses the persistence of the terms 'kiss' and 'hand' in later Germanic laws referring to contractual service.

[3] Hill, 1995

[4] *oret* 'challenge' is from *or-hat* 'calling [another to come] out'. See Green, 1998

The utterance of the *beot* was accompanied by strong drink. This was at least originally sacramental – speaking under the influence of alcohol, a man was less able to deceive others or hide his true feelings. Tacitus[1] noted that it was Germanic custom in his day to debate all important issues with the accompaniment of strong drink, but to avoid taking decisions until all were sober.

In *Beowulf*, the hero cannot promise success in his undertaking, and the gathering acknowledges this; he can only promise to slay the attacker or to die in the attempt. Hroðgar has already made plain that others have made similar *beotas*, and have not lived to see success. The importance of the *beot* as part of the *symbel* is crucial: there are many references in Old English verse (*Beowulf*, *The Battle of Maldon*, *Brunanburh*, *Finnsburh*, *The Wanderer* and elsewhere) to men fulfilling what they had promised over their mead. The *scop* would then sing of their courage and honour, spreading their fame.

This notion of fame is central to the warrior ethos. The goal of every warrior was to be considered worthy and honourable in the hope that, after death, his name would live on in stories and poems to be told for generations to come. It was crucially important to his worth to avoid swearing false oaths - that is to say, either knowingly stating as truth something which he knew not to be, or undertaking to do something he could not achieve. Carefully wording the oath to avoid both these dishonourable outcomes would have been a wise precaution.

Gebeorscipe

While the *symbel* was a heavily symbolic, ritually rigid and controlled form of event, there is evidence for a less restrictive social occasion. This appears in the literature as the *gebeorscipe* which can be rendered 'beer-drinking' or 'drinking party'. It seems that this kind of occasion could have elements of the *symbel* attached to it, although it may not always have done so.

It is suggested that the standard feast was a day-long event and the guest was expected to stay to the end;[2] the ceremonial part of it may have been only a small but important section of the overall festivity. Special events were celebrated with a party lasting three days (and we noted above, p.37, that the host's responsibility was to provide for his guests for a maximum of three days).

The tale is told of King Oswold's murder by his rivals, Penda of Mercia and Cadwallon of Gwynedd, and the miracles which occurred at the spot where the king's body had been hung. Eventually, people began to take away portions of the soil from the spot in the hope of securing some of the king's (later, a saint) remedial powers. The story continues:[3]

---

[1] *Germania*, ch.22
[2] Hagen, 1992
[3] Needham, 1976

*Eft siððan ferde eac sum ærendfæst ridda be ðære ylcan stowe 7
geband on anum claþe of þam halgan duste þære deorwurðan stowe 7
lædde forð mid him þær he fundode to. Þa gemette he gebeoras bliðe
æt þam huse: he aheng þa þæt dust on ænne heahne post 7 sæt mid
þam gebeorum blissigende samod. Man worhte þa micel fyr tomiddes
ðam gebeorum 7 þa spearcan wundon wið þæs rofes swyðe oð þæt
þæt hus færlice eall on fyre wearð 7 þa gebeoras flugon afyrhte aweg.
Þæt hus wearþ ða forburnon buton þam anum poste þe þæt halige on
ahangen wæs ....*

Afterwards a certain rider on an errand rode by that same place, and
bound up into a cloth some of the holy dust from that precious place
and carried it off with him to where he was heading. When he met
happy beer-drinkers at the house, he hung up the dust onto a high post
and sat with the beer-drinkers, making merry together with them.
Then a great fire was made in the middle of the drinkers, and the
sparks spun up fiercely towards the roof, until suddenly all the house
was on fire and the frightened drinkers fled away. The house was
burnt down then, except for the one post on which the holy dust had
been hung up ...

Life of St. Oswold, l.183-92

These *gebeoras* 'people who take beer together', do not sound like the nobles one finds at the *symbel* in *Beowulf* and the other verse. They are *bliðe* 'happy', but their happiness in combination with their drinking has made them very careless. When the house catches fire, they flee in terror, rather than staying to extinguish the flames. We are not told whether these are freemen, servants or bondsmen, but the fact that they have organised a social event with a supply of strong drink suggests that they are not members of the unfree classes. It may be that the *gebeorscipe* was an impromptu affair, a small-scale celebration or casual social event. This is borne out by the story of Cædmon (see Appendix 2 for more of this story):[1]

*Wæs he se mon in weoruldhade geseted oð þa tide þe he wæs gelyfdre
ylde, 7 næfre nænig leoð geleornade. Ond he forþon oft in
gebeorscipe, þonne þær wæs blisse intinga gedemed, þæt heo ealle
sceolden þurh endebyrdnesse be hearpan singan, þonne he geseah þa
hearpan him nealecan, þonne aras he for scome from þæm symble 7
ham eode to his huse.*

---

[1] The Cædmon story was a popular tale, and at least two version of the hymn survive. Henry, 1966, argues for a British origin for the poet, and Irish Latin influence in the verse.

Feasting and Society

That man was established in secular life until the time when he was quite old, and never learnt any verse. And for that reason often at a beer-drinking, when a cause for celebration had been determined, so that they must all sing with a harp in turn, when he saw the harp nearing him he then rose from the feasting for shame and went home to his house.

From the Old English version of Bede's
Historia Ecclesiastica Gentis Anglorum

It is clear that the *gebeorscipe* here is a celebration or commemorative rejoicing: *þonne þær wæs blisse intinga gedemed* "when a cause for celebration had been determined". It also clear that the entertainment aspects of the evening – the singing and music – are *symbel*-related, because Cædmon escapes *for scome from þæm symble* "from the *symbel* for shame". They are provided by members of the gathering, not by professional entertainers.

The story of Apollonius of Tyre was known in Anglo-Saxon England, and a vernacular version of the tale survives. Having suffered shipwreck, Apollonius seeks out some nearby dwellings, which are the quarters of the king of the land:

Ða eode se man in beforan to ðam cynge 7 cwæð "Se forlidena man is cumen þe ðu æfter sændest. ac he ne mæg for scame ingan buton scrude". Ða het se cyngc hine sona gescridan mid wurðfullan scrude. 7 het hine ingan to ðam gereorde. Ða eode apollonius in. 7 gesæt þar him getæht wæs, ongean ðone cyngc. Ðar wearð ða seo þenung ingeboren 7 æfter þam cynelice gebeorscipe. 7 apollonius nán ðingc ne æt. ðeah ðe ealle oðre men æton 7 bliðe wæron

Then the man went in before [him] to the king and said "The shipwrecked man whom you sent for has come, but he cannot enter without clothing, for his shame." Then the king straightaway ordered that he be clothed and bade him go in to the meal (*gereord*). Then Apollonius went in and sat himself down where it was indicated to him, across from the king. Then the meal was carried in, and after that a kingly beer-drinking (*gebeorscipe*) and Apollonius ate nothing, although all the other men were eating and were happy.

From *Apollonius of Tyre*[1] Chapter 21

---

[1] ed. Thorpe, 1834; Goolden, 1958

Chapter One

Fig.4 Feasting scene. The lack of drinking horns among these Norman diners is noticeable, as is the rather aggressive posture of the bearded figure on the left who is crowding out his neighbour. Scene from the Bayeux Tapestry, redrawn by Lindsay Kerr.

Here, the king's meal is followed by a convivial gathering with strong drink, called in this text a *gebeorscipe*. Presumably the lack of formal gift-giving, speeches and ritual prevent this occasion from being presented as a *symbel*. Later (Chapter 24) Apollonius has explained that the sight of all the happiness and pleasure at the king's court has reminded him of the happiness and pleasure he has lost through his misfortunes. He calls for a harp to show the king's daughter his skill:

Đa het se cyng sillan apollonige þa hearpan. Apollonius þa út eode 7 hine scridde 7 sette ænne cyne-helm uppon his heafod 7 nám þa hearpan on his hand 7 in-eode. 7 swa stód þæt se cyngc 7 ealle þa ymbsittendan wéndon þæt he nære apollonius ac þæt he wære apollines ðara hæðenra god. Đa wearð stilnes 7 swíge geworden innon ðare healle. 7 apollonius his hearpe-nægl genám. and he þa hearpe-strengas mid cræfte astirian ongan. 7 þare hearpan sweg mid winsumum sange gemægnde. 7 se cyngc silf 7 ealle þe þar andwearde wæron micelre stæfne cliopodon 7 hine heredon. Æfter þisum forlet apollonius þa hearpan and plegode 7 fela fægera þinga þar forð teah. þe þam folce ungecnawen wæs 7 ungewunelic. 7 heom eallum þearle licode ælc þara þinga ðe he forð teah.

> Then the king ordered that Apollonius be given the harp. Apollonius went out and clothed himself and set a crown upon his head and took the harp in his hand and went back in, and he stood so that the king and all those seated there believed that he was not Apollonius, but Apollo the god of the heathens. Then calm and silence came about in the hall and Apollonius took up his plectrum and began to stir the harpstring with skill and mixed the harp's music with joyful song, and the king himself and all those who were present called out with a great clamour and praised him. After this Apollonius put aside the harp, and he played and brought forth many fine things which were unknown and outlandish to the people, and each thing he brought forth pleased them all greatly.

Here again we have something closer to the entertainment and merriment of Cædmon's nocturnal gathering than to the formal, structured seriousness of the *symbel* at Heorot. While the details of the Apollonius story were already fixed before the Anglo-Saxon scribe wrote them down, the English words used to describe them were not. Nowhere does the translator suggest that the king's meal and drinking party is a *symbel*; it is always a *gebeorscipe* or *gereord* (communal meal, gathering to talk), neither of which seems to have the specific ritual nuances of the *symbel*. Even the traveller's harping – a feature of the Cædmon story no less than the present one – cannot transform this serious but informal occasion into a ritual event.

An indication of the expectation among an early English community of a formal gathering occurs in the *Vita Sancti Æthelwoldi* written by Wulfstan of Winchester. King Eadred and his hearth-troop visited Athelwold's monastery at Abingdon and they were treated to a public gathering of the monastic community at which the traditional drinking bouts took place; miraculously the supply of drink was not exhausted, even though the group sat drinking all day.[1] A similar story is told by Ælfric, and Bede tells of St. Cuthbert turning water into wine, which has a clear biblical precedent in the 'wedding at Cana' episode.

Other Old English terms for high-status feasting are *ætwela* 'well-being through eating', *gereord* 'discussion' and its compounds *beodgereord* and *symbelgereord*, *feorm* 'hospitality meal', *winþegu* 'wine-tasting' (as wine was an expensive and high-status drink) and *wiste* 'abundance' (because there was no stint of any food or drink). The Christmas period of enforced inactivity was celebrated with a *winterfeorm*, and Easter with an *easterfeorm*, while a meal provided for travellers was a *cumfeorm*.

---

[1] Magennis, 1996

Chapter One

Feasts, Marriages and Alliances

With the emphasis on warbands and oaths and heroic deeds, it may seem that Anglo-Saxon feasts were essentially military events. Yet we refer below (p.104) to the wedding feast of Ingeld and his bride, whose marriage was supposed to heal the rift between two communities (see *Widsið* l.45-9 for Ingeld's failed attack on the Danes at Heorot). Weddings and funerals seem to have been two occasions which demanded a communal meal – a tradition which has not entirely died out yet.

The wedding celebrtion was called the *brydealoþ* 'bride-ale', indicating that the union of man and woman had to be toasted with strong drink.

Despite the political history of the time appearing to consist almost exclusively of conflicts, battles, long-running wars and feuding, there is good evidence that peaceful, even friendly relations could exist between Anglo-Saxon polities and their British neighbours fostered through exogamous marriages. The following are a handful of northern examples:[1]

> *King Oswiu of Northumbria was connected with Princess Fin of the northern Ui Neill, and their son was King Aldfrið of Northumbria;*
>
> *King Oswiu of Northumbria married Princess Rhiainfellt of Rheged, as part of an alliance;*
>
> *King Talorcan of the Picts was the son of King Eanfrið of Bernicia and an unnamed Pictish noblewoman*

These relationships happen to be traceable today due to the testimony of Nennius and Bede, and it seems likely that all Anglo-Saxon kingdoms would have attempted to weave a network of trust and good relations with their neighbours of whichever language or religion.

The complex inter-relationships of Anglo-Saxon, British, Dal Riadic and Pictish nobility in the 7th and 8th centuries is well recorded. Likewise, the involvement of Iona and the Irish in the spread of Christianity in England has long been recognised. Cultural, political and personal contacts between Ireland and Northumbria are evidenced by the history of the region, including the exile of one branch of Northumbrian kings among the men of Dal Riada. On their return, they brought Irish devotional traditions with them to their kingdom. Great works such as the Lindisfarne Gospels or the Book of Durrow arose from the fusion of insular art styles and the Germanic decorative tradition of the Anglo-Saxons.

---

[1] See Cessford, 1996

It is not too fanciful to see in these connections one explanation for some of the apparently intrusive items in the archaeological record – for example, an Anglo-Saxon sword-bead and button brooch from South Cadbury, Dorset, dating from as much as a century before the area fell into English hands; or some pieces of Germanic glasswork from southwest Scotland; or the burial in a prone position of a woman at Blackness, near Glasgow, with a Germanic bracelet.[1] While it is perfectly possible that some of these items were traded in, and others arrived with captives from Anglo-Saxon areas, there is a good chance that many were in fact part of the system of gift exchange among hosts and guests.

If this is so, then it would also explain the remarkable incidence of British elements in the Sutton Hoo ship burial. Some of the feasting-gear featured enamelled escutcheons of certain British workmanship (Fig.20 p.165, inset), while the whetstone may also have been influenced by Celtic traditions.[2] If the cauldrons were indeed made by British craftsmen and had found their way to East Anglia as part of the diplomatic exchanges of the 6th century, they would sit happily alongside the Byzantine silver, Roman tableware, Indian garnets, Baltic armour, Egyptian bowl and other exotic items which this powerful leader had acquired.

The mound burial complex was not the only important group of interments on the site. About half a mile to the north a farmer discovered a large bronze bucket with a Greek inscription. This find – the Bromeswell Bucket – dates from approximately the 6th century AD; it was probably made in Antioch, and is one of a class of similar objects found in late 6th to early 7th century graves in England.[3] Possibly even more telling is the evidence uncovered in the construction of the new Sutton Hoo Visitor Centre: 19 inhumations and 17 cremations in a tight group centred on a Bronze Age barrow. One of the cremations was the focus for a group of four neighbours; it was contained not in an earthenware pot, but in a magnificent bronze hanging bowl (Fig.20 p.165). Each of the four satellites contained a portion of a similar vessel, presumably emblematic of joint feasting in this life and the next. As with some of the finds from Mound 1, the vessel was of British workmanship with finely executed La Tene style escutcheons. This smaller cemetery was possibly a century or more earlier than the larger, more imposing mound-field, and it had strong symbolic ties to Germanic burial traditions: nine of the cremations were enclosed within ring-ditches, a common feature in northern Germany but less frequent in England. The burial in the bowl can hardly be anything other than that of an important man with strong (family?) links to northern Germany and with access to high-quality British metalwork.

---

[1] Proudfoot & Aliaga-Kelly, 1996 have a listing of known Anglo-Saxon artefacts from Scotland from the 5th to the 9th centuries. O' Sullivan (same volume) has tracked down an apparently pagan-period Anglo-Saxon group of burials from the Eden valley, Cumbria.

[2] The whetstone is a unique item, but there are known parallels of symbolic whetstones from Celtic Britain. While none of them is even superficially similar to the Sutton Hoo example, it remains the case that there are no known comparable Germanic finds either.

[3] See *Current Archaeology*, 180.

Chapter One

It is perhaps worth noting that there was a persistent Germanic tradition of 'funeral feasting' whereby the burial of a prominent person was marked with a ritual meal, taken by the kinsmen of the departed and his friends and followers. This points up the use of a communal meal as a shared event. Evidence suggests that, in concluding the commemorative event, ale was drunk to the well-being of the dead on his or her journey to the next world, and songs were sung praising good and noble deeds. Thus in *Beowulf* (1.3156-82) the king's passing is mourned by his followers and folk:

> Geworhton ða Wedra leode
> hleo on hoe, se wæs heah ond brad,
> wægliðendum wide gesyne,
> ond betimbredon on tyn dagum
> beadurofes becn, bronda lafe
> wealle beworhton, swa hyt weorðlicost
> foresnotre men findan mihton.
> Hi on beorg dydon beg ond siglu,
> eall swylce hyrsta, swylce on horde ær
> niðhedige men genumen hæfdon,
> forleton eorla gestreon eorðan healdan,
> gold on greote, þær hit nu gen lifað
> eldum swa unnyt swa hit æror wæs.
> Þa ymbe hlæw riodan hildediore,
> æþelinga bearn, ealra twelfe,
> woldon ceare cwiðan ond kyning mænan,
> wordgyd wrecan ond ymb wer sprecan;
> eahtodan eorlscipe ond his ellenweorc
> duguðum demdon, swa hit gedefe bið
> þæt mon his winedryhten wordum herge,
> ferhðum freoge, þonne he forð scile
> of lichaman læded weorðan.
> Swa begnornodon Geata leode
> hlafordes hryre, heorðgeneatas,
> cwædon þæt he wære wyruldcyninga
> manna mildust ond monðwærust,
> leodum liðost ond lofgeornost.

Feasting and Society

Then the nation of the Weders[1] made
a barrow on a headland – it was high and broad
widely seen by seamen –
and in ten days they built
a beacon for the battle-fierce man, about the fire's leavings
they made a wall as, most worthily,
the wisest men could devise it.
Into the mound they put a ring and standards,
all such war-gear as from the hoard before
battle-brave men had taken it –
they let the earth hold the treasure of heroes,
gold in the ground where it now still rests
as useless to men as it was before.
Then around the mound rode the war-brave ones,
sons of nobles, twelve in all;
they wished to tell their sorrow and mourn the king,
make a lament in words and speak of the man;
they told of his heroism and his deeds of courage
with warriors they praised, as shall be fitting
that a man praise his friend-lord with words,
love him in his heart when he must take his leave,
be led forth from his body.
Thus mourned the nation of the Geats -
his hearth-companions -their lord's fall
they said that he had been among the world-kings
the mildest of men and the kindest,
the gentlest to his people and the keenest for praise.[2]

This tradition of funeral commemoration was Christianised into the formal anniversary feast celebrating the leading members of the community.[3] With feasts on saints' days and other important festivals, monasteries must have been as often the scenes of ritual meals as were secular halls.

Bede says that Pope Gregory specifically encouraged the continuation of 'pagan' feasts among the English but re-dedicated to the god and saints of the incoming religion, so that the locals would see that their time-honoured traditions were not swept away by the new faith, and thus would come to accept it the more readily.

---

[1] Beowulf's folk are variously named as *Wederas* 'Weders' and *Geatas* 'Geats'. The two terms seem to be interchangeable in this poem.

[2] It is interesting that Beowulf's folk find it most praiseworthy of him not that he was boldest in battle, or greediest for slaughter, but that he treated his own folk with dignity and kindness.

[3] Hagen, 1992

Chapter One

Aside from religious gatherings and events staged by secular or military leaders, there is evidence for the observance of regular feasts by guildsmen – communities of traders or craftsmen whose work involved them in inward-focussed communities. Non-members could buy a seat at the high table of a guild feast with a payment.[1] Guild meals were evidently quite an important social occasion in later Anglo-Saxon England, and the leftover food was distributed to the needy as alms.

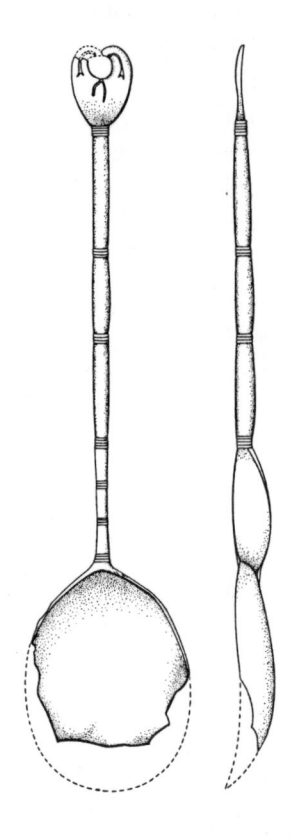

Fig.5 Fragment of a silver spoon with waisting on the shaft and opposed animal heads on the finial. Found at Desborough, Northamptonshire. Possibly early 7th century.

---

[1] Hagen, 1992; the Cambridge Thegns' Guild demanded one *sester* (large pot?) of honey if a retainer wished to purchase this privelege; the retainer is described as a *fotsetla* 'foot-sitter' or subordinate.

2 The Hall – construction & furniture

The Hall and its Settlement

One of the problems facing historians of the Anglo-Saxon period is the difficulty of matching up the written record with the surviving artefacts and archaeology. In many parts of the country, settlement remains are quite insubstantial and easily overlooked or destroyed. Also, it must often be the case that the remains of human habitation founded in the Anglo-Saxon period lie directly beneath the subsequent mediaeval and modern buildings on the same site. Unless there happens to be a sizeable concentration of pottery or metalwork, dating any structures that are found can be problematic.

In many parts of the country, the majority of secular architecture until quite recent times was made from timber, which survives only in exceptional circumstances, such as waterlogging. This means that inferences about the construction of mediaeval and earlier houses are based largely on the position and depth of postholes.

The evidence of dating available to historians of ecclesiastical architecture – shapes of windows and doors, thickness of walls, surface decoration, etc. – are totally absent where the building material has perished or been removed. The Anglo-Saxon period secular buildings appear to have been uniformly rectangular, and the main differences between the houses of yeomen and kings lie in the scale of the buildings and the materials used in constructing them.[1]

Given that in many cases the inhabitants would periodically take down buildings and re-erect them elsewhere – it perhaps was easier to repair damage and replace rotten timbers in so doing - archaeologists often face challenging situations on Anglo-Saxon sites, because the mass of post-holes and trenches do not necessarily relate to a single structure at a single phase of its existence. It may even have been traditional for each new owner, on acquiring or inheriting the site, to build a new home because living in an old house implied poverty.[2] Fortunately, some of the most characteristic early Anglo-Saxon structures – the Sunken Featured Buildings (SFBs) – were used intensively and often have a useful quantity of domestic material in their infill, possibly indicating that they

---

[1] Dixon, 1991

[2] Dixon, 1991 On this reading, the 'eternal' structures were the churches which would be free from this social constraint. Yet Anglo-Saxon churches show a developmental history every bit as complex as the halls and other buildings.

were erected as workshops but when they began to need major repair the superstructure was removed and the internal cellars were converted to rubbish pits.[1]

Settlement layout is difficult to determine since only exceptionally is a large area of an Anglo-Saxon settlement available for excavation.[2] Those which can be explored in this way are by definition failed settlements; most Anglo-Saxon villages underlie modern towns, villages and hamlets. Many early sites appear to have been laid out as large central dwellings surrounded by a scatter of SFBs. It is seldom possible to determine accurately how long any single structure lasted, to be able to assess how many buildings are strictly contemporary.

Landscape features such as wells, droveways, boundary and drainage ditches are sometimes traceable though many such features are difficult to date. Cots – small, isolated workshops or temporary dwellings – must have been plentiful judging by place-name evidence (Caldecot, Didcot, Walcott, etc.) but are virtually invisible archaeologically.

Key:
A – Main Door
B – Private Door
C – Antechamber
D – Dais (*yppe*)
E – Hearth (*heorð*)
F – Lord's high seat
G – Lady's high seat
H – Guest's high seat
I – Mead-Bench (*medubenc*)
J – *Þyle* (spokesman)
K – *Byrele* (cupbearer)
L – *Duruþegn* (doorkeeper)

Duguð – nobles / older, experienced warriors
Geoguð – young warriors

Fig.6 Schematic plan of an Anglo-Saxon hall. - opposite

---

[1] Welch, 1992; Dixon, 1991. On the basis of finds of hearths within SFBs it used to be assumed that they were primarily built as dwellings. However, hearths are needed for many industrial processes; also, broken fragments of fireside material are among the many types of domestic rubbish. Another possibility is that SFBs were used to house slaves, as they may have been in Frankish and Viking contexts (Faith, 1997), although they seem far too numerous for this purpose. In Anglo-Saxon tradition, 'slaves' were agricultural workers who had to render most of their produce to their owner without payment; although they could be traded, they were not generally a mobile asset but one of the appurtenances of an estate.

[2] Rahtz, 1976

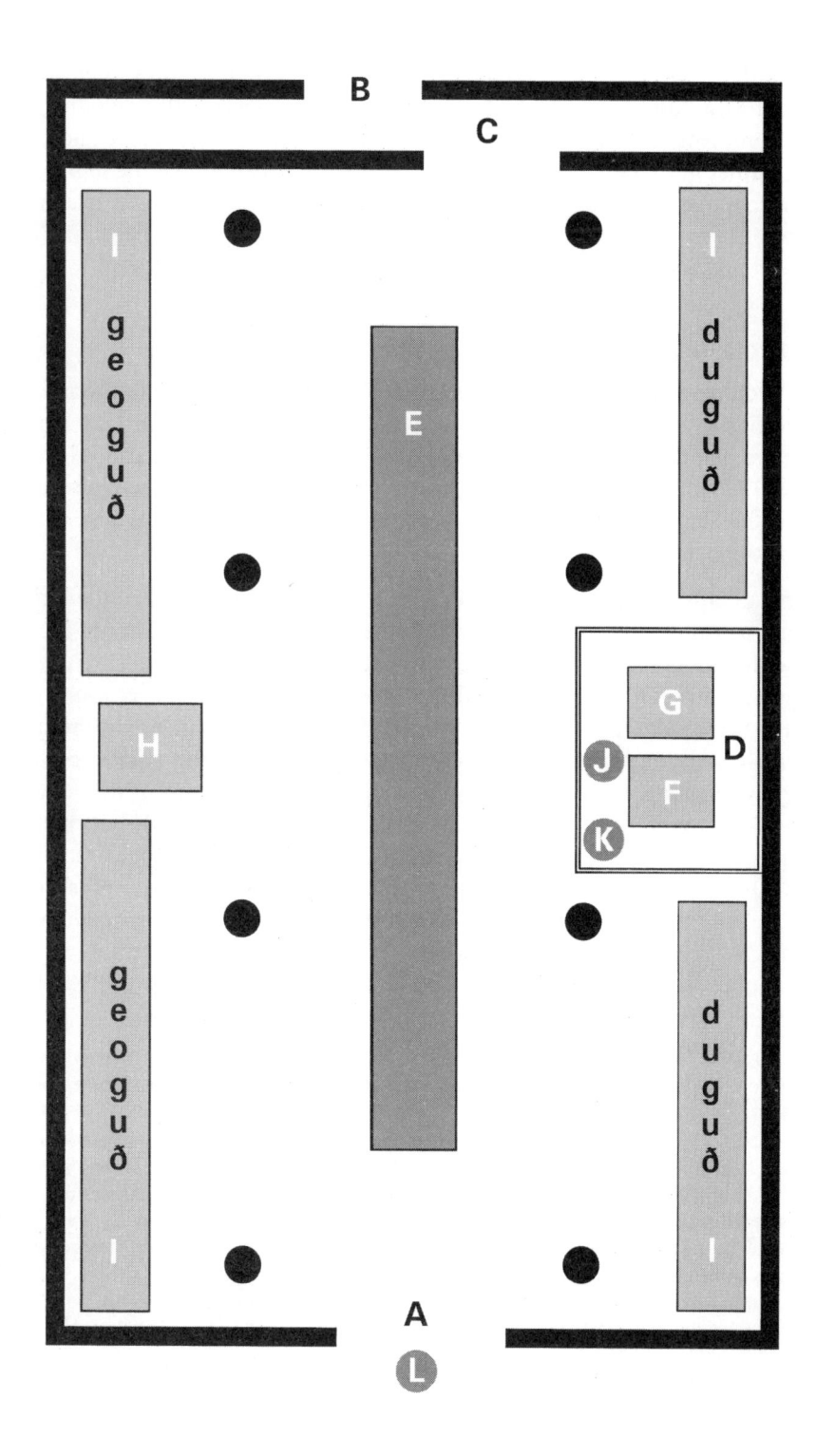

The Hall – Construction and Furniture

The Germanic origins of the English hall appear to lie in the Iron Age where it was customary for each settlement to have a large structure, presumed to have been used as a communal meeting room (*Volkshalle*) among the dwellings of a single, dominant family in the settlement.[1] The role of the most successful, leading farmer gradually merged with that of political leader, and the hall became the private stage for public acts carried out by this chieftain. The leader then began to act for the other members of the group, and could take decisions on its behalf and provide leadership.

Construction & Layout

As has been mentioned above, Old English literature is not very forthcoming on the specifics of hall construction and layout. The evidence from Old Norse is much more helpful, but it is often specific to Icelandic conditions and it is mostly from the 13th century. These two facts mean that it is unwise to use Norse details to fill in the English picture, although some reasonable inferences and cautious interpretations may be possible.

The typical halls or long-houses of the Germanic homelands, where the building traditions of Anglo-Saxon England were developed, are similar but not identical to those found here. Similar is the basic idea of an organised (usually sub-rectangular) farmyard marked off with a boundary fence, which is found along the North Sea coast from Vorbasse, Jutland (Denmark) to Wijster (Netherlands). Some of these littoral settlements were abandoned around the middle of the 5th century, suggesting dislocation in the population; sometimes this may be attributable to settlement-shift (such as is later seen at Mucking), but one other strong possibility is emigration to the south-west, either to northern France or to Britain. Overpopulation, soil exhaustion, climatic decline, marine transgression and numerous other causes have been suggested as the spur for this movement of peoples.[2]

---

[1] Herschend, 1998. The word *heall* 'hall' is based on the same root **kel-* as *helm* 'helmet' and *hel* 'Hell'; the idea is of covering and concealment. The Latin word *cella* 'cell, room' is based on this root also.

[2] Anthony, 1997, discusses theories of prehistoric migration in detail. In order for significant movements of people to take place there are four pre-conditions: a 'push' factor, or reason to move; a 'pull' factor, or belief that the reason to move does not apply elsewhere; information flows, in order to select a destination where the 'pull' factor applies; transportation costs, which must not outweigh the 'pull' factor. In the Anglo-Saxon case, where Old English appears to have replaced the previous British language(s), he notes: "In the absence of states, it is not likely that a small group of immigrants could bring about substantial language shift merely by attacking, defeating and enslaving the indigenes (witness the Normans in England and the Celts in Galatia). Those who shift to a new language must see a clear advantage in doing so, and must have enough contact with speakers of the target language so that they can learn that language. In 'plantation' situations, where the indigenes are enslaved, denied access to positions of power and excluded from social contacts with the conquerors, creoles may develop on the plantations, but these may or may no[t] be widely adopted beyond. In the case of the Anglo-Saxon migrations that brought English (not a

The Hall – Construction and Furniture

The construction and use of the sunken-featured building (SFB) remain a constant feature of the Germanic building tradition in all areas.[1] Loom-weights are common finds,[2] as is also evidence for keeping livestock in them, using them as workshops and for storage. They may have been used for human occupation when circumstances dictated,[3] but this was not their main purpose.

Dixon[4] discusses the construction of the SFB. The pit – usually the only surviving constructional feature – is subrectangular, with rounded corners. The cob[5] walls must have followed the pit's outline, or else the pit would have partially collapsed, and the pit cannot have been timber-lined as this would have resulted in sharp corners. A wooden block acting as a threshold must have been placed by the doorway, as otherwise the entrance would have been eroded by the users entering and leaving; the eroded hollow would have allowed draughts and rainwater to enter the interior of the hut. But, with people using the hut regularly, if not necessarily often, it would be expected that the dynamic pressure rocking the threshold would have left a sizeable impression in the soil. Such does not seem to be the case – the impression of removed timber and even rotted timber can be detected, but no thresholds are known to have survived into the excavation records. This is probably due to the fact that the pit, as it exists in the soil record, was the part of the hut below the ground surface at the time of construction, and any threshold would have been placed above and outside the pit, i.e. in a position which would already have been removed in the process of excavation before the shape and size of the pit became apparent.

The halls in the homelands are often claimed to be very different from the types found in Britain. The normal Continental structures are huge, with one end divided off and segmented into individual stalls for cattle (the 'byre-house' type

---

Celtic-Germanic creole, but a purely Germanic language) to Britain .... if the Germanic immigrants were few in number we might expect to see evidence that they deployed .... small-group strategies. That evidence appears to be lacking, which perhaps makes a demographic explanation – massive immigration and population replacement – more likely."

[1] Todd, 2001; the Germanic spread into eastern and southern Europe, evidenced by e.g. the Cjernjakhov culture, is likewise demonstrated by the association of long-houses and SFBs.

[2] The elder Pliny refers to Germanic women who know of no clothing more beautiful than linen, which they weave "underground". This would seem to be a clear reference to the use of SFBs for weaving, since the sunken floor is beneath ground level. (See Rives, 1999, p.200.)

[3] Dixon, 1993 p.130 suggests a parallel with *cots* (small, one-room, sunken-floored cottages) in use at Athelney, Somerset up to the 1880s, made from cob with wattle-and-daub gables. The walls were constructed from the clay dug out to form the floor in these very basic dwellings. Nevertheless, the cot-dwellers were noted for their neatness and clean appearance.

[4] Dixon, P.H., 1995

[5] Cob is a building material made from straw and clay sub-soil, formed into blocks and air-dried. Cob walls have the advantage of drawing damp out of a building. They are quite substantial – the blocks are heavy and dense – but have to be insulated against damp from above and below. All-timber walls with daub caulking are an alternative possibility.

evidenced at Feddersen Wierde, Germany).[1] There is no real evidence to suggest that English halls were ever built in this way or intended for this purpose, possibly because the climatic and social conditions here did not make it necessary. The English tradition is one of smaller, simpler dwellings.

It is sometimes suggested that (Romano-)British techniques and traditions have influenced the layout of early Anglo-Saxon buildings,[2] and this cannot be ruled out as an explanation for the divergence from Continental practice, yet it would be remarkable that halls and huts from Northumberland to Hampshire could be affected in precisely similar ways. (For example, the majority of late Romano-British farm buildings were erected on stone foundations, not the timber posts and sill-beams of the Anglo-Saxon tradition.) The smaller, rectangular dwellings which are typical of Anglo-Saxon sites are also occasionally found on the Continent, mainly in the area around the mouth of the Rhine.[3] Furthermore, while the whole byre-house design does not appear in England, some English houses replicate the human habitation end of the byre-house. On balance, while there are aspects of the Anglo-Saxon hall which are parallelled in the late Roman period, the closest similarity is with houses in the Continental homeland. Indeed, Herschend[4] remarks that the "Anglo-Saxon hall preserves an older building tradition with ancient traits such as the juxtaposed entrances in the centre of the façade and thereby it links the aristocracy with its continental roots. In South Scandinavia the central entrance room in Gudme may be viewed in a similar perspective, but there the hall develops in such a way as to show influences from the Roman basilica...". The significance of the entrance room is that it can function as an interface area where potential guests and visitors can be dealt with outside the leader's presence, thus saving him the necessity of giving an official response without pre-warning. It also serves to keep the interior secure from direct attack, and protected from the weather.

The absence of the byre-house[5] from the Anglo-Saxon records remains an unresolved question when so much else of Germanic material culture was embraced and spread in lowland Britain. Familiar architectural styles are an important part of the mental image of 'home' and are necessary for a comfortable life. Probably, the byre-house had already begun to mutate into another, simpler form of dwelling before the bulk of Anglo-Saxon settlers left the Continent.

---

[1] Welch, 1992; it has been suggested that there is a distinction to be drawn between the private *Herrenhof* (lord's farm) and the communal *Volkshalle* (folk-hall), but there is little in the archaeology to support this. See Herschend, 1998.

[2] e.g. Rahtz, 1976 or Dixon, 1991

[3] Hamerow, 1997 s.v. '*The Evidence for Anglo-Saxon Migration: Settlements*'; Herschend, 1998. The 4th century hall dwelling at Wijster is a close parallel to the English hall at Cowdery's Down.

[4] Herschend, 1998, p.20

[5] Herschend, 1998. The 'byre-house' is itself an abstraction: there are considerable differences even between Scandinavian regions: e.g. the southern area favours a central entrance room, while the middle area typically has two entrance rooms at the ends of the hall.

There may simply have been no need for the huge, complex buildings which were designed to accommodate large numbers of people; perhaps, in the settlement of England, the more unwieldy aspects of the tradition may have been shed because there was a smaller workforce to implement it, and the smaller settlement households did not require such large buildings.

In time, an insular style of architecture does emerge, but not until the 7th century (e.g. Cowdery's Down, see p.90), and even then in conjunction with standard Anglo-Saxon rectangular buildings. The two-room structure seems to extend across the entire social scale.

Many early sites, both rural and urban, are clearly related in their location to earlier Roman structures. The nature of the relationship is not at all easy to define, and indeed need not have been invariably the same in all places, even in the early years of Anglo-Saxon settlement. Some appear to be sited near or on villa estates, which may suggest continuity of occupation; it may equally show that the early Germanic settlers had a close (but subservient?) relationship to the late Roman authorities.[1]

Building Techniques

Details of the construction of an Anglo-Saxon hall can be revealed by archaeology, although interpreting physical remains of foundations to understand superstructures is not always possible without relying on speculation. Buildings identified as 'halls' are found on many sites, from the earliest Germanic settlements such as Mucking, Essex, to the latest fortified houses such as Goltho Manor, Leicestershire. One common feature of buildings interpreted as halls is that they generally have a large central open space, ideal for use as an assembly room. Commonly, at one or both ends a smaller chamber is constructed which may be interpreted as a private room, a reception area or storage room;[2] these rooms usually have their own outside door.[3]

The well-developed craft of woodworking (or carpentry) was widely used in manufacturing a range of products in Anglo-Saxon England, not least the timber houses, halls, byres, sheds, huts and churches in which daily life took place. Skilfully made buildings required as much thought and care as fine weapons or jewellery, and a greater expenditure of effort. Cowdery's Down (see below p.90) is a good example of this.

---

[1] Todd, 2001 notes that early Alemannic settlements in former Roman territory are sited in close association with Roman villas, but in time they appear to deliberately shift away from them. It is as if attitudes to the Roman past changed totally, and what was formerly embraced was now shunned. A similar re-alignment of settlement distribution apparently took place in Anglo-Saxon England.

[2] Dixon, 1991; Hamerow, 2002

[3] Some archaeologists reconstruct the entrance room as a kind of ante-room or porticus; others see it is an internal subdivision of a unitary hall.

Chapter Two

The quality of Anglo-Saxon woodworking[1] was such that the most elaborate jointing could be safely executed with wooden pegs (trennels), even in such lofty and awe-inspiring structures as the palaces at Yeavering and Cheddar. In poetry, the magnificent hall Heorot was clamped together with iron bands - *innan 7 utan irenbendum* (1.774) "with iron bands within and without" - but the majority of Anglo-Saxon halls needed no such anti-terrorist measures.[2]

Among the tools known from the period are axes in various forms, hammers, adzes, boring-bits, chisels, gouges, draw-knives (spokeshaves), saws and wedges.[3] T-shaped axes appear to come into use in the post-pagan period, and reach a highly developed form by the 9th century. The back of an axe will serve as a hammer, while no claw-hammers survive from the period. The Sutton Hoo "axe-hammer" is certainly a weapon, but demonstrates that the two items were used in combination at this time. Adzes were used for dressing timber, and could be used as makeshift wedges; a few examples survive. A set of Viking wedges was found at Mästermyr, Sweden, and a lone English example comes from Sarre, Kent (grave 233). The use of saws is known from tooling marks on timber, and from some fragmentary remains. A box-plane from Sarre (grave 26)[4] is the only known English example, but a similar tool was found at Finkum, Friesland. The chisel, gouge and draw-knife are also attested only once. Spoon-bits survive from a handful of sites in East Angia while boring-bits are known from Viking Scandinavia.

A group of woodworking tool-names are found in the Old English records. A cutting tool was a *þwearm* in one glossary. Specific types of tool are the 'knife' (*cnif, seax*), 'saw' (*sagu*), 'chisel' (*heardheaw*), 'adze' (*adesa*), 'wood-axe' (*wudubill, æcs*), 'plane' (*locor, sceafa*), 'file' (*feol*), 'awl' (*æl, byres, næfebor*) 'drill' (*searopil, timbor*). A two-edged axe was a *twibil*. A 'hammer' was a *bietl, hamor, slecg* or *slic*; a dowel was called *dyfel*. To ensure accurate alignment a plumb-line was used – *colþræd* 'coal-thread'[5] or *rightungþræd* 'righting-thread'.

Other constructon tools included the *stanbil* 'stone-cutter' and *cweornbil* 'quern-stone cutter'; the *bedd* a frame or assembly area; the *anfilte* 'anvil' and *onheaw* 'cutting block'; the *græfseax* 'engraving tool'; the *handæx* 'hand-axe'; the *mattuc* 'mattock, pickaxe'; the *clawu* 'pincers'; the *yppingiren* 'upping-iron, crowbar'; the *tygehoc* 'drawing-hook' and *wince* 'winch, pulley'.

---

[1] Hewett, 1980; the author criticises the archaeological assumption that 'archaic' = 'crude' in the matter of Anglo-Saxon carpentry, and the persistent reconstruction of posthole and earthfast buildings at the lowest level of technological skill and achievement.

[2] Iron bands were used in the manufacture of coopered buckets, coffins and caskets, but no archaeological evidence for the technique being used on buildings survives.

[3] Wilson, 1976

[4] Dunning, 1959

[5] Presumably this refers to a length of thread covered in soot, drawn tight between two points and plucked to leave a dark trace of soot on the surface, a perfect straight line. Similar devices employing chalk are in use today.

Spades and shovels came in many types. For digging, a *delfisen* 'delving-iron' or *spadu* 'spade' was used; a smaller version was the *handspitel* 'hand-spade'. For clearing up loose material, there was the *pal* or *scofl* 'shovel'. There are many words for various kinds of post or rod, including *beam* 'beam', *gierd* 'yardstick', *pal* 'pole', *post* 'post', *sagol* 'rod, club', *sceaft* 'shaft', *stæf* 'staff', *stocc* 'stock'. Joints were made by means of a *nægl* 'nail', *pinn* 'pin', *spicung* 'spike', *sprota* or *sticca* 'peg'. Nails were fastened off with a *cleot* 'cleat'.

Construction was called *getimbre* 'timbering'. A wooden building was called a *treowgeweorc* 'tree-work' and the wooden materials used were *bohtimber* 'bough-timber', *boldtimber* 'house-timber' or just *wudu* 'wood'. Boards and planking were called *þiling*, while an individual board was a *bord, bred* or *þel* and wattle was *watel*. Limewash (*weallim* 'wall-lime') was applied, as well as plaster (*clam*) made from chalk (*cealc*) or gypsum (*spærstan*). Brick (*bryce*) or tile (*tigele*) was also in the list of builders' materials; brick- or tile-making (*tigelgeweorc* 'tile-work') was handled by a *tigelwyrhta* 'tile-wright'.

Roofing was carried out by a *hrofwyrhta* 'roof-wright'. The main materials were wooden shingles (*scindelas, scingalas*) or thatch (*þæc*). The roof-ridge (*hrycg*) was formed with a ridge-pole (*first*) and various pieces of woodwork (*hrostbeag* 'roost-collar, *hroftimber* 'roof-timber'). The gables (*hornas* 'horns', *scylfas* 'turrets, ledges') were shaped for display.

Measuring and Laying-Out

There have been some few studies of the standard measurements used in laying out Anglo-Saxon buildings.[1] Analysing data from archaeological reports, from different periods and by various hands, is problematical when a consistent approach to taking measurements cannot be assumed. Even for the better documented Roman period, where a standardised 'foot' of 296mm is believed to have been in use, a survey of nine folding footrules failed to produce one of the expected correct length (values ranged from 290 to 294.5mm). Analysis of data from the Anglo-Saxon monastery at Jarrow[2] produced a standard base unit of measurement of 280mm; at contemporary Yeavering, the base unit of measurement was 281mm, suggesting that there was a local Northumbrian standard 'foot' in the early 7th century.

The other main basic unit of measurement for timber buildings is the 'rod' divided into thirds and sixths; unfortunately there are two clusters of possible values for this, one of 4.65m and the other of 5.03m (16ft 6inches or 5.5 yards).[3]

---

[1] Summarised in Bettess, 1991; see also Huggins, 1991

[2] Bettes, 1981; the building analysed is the nave of St. Paul's church which is believed to have been part of the first construction on the monastery site,

[3] Huggins, 1991, from which the data for the table are drawn. The 'rod' is also known as a 'pole' or 'perch'. See also Fernie, 1985 and 1991 for an attempt to establish a Roman origin for the perch, acre and foot.

Sites using a rod of 5.03m

Region	Site	
Northumberland	Yeavering	1 building reset from previous rod of 3.77m?
	Thirlings	1 building
Northamptonshire	Northampton	annexe to palace
	Raunds	2 possible examples
Suffolk	West Stow	1 building
Essex	Mucking	25 buildings
	Springfield Lyons	
	Wicken Bonhunt	6 buildings
Sussex	Bishopstone	3 buildings
Hampshire	Cowdery's Down	2 buildings
Somerset	Cheddar	1 building

Sites using a rod of 4.65m

Region	Site	
Northumberland	Thirlings	1 building
Staffordshire	Catholme	3 buildings; some evidence for rod of 4.33m?
Suffolk	West Stow	9 buildings
Essex	Mucking	40 buildings
	Springfield Lyons	
	Wicken Bonhunt	6 buildings
Sussex	Bishopstone	1 building
Hampshire	Cowdery's Down	12 buildings

The distribution of the two types of Anglo-Saxon 'rod'

All the above sites show the use of multiples and fractions of the base unit. The fractions are usually thirds and sixths, suggesting that the 'rod' was subdivided into thirds, and these thirds could in turn be halved. The use of standard (folding?) measures is one possibility, although there are no finds to support this idea. It is not unusual for different measuring systems for different purposes to co-exist: for example, where feet and inches are used to measure building materials, while rods are used to measure land.

Contemporary documents record the *geard* 'yard' and *elne* 'ell' as smaller units, as well as the *fæðm* 'fathom'. It is unlikely that these corresponded, other than in name, to the standardised measurements which remained in use into the 20th century, where 3 feet = 36 inches = 1 yard and 1 ell = 16 inches. But it should be noted that 5.5 ells = 1 rod (16.5 feet) which is 5.03m, the length of the longer 'rod' of Huggins's analysis.

At Yeavering, Hope-Taylor[1] noticed that the interior of the halls was subdivided by the two lines of roof-posts which ran down the long axis of the building. The proportions were (in whole units):

The distance between roof-posts

	Ratios
Building A2	6 : 12 : 6
Buidling A4 (original plan)	6 : 8 : 6
Buidling A4 (final plan)	6 : 9 : 6

The relatively greater amount of internal space between the roof-posts in building A2 is obvious, and indicates a larger middle passageway in relation to the seating areas outside the roof-posts.

Woodworking techniques

The only timber building of Anglo-Saxon date known to survive is the tiny church at Greensted-juxta-Ongar, Essex, which presently sits on a Victorian brick sill. Hewett[2] does not discount the possibility that the vertical timbers of the church were originally earthfast, but a wooden sill was added in Tudor times. The building is unique in that the vertical oak timbers are halved, and the outer surfaces are still semi-circular in section. It is thought that this tradition was already in decline by *c.* 960 AD for religious buildings. There are Anglo-Saxon timbers surviving in some church architecture, for example the church spire at Sompting, Sussex, with its characteristc "Rhenish helm" profile.

Woodland was a valuable resource which was prudently managed in Anglo-Saxon England. Where it can be identified, the timber was very carefully selected

---

[1] Hope-Taylor, 1977
[2] Hewett, 1980

for most projects, with the occasional inclusions of poor materials possibly being due to civil and political disturbances, such as Viking campaigning, making non-local supplies temporarily unobtainable. Some of the techniques have a background in shipwrighting, as for example the use of three-quarter round timbers for door ledges, and of iron roves and clenches, e.g. Hadstock, Essex.[1] Hewett has determined that, on the basis of the available evidence, the Anglo-Saxon craftsmen were developing a highly capable woodworking tradition which accelerated towards the end of the period.

It is doubtful that the Norman invasion introduced any revolutionary new techniques to England; its main contribution seems to lie in the sudden stimulus for very large construction projects, coupled with demolition of many existing structures. Anglo-Saxon buildings were generally built on a 'human scale', and very few large edifices survive (but see below for large, high-status residences). The poem *The Ruin* may describe stone walls as "the work of giants" *eotena geweorc* (l.2) but masons were to be found who could raise similar structures.

Discussing the evolution of the 'notched lap joint' Hewett suggests that the traditional English lap-joint was augmented by a notch which appears in the debated 'Saxo-Norman' period when English-trained woodworkers laboured under Norman direction; it may be that some refinements of existing techniques were developed at this time (c.1066-1100). On this basis, applying the principle of 'overlap' between traditional Anglo-Saxon techniques and the traditions of the incomers, Hewett suggests that the following carpenters' joints were known and used in the late Anglo-Saxon and Saxo-Norman periods:

- Lap-dovetail joints
- Mortise and tenon joints (both 'through' and 'stub' varieties)
- Squint lap-joints
- Bridle-joints
- Cogged clasping joints
- Splayed scarf joints (with butts under the squints)
- Chase-tenon joints
- Rebates (square and splayed)
- Tongue-and-groove joints
- Fox-wedged peg joints
- Butt-notching
- In-pitch wall-plating
- Arris trenches
- Cross-halving
- Hewn outsets

---

[1] Hadstock has the only known examples of carpentered windowframes, rather than a single plank with a suitable aperture cut through it. (Hewett, 1980)

The Hall – Construction and Furniture

The following practices and structural concepts were also in use in the period:

- Use of wild timber (i.e. not from managed woodland, or grown for construction purposes)
- Fine quartered oak planking, cleft not sawn
- Steam- or heat-bending of timber
- Stability of timber frames at tie-beam level (due to earthfast outer walls)
- Wall-plates which clasp their spans (no inward or outward thrust)
- Wickerwork to shutter mortar-set rubble
- Use of cleft or triangular timbers as put-logs
- Outward-angled put-logs at returns
- Bonding timbers inserted into rubble masonry

At Feddersen Wierde, the identifiable jointing techniques were the scarf, tongue-and-groove and mortise-and-tenon.[1]

The 'halls' found on rural sites such as Mucking or West Stow were domestic buildings, meeting rooms or houses. They are not necessarily the same type of building as the joyous establishments, such as Heorot, where the king slept in an external structure while the hall was used for formal gatherings. It is nonetheless possible that they fulfilled this role within their own settlements, and that the house was the building where visitors were quartered and rituals enacted for the owner, his blood-kin and his hirelings. Within these small communities of perhaps a few dozen people, the normal dwelling could double as the ritual space.

Dixon[2] has estimated that a standard SFB, as found at Mucking, would have taken 140 man-hours to build, with a further 40 man-hours to gather and prepare the materials. He envisages the sunken floor dug out first, and the spoil from this process mixed with fibrous material and used to build the walls, which would be dried by the heat from the hearth. A single settler family could therefore have built an SFB as a first shelter within 5 or 6 days of arrival, or much sooner with help.

When used as a workshop, as in the case of the woodturner's workshop at Bucklersbury Common, Berkshire,[3] the thick floor-covering of woodshavings gives good insulation and the low profile is more able to withstand extremes of wind; no additional source of heat or light was used or needed.

The Anglo-Saxon love of display and decoration makes it vey likely that many buildings featured carved decoration on the woodwork, both inside and out. The almost total lack of wooden architectural remains from the period makes further comment impossible.

---

[1] Rives, 1999, p.194
[2] Dixon, 1991 p.135
[3] Dixon, 1994

Chapter Two

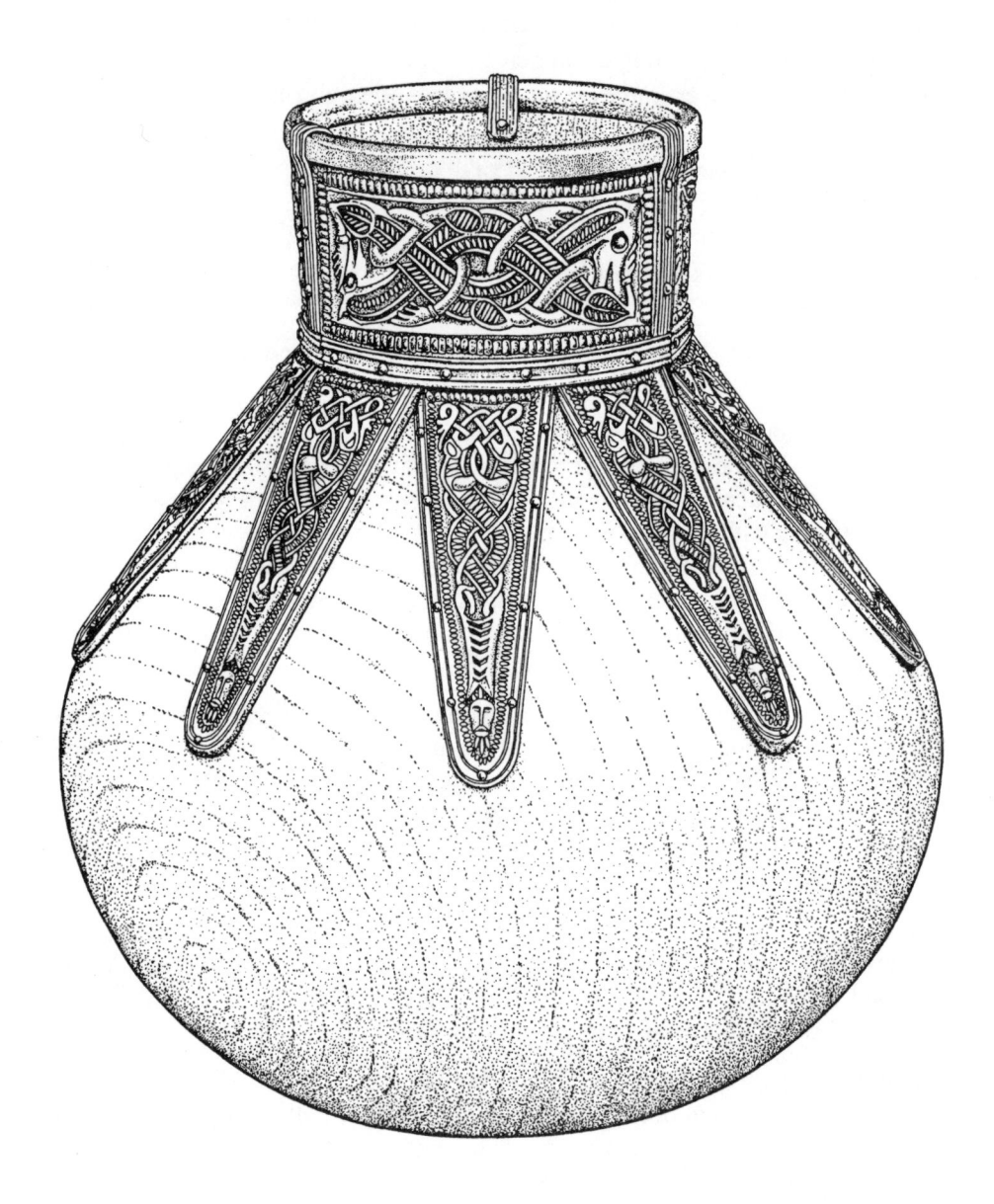

Fig.7 Wooden 'bottle' or serving vessel with gilded copper-alloy mounts, from Sutton Hoo, Mound 1. The bottle was turned on a pole-lathe from a block of dried timber.

Hearth

In the larger Anglo-Saxon hall, the function of the hearth was not for cooking but rather as a source of light and heat. Cooking took place in another building on the site where large coarse vessels were used to heat water, seethe meats and vegetables and brew strong drink.[1] The hall's hearth was not usually used for such mundane purposes, and those who had a seat at the leader's hearth were not there to work. Indeed the OE nouns *heorþgeneatas* 'hearth-companions' and *heorþwerod* 'hearth-troop', used of a nobleman's military entourage, indicate that a seat at the leader's hearth was the right of every retainer.

The Old English word *heorð* 'hearth' describes the standard fireplace arrangement. Hearthside equipment might include a shovel (*fyrpanne, fyrscofl, gledscofl*), tongs (*fyrtang*), rake (*furræce*), firedogs (*brandiren, brandrad, brandrida*) and bellows (*blæstbelg*).

A curious find from Sutton Hoo, Mound 1, was the small iron lamp consisting of a cup held in a cage of three iron strips, joined together beneath the bowl and splaying into three feet[2]. The fuel was beeswax, of which traces remained, but no wick was found. The only known parallel find was from Broomfield,[3] Essex, a broadly contemporary high-status barrow inhumation.

Lighting must always have been a problem in areas away from the hearth, in dark corners of the hall and in the ante-rooms and outhouses. Candles made from tallow (an animal fat) or beeswax were produced in the Anglo-Saxon period, the latter a very costly product associated with ecclesiastical contexts. King Alfred gave instruction for the construction of a timepiece based on slow-burning candles in a horn-sided lamp.[4] A cheap, home-made alternative to the candle was the rushlight, a rush core dipped in fat. For the wealthy, cressets holding a wick in a measure of oil would have provided lighting.[5]

The vocabulary of lighting includes the torch (*blæse* 'blaze', *brand* 'firebrand', *bryne* 'burner', *cen* 'torch', *fæcele* 'torch'), taper (*sceaft* 'shaft', *speld* 'spill', *tapor* 'taper'), candle (*condel, weaxcandel*), lantern (*blæcern* 'light-tower') and lamp (*fyrencylle* 'fire-vessel', *glæsfæt* 'glass-vat', *leohtfæt* 'light-vat', *leohtstan* 'light-stone'). A candle needs a candlestick (*candelstæf* 'candle-staff', *candelsticca* 'candle-stick', *leohtisern* 'light-iron') and a wick (*weoce*).

---

[1] Herschend, 1998 Figs.12a and b for a comparison of ceramic vessels from kitchen and hall at Vallhagar, a Swedish site.
[2] Care-Evans, 1986
[3] Page, 1903
[4] Keynes & Lapidge, 1983, *Life*, ch.104
[5] Messent, 1999

Seating

There were many words for kinds of seating: *benc* 'bench', *bencþel* 'benchboard', *formelle* 'ecclesiastic or monastic bench, pew', *hleda* 'seat', *scamol* 'bench or table on tressles', *sess* 'place to sit', *setl* 'seat, chair'. Some seating was associated specifically with drink: *beorsetl* 'beer-seat', *ealubenc* 'ale-bench', *medubenc* 'meadbench'.

The total lack of reliable archaeological evidence for the internal fittings of the Anglo-Saxon building makes it very difficult to determine what form the 'bench' of an English hall might have taken. The woodworking skills needed to construct an artefact like the bed used in the rare burial from Swallowcliffe, Wiltshire, would have been similar to those needed for the construction of benches and other seating. The bed was made of ash planks, with iron fittings and leather webbing.[1] Benches constructed with a low seat and their backs directly against the long walls of the hall would seem to be the most efficient solution to the seating problem.

Chairs & Stools

The Old English word *stol* means both 'chair' and 'stool' i.e. any free-standing seat, with or without a back. A covering for a chair or seat was a *sethrægl*. Individual seats of 'stool' or 'chair' type are mentioned in the literature. The figure moulded onto the lid of a funerary urn from Spong Hill, Norfolk, depicts a seated male, possibly representing the cremated person in the urn. The chair is depicted as solid-based with inset panels of decoration which may be intended to show the hollow framework of the chair's legs without weakening the pottery fabric of the model.

Examples of free-standing chairs from the Anglo-Saxon period are few. Possibly the most famous is the one in the church at Jarrow, Northumberland, said to have belonged to St. Bede. It is of a simple design, high-backed and made from slats of wood pegged into the frame. The association with Bede is unproven, but appears to go back a long way.

From St. Peter's church, Monkwearmouth, Northumberland, comes an 8th or 9th century stone animal head, which is usually assumed to be a finial from a chair frame.[2] The features are finely carved, and may represent a seal. A similar item from Lastingham, Yorkshire,[3] is also dated to the 8th or 9th century, and is associated with a fragment of stone with a straight rear edge and sloping front, probably part of the supporting structure of the freestanding chair.

---

[1] Speake, 1989
[2] Hawkes, 1996; Webster, 1991, item 111
[3] Webster, 1991 item 112

A rare find, now in the British Museum, consists of an iron folding-stool of probable sixth century date.[1] The Old English word *fyldestol* describes these items, and one MS illustration shows a king sitting on such a seat. A separate footstool was called a *fotsceamol* 'foot-bench', *fotsetl* 'foot-seat', or *fotspure* 'foot-heel'.

Frithstool

In Hexham Abbey,[2] Northumberland, there is a simple sandstone block carved into a chair, known as the 'frith stool', which is claimed to be of Anglo-Saxon date. It is associated in local legend with St. Wilfrid, and would therefore have been carved in the 7th century, as he founded the minster in 671 AD. Since Hexham Abbey was then a cathedral, at the centre of a diocese, from c. 678 to c. 821, this simple stone chair may have been the bishop's official *cathedra*. The minster at Hexham was apparently constructed from re-used Roman stone taken from the disused Roman fort at nearby Corbridge. The stone block may have likewise come from there, and been re-worked in Wilfred's day. Its only decorative features are simple, incised lines which follow the outline of the seat, and an interlace panel on each of the upper arms, ending in a three-way knot (*triquetra*). A very similar pattern appears on an illustration of St. Matthew, painted about 750 at Canterbury. The seat was probably originally set against a wall and surrounded by benches for the other clergy. It may have been sited on a stone plinth to raise it above the level of the assembly.

The chair was used to guarantee sanctuary (*friþ*) to fugitives until the late Middle Ages, after which it became redundant and was re-sited several times. In the mid-1800s, during one of these moves, it was broken in two; its clumsy repair could not undo the damage the seat had sustained. Its present position in the abbey is based on the surviving foundations of the Anglo-Saxon church. A similar abbot's seat is to be found at Beverley Minster, Yorkshire.

Gift-Stool (Giefstol)

The lord of the hall customarily had his own free-standing chair in which he sat to give judgements, hear legal cases, greet visitors and reward followers. In the latter guise it was referred to as the gift-stool (*giefstol*). Although it was not part of the bench structure, the posts which supported its back were probably earth-fast. The position of the chair in the hall was significant, and was confined to either the middle of one of the long walls, or a corner position.[3] The latter is assumed to have developed from the continental tradition of placing the main

---

[1] Arnold, 1997

[2] Webster, 1991 item 148

[3] Herschend, 1998, p.25. The corner or short-end position is not possible in the byre-house, as there it is occupied by beds or kitchen equipment.

Chapter Two

seating positions in side aisles on either side of a central hearth; these opposed seats are known in Norse as the *hásæti* "high-seat" and the *undvegi* or *öndvegi* "opposed(-seat)". The high-seat was the seat of prominence and, from Gotlandic pictorial evidence, appears to have been sited on a dais. Terms in Old English used for this include *solor*, (based on Latin *solarium* 'upper room') and *yppe* (derived from 'up'). Possibly *scilfe* 'shelf, ledge' may refer to the same idea. In *Beowulf* (l.1926-7) we read of the *bregorof cyning hea on healle* 'powerful king high in the hall' which may be figurative, but could be a literal description of his elevated position.

In *Egil's Saga*, after the battle of *Vínheiðr* (plausibly identified with the OE *Brunanburh*), the Icelandic mercenary Egil and his men, who have played a decisive role in winning the day for King Athelstan, enter the king's hall:

Síðan fór Egill með sveit sína á fund Aðalsteins konungs og gekk þegar fyrir konung, er hann sat við drykkju; þar var glaumur mikill; og er konungur sá, að Egill var inn kominn, þá mælti hann, að rýma skyldi pallinn þann hinn óæðra fyrir þeim, og mælti, að Egill skyldi sitja þar í öndvegi gegnt konungi.

Then Egil went with his troop to the table of King Athelstan and strode up before the king, where he sat at his drink; there was great merriment; and when the king saw that Egill had come in, he said that the bench before him should be cleared so that Egil should sit there in the *ondvegi* across from the king.

Egils saga Skallagrímsonar, ch.55

It seems likely from this sequence that, in Anglo-Saxon England at least, the guest's seat was not a permanent fixture of the hall but was brought out or made up for guests when necessary. There is no evidence for it in the feasting scenes on the Bayeux tapestry. The gift-stool role of the leader's seat is further demonstrated in the same chapter of this saga:

Aðalsteinn konungur sat í hásæti; hann lagði og sverð um kné sér, og er þeir sátu svo um hríð, þá dró konungur sverðið úr slíðrum og tók gullhring af hendi sér, mikinn og góðan, og dró á blóðrefilinn, stóð upp og gekk á gólfið og rétti yfir eldinn til Egils. Egill stóð upp og brá sverðinu og gekk á gólfið; hann stakk sverðinu í bug hringinum og dró að sér, gekk aftur til rúms síns; konungur settist í hásæti. En er Egill settist niður, dró hann hringinn á hönd sér.

King Athelstan sat in the high-seat; he also had laid his sword across his knees and when they had sat so for a while the king drew his sword from its scabbard and took from his hand a golden ring– a large and fine one – and hung it on his sword-point; he stood up and went

The Hall – Construction and Furniture

onto the hall-floor, and stretched over the fire towards Egil. Egil stood up and brandished his sword and went onto the hall-floor; he stuck the sword into the arc of the ring and drew it towards himself, and went back to his place; the king seated himself in the high-seat. But when Egil sat back down, he pulled the ring onto his own hand.

It is interesting that the king must step down onto the floor from his raised position, as must his guest. The hearthfire separates them in this tale. However, we should bear in mind that this is a mediaeval Icelandic account and there may be elements of contemporary hall-layout in the text.

It seems likely that originally the leader's reserved seat was marked out by its position of prominence, and that lower ranks stood before it to address him. However, when a guest was to be shown special honour he would be offered a similar, but less prominent, seating position – hence the use of the dais to raise the householder above the level of other men. Construction details such as a high back, decorative carving and other ornament could have been used to show the rank of the incumbent, as well as textile covers, cushions and furs. The householder's seat was close to the hearth, while the less prominent hall-users were ranged away from it hierarchically.

The Icelandic *Eyrbyggja Saga*, chapter 3,[1] concerns the arrival and settlement of Þórolfr Mostrarskegg, a devout Þórr worshipper from Norway. Nearing the Icelandic coast, Þórolfr decides to let his favourite divinity take a hand:

> *Þórolfr kastaði þá fyrir borð öndvegissúlum sínum þei, er staðit höfðu í hofinu: þar var Þórr skorinn á annarri. Hann mælti svá fyrir at hann skyldi þar byggja á Íslandi sem Þórr létu þeir á land koma. ... þar lét hann reisa hof ok var þat mikit hús, váru dyrr á hliðvegginum ok nær öðrum endanum, þar fyrir innan stóðu öndvegissúlurnar ok váru þar í naglar, þeir hétu reginnaglar.*

> Þorolf cast overboard his own high-seat pillars which had stood in the hall;[2] Þórr was carved there on one of them. He said that he would dwell in that place wherever Þórr allowed them to come to land .... There he had a hall raised and that was a great house, there were doors in the sidewalls and towards either end, before them inside stood the high-seat pillars and there were nails in them, which were called 'power-nails'.[3]

---

[1] Text from Garmonsway, 1928

[2] ON *hof* means a large meeting room, and can signify 'hall' or 'heathen temple'.

[3] ON *reginnaglar* – 'nails of *reginn*' the name for any god or powerful being; it is understood that the purpose of these nails was to strike a fire from them (with flint?) in a heathen ritual.

Chapter Two

The central position of the high-seat in the symbolism of the hall is echoed in the word *frumstol* which apparently means 'principal dwelling' but is literally 'first seat'; a son's right to his *frumstol* – and therefore his own authority – is enshrined in *Laws* of King Ine of Wessex from the 7th century.

The treasures which a follower could expect might include war-gear and feasting-gear of various kinds:

> *Forgeaf þa Beowulfe bearn Healfdenes*
> *segen gyldenne sigores to leane;*
> *hroden hildecumbor, helm ond byrnan,*
> *mære maðþumsweord manige gesawon*
> *beforan beorn beran. Beowulf geþah*
> *ful on flette; no he þære feohgyfte*
> *for sceotendum scamigan ðorfte.*
> *Ne gefrægn ic freondlicor feower madmas*
> *golde gegyrede gummanna fela*
> *in ealobence oðrum gesellan.*

> Then Healfdene's son gave to Beowulf
> a golden standard as reward for his success,
> an adorned battle-sign, a helmet and byrnie,
> many saw a famed treasure-sword
> brought before the warrior. Beowulf received
> a cup on the hall-floor; of that wealth-giving
> he had no need for shame before the warriors.
> I have never heard of four treasures
> made from gold, from many nobles
> more lovingly given to another on the ale-bench
>
> *Beowulf*, l.1020-9

Rewards of this nature were the counterpart of the follower's loyalty, either previously or still to come. A military follower would customarily receive a gift of weapons on admission to the lord's service, and was expected to wield them in defence and service of the leader thereafter. The *giefstol* is therefore both a recruiting device for renewing the warband, and a means of demonstrating the power and prestige of the man who sits upon it.

While not a *giefstol* in the accepted sense, it is worth recording that clergymen had adapted the *comitatus* structure to their needs to the extent that a religious leader could have a 'reserved' seat in the communal meeting room, as when Bede records that Bishop Aidan took up his customary seat (*residebat in suo loco*) at a gathering.[1]

---

[1] Evans, 1997, p.93

Mead-benches

The 'mead-bench' was the seating of the rank-and-file members of the lord's household, and his guests. The Old English words include *meodusetl* 'mead-seat' and *medubenc* 'mead-bench'; *ealubenc* 'ale-bench' appears in *Beowulf* whereas wine- and beer-benches do not occur.

The removal of the benches by Scyld Sceafing (see p.32 above) signified the leader's having overcome his neighbours and deprived them of their group identity. A lack of mead-benches implies a lack of warriors to sit along them, and therefore military defeat and societal annihilation or absorption.

Herschend[1] suggests that the occurrence at a number of Danish sites of large pieces of broken glass drinking vessels inside post-holes implies that the glasses were smashed at the same time as the buildings were pulled down. Fragments of pottery were found in the postholes at Yeavering, Northumberland.[2] The prominence given to the hall and its meadbenches in *Beowulf* and *The Fight at Finnsburh* demonstrates the thematic link between strong drink, leaders and halls.

Boards & Tables

Old English had a few words for types of table: *beod, bord, mese, þiling, þroc*. Archaeology has little to tell us about Anglo-Saxon tables, although the generally high level of competence in woodworking suggests that they should have been both efficient and decorative. Tables were not generally a permanent feature of the hall, but were made up from a flat top (*bord*) and trestle legs, which could be collapsed and folded away when not required.[3] The fact that people were sometimes able to sleep in the hall would dictate that the maximum space possible should be available for bedding. Since the hall was at other times used as a court and a workroom, the best use of limited space was vital.

The symbolic relationship implied by sharing a table together is indicated by the OE word *beodgeneatas* 'table-companions', used in *Beowulf* of the warband.

Tacitus describes in passing the dining arrangements in the Germanic halls of his day. The text (Chapter 22) indicates that at breakfast each diner had his own individual seat, trestle and board. While this is not impossible,[4] it would presumably only be workable when not all members of the group would have been sitting to eat at the same time, since otherwise a large number of small tables would be required.

---

[1] Herschend, 1998, p.36

[2] Hope-Taylor, 1977

[3] Yarwood, 1979

[4] It was customary in Roman and Greek practice to recline on couches around a low, common table; it may be that Tacitus is here just indicating the alien ways of the *Germani* as other writers did of the Thracians and Celts (Rives, 1999).

Evidence from other sources is needed to fill out the picture. Here, the Bayeux Tapestry is perhaps our most important single document, since, unlike many manuscripts, it was not copied from an older source. Its depiction of the houses, palaces and churches is fresh and probably drawn from life[1] – even if sometimes limited by the medium of embroidery. (See Fig.2 p.40)

Flooring

In *Beowulf* (1725), the curious expression occurs: *on fagne flor feond treddode* "the enemy trod the coloured floor". Wrenn[2] saw in this a "reference to the hall having a floor of variegated colouring" which he thought might "refer to traces of Roman tessellated paving which may have remained in early times after Anglo-Saxon halls had been built on the sites of Roman-British villas". There is no real evidence that Anglo-Saxon halls ever were built directly over Romano-British villa buildings, but still there is the intriguing place-name "Fawler" (Oxfordshire) which is from the same Old English expression - *fag flor* – where a Roman mosaic floor was found in the 19th century. This is not the only such reference – there are parallel expressions in some charter bounds – but it is the only one to have given rise to a modern English place-name. However, it is not a necessary reading of *fag* to mean 'tessellated' since any form of coloured decoration could give rise to the term; neither can the homonym *fah* (sometimes spelt *fag*) 'hostile' be ruled out entirely[3] where the walker is explicitly referred to as *feond* 'enemy'.

The common Old English word for any form of flooring is *flor*, which presumably could cover everything from boards to packed earth. The hall's sprung wooden floor is called *bencþel* 'bench-plank', the wooden structure on which benches are raised. In *Beowulf* (1.1316-7) we read that Beowulf's warband *gang ða æfter flore ... healwudu dynede* 'went across the floor then ... the hall-wood thundered'.

Another name for the floor is *flett*,[4] which has connotations of hall-life: a *fletsittend* 'floor-sitter' is one who has a place in the hall, and *fletræst* 'floor-bed' is a place of rest inside the hall itself. The defensive company of warriors inhabiting the hall is the *fletwerod* 'floor-troop'. These terms suggest that *flett* meant 'wooden floor of a hall' and had a rather high-status connotation.

---

[1] Wilson, 1985, doubts that all the scenes are new creations. He sees the depiction of royal thrones as typical of an artistic tradition dating from Carolingian times, and the reliquaries on which Harold allegedly swears the fateful oath to support William "can hardly be regarded as accurate renderings of the actual shrines available at Bayeux." Even accepting that the artist may have made concessions for the sake of convention and clarity, it remains the case that we do not know what Edward's, Harold's or William's thrones looked like.

[2] Wrenn, 1973, footnote to line 725.

[3] The acc.sing. masc. of *fah* is usually *fane*, not *fagne*, but confusion of the two words is not impossible.

[4] This is the source of Tolkien's word 'flet' to describe platforms built into trees.

The Hall – Construction and Furniture

Building A2 at Yeavering[1] was unusual in its layout, a large hall built from massive timbers but with a door in each of its four walls. The west door was detectable through a pair of deep post-pits but the wall-line continued between the doorposts, which presumably means that the door itself was situated higher up in the wall. This would coincide with a raised chamber above the living space of the hall, its flooring carried on the rafters of the hall. This building's interior was "thickly punctuated" with a series of post pits which may have supported a raised floor. These pits respected the gangways from door to door, which were entirely free of soil-based features except for three post holes placed slightly off-centre (to the south of the east-west median line) in the middle of the western end of the hall. These posts have been interpreted as supports for the gift-stool.

There is good evidence for the building of two-storeyed structures in Anglo-Saxon times. The Bayeux Tapestry depicts several such buildings; one, adjacent to the Godwinessons' church at Bosham, Sussex, is shown as a standard feasting hall erected above a vaulted basement (perhaps a storage area?) (fig.2 page 40).[2] It is known that a two-storeyed building stood at Calne, Wiltshire, because the *Chronicle* records its collapse in 978:[3]

> *Her on þissum geare ealle þa yldestan Angelcynnes witan gefeollon æt Calne of anre upfloran, buton se halga Dunstan arcebiscop ana ætstod uppan anum beame 7 sume þær swiðe gebrocode wæron 7 sume hit ne gedydon mid þam life.*

> Here [in the chronicle] in this year all the eldest counsellors of the English nation fell from an upper floor at Calne, except the holy archbishop Dunstan remained standing upon one beam, and some there were badly injured and some did not escape with their lives.

Many Anglo-Saxon church towers survive to a height of three storeys or more, so clearly the prospect of building tall buildings was not too daunting.[4] Internal ceilings were called *firsthrof* 'ridge-pole-roof'; each storey was a *flering* 'flooring'.

Finding suitable timbers of sufficient strength and height may have been a limiting factor in construction, since the ideal wood types for this purpose, such as oak, will take more than one human generation to reach the necessary proportions.

---

[1] Hope-Taylor, 1977
[2] Thorpe, 1973; Wood, 1965
[3] ASC MS 'D', s.a. 978 (Cubbin, 1996)
[4] An Anglo-Saxon illustration of Noah's ark in the Bodleian Library shows a three-storeyed building as the superstructure of the vessel.

Hall Development in Anglo-Saxon England

Some of the more important stages in the development of the Anglo-Saxon building tradition are typified by excavated houses from a small number of sites. They can be divided into three main periods:

Early-Saxon Period – 5th to 7th centuries

Sutton Courtenay, Oxfordshire, was one of the most influential early excavations of Anglo-Saxon buildings. The finds of SFBs with an array of domestic items in the infill suggested that these squalid huts were inhabited, the real "halls" of kings. In fact, the squalor was due to the SFBs having been built as workshops, then the pit used as a convenient rubbish dump once the superstructure had been re-cycled.

Mucking,[1] Essex, is one of the earliest Anglo-Saxon habitation sites to be identified so far, possibly founded as early as *circa* 420 AD. It extended over a gravel terrace on the north bank of the Thames, and was partially excavated prior to its destruction in the course of commercial gravel extraction. Its elevated position on the bend of the river gave it an excellent view both seawards and up-river towards London, some twenty miles to the west. In total, 210 SFBs and 50 larger buildings – the putative 'halls' – were discovered, the largest single Migration Period site ever discovered in England. The settlement was, characteristically, built and re-built over a considerable period, with the nucleus wandering across the terrace through time. There were nine wells in the settlement area, some of which had been in use in the Roman period, and a villa had existed in the vicinity. The Mucking buildings predictably owed far more to Germanic than to Romano-British traditions of construction.[2]

Settlement began at Mucking in the early/mid-5th century ('phase A') with an occupation area in the south-west of the site and a large cemetery to its north. In the late 5th-6th century ('Phase A/B') this settlement developed while another grew up on the further (north-east) side of the cemetery. In the 7th century ('Phase B/C') this northern settlement moved further north-east, and in the final period ('Phase C') occupation areas were scattered to the south-west, west and north-west of this centre. An 8th century coin hoard was among the last items deposited on the site. An area between the gravel terrace and the river was not excavated, and more material from the early phases may await discovery there; the buildings were traced through their post-holes. In Phase A there were no less than 67 SFBs on the part of the site excavated, but only two halls could be identified.[3] This may be viewed as a small number (but probably more than just

---

[1] M.U.Jones, 1980; W.T. Jones, 1980; Welch, 1992; Dixon, 1993; Barford, 1995; Arnold, 1997.

[2] Todd, 2001 p.85

[3] Dixon, 1993, suggests that SFBs were first erected as dwellings, and only with the passage of some years could the erection of a more substantial hall be contemplated, requiring large resources and some specialist expertise. In the intervening period, Dixon further suggests that the settlement was supported by relations with the local Britons. The possible use of late Roman measurements

two?)[1] of separate settlements, each consisting of a hall and its outbuildings. In Phase A/B there were 9 halls and 14 SFBs (a hall : SFB ration of 1:1.5), and in B/C 19 halls with 56 SFBs (1:2.9); in C 21 halls stood with 56 SFBs again (1:2.7).

The evidence of the cemetery[2] implies around 900 persons lived and were buried on the site over about three centuries (c.420 – 750AD), so that with three generations to a century there was an average population of 100 people resident on the site at any time. Hamerow[3] suggests that there were originally 65 halls on the site and that each remained in use for 40 years, while the adjacent SFBs lasted around half this time. Therefore at any one time there would be 10 halls and 14 SFBs in occupation, each hall housing 10 people. It appears that each generation renewed the 'village' by building on open land next to the existing settlement, re-using timbers from the older structures and recycling it into the SFBs, which were built in a very conservative manner showing little variation over the whole timespan of occupation. The area had been under cultivation in the Roman period but seems to have been abandoned before the Anglo-Saxon settlement was established.

Sunken Featured Buildings are also a feature at the **West Stow,**[4] Suffolk, site which has been made famous by the reconstruction of experimental buildings on the original locations denoted by the discovery of post-holes. It throve between the mid-5th and mid-7th centuries, roughly 200 years or around six to eight generations. It seems to have been a grouping of at most four nuclear settlements, each with a number of outbuildings surrounding a larger dwelling (a 'hall') and by the mid-7th century it had shrunk to just two halls with outbuildings. Some of the halls may have been used for over 50 years, or two generations.

At **Carlton Colville**, also in Suffolk,[5] the excavators noted a great range and variation in the SFBs on the site, both in size and in structural type which is in keeping with the evidence from other excavations in the region (East Anglia and Essex) where a number of different types of construction have also been observed; these are classified by the number of earthfast posts used. In contrast, other parts of England show considerably greater uniformity, particularly amongst the two-post structures. This might be due to the fragmented nature of

---

(*pedes*) in some of the halls may support this idea, although it should be borne in mind that the earliest buildings (c. 420) must have been erected in a late Roman context with the approval of the contemporary local authorities, and that the 'Saxon' settlers were therefore familiar with Romano-British culture and practices.

[1] On the basis of the lower hall : SFB figure given below, 67 SFBs should have been attached to about 40 halls.

[2] There were actually two cemeteries, only one of which was recorded. Cemetery I yielded 50 burials but the larger Cemetery II consisted of around 800 burials.

[3] Quoted in Welch, 1992.

[4] Arnold, 1997; Welch, 1992; Rahtz, 1976

[5] Cambridge Archaeological Unit, 1998

the early coastal settlements; within a generation or two, distinct traditions of construction would have developed and stabilised. The settlement appears to have lasted from the 6th to 8th centuries, with buildings incorporating one, two and six posts as well as others which were apparently not based on a post-built design. One of these (F134) had clear evidence of a plank-lined slot in the base of the sunken floor and plank-lined sides. Another (F5) had posts around the inner base. Of the nine SFBs excavated on the site, five are of standard two-post design, two have six posts, one has one post and one has none - this may have had its posts set on stone post-pads, a feature known from European sites. One had been repaired and may have had additional posts added. The SFB pits were rectangular and aligned east to west, ranging in size from *c*. 3m x 4m up to *c*. 5.4m x 4.8m. One of the two-post structures was square, measuring 4.6m x 4.6m. None of the SFBs had any evidence for internal structures, but one provided a quantity of iron and slag in a pit which might be the result of smithing in the settlement, although there was no hearth in the SFB itself. A separate metalworking area was found elsewhere on the site. Many of the pits had been refilled with rubbish, after the buildings had been taken down. There were also a number of other pits and at least three ovens identified during excavation.

A chalkland settlement on the edge of the South Downs at **Rookery Hill, Bishopstone,**[1] East Sussex got underway in the late 5th century. Its adjacent cemetery contained 118 burials, extending from the 5th into the 6th centuries. Twenty two separate buildings were excavated, of which only three were SFBs; two of these contained spindle-whorls. There was only one identifiable hall, the rest of the buildings being smaller rectangular structures, one with slightly bowed walls. Traces of fence-posts remained, though not enough to be able to determine property boundaries. The hall had been destroyed by fire, leaving remains of its trench-based timber walls; the pottery found within this building was different from that found elsewhere on the site, suggesting difference in usage and probably also date, since the trench-based walls replaced post-built structures in the 7th century.

At **Cowdery's Down**, Hampshire, the largest and most elaborate of the buildings excavated was labelled 'C12' in the report,[2] dated by the calibrated radiocarbon method to 609 AD +/- 57. Thermoluminescence dating of the daub from the excavation puts the destruction by fire at 720AD +/- 147.[3] The three successive phases of construction detected in the building may indicate three generations inhabiting and improving or repairing the hall, which lasted for around a century, although a 'generation' in this context might be as little as 25 years or as much as 35. Whether such a structure could realistically endure for 50 years without some thorough repair-work is not presently known.

---

[1] Arnold, 1997; Welch, 1992; Rahtz, 1976
[2] Arnold, 1997; Welch, 1992
[3] Welch, 1992

Arnold estimates that the initial construction of the building would have entailed moving 45m^3 of topsoil, chalk and clay weighing around 81 tonnes for the footings, which would have taken around 90 man-hours to complete. The building materials (timber, thatch for the roof, daub for the walls) would have weighed about 70 tonnes.[1]

Without knowing the methods of construction, the available tools and the preferred working methods it is impossible to gauge just what went into the erection of the building. There is no evidence for large timber saws from the early AS period,[2] so it may be the case that the individual planks were radially split from felled trees. Posts would presumably have been worked with adzes from trunks. It is estimated that about 55m^3 of oak would have been required, equivalent to eighteen mature trees representing 2 hectares of oak forest. This excludes any flooring or household equipment.

The presumed sequence for preparing and constructing a building like C12 would begin with excavation of the wall trenches from the chalk subsoil, in this case using a pick to peck away at the chalk. The rectangular area marked out, with doorway gaps, measured 22.1m x 8.5m, and slightly wider where the long sides were bowed. Vertical posts were fixed in the trenches in a staggered arrangement, then horizontal stringers were positioned between them to house the infill panels of daubed wattles; these sections may have been fixed together flat on the ground then raised into position and pegged to secure them. A wall-plate finished off the construction. As there was no evidence for internal supports for the roof, it may be that there was a pair of crucks at each end supporting a horizontal beam, from which king-posts held up the roof-ridge. Rafters would have run horizontally from the wall-plates to the ridge, supported on purlins. There may have been a plank floor supported on joists. As the wall plates carried most of the load, a series of 'buttress' timber posts were placed around the exterior to support the weight. Arnold declines to estimate the man-hours involved in constructing the building, and notes that although it is the largest building on the site the effort required to construct some of the others would not be much less.

Even with a well-studied site such as this, there is no recognised evidence for the roofing, which has allowed a number of very different reconstructions to be made.[3]

---

[1] Dixon, 1993, cites comparative figures for the construction of an aisled house compiled by Dr. Harsema: allowing for modern tools, the total man-hours is put at 1800 for building plus an additional 1800 man-hours for resource-gathering within a maximal 5-mile radius. The project would have to be overseen and co-ordinated by a skilled craftsman. A detailed costing model is provided in his Appendix.

[2] Evidence for Anglo-Saxon tools is generally poor, with a few exceptions. A handful of archaeological finds and some manuscript illustrations are all we have to go on. It is premature to conclude on this basis that large saws - and many other types of equipment - were unknown.

[3] See Welch, 1992 figs. 32-4 for differing views of the final construction.

Chapter Two

A sequence of four building phases may be represented at **Chalton**, Hampshire,[1] where 61 separate buildings may indicate fifteen or sixteen buildings per generation (building phase), possibly three or four farm-units grouped together. The site lasted up to 140 years, and represents a nucleated settlement, smaller than a village but larger than an individual farmstead. It was probably involved in supplying the markets at *Hamwic* (Southampton) as traces were found of wheel-thrown pottery from northern France which are difficult to explain except as products of cross-Channel trade through the local port. The indications from the sparse finds suggest a date range beginning in the sixth century and extending into the eighth: a hanging bowl mount, a link from a chain and an assortment of knives and pins.

A rare example of a grand – probably royal – hall from the early period is the famous building complex at **Yeavering**, Northumberland, known to Bede as *ad Gefrin*, a seat of the Bernician kings.[2] In the late 620s the newly converted King Edwin of Northumbria visited the site with his Kentish queen and the missionary bishop Paulinus, who preached and baptised in the area for a whole month. After Edwin's day, *Gefrin* was abandoned and a new palace erected at *Maelmin* (possibly Milfield).

The site was divided into areas of habitation and human activity by its excavator, Brian Hope-Taylor.[3] Central to the importance of the site was the main dwelling site ('area A') where the first building was a post-built hall (similar to Mucking or West Stow) followed by a series of trench-built successors. A large hall, 82' (25m) long and 36' (11m) wide, was then built on one part of the site, and nearby an even larger one paired with a smaller dwelling; these were all destroyed by fire. Fragments of yellowish wall-plaster were found in the postholes. This probably happened around 630-40 AD, on the evidence of a Frankish buckle found beneath the fire-damaged layers, and would tie in well with the ravaging of Northumbria in 632-3 AD by Edwin's enemies, Penda of Mercia and Cadwallon of Gwynedd.[4] Another hall and secondary building were erected on the site, but these too burnt down and were replaced yet again with a great hall and secondary building. This is roughly dated to the mid-600s by the discovery of a copy of a Frankish coin, and again has been associated with the second invasion of the kingdom by Penda in 651-5. Within a relatively short time, the whole complex was taken out of service but the timber may have been re-used, as the first hall at nearby Milfield is of similar proportions to the last phase hall at Yeavering. East of this complex of buildings stood a large palisaded area, possibly an enclosure for livestock.

---

[1] Welch, 1992

[2] Hope-Taylor, 1977

[3] Hope-Taylor, 1977; Rahtz, 1976

[4] The accident of a historical context for these fires should not blind us to the fact that even the most damaging fire can have accidental causes and need not demonstrate hostile activity.

A unique feature was a large wooden 'grandstand' which dates from the period of the first hall on the site. This might be associated with the Christian preaching of Paulinus, but can also be seen in the context of the need for pageantry and display in mediaeval kingship. The nearest parallel structures are, however, the amphitheatres of the classical world. The grandstand had been enlarged once during its period of use, which suggests an increased importance for whatever kinds of gatherings were held there.

There is evidence for similar structures to the Yeavering hall complex at a series of sites around the country, which may indicate that this royal villa was not actually unique, or perhaps even unusual.

Early English settlements as a group show little evidence for defences or barriers. The only early site in which defence seems to have played a major role is **Bamburgh**, Northumberland.[1] Habitation sites, from isolated farmsteads to royal hall complexes, seem to have had at best only palisade defences in the early Anglo-Saxon period. This may indicate that warfare at this time was governed by ritual or formal structuring, and that both the Germanic and Brythonic polities knew and observed the rules of engagement.

Mid-Saxon Period - 8th & 9th centuries

As an example of a middle-status site, the excavations at **Catholme**, Staffordshire, produced evidence for a small settlement featuring SFBs, post-built and trench-based rectangular structures. The individual plots were marked out with hedges and ditches. There were no artefacts with which to date the site but radiocarbon samples from wooden remains range from the 5th to 9th centuries with a concentration in the 7th-8th. Interestingly, the construction methods used were similar to others found in the Roman period (3rd century) in Nottinghamshire, suggesting that some of the Romano-British building traditions were taken over by Anglo-Saxon farmers (if, indeed, the farmers were not themselves descendants of the Romano-Britons) although so little is known of vernacular, non-villa-related buildings in Britain at that time that no safe conclusions can be drawn.

In the 1960s a series of archaeological excavations revealed a substantial hall complex at **Cheddar**, Somerset; the long timber buildings spanned a period of several centuries, beginning in the 800s.[2] The hall complex is sited at the mouth of the gorge; it consisted of five timber buildings situated south of a major drainage ditch. A coin from the reign of Æþelwulf is the earliest find from the site, dating to c.845. The main hall was trench-built, using squared timbers; it measured 24m long and 5.5m wide at the ends, 6m in the middle due to the bowed plan of most large Anglo-Saxon wooden buildings. Midway along the long (east- and west-facing) sides were large opposed doorways, with a further

---

[1] Evans, 1997

[2] Reynolds, 1999; Arnold, 1997

smaller entrance on the eastern side. A section of the western wall had doubled posts, suggesting that there may have been an upper storey in this area. A possible hearth area lay to the south of the crossed doors. The hall may have had a suspended wooden floor.

Three outbuildings lay to the west, south-west and north of the hall which may have served for storage or housing the administration of the estate. A further structure, lightly built from posts, lay to the east of the hall's north end. Near this enclosure was a human burial, possibly that of an executed criminal as the hands were secured behind its back. During the late ninth century the ditch began to silt up, and this may have flooded the site.

In the centre of **Northampton,**[1] in the region of the present St. Peter's church, remains of a substantial timber building were discovered, assumed by the scale to have been the hall of a major aristocratic or royal figure. The feature dates from the $8^{th} - 9^{th}$ century (radiocarbon dates are 840 AD +/_ 60) and resembles in plan the Yeavering hall of King Edwin and some other sites (Millfield and Sprouston, Northumberland; Atcham, Shropshire; Malmesbury, Wiltshire and others). The timber hall was built to the east of the present St. Peter's, itself the probable site of a minster church, and was an estimated 97.5' (29.7m) by 28' (8.6m). It was built as a main rectangular cell with a smaller (21', 6.2m square) annex at each end; it is believed that the building was planned and constructed in one operation as there is a single 3'3" (1m) wide and deep foundation trench running the entire length of the walls. The design or execution of the construction may have been flawed, as a number of external post-holes indicate some form of shoring to counteract the spreading of the massive roof. It was surrounded on the north- and south-west by smaller timber structures, interpreted as outbuildings for storage or temporary accommodation. This is similar to the arrangements known to have existed at Cheddar and Yeavering.

About a century later, the timber hall was dismantled and replaced by a stone-built, rectangular structure which began as 123' (37.6m) long by 37' (11.4m) wide but was extended to 142' (43.3m) long, with foundations more than 4' (1.2m) wide and 2' (0.6m) deep tightly packed into the earth. The walls may have been as much as 3'3" (1m) thick, and mortared together. The interior was plastered and lime-washed. The source of the stone may have been robbing out some local Roman structures, possibly the villa at Duston. The roof remains a mystery as no identifiable roofing materials were recovered, suggesting that an organic, perishable substance such as reed thatch or wooden shingles was used. The archaeological evidence does not indicate whether the stone hall was a secular or a religious structure. Strangely, it was abandoned by the end of the 10th century, at which point the nature of Northampton's settlement changed: there is evidence for industrial processes and metalworking. This may be associated with the capture of the area by the Danes in the early 900s.

---

[1] Zaluckyj, 2001; Williams, Shaw & Denham, 1985; Welch, 1992

The dimensions of the stone hall at Northampton are quite exceptional for an Anglo-Saxon building, and very few contemporary structures are known to have been so large; perhaps the impressive nearby church at Brixworth, Northants, was designed and built by the same team?

Late-Saxon Period – 10th & 11th centuries

Knowledge of late Anglo-Saxon high-status sites is based largely on the later phases of the **Cheddar** site.[1] Historical records indicate that the *witan* (the king's counsel) met at Cheddar on three occasions (941, 956, 968 AD) under Kings Eadmund, Eadwig and Eadgar respectively.

A major alteration took place in the early 10th c., probably attributable to King Æðelstan around 930.

A new hall was built on an east-west alignment to the south of the preceding hall, and a small stone-built chapel was constructed over the site of the latter. The chapel was built from limestone, and had moulded windows and doorways. The hall was 17m long and 9.1m wide, made from substantial (0.3-0.6m square) posts set into post pits 2.3m apart. The new hall had doorways in both the short, end walls. A latrine was situated outside the western doorway.

A remarkable structure to the west of the main habitation complex consisted of two rectangular buildings joined by a circular structure with a scooped out floor. This has been interpreted as a fowl house,[2] one end being the keeper's house and the other the storage building, with the birds kept in the circular middle component. Iron-working was also carried out on the site, as well as casting in precious metals. A boundary ditch to the east was dug and an entrance was sited opposite the eastern doorway of the hall; next to this a large timber was set up in a pit 1m in diameter and 1m deep, which has been interpreted as a flagstaff or wooden post.

Further reconstruction took place towards the end of the tenth century, possibly commissioned by King Æþelred ("Ethelred the Unready") in the 990s. The hall was reduced to 7.6m in width, at the same time as the chapel was rebuilt on a grander scale.

Throughout its history, the timber halls dominated the site, which featured relatively few outbuildings, suggesting that most activity here was intended to take place within a single building, the main hall. The complex seems to have been a royal villa from the outset, but the reduced nature of the later structures may indicate that towards the end of its life it was used for official purposes only periodically.

In the tenth century, settlements of a 'manorial' character began to spread, probably the residences of local magnates, the class of *þegnas* 'thanes'. These

---

[1] Reynolds, 1999; Rahtz, 1976

[2] The identification is based on a manuscript from St. Gall, Switzerland which shows a square building between two round ones, one for geese and the other for hens.

new estates are smaller than those of the previous period, and represent the many grants of land made to the warrior classes in return for military service and local peace-keeping. These replace the previous large estate centres, suggesting both diversification in the economy and tighter local control over living conditions. These late Anglo-Saxon estates, with their quasi-military character, in some ways prefigure the early Norman castles of the late 11th century.

The estate known as **Bonhunt Farm**[1] in north-west Essex is the eastern sector of Wicken Bonhunt parish. It covers some 211 acres (including 10 acres of meadow); at the time of the Domesday survey (1086) it was assessed as 'two hides'. The normal rule-of-thumb is that hide is equivalent to 120 acres of land, giving a notional 240 acres for the holding. Bonhunt Farm therefore may well continue a Middle Saxon two-hide estate, the nominal landholding of the *ceorl* (yeoman) class. The farm was partially excavated in 1971-3 and contained a Middle Saxon settlement overlaid by an 11th century 'demesne farm' of four elongated plots; there were four bordars recorded here at Domesday. Later in that century the site was transformed into a village with a large, aisled hall, a standard mediaeval manor estate.

The outer wall of **Portchester Castle**, Hampshire, was constructed as a Roman fort of the *Litus Saxonicum* or 'Saxon Shore' in the 4th century.[2] This was a series of strongholds along the southern and eastern seaboards designed to deter raiding by Germanic pirates in the late Roman period. By the tenth century the site had resumed an importance position, this time defending the successors of those Saxon raiders against a fresh wave of Scandinavian incursions, those of the Vikings. The site is mentioned in the *Burghal Hidage*, an administrative document of the 9th century. Evidence of finds made on the site suggests that it was occupied in the 8th century in a rural, agricultural capacity but from the late 9th century it began to see high-status occupation.

In the mid-tenth century, four buildings were present of which the largest was a hall residence, 12.8m by 9.45m, lightly constructed and with rounded corners. Three pairs of internal posts supported the roof, each set into a square posthole up to 0.75m deep. The internal arrangement was subdivided by walls of wattle with a daub overlay. The doors were placed opposite each other, midway along the long walls, but there were no physical remains of a hearth. A smaller building to the north was 7.0m by 4.9m and was interpreted as a storeroom. To the hall's south-west was another building, erected using the post-in-trench method, of 12.5m by 6.7m; this had an internal feature interpreted as the bottom end of a stairway, indicating an upper floor. It had a small hearth in the western end. A further post-built structure lay to the west. An unlined well was dug, and a group of cesspits mark the site of the latrine. Rubbish pits were dug around the northern and western perimeters.

---

[1] Wade, 1980
[2] Reynolds, 1999.

Later in the tenth century the latrine was filled in and a storeroom was erected over the site; the hall was replaced with a similar structure with square corners. The well remained in use and more rubbish pits were dug, suggesting increased activity on the site, if no change in status. Early in the 11th century the inhabitants built a masonry tower (4m by 5m) to the south of the main hall,[1] and it was probably in this phase that the Watergate, a late Saxon tower, was added to the perimeter walls (this was actually the rebuilding of a Roman structure which had fallen into disrepair). By the mid-10th century the stone tower was made larger and stronger (20' / 6m square). The hall fell into disuse and may have collapsed, or had its timbers removed and recycled elsewhere. A small cemetery was laid out on the site, to the north of the tower; by this time the site may have been in Norman hands, and the construction of the castle would then have been underway in the north-west corner of the fort.

Goltho, Lincolnshire, is another of the class of 'thanely' residences.[2] In mid-Saxon times the land was agricultural but from the early tenth century the nature of the site changed: the modest domestic structures were replaced by a series of halls and outbuildings disposed around a central courtyard. To the north were weaving sheds, and to the west kitchens. These stood within a sub-rectangular enclosure, although the church lay outside it. The kitchens were enlarged later in the century, and further rooms added to the east of the new main hall.

In the eleventh century, a substantial enclosing ditch was added to the site, 110m long and 100m wide (a bigger area than the later Norman fortifications). The site showed evidence for high status ceramics, and for metalworking.

Manorial complexes of a similar kind have been identified at a number of sites – Raunds, Northamptonshire, Trowbridge, Wiltshire and elsewhere – and must have been relatively common towards the later end of the Anglo-Saxon period.

The British tradition

It is perhaps not surprising that the hall-based *comitatus* societies of the Anglo-Saxons' neighbours should have been broadly similar in many respects. Both Anglo-Saxon and British societies were founded on networks of kinship, loyalty and favour; both had evolved during the sub-Roman and post-Roman periods; both faced similar problems of organisation, supply and political survival. There are some significant differences in the strategies adopted to meet these problems, as well as cultural differences. The British spoke a Brythonic Celtic language which, when committed to writing, is called Old Welsh. Many were probably Christian in their religion, and some of their political and social structures were of Roman origin.

---

[1] A fortified gate and a bell-tower were two of the requirements for the residence of an English *þegn* in the late Anglo-Saxon period.
[2] Reynolds, 1999

Chapter Two

British and Anglo-Saxon halls were similar in design:[1] rectangular, up to 80' in length and constructed from timber, thatched and with a wooden floor. A high-status structure excavated at **Doon Hill** was 70' long by 32' wide, with doors in the long sides and a separate room at either end. This is one of a small number of British princely halls (*neuadd*) which commonly consist of a large assembly space and a small chamber offset.

One exceptional structure built on a *crannog* – an artificial island – at **Buiston**, East Lothian was circular. It has been identified as a high-status hall on the basis of the finds (weapons, metalworking residues, imported pottery) and the open space within. This structure dates from the 7th to 8th centuries. It was 56' in diameter and featured a central hearth. It may not have been necessary that a lord's hall be any specific shape or size, since its main purpose was to house the *comitatus*.

The warbands of the British and Anglo-Saxon communities seem to have been similar in structure and outlook, although there is less evidence from Old Welsh literature. The praise-poetry of Taliesin fits well with the function of the poet as eulogiser of his patrons, but it concentrates rather more on the gifts he received than on the circumstances of the award. Another important source, the *Gododdin*, clearly has the hall-culture as its background and social setting.[2] References are made to the hall's hearth, the candles lighting it, the warriors' benches, the drinking horns passing among the men. The highlighted event is the 'feast' (*gwledd*), a formal meal at which gifts are given, speeches made, friendships reinforced. The drinks are mead and wine (*medd, gwin*) which are taken from mead-horns, cups or glasses. One interesting deviation from the English tradition is that the *Gododdin* poem refers to mead as 'bitter'.[3] Normally, mead is a honey-based alcoholic drink retaining a certain residue of sugars and is moderately sweet to the taste; the usage here may be figurative, in that the 'bitterness' associated with being a mead-drinker is the duty to kill and to die in exchange for it.

The warbands of the early British polities have been considered to be smaller in numbers than the Anglo-Saxon equivalents,[4] due in part to their reliance on the horse (as at the battle of Catraeth) and also, in time, on their confinement in less agriculturally productive areas. However that may be, the alliances formed between English and Welsh states in support of a common aim demonstrate clearly that whatever the linguistic, religious or cultural barriers between them, they shared enough common ground to work together. The 7th century pagan king of Mercia, Penda, was notoriously allied with the Christian King Cadwallon of Gwynedd in their joint effort to destroy the power of Christian Northumbria.

---

[1] Evans, 1997, ch.7

[2] The literal historicity of the events described in the *Gododdin* has been doubted, but the fact remains that the verse deployed seems to be typical of the period.

[3] Evans, 1997, p.108

[4] Evans, 1997, p.28-9

3 Ritual Space: The Hall in Ideology

The Hall as the Ideal Dwelling

It has been suggested that the Germanic notion of 'goodness' involved a willingness to share resources; it was however an outward, public rather than an inward, private quality, and involved public recognition of worth as part of its reward.[1] A 'good man' in this early Iron Age society was one who acted in a practical, utilitarian way to preserve the society and to promote its aims. This 'good man' was a man of means, a leader or prominent member of his social group, economically independent and dominant in his settlement; the room in which his public acts of distribution took place was the hall of his household. The hall was therefore the interface between the public and private aspects of the leader's life. In this way, the hall became associated with wealth and with gifts, and this ideology took firm root as social trends led from a communal to a more individual approach to social structures. The individual householder, as head of his nuclear family and its dependants, thus came to stand aside from the collective workforce.

The notion of the hall as the place of assembly for the social group goes hand in hand with the rise of a well-defined social élite in the Celtic Iron Age (c.500-100BC).[2] The traditional, open *þing* assembly of freemen was gradually replaced as the central social institution by the hall-based gift-giving ritual; the gathering of many free equals became an assembly of élite leaders and their warrior-followers. The open, democratic nature of the *þing* was subverted, over a period of time, by the dominance of a few decision-makers; while the *þing* continues to be important even into late Anglo-Saxon England, its original purpose is lost in the multiplication of layers of hierarchy, shifting power into the hands of kings. The first 'kings' – the *reges* of Tacitus's time – were simply leading men; Tacitus himself states that they are *primus inter pares* 'first among equals'.[3] Due regard for the base of their power was always necessary: without showing generosity and recognition of merit, they would gain no support.

The unusual grandstand at Yeavering, Northumberland, can be interpreted as a purpose-built structure in which to hold such large assemblies, but it is carefully

---

[1] Herschend, 1998; Herschend links modern notions of private goodness to the world-rejection of Christianity.

[2] Herschend, 1998; Kershaw, 2000

[3] Tacitus, *Germania*, Ch.7

positioned next to the royal hall in which the king's wealth was housed. It may have been constructed with this balance of power in mind. Symbolising the notion of a hierarchical society, dominated by the king at its apex, the huge hall at Yeavering emphasised the wealth and political success of its owner and his folk.

The literary references to hall-life are concerned almost exclusively with the halls of the powerful, important and wealthy. There must have been lowlier, less ambitious halls on every settlement in which the householders demonstrated their generosity and wisdom: the differences are apparently of quantity, not quality.

It is notable that the halls identified archaeologically are seldom on defended sites (but less so at the very end of the Anglo-Saxon period). Typically the hall sits within its community of dwellings and workshops, with only fences to mark off the home-acre from the rest of the area. It may be that the hall had to be accessible by definition, and that a chief who could not defend his hall through the power of his reputation would be deemed unworthy to lead.[1]

There is some indication in Icelandic literature that a young man built his hall when it was his intention to marry. For the English warrior class this meant around twenty five years of age, when he was no longer on constant military service with the king and could take on the responsibility of household and family as well as the social role of *eorl* or member of the *duguð*.

The Anglo-Saxon hall was not just a living-space, the scene of revelry and entertainment. It was the only available public arena in which events of many kinds took place. Its large, central, open space must be seen as both an assembly room and as a court of law. As the hall was the centre of political and social life for leaders and kings, the discussion in the hall would encompass all aspects of leadership – it was a public forum in which policy could be made. Therefore what happened in the hall impacted upon the 'real world' beyond its walls. This impact may have taken the form of initiatives in peace or war, trade, laws, religious ritual and tradition.[2]

The hall stood at the centre of a cluster of buildings, which were themselves the nucleus of the human geography of the area in which they sat. As the central place of the lands attached to it, the hall was the stage on which all significant public life was enacted.

---

[1] Herschend, 1998

[2] Herschend, 1998, p.168ff sees a development from the unquestioned, normative leadership of the early or legendary period (e.g. that of Hroþgar as presented in *Beowulf*) to the more human, fallible leadership of the historical period (e.g. that of Byrhtnoð in *The Battle of Maldon* whose decision to fight is implicitly criticised in the poem). This notion would carry more weight if we could be certain of the date of *Beowulf*'s composition; its manuscript dates from within a decade or two of the *Maldon* poem.

The hall at Cowdery's Down is situated between the fenced-off farm area and the path outside,[1] demonstrating its function as the interface between the community and the world at large. Here the leader met and greeted guests, and enacted his public role as spokesman for the group. Here also the lady of the household offered the customary drinks and hospitality to her guests. These occasions were opportunities to display wealth, social grace and benevolence to the world at large. In so doing, the leader and his family emphasised their high status and access to resources.

Heorot

The best-documented hall from contemporary literature is Hroðgar's building *Heorot* in *Beowulf*:

> .... *Him on mod bearn*
> *ðæt healreced hatan wolde*
> *medoærn micel men gewyrcan*
> *þonne ylda bearn æfre gefrunon*
> *7 þær on innan eall gedælan*
> *geongum 7 ealdum swylc him god sealde*
> *buton folcsceare 7 feorum gumena.*
> *Ða ic wide gefrægn weorc gebannan*
> *manigre mægðe geond þisne middangeard*
> *folcstede frætwan; him on fyrste gelomp*
> *ædre mid yldum þæt hit wearð ealgearo*
> *healærna mæst, scop him heort naman*
> *se þe his wordes geweald wide hæfde*
> *He beot ne aleah beagas dælde*
> *sinc æt symle sele hlifade*
> *heah 7 horngeap .....*

> ... it came into his mind
> that a hall-building he would order
> his men to build, a mightier mead-hall
> than the sons of men had ever heard of
> and there in the rooms he would deal out all
> that God gave him to young and old ones
> - except for the tribal lands and the lives of men.
> Then I heard widely of the work ordered
> in many nations throughout this middle-earth

---

[1] Herschend, 1998

Chapter Three

to adorn the meeting-place; it happened in time to him
after a while, that it was fully finished
- the greatest of hall-buildings – he made its name 'Heorot',
he who widely held his word's rule.
He did not fail in his oath, he handed out rings,
treasure at the feast, the hall towered up,
high and wide-gabled ….
                Beowulf, l.67-82

Contemporary records indicate that it was customary for the landed classes to receive visitors in the hall. On his arrival at the Danish court, Beowulf and his men travel to Heorot:

… guman onetton
sigon ætsomne oþþæt hy sæl timbred
geatolic 7 goldfah ongytan mihton
þæt wæs foremærost foldbuendum
receda under roderum on þæm se rica bad
lixte se leoma ofer land fela

… the warriors hastened
they went down together until a timbered hall
they could make out, furnished and gold-fair,
- it was the most renowned among dwellers on earth
of buildings beneath the sky – in which the great man dwelt;
its brightness shone out over many lands …
                Beowulf, l. 306-11

They present themselves at the doors of Heorot, where they are greeted by the king's door-keeper, Wulfgar, whose function it is to announce guests requiring an audience and turn away those having no business with the king. Beowulf declares his name and purpose, and his journey thither. The poet says:

Wulfgar maþelode – þæt wæs Wendla leod
wæs him modsefa manegum gecyðed
wig ond wisdom "ic þæs wine deniga
frean Scyldinga frinan wille
beaga bryttan swa þu bena eart
þeoden mærne ymb þinne sið
ond þe þa ondsware ædre gecyðan
ðe me se goda agifan þenceð."

Ritual Space – The Hall in Ideology

hwearf þa hrædlice þær Hroðgar sæt
eald ond anhar mid his eorla gedriht
eode ellenrof þæt he for eaxlum gestod
Deniga frean, cuþe he duguðe þeaw.
                                    Beowulf, l.348-59

Wulfgar spoke – he was a prince of the Vandals
His courage was known to many
his valour and wisdom "The friend of the Danes
Lord of the Scildings, I will ask for this
to the giver of treasures, as you are a boon-asker[1]
to the famed prince, concerning your mission
and soon declare to you the answer
which the good man thinks to give me."
He quickly turned then to where Hrothgar sat
old and white-haired with his troop of nobles.
the brave-hearted man went so that he stood before the shoulders
of the Danes' lord - he knew the customs of the court.[2]

It is interesting that Beowulf must treat with Wulfgar before entering the hall: some Scandinavian halls are laid out with no ante-room so that, on approaching the open door, the guest immediately becomes the focus of attention for those within. Likewise, some later halls have a separate doorway behind the high-seat through which the householder is able to make a staged entrance into the upper, prominent area of the hall without having to pass the door-warden; this is itself a mark of high-status for the owner, his family and any guest afforded the honour of using it.[3]

As a meeting-room, the hall was the scene of petitions and requests; bargaining, buying and selling; presentations and rewards. It must equally have been the place where public humiliation took place, punishments were enacted and fines exacted.

---

[1] *bena* 'petitioner, suppliant, one who makes a request'. The word has no elegant modern equivalent, but in the original it conveys the sense of someone who has travelled to the leader's hall with a request to make – in this case, to offer his services as the king's defender.

[2] The OE says he knew *duguðe þeaw* 'the custom of the *duguð*', these being the older, doughty, trusty warriors of the king's company; as the more experienced men in the warband, they formed the king's advisers and, it may be assumed, held an élite position in the social group.

[3] Herschend, 1998

Chapter Three

Tacitus[1] implies that the Germanic folk of his day used hall-feasts as the occasion for reconciling enemies, patching up feuds, brokering alliances, match-making, choosing leaders, striking deals. A feast as a communal, inclusive occasion would have been the ideal opportunity for the negotiation of peace and brotherhood among groups with a history of hatred or rivalry. In reality, with strong drink flowing and unsettled scores, halls were probably just as often the site of fighting and declarations of war on neighbours or enemies further afield. Old English heroic verse does not shrink from depicting this aspect of the hall as *maþelstede* 'discussion-place' or *mæþelern* 'assembly-hall' since the undertone of menace gives greater poignancy to the joy to be found in the halls of the great and the good. The assembly itself was protected by *mæþelfriþ* the legal 'peace' surrounding a public assembly. The *mæþel* in question is public discourse, meant to sway the listeners – the audience of warriors, leaders and advisers – to some course of action, be it acceptance of former enemies or renewing strife.

The *Beowulf* poet gives us a clear example of the manner in which hatred can flare up at even a wedding banquet, meant to seal a compact of peace, when the bride's escort of armed followers must share a bench with their host's men:-

> *þonne cwið æt beore se ðe beah gesyhð*
> *eald æscwiga se ðe eall geman*
> *garcwealm gumena him bið grim sefa*
> *onginneð geomor mod geongum cempan*
> *þurh hreðra gehygd higes cunnian*
> *wigbealu weccan ond þæt word acwyð:*
> *"Meaht ðu, min wine, mece gecnawan*
> *þone þin fæder to gefeohte bær*
> *under heregriman hindeman siðe*
> *dyre iren þær hine Dene slogon*
> *weoldon wælstowe syððan Wiðergyld læg*
> *æfter hæleþa hryre hwate Scyldungas?*
> *Nu her þara banena byre nathwylces*
> *frætwum hremig on flet gæð*
> *morþres gylpeð ond þone maðþum byreð*
> *þone þu mid rihte rædan scoldest."*
> *Manað swa ond myndgað mæla gehwylce*
> *sarum wordum oð ðæt sæl cymeð*
> *þæt se fæmnan þegn fore fæder dædum*
> *æfter billes bite blodfag swefeð*
>   *Beowulf*, 1.2041 - 60

---

[1] *Germania*, Ch.2

Then he who sees a ring speaks over the beer,
an old spear-fighter who remembers well
the war-death of warriors – his heart is grim –
of a young champion he begins, in sorrowful mood
through his mind's thoughts, to test the courage,
waken the war-bale, and says those words:
"My friend, can you recognise the sword
which your father bore to the fight
wearing his war-mask for the last time,
- that beloved weapon – where the Danes slew him,
controlled the battlefield once Wiþergyld lay dead,
after the fall of the heroes – those brave Scyldings[1]?
Now, a son of one of those killers
walks on this floor proud of his adornments
boasts of murder and bears that heirloom
which by rights you should own."
He urges and reminds thus at every opportunity
with bitter words until the time comes
that for his father's deeds the lady's thane
dies blood-drenched after the sword's bite.

The short-lived marriage of Ingeld and his bride Freawaru must have been a commonplace of Old English story. The same tradition, differing in detail, is known from mediaeval Denmark in Saxo Grammaticus's *Gesta Danorum*; here, the most renowned warrior-adventurer-hero-troublemaker of the north, Starkaðr, stirs up strife so that the Danish Ingeld kills his (Saxon) wife's brothers.

Mead-hall and Men's Hall

An interesting attempt to apply techniques from psychoanalytic anthropology to *Beowulf* by Earl[2] sets the architecture of the Anglo-Saxon period into its context of customs and institutions of the fictionalised world of the poem. Taking as his starting point the notion of the hall as 'ritual space', he tackles the loaded question of the role of hall culture in the development of Anglo-Saxon civilization. Specifically, he deals with the conversion from heathen polytheism to Christianity, and with it the social and cultural movement from tribal to

---

[1] The *Scyldingas* are the leading or royal family of the Danes in OE tradition – the *Skjoldungar* of Norse sources.

[2] *Beowulf and the Men's Hall* in Earl, 1994. Earl notes that the structuralist approach reduces a complex reality to a set of binary oppositions, and thus it idealises historical fact; however, works of human imagination such as *Beowulf* itself do no less. See also Hennessy Olsen, 1997; Hill, 1995.

civilised mind-set.[1] By the 6th century, a ruling (or, at least, leading) warrior class had emerged from the melting-pot of the migrations with the hall as its central cultural artefact; the hall was used to inhibit violence, to bring structure and dialogue to human interactions, to control society.

Kinship – the bloodline and genetic relationsips – was the cornerstone of the social structure, yet the conflict between the ties of blood and those of marriage, or friendship, or oath-binding were among the most persistent themes of Germanic literature. The kinship system was bilateral in the sense of taking both maternal and paternal lineages into account; no two people could have the identical *cyn* (kindred) because they each had a unique set of relations.[2] Therefore, the kindred system was a social institution but individual kindreds were not shared, and so could not become powerful institutions in themselves. While the male-centred paternal aspects of the *cyn* were emphasised in many contexts, the female and maternal elements were no less important; the word *mæg* or *mægð* could mean both 'woman' and 'family, folk'. The early tribal legal system regarded the *cyn* as the principal legal entity;[3] individuals were answerable to their folk, and it was to the folk of the perpetrator that victims of crime turned for redress. Nevertheless, the warband's oath-based relationships cut across this social structure based on the bloodline (see Appendix 3). The oath-brotherhood of lords and warriors distinguished the class of leaders from the mass of ordinary people whose social ties were genetic and agnatic, whose occupations were agricultural or industrially productive and whose organisation was kin-based and led by the *Cyning*.[4]

In the migration to Britain, Earl suggests that the balance of the traditional Germanic system was disturbed. The warband assumed an undue importance as the means of winning and administering territory, and the lord (*dux*, warlord)

---

[1] Crudely, one might characterise a tribal/traditional culture as one where shame (public disapproval) is the moral negative, while in a civilised/modern society it is guilt (private conscience). The role of Christianity in promoting private guilt is hardly to be doubted.

[2] For example, two brothers will share most of the same kindred, but each has a different person as his brother; the kindred is therefore egocentric and unique to the individual. (See Haymes, 1998.) An ego-centric kinship grouping allows the central 'focal figure' to reposition him- or herself in relation to multiple descent groups. This is the opposite of the clans where descent from a common ancestor is paramount. Ego-centric groupings are by definition impermanent, yet the flexibility in the system allows for one or more lineage to be emphasised as needs dictate. See Hill, 1995. The term *cyn* then can mean whatever part of the genetic background the individual chooses to identify with, which will be determined to a large extent by the benefits or otherwise of belonging to group A over group B. In *Beowulf* there seems to be an upper limit of four preceding generations, beyond which living memory specific forebears are merged with the legendary background of the tribe. This murky fluidity in the ancestral past enabled court poets to manipulate the common traditions of many groups to reflect contemporary arrangements.

[3] The pre-eminent male of the kin-group was called the 'scion of the kin' – *cyning* – which is the standard OE word for 'king'.

[4] This division lies behind the warrior-aristocratic Æsir gods Oðinn and Þorr who stand apart from the peace-and-plenty Vanir gods such as Freyr and Njorðr in Norse myth.

assumed powers and responisbilites normally associated with the king (*rex*, tribal priest-king). The tensions arising from this redefinition of roles were not wholly destructive but they did cause a re-alignment of social-standing, a division into high- and low-status groups, religious cults and priorities. When Christianity was introduced in the early 7th century, it became another means by which the aristocratic tendencies of the leaders and warriors could be given a religious dimension; the new religion sanctioned the power and position of the lord while it may have been resisted by the adherents of the kin-based social order. In a sense, the advent of Christianity was well-timed to take advantage of the move among early Anglo-Saxon societies to subjugate the kin-based structures to the new oath-based system which could be extended to incorporate ever larger numbers of people; thus the primary focus of loyalty became the nation (and the state) rather than the kindred, and in time the administration of the law became a state, rather than a family, responsibility.

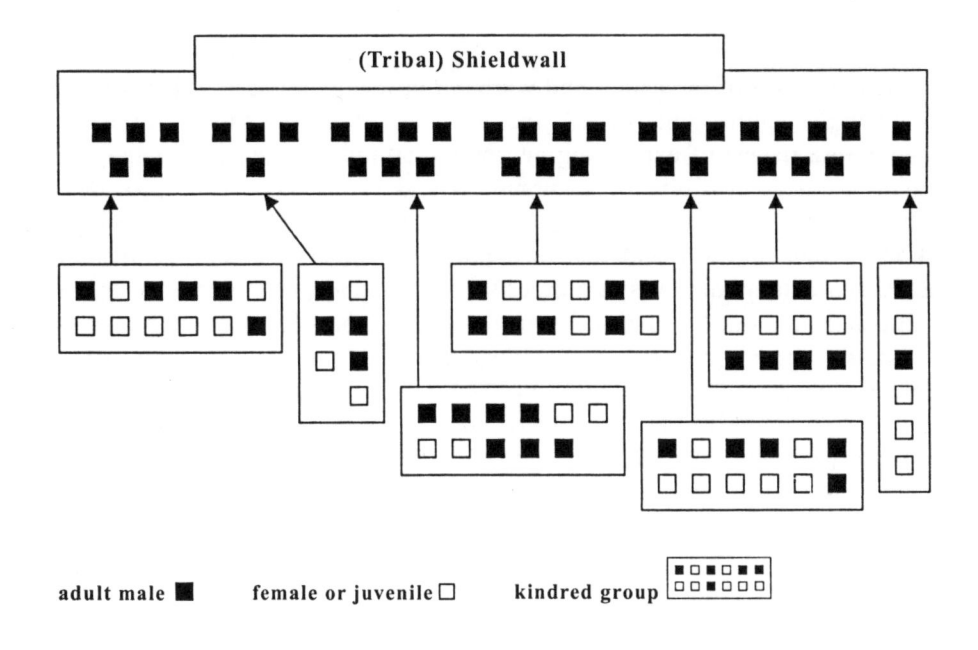

Fig.8 The traditional Germanic military structure

The contention was played out between two social institutions symbolising love (the kindred) and aggression (the warrior class) in a paradigm of Freud's theory that civilization relies on the suppression of the twin instincts of sexuality and violence (procreation and destruction). As the role of the kindred diminished under Christian civilizing influence, so too did the importance and influence of the trustee of the kindred's power, the freeborn Germanic woman.[1] It should be noted that Earl's ideas are not entirely supported by the research of other scholars. The Vanir-worshipping agriculturalists and artisans, for example, apparently shared the egocentric bilateral kinship model of the Æsir-worshipping leaders and therefore bloodline was not the sole determining factor in membership of their culture. Just as important was vicinage, and although Tacitus (*Germania*, ch.7) explicitly says that family members go to war alongside each other, in village settlements one's family are one's neighbours, due to inter-marriage between a small number of kinship groups. Equally, the identification of SFBs with dwellings is not at all secure - as we saw above (p.65) there is very little evidence for these huts having been used for long-term occupation. Nevertheless, the opposition of male-dominated public meeting hall versus female-dominated domestic house is one that has persisted in English society to some extent down to the present and, while there may be some truth in the idea that public affairs were largely the preserve of men, free women in historical times had access to justice and policy-making through the meeting hall while thralls of both sexes had no such legal access.

Now, the position of the leader and warband in this is not strictly limited to the promotion of aggression; indeed, the warband offers a channel for existing aggression, a means of expressing aggressive attitudes which externalises them (turning them away from the community) and at the same time provides an opportunity for bonding; in jointly breaking the traditional taboos on violence and aggression, the warband fosters feelings of solidarity among its members. The warrior cult upholds and reinforces the social bonds, and imposes a strict ban on internally-focussed violence. In Anglo-Saxon times this was known as *grið*, the 'king's peace', an area surrounding the king's person in which it was forbidden to use violence or threats, or even to carry weapons.[2] Whereas the kin-based system could lead to blood-feuds and escalating violence,[3] the oath-based warbands were able to contain this violence through legal mechanisms such as the payment of *wergield* 'man-price', a compensatory and voluntary surrender of wealth for a killing. The payment went to the dead man's kindred, but a portion was taken by the king as a 'fine'. Eventually, fictive kindreds were accepted in law, composed of groups of unrelated people who resided or travelled together. These people usually had an economic relationship, and were styled *gegieldan* 'co-payers', the basis of the mediaeval guilds.

---

[1] This process did not reach its logical culmination until the new regime of Norman England finally disenfranchised women and rendered them legally incompetent to administer their own affairs.

[2] Earl, 1994 p.112ff. One law-code sets the *grið's* perimeter as extending from the gate of the king's residence in all directions for a length of 3 miles + 3 furlongs + 3 acres + 9 feet + 9 shaftmunds + 9 barley-corns. The ritual nature of this preceinct is demonstrated by the symbolic measurements stated.

[3] The potential for violent exaction of revenge by the kindred was nevertheless a strong inhibitor of violent behaviour.

Ritual Space – The Hall in Ideology

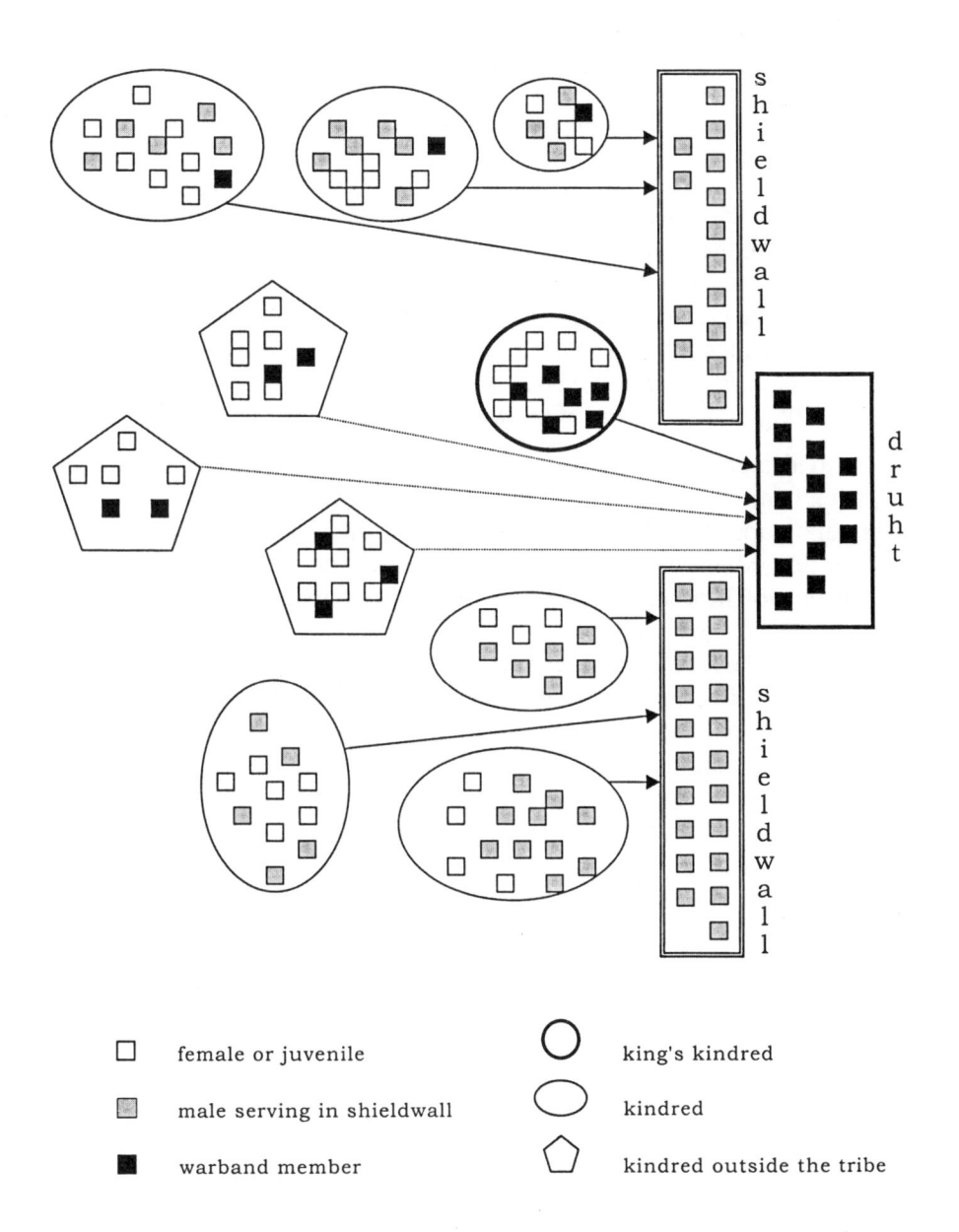

□	female or juvenile	○	king's kindred
▨	male serving in shieldwall	⬭	kindred
■	warband member	⬠	kindred outside the tribe

Fig.9 The Germanic military structure with Warbands

Chapter Three

Earl relates the stubborn adherence to wooden hall-building traditions, even when good building stone was available and stoneworking was a common trade, to the Anglo-Saxon devotion to the symbolism of the traditional hall, which was not a dwelling but a symbolic space, a *mæðelstede* 'meeting-place'. The hall evoked and defined the traditional way of life, which was immensely important to the Anglo-Saxons; rather than adopt palaces or villas, they clung to the time-honoured building forms.[1] The story in the *HE* of the sparrow flying briefly through the king's hall on a winter's night, encapsulates the northern view of the cosmos in which the outer chaos was an ever-present threat to the warmth, order and comfort of human society.[2] One can see in this imagery the position of the warrior-king as upholder of man's fragile achievements in the fight against the surrounding darkness – an image from the heathen religion which nevertheless resonated well within a mediaeval Christian framework. Likewise, the raising of the hall *Heorot* in *Beowulf* is symbolic of the rise of human society, accompanied by a song telling of the creation of the world.

Heorot provides an inviting picture of the hall as ritual space, yet it is only a house, not a home: there is no mention in the poem of servants, or women, or the agricultural workers whose labour provided the raw materials for the heroes' feasting. Men eat, drink and talk in the *mæðelstede*, but they do not sleep[3] there, we do not hear that they bring their wives and children to hall-based events. Family life goes on, in Earl's view, in the spread of domestic buildings which surround the hall; in the early period, these huts could be SFBs. Adducing cultural parallels from modern tribal societies, he sees the hall as the men's "ceremonial house" and bachelor quarters. Its function and importance are defined by its relationship to the surrounding domestic homes: as the backdrop to matters of lordship, feasting ritual and public discourse, oath-making and gift-giving – the whole context of the warband lifestyle – the hall functions as a symbolic public arena. The huts, by contrast, are the domain of women, of kindred-based groups, of daily family life. In as much as warriors and farmers had contrasted religious needs, the hall functioned as the cult building for the Æsir-worshipping, oath-based warbands while kindred-based groups worshipped their Vanir gods in different locations.[4] The use of strong drink in the hall rites is

---

[1] Earl, p.115, notes "Dwellings are cosmic symbols, guiding the behaviour, belief and thought of those who dwell in them by organizing their notion of the world."

[2] The only consistent image of the afterlife from northern mythology is *Valholl*, the hall of the noble slain warriors under the leadership of the god Óðinn. Here again, the hall stands for the home of men and gods which must be defended against the wolf, ogres and monsters of Hel.

[3] Beowulf and his party do rest in the hall on the first night of their stay, as a means of ensuring that they can counter-attack when Grendel visits. Significantly, once the Grendel-menace is believed to be over, the guests sleep in outside quarters.

[4] Taking the contrastive symbolism even further into Freudian territory, halls are tall, awe-inspiring masculine erections while earth-fast huts are comfortable feminine holes in the ground. The domestic life in the huts is therefore female-dominated and 'telluric' and natural, while the hall is cultural.

explained by reference to the Norse tale of the treaty between the two groups of gods, which was confirmed by jointly spitting into a bowl; the result was made into a man, Kvasir, who surpassed all others in wisdom. When Kvasir was killed by the dwarfs, his blood was collected and from it was made the mead of poetry, one draught of which could turn the drinker into a poet. The poet was originally a cult figure, a leader in ritual, but by historical Anglo-Saxon times this aspect seems to have been lost, forgotten or suppressed.[1] Nevertheless the passing of both harp and drinking-horn in the tale of Cædmon (Appendix 2) suggests that a communal bond was created by participation in a joint cultural and social activity.

The Hall as Central Place

Another attempt to understand the relationship between the hall and its surroundings is based on Scandinavian evidence, where the development of administrative centres – hall settlements – is a crucial phase in the progress towards the development of the mediaeval nations of the kingdoms-states of Norway, Sweden and Denmark.[2] Parallel trends were at work in Anglo-Saxon England, probably facilitated by the long tradition of villas, *vici* and administrative centres created in the Roman occupation, building in turn on existing networks of *oppida*.[3] Although many Roman towns remained in occupation in the sub-Roman[4] period, they often lost their specifically urban character. Only later in the sixth century did emporia begin to play a part in trade networks, situated on the coast or navigable rivers.[5]

The Anglo-Saxon hall within its settlement surrounded by ploughlands, woodland and *feld* (open land) appears to have the characteristics of the "central place", used in archaeological theory to describe sites which act as focuses for administration, religion, justice, economic activity, distribution and so on.[6] The hall, in its function as meeting-place, acts as a centre of various kinds of activity for the district which it serves. In the northern European context, the "central place" may be identified by special buildings (such as the hall, and later the church); specialised artefacts, such as regalia, weapons, tools or jewellery; distinctive monuments, such as burial mounds; and sometimes specific site nomenclature. The function may be dispersed over a number of buildings or sites within a small district.

---

[1] Calvert Watkins, 1995; Pollington, 2001

[2] Brink, 1996

[3] Grant, 1986

[4] The adjective 'sub-Roman' is curious: chronologically, the period is post-Roman and archaeologically, since Anglo-Saxon remains usually sit on top of Roman ones, they should be termed 'super-Roman'. Yet the use of the term persists.

[5] Hodges, 1989

[6] Aston, 1986

Chapter Three

In the early Anglo-Saxon period, when boundaries were fixed between groups by mutual agreement, or the assertion of one group's power, the hall stood as a fixed geographical structure in a changing political landscape. The lord of the hall was the lord of those people living round about who acknowledged his leadership.[1] Later, as physical boundaries became more important, the hall continued to act as the social centre for the group who were now those people living within a given boundary. The lord was by this time the leader of a pre-defined district, not of a group. This coincides with the idea of the king as an itinerant ruler, constantly moving from one settlement – from one "central place" - to the next to collect his dues, meet his people, dispense justice and make awards; in the pre-Christian period, doubtless the king took part in religious activities as well. The fact that the king was constantly moving necessarily meant that the districts under his leadership displayed considerable autonomy – it is possible that only the regular presence of the king and his court kept the local leadership loyal.

The circuit taken by kings of small kingdoms - the 300 hide units of the *Tribal Hidage*, for example the *Færpingas* in the Cotswolds or the *Hicce* in the Chilterns[2] - would presumably have included all the central places of the polity. By the time a kingdom was in the order of 7,000 hides it would have been impossible for an individual to visit all the settlements, even briefly. It may have been the case that kings then visited the halls of the leading men of each district, and these men - the *subreguli* and *ministri* of the charters - in turn visited the halls within their territories. Local government was administered by such means, as well as through the hundred organisation (and its predecessors) and regional meetings.

"Central places" or CPs acted as focal points for a range of specialist skilled workers, such as weapons-makers, armourers, jewellers, and the rest. Once Christianity was established, minsters became central places of a similar kind, where the crafts also included manuscript production, religious services and librarianship. It is quite likely that pagan period CPs were the settings for cult enactments, religious rites, worship and sacrifice.

There are a number of words which describe the CP, but they are not easy to identify or to analyse. In Scandinavia, place-names such as *husaby*, *bo* and *kungsgardar* appear to correlate with local assembly points and centres of administration but none of these names occurs in the Anglo-Saxon records. (English place-names ending in -*by* are generally of Scandinavian origin, but do not appear to reflect the same social structure or distribution. There are English place-names with the element *cynges* "King's" but as they date from a variety of periods, their distribution may not reveal a comparable system.) The word *heall*

---

[1] It is tempting to associate this 'leadership by consent' with the quasi-tribal groupings whose titles are based on a personal name: the –*ingas* groups which are commemorated in many English (and other Germanic) place-names.

[2] Based on the suggested placements of Hill, 1981

or *hall* is not found as the second element in place-names from the Anglo-Saxon period, although it may appear as the first (e.g. Halstead, Essex) and has been used since mediaeval times to refer to the centre of a manorial estate. Neither is it found in Scandinavia in the pre-mediaeval period, and indeed it may have been borrowed from contact with West Germanic speakers as a name for a king's residence or main chamber, whence its occurrence in the mythological name *Valholl*. *Heall* is easily confused with the word *healh, halh* 'nook, corner' which occurs in some English place-names (e.g. Haltwistle, Northumberland).

An alternative term for 'hall' is OE *sele*, ON *sal*, which occurs regularly in *Beowulf* and forms a common poetic term for a large building for gatherings. The Lombard word *sala* 'barn' is related. OE has a by-form *salor* which is of an ancient type.[1] OE *sele* seems always to be a rather poetic synonym for *heall*, with perhaps royal, cultic or merely grand overtones, based on the usage in *Beowulf*. Its original meaning appears to have been 'long house with one large room', as distinct from the sub-divided byre-houses of the agricultural classes.

The word *hof* is rather difficult to pin down. In OE it seemingly means 'building' but originally it may have meant 'something lifted, a raised up place' (from *hebban* 'heave, lift'). It is used in Scandinavian toponyms to indicate the site of a cult-place (*Njarðarhof, Ullinshof*, etc.) but this usage is not evidenced in English. Since buildings were erected on sites which were already sacred, the transfer of meaning may not have taken place in this country. Sacred sites were characterised by the presence of a *weoh* 'cult-site'[2] in pagan Anglo-Saxon England, which rarely survives into modern place-names (Weedon is an exception); the Scandinavian form *vi* is much more productive in theophoric names such as *Torsvi* (Þórr's *vi*) or *Odensvi* (Óðinn's *vi*). Another word of similar meaning is *hearh, hærg* 'cairn, pile of stones' which had associations with ritual; it survives into modern English place-names as 'harrow' (as at Harrow, Middlesex, the *Gumeninga hearh* of one Anglo-Saxon document). In *Beowulf* (l.175), the heathen Danes turn to sacrifice to rid themselves of Grendel *æt hærgtrafum* 'at idols', sites of pagan worship.

The mid- and late-Anglo-Saxon CPs were the sites in the *burh* system, created in 9th century Wessex as a range of strongholds for local defence, but expanded into the greater part of modern England in the 10th century. These fortified centres took on the function of market towns in due course. With an increasingly centralised administration, it is likely that the small, local focal points were outgrown and many hall-based settlements would have reverted to the status of estate centre or manorial grange by the 11th century.

---

[1] Campbell, 1987, section 636. The type is the ancient neuter *es-/os-* stem nouns.
[2] Wilson, 1985a

Chapter Three

The Hall Of Dreams

The hall in the imagination of the audience appears as a male-dominated structure in a patriarchal society, and the heroes of old who swagger through the halls of this tradition are men larger than life, bound by terrible oaths, haunted by implacable nightmarish spirits, forsaken by loved ones and kin. Despite this powerful imagery, from the 7th c. at least, with the introduction of Christianity, a transformation took place in attitudes to the idealised hall of the imagination. Expanding on its association with negotiations and discourse, the hall became the appropriate venue for the display of power, both secular and religious. Power was visible through ritual; through the deference of others in power; through the careful use of rich display. Anglo-Saxon taste in the visual arts seems to have centred on the costly, the sumptuous, the eye-catching. Gold, silver, gemstones and rich coloration are all characteristic of the Anglo-Saxon style.[1]

Yet the symbolic power of the hall was not confined to the imagination: the Anglo-Saxons knew their own halls as a tangible reality, and life within them was no mere poetic fiction even at the end of the period when the trend towards private dwellings away from the eyes of followers and petitioners was already underway. The primacy of hall-based leaders was not threatened by early Christianity.[2] The lord still ruled his folk and lands from his high-seat, even as the bishop kept watch over his flocks from his *cathedra*. The two traditions were intertwined, and in the end indissoluble. By the tenth century there was a close correspondence of élite or royal dwellings with religious buildings, some of which may be interpreted as private chapels.[3] The power of secular and religious authorities was perhaps by then a unity.

In Christian religious poetry, the hall-complex largely replaces the image of the *civitas* or 'civilized (Christian) community' in many texts; the hall-society may even denote the 'brotherhood of the kingdom of heaven'. Heaven as a city reflecting 'splendour and community under God'[4] is an image associated with St. Augustine who was instrumental in bringing the Christian faith to the pagan Anglo-Saxons. Indeed, it has been argued[5] that the Anglo-Saxons were most impressed with the substitute lordly halls of Christendom – the monastic centres where a simple yet fulfilling way of life could be led by those whose allegiance was true; this vision of Christianity as a dimension of the idealised heroic life resulted in the speedy adoption of the new religion with little outright resistance, but considerable reservations were expressed when the practices of the new faith conflicted with the pre-existing moral certainties of the folk tradition. The church

---

[1] Dodwell (1982) lists this as one of the three 'prejudices' of Anglo-Saxon art, the others being a 'partisanship for relics' and an 'easy mingling of the arts of the secular and monastic worlds'.
[2] Herschend, 1998
[3] Magennis, 1996; Herschend, 1998
[4] Magennis, 1996,p.41.
[5] Earl, 1994 "The Hall and the Church", p.124ff.

learnt to express its mission in militaristic, masculine terms likely to appeal to the warrior classes. This resulted in the adoption of aspects of the hall-based lordship culture into the early church – for example, the traditional heroic songs sung at monastic mealtimes (see p.192). In time, the commonplace themes of heroic story would be transformed by cultural innovators into metaphors of Christian ideals – Beowulf's fight with the firedrake becomes an allegory for St. Michael's fight with the dragon.

In the pre-Christian period, it is likely that the geographical relationship between settlement and graveyard held some special significance. Some graveyards are characterised by large, dominant tumuli in which some important individual – often a putative ancestor – was interred. This notion, the relationship between ancient burial and estate, seems to have been critically important for some groups; so much so that they took over pre-existing Bronze Age or Roman tumuli for this purpose.[1] This may have been an act of adoption – staking a claim in Britain and taking possession of the ancestral spirits for their own purposes.

Likewise the positioning and construction of the dwellings and outhouses may have had some religious or ritual importance, which can only be guessed at today. In Scandinavia, it is not unknown to find thin gold foils (*guldgubbar*) in the filled-in post-holes of longhouses. These foils show a consistent image: a man and woman embracing, thought to be an icon of the divine pair Freyr and his wife Gerd. Freyr[2] is strongly associated with fertility, wealth and sexual love. The implication appears to be that these are amulets designed to promote fecundity, well-being, health and harmony in the household.

The importance attached to seating positions may have been a social phenomenon, an outward sign of hierarchy. It is nevertheless possible that the householder's highseat functioned as the focus of attention in some rituals, just as Oðinn's highseat *Hliðskjalfi* played a part in some myths. From Hliðskjalfi the god could see out over all the nine worlds; from his high-seat the householder could see out over the entire hall.

The terminology of lordship permeates early English Christianity, as we have seen in the early translation of the Hebrew Creation myth into its Old English verse by Cædmon (Appendix 2). God is here referred to as *ece drihten* 'everlasting lord', *heofonrices weard* 'keeper of the kingdom of heaven', *frea ælmihtig* 'almighty lord'. This theme is developed in later Christian verse and becomes one of the commonplaces of the tradition, of which examples will be found in religious verse such as *Christ and Satan, Genesis* or *The Dream of the Rood* (p.20).

---

[1] Williams, 1997

[2] Herschend, 1998. There is circumstantial evidence for a similar cult in Anglo-Saxon England, specifically the word *frea* (the god's name) meaning 'lord', and the use of Freyr's boar-imagery in high-status pagan Anglo-Saxon art (e.g. the crests of the Wollaston and Benty Grange helmets, and the eyebrows of the Sutton Hoo helmet).

Chapter Three

The Joys Of The Hall

The image of the hall is, then, very much the image of 'the good life' in Anglo-Saxon thinking, and this is true of the Scandinavians, the Irish and many other folk of the period. We shall look below (Ch.6) at some of the entertainments available to dwellers in the hall, to pastimes and feats of showmanship. No less important than the individual 'joys' of the hall was the fact of their availability only through the hall. For the loner, the traveller, the outcast, there could be no hall-joys because there were no hall-fellows with whom to enjoy them. The fellowship of hall-meetings was the whole point of them.

One Anglo-Saxon manuscript illustration[1] demonstrates the equivalence of mead-hall trappings with the desirable things in life. It shows the temptation of Christ, and among the worldly treasures offered to him are a metal bowl, two arm-rings, an ornate shield, a smaller finger-ring, a sword in a decorated scabbard, a drinking horn and a metal cup. All these items are direct from the material culture of the weapons-bearing freeman, celebrating with friends in the hall.

The following curt description from *Beowulf* brings in the majority of the salient feast features:

> ... *leoð wæs asungen*
> *gleomannes gyd, gamen eft astah*
> *beorhtode bencsweg, byrelas sealdon*
> *win of wunderfatum. Þa cwom Wealhþeo forð*
> *gan under gyldnum beage, þær þa godan twegen*
> *sæton suhtergefæderan* ....
>
> '... a song was sung
> the gleeman's lay, merry-making rose up again
> the bench-noise brightened, servants dealt out
> wine from wondrous vessels. Then Wealhþeow came forward
> walking beneath a golden circlet where the two good men
> uncle and nephew sat ....'[2]
> *Beowulf*, 1.1159-64

It is undeniable that quantities of strong drink were among the anticipated hall-joys of the Anglo-Saxon audience. Drunkenness was not apparently an end in itself, but might be the result of over-eager merry-making. It is not condemned

---

[1] BL Cotton MS Tiberius C VI, fol,10v. reproduced in Dodwell, 1982

[2] There is an irony in this passage, in that the uncle and nephew who sit together here in friendship would eventually become bitter enemies. But for the purposes of the audience *at this point in the story* there is not yet any hint of the bitterness to come. The motif of the feast in reinforcing social harmony and relaxation serves to underscore the disunity which is to follow in some years, and the further monstrous attack which is to follow that same evening.

for itself outside narrowly clerical works, but neither is it praised or held up as admirable. The objection to drunkenness appears to be that a drunken man cannot control his words or actions, may give offence unduly and may be unable to defend himself if necessary. These all are practical rather than moral considerations. Norse tradition likewise stresses the inherent danger of ale for the sons of men, as in the Icelandic *Hávamál* stanza 12:

Er-a svo gott
sem gott kveða
öl alda sonum,
því að færra veit
er fleira drekkur
sins til geðs gumi.

Not so good
as men say
is ale for the sons of men:
For he knows less
who drinks more,
appears a foolish man.

However, some Christian churchmen had very firm views on the subject and were vehement in their opposition to drunkenness, if not always to drinking alcohol. There were good biblical precedents for sharing wine among companions, after all. The eleventh century writer, Ælfric, refers to drunkennes as *cwylmbære ðing 7 galnesse antimber* 'a deadly matter and foundation of lust' yet from his correspondence with his clerical colleagues it is clear that they did not all share his abstemious inclinations. One Anglo-Saxon ruler, King Harðacnut, was at a wedding celebration enjoying his drink when he fell to the floor, unconscious, and died there.[1] Whether the king suffered a stroke or seizure is not known, but there is no suggestion that he had overindulged.

In *Beowulf*, the upright and very proper lady of the hall, Wealhþeow, refers to her *druncne dryhtguman* (line 1231) in clearly approving terms. The phrase is often taken to mean 'drunken warriors' (or variants such as 'wine-glad', 'carousing'). However, in the context in which it occurs, it surely refers to the in-group, the band of warriors who have jointly taken part in the ale-ritual (p.42) and bound themselves to each other and their lord in so doing.[2]

Nevertheless, as far back as the 1st century AD, Tacitus could note of the Germanic people of his day that a fondness for strong drink was one of their main vices (along with gambling and fighting). The ale which flowed as reward

---

[1] Hagen, 1995
[2] Hill, 1995 p.103ff.

for warrior service may well have seemed the only anaesthetic to the minds and souls of men who had seen friends cut down before their eyes, and who knew that they risked meeting a similar fate themselves.

The guiding principle in the religious and secular literature seems to be that of moderation in alcohol consumption, which is also picked up in the Norse material such as *Hávamál*. Drinking itself seems to be taken as a normal part of life, but to drink *ofer gewunan* 'beyond one's customary limit' is considered sinful, or at least reprehensible. In a society where everybody drank some form of alcoholic drink, everybody had to know where to draw the line.

In the light of the large quantities of alcohol available in the hall, the conclusion seems inescapable that some feasts must have ended in arguments, brawling and all-out fighting. Indeed, if the Icelandic image of Valhöll as an ideal warrior's hall is to be believed, fighting during the day and feasting during the evening were among the most desirable aspects of the afterlife. The temptation to drink too much, then lose one's temper or overstep the bounds of good behaviour must have been among the factors leading to the notion of *frið ond grið* 'peace and security', the guaranteed safety of guests and others under one's protection. It was, in its nature, a temporary and limited condition – such as when enemies met to negotiate a truce. Yet its violation was a serious affair, and injuries had to be compensated by the attacker[1] - both to the injured party who had sustained physical damage, and to the householder whose *grið* (protection) had been trampled and despised.

---

[1] Griffiths, 1995

4 Food and Feasting Equipment

The best evidence for the movable and personal equipment associated with feasting comes from the later pagan period, when the burial rite for the wealthy could involve deposition of large amounts of household goods with the deceased. The barrows at Sutton Hoo (Mound 1) and Taplow are the most significant finds, but there is a wide distribution of goods of this type. The most spectacular finds date from the early 7th century. As we noted above in Ch.1, conspicuous consumption and provision for the household were central themes in later pagan culture.

More goods survive in a partial or fragmentary state than as substantially whole or intact items. This means that understanding the remains necessarily involves an element of interpretation, when all that comes to light is a fragment of metal with perhaps some organic material adhering to it: what was the nature of the object originally? Was the metal itself re-used in antiquity? The majority of metal rims – usually associated with drinking horns – occur in (presumed) male graves, but there are fittings from metal cups in (presumed) female contexts.[1]

The tenth century bequest of one Wynflæd, a wealthy noblewoman, mentions *hyre goldfagan treowenan cuppan ... hyre twa treowenan gesplottude cuppan* "her gold-adorned wooden cup ... her two wooden spotted cups" indicates that fine tableware could be among the possessions of noblewomen in the late Anglo-Saxon period.[2] Whether *gesplottude* means 'spotted' (and therefore refers to a speckled wood, such as maple) or not is unclear from the context.

Cherry wood was identified as the likely material at one probably royal grave (Broomfield).[3] Willow or poplar was used to make the beaker recovered at Soëst, Norway; birch was chosen for the beaker from beneath Cologne cathedral, and for the yarn cups from Oseberg, the latter with a twisted grain. At Oberflacht, Germany, a bowl was found, made from pear-wood. The maplewood (OE *mæsen*) so common at Sutton Hoo is a native British tree, specially selected for the purpose of making wooden tableware. Walnut also occurred at Sutton Hoo; it

---

[1] Two notes of caution must be sounded here. First, in graves with sparse grave-goods the odd find of a spearhead is not necessarily indicative of a male burial, as modern skeletal studies have demonstrated. Therefore, where excavation was carried out without careful records and the skeletal material is no longer to hand, we cannot be certain that the ascribed sex is correct.

Second, objects which resemble cups were recovered from the (female) Oseberg ship burial, Norway, where they are believed to be yarn-cups used in spinning, not connected with drinking.

[2] East, 1983; Owen, 1979

[3] Page, 1903

may have become an unusual species by this time, although it had been introduced to Britain in the Roman period.

Other wooden items must certainly have perished in many cases, and even such as did survive would not have been recorded by grave-robbers and treasure-hunters. The princely burial from beneath Cologne cathedral, roughly contemporary with the later pagan burials of England, contained many high-status wooden items which would ordinarily not have been recognised, among them a flask, bowls, a flat dish and a conical beaker. Clearly, well-made wooden articles did not need metal fittings to make them lavish and desirable.

The prestige of a leader's court was measurable by the costly tableware on display. Among men of leader status the invitation to a meal was an open offer of friendship, with a view to forming a social (and therefore military and political) alliance. For the invitee to decline such an offer was considered an act of repudiation, and could lead to enmity.[1] In order to impress their guests and their own followers, barbarian leaders of many nations sought out the most costly and decorative tableware available. No-one, it seems, could aspire to kingship unless he owned an array of fine dishes and other vessels, along with knives and other eating implements. King Chilperic of the Franks had a great golden salver, fitted with gems and weighing 50 pounds, according to Gregory of Tours, while Queen Brunhild had a similar platter and two gold-fitted wooden bowls.

The aged King Beowulf, at the end of the poem, lying mortally wounded outside the dragon's treasure-filled lair, bade his young kinsman Wiglaf enter the cave and bring out the hoard; this consisted of

> ... *orcas stondan*
> *fyrnmanna fatu feormendlease*
> *hyrstum behrorene, þær wæs helm monig*
> *eald 7 omig, earmbeaga fela*
> *searwum gescæled.*

> ... cups standing,
> vessels of ancient men lacking polishers,
> deprived of riches, many a helm was there,
> old and rusty, many arm-rings
> skilfully bound.
> Beowulf, l. 2760-4

---

[1] Enright, 1996Ch.2

as well as a battle standard and sundry golden articles. Beowulf considers them a fitting gift to have won for his people, even at the cost of his own life; his people, conversely, consider them a fitting set of grave-goods for his mound.

One late bishop of Worcester is recorded to have exchanged a parcel of church land for a set of splendid feasting equipment.[1] The desirability and usefulness of good tableware when entertaining high-status guests had not declined with the introduction of the new faith.[2]

Consumables

Anglo-Saxon kings did not live full-time in one area or at one site. It was customary for them and their retinues to tour the estates in the territory consuming the food owed by their vassals. Taxation in a pre-coinage economy consisted of food-renders and services. The farmers of a whole region were bound to supply the royal court with a range of foods and other products which they would consume on their journey round the kingdom. Storage must have been provided at the estate centre (the *worþig* or *tun*) where the king's hearth-troop and other officers would be housed.

Livestock would be brought to the king's estate in time for his visit, as well as dry goods, grain, drink and other consumables. Freemen had a duty of *feorm* or food-rent, originally 'hospitality', which was the principal means of supporting the monarchy in a pre-coinage society; later in the period, payments of tax were to supersede provisions in meeting this obligation, which stemmed from the landholder's ancient duty to host the king's entourage for a single night. Farmsteads grouped together into larger units to meet the payment, and were also assessed for tax and military service in these groupings. By the time of Edward the Confessor, the cash equivalent of *'firma unius noctis'* (one night's *feorm'*) was eighty pounds.[3]

A series of such royal estates situated round the kingdom provided the king's company with a constant food supply and gave the king the opportunity to dispense justice, hear law suits, make grants, hand out rewards, encourage his supporters and intimidate his foes. The personal nature of the ties of loyalty which held the system together was reinforced by the personal nature of the encounter – the king was a house-guest as well as a ruler. The king's local representative - his *gerefa* 'reeve' – was responsible for organising the collection and storage.

---

[1] Zaluckyj, 2001

[2] Whitby Abbey yielded evidence for ten hanging bowls. Some may have been used in liturgical operations, but it is likely that others were used for social entertaining purposes. See p.164

[3] Stenton, 1971

Chapter Four

A site such as Yeavering[1] (see p.92) would provide a good example of such an estate centre with its large, roomy buildings and palisaded cattle enclosure. The many outbuildings may have provided storage and temporary accommodation for the visitors.

Harke's work[2] on the skeletal evidence from Anglo-Saxon graves showed that, despite the wealth and importance displayed through grave-goods and dimensions, all individuals seem to have been exposed to the risk of malnutrition. Therefore, in Anglo-Saxon England, nobody could ever be certain of the continued good fortune of abundant or sufficient harvests, no matter how much prudence they exercised or effort they put into husbandry. Nor was danger confined to starvation. In 716, King Ceolred of Mercia was feasting with his men when he died, possibly from some kind of convulsion or from choking on his food.

An understanding of the scale of food-renders can be gleaned by examining a charter of Christ Church, Canterbury, detailing the annual payment to be made from one estate (*et burnan*, somewhere in Kent) dating from c. 850:[3]

> *... xl ambra mealtes and xl and cc hlaba i wege cesa i wege speces i eald hriðer iiii weðras x goes xx henfugla iiii foðra weada .... And suelc mon se ðet lond hebbe eghwelce sunnandege xx gesuflra hlafa to ðare cirican .....*

40 measures of malt and
240 loaves
1 weight of cheese
1 weight of lard
1 adult heifer
4 wethers
10 geese
20 hens
4 loads of wood ....

and whoever may have the land [shall give] each Sunday 20 buttered loaves[4] to the church ...

---

[1] Welch, 1992; Hope Taylor, 1977
[2] cited in Enright, 1996, p.94
[3] MS Cotton Augustus ii.52 published in Sweet, 1967
[4] *xx gesuflra hlafa* is properly 'twenty loaves provided with filling', some kind of accompaniment to bread.

We do not know how large the estate at *Burna* was, but the quantity of provisions due from it suggests that common farmsteads could be expected to produce a reasonable surplus without compromising their viability. In the OE text *Dialogue of Solomon & Saturn* it is stated that

> *On xii monðum ðu scealt sillan ðinum þeowan man vii hund hlafa 7 xx hlafa buton morgemetum 7 nonmetum.*

> In twelve months you must give to your serving man seven hundred loaves and twenty loaves besides morning-food and afternoon-food.

This suggests that a dole of two loaves a day was the staple rations of the common man, and that breakfast and lunch were additional. The laws of King Æðelstan suggest that the normal accompaniment to bread was meat, cheese or other seasonal fare.[1]

Food

Anglo-Saxon farming and husbandry must have been relatively well-developed, and few resources appear to have been wasted. Food products such as pies and sausages were made from poorer pieces of meat, and being sealed in an air-tight covering, they were less likely to decay. Among the more exotic items consumed by Scandinavians, according to saga evidence, we find whole sheeps' heads.[2]

Animal by-products were also valued: bone, hide, horn, antler, sinew, fur, wool, tallow and urine all had a place in the inventory of industrial processes deployed at this time.

Cultivated vegetable resources included a number of edible crops, such as peas, beans, turnips, radishes, beets, carrots, parsnips, cale, cucumbers, lettuce, onions, leeks and flavourings such as garlic, mustard and horseradish. Peppercorns were known, although they were a luxury item.

Wild mushrooms were gathered from the woods, as well as nuts and berries. Fruits such as apples, pears, medlars and plums were cultivated in reserved orchard areas.

The staple vegetable crop for the Anglo-Saxon diet was wheat, which was used for baking and brewing.[3] The seed was sown in spring, and the crop was harvested and dried in autumn, then threshed and winnowed in winter. Milling was carried out on a small scale using a hand quern – either a saddle quern, with a side-to-side motion, or the rotary handmill. Larger mills used a long pole which

---

[1] Hagen, 1992, p.67
[2] Healey, 1998 citing an incident in the Icelandic *Hrafnkelssaga*
[3] Hagen, 1992

could be turned by human or animal power. Having been introduced in the 7th century, watermills were presumably common by the end of the Anglo-Saxon period, and Edward the Confessor found it necessary to restrict their construction as they had become a hazard to navigation.

Having milled the corn to produce wheatmeal, the product was sieved to remove impurities and insect inclusions. (Other meals were made from rye, barley, oats, acorns and beans for different purposes.) The meal was worked with water and salt to make a dough to be made into flat cakes; the addition of yeast produced the traditional form of leavened loaf. Flat bread could be baked under a pot, on a bakestone or griddle by the hearth. Yeast could be of the naturally occurring airborne varieties, or perhaps the residue from brewing. Depending on the fineness of the sieving, the resultant bread could be brown, yellowish or white (like modern varieties). Loaves were round and of varying sizes, similar to cottage loaves and bread rolls today. Larger loaves would have needed to be baked in a bread oven to ensure they were properly cooked; such ovens were found in a bakehouse from the 8th century at North Elmham. The trade of baker (OE male *bæcere* or female *bæcestre*)[1] was well established, either attached to a large monastic or secular estate, or in free trade within an urban commercial district. Payments of alms often took the form of bread; it is possible that loaves intended for this purposes would have been hardened to a rusk in order to preserve them longer.

For special occasions, extra fine white flour was used to give a very pure white bread. The loaves could be spiced or flavoured with seeds such as dill, caraway, poppy, fennel or sweet cecily, which may have been ground into the dough or sprinkled onto the unbaked ingots. A richer form of bread could be obtained by adding egg, milk, cream or vegetable oil to the mixture. Crumpets and pancakes were made in the Anglo-Saxon period, cooked in pans.

Animal resources used by the Anglo-Saxons included the cow, goat and sheep for dairy farming; these as well as the pig and various fowl were kept for slaughter. Dairy farms were an important economic resource providing milk, butter, cheese and eggs; calves, lambs and kids would have been slaughtered once a replacement for the adult had been selected, although some cows may have been used as draught animals. Cowherds, shepherds and goatherds - presumably male - were members of recognised occupational groups in the Anglo-Saxon period, with traditional rights over the produce of their herds. Static dairy workers, such as cheesemakers, seem to have been female and also had an entitlement to a portion of their output. Cream, curds and whey were all milk-based products which were valued for food. Likewise, in making butter, the drained buttermilk was saved, and may have been drunk, or have gone into animal feed.

---

[1] Hence the modern surnames 'Baker' and 'Baxter'.

Apart from domesticated animals, hunting was an important means of supplementing the communal diet and also served as a popular pastime for the wealthy. As well as chasing deer and boar with hunting dogs, Anglo-Saxon nobles also practised falconry as a sport.[1]

Animals for butchery were usually processed on the farm, but some may have been driven to town for sale and slaughter there. Once stunned and slaughtered, the carcass would be hung, jointed and salted. Carcasses for immediate consumption may have been only partially de-boned so that they could be roasted on a spit. Large bones were split to allow extraction of the marrow, which could be added to stew as a nutritious thickening agent or used in the manufacture of salves and ointments. Offal, tongue and brain were all consumed, possibly in conserved forms such as sausages. Fat was collected for use in frying, and in medical treatments.

Fig.10 Preparing food in the open air. To the left a cauldron is boiling over an open fire, attended by two servants who have impaled some pieces of food on spikes. Centre, a bearded cook uses a "meat-hook" to take what appears to be bread from an oven and place it on a platter. Right, a table-servant takes the spitted meat to the table. Scene from the Bayeux Tapestry, redrawn by Lindsay Kerr.

Food for preservation had to be treated. Drying was a common method used for meat and vegetables, either by sun-drying, placing by the hearth or by means of a kiln. Items such as mushrooms, herbs, fish and seaweed were routinely dried. Smoking was no doubt a popular treatment, since any food hung in the rafters of

---

[1] The opening image of the 10th century poem *The Battle of Maldon* is of a young man letting his hawk fly off before dismounting to fight. The 7th century Sutton Hoo purse lid shows a duck being seized by a falcon. A manuscript illustration of a falconer is found in an 11th century calendar (BL Cotton Julius A.vi. See Owen-Crocker, 1991.

a hall would be treated with smoke from the hearth. The flavour of foods can be affected by the wood used to produce the smoke, a fact which was certainly known in this period. Pickling in brine, vinegar or honey was also a traditional method of conserving some foods. Berries, fruit and rosehips were boiled down to a thick paste for storage in jars; this may have been spread on bread.

Storage vessels included a range of jars, coopered barrels, tubs and boxes. Old barrels were routinely used as lining for wells. It would have been necessary to have some form of secure storage due to the presence of mice and rats, weasels, moths, lice and other small creatures likely both to eat and contaminate stores. The most effective means of direct conservation was salting, using a mixture of refined and bay salt or immersion in brine. Salt was essential for the production of bacon and hams, which were further treated by salting.

Wood-gathering for fuel was a never-ending task, but the main alternatives of charcoal and coal were probably too expensive to use for everyday domestic purposes. Peat, reeds and straw may have been used when a slow- (peat) or fast-burning (reeds, straw) effect was needed. Firesteels were used with flint and tinder to start a fire, but most settlements would have had a fire going for some process at all times. Fire-tongs, bellows, a fuel shovel, pokers and covers are all referred to in the literary records. Fire-dogs were used to assist with domestic tasks requiring heat.

Domestic life centred round the hearth, a stone-lined fire-pit in the centre of the hall. Late Anglo-Saxon stone-built dwellings may have had the hearth against one of the stone outer walls. Cooking and other activities probably took place round open-air fire-pits when the weather was clement. Hot water was required for a number of purposes – cooking, washing, cloth-dying among others; where the direct application of fire to the pot was not possible, stones were heated and dropped into the liquid. The Bayeux Tapestry (fig.10 page 125) clearly shows in one of its scenes the preparation of food outdoors, with a cauldron suspended over a fire from a transverse bar and what may be a portable oven nearby; the servants are laying out food on a makeshift table formed from shields (fig.22 page 177). Spitted meats served by stewards and a bearded cook with a fork or meat-hook are also included. One of the diners is raising a horn, but as he has the narrow end to his lips, he may be summoning his fellows to eat.

Purpose-built ovens were constructed, either sunken pits filled with hot stones into which the meat was packed and the whole covered with turf, or air-draught ovens with a flue. These would have been housed in a separate kitchen or bakery building away from the main hall, thus reducing the fire-risk. Professional cooks certainly existed, attached to large households and monasteries; aside from their skill at producing palatable food, they would have needed to be physically strong to move around the carcasses and cauldrons involved in early mediaeval cooking.

Food and Feasting Equipment

Fish was a valuable food resource, both freshwater varieties and seafish. Fish weirs dating back to Anglo-Saxon times have been found in the Thames and the Blackwater. Shellfish such as mussels and oysters were enjoyed as a variation in the diet. Some Christian Anglo-Saxons were careful to follow the biblical dietary code and avoid certain types of seafood. Nevertheless, eels seem to have been an important part of the diet in some districts.

Bees were kept for their wax as well as their honey. Wax was used in the manufacture of the finest quality candles, while honey was valued as a sweetener and for its antiseptic and preservative qualities.

Green salad was a common summer dish, requiring little preparation beyond washing, along with fruit, nuts and berries. Puddings of bread and fruit served with cream may have been known. It is possible that a form of jelly made from cows' heels was produced.

The cooking processes available to the Anglo-Saxons included boiling, roasting, frying, grilling and baking in an oven. Boiling seems to have been commonest, with even some oily meats such as duck or goose being boiled. Apart from the nutritional benefit that boiled meat remains soft and juicy, it may be that a pot of stew was always on the hearth and it was comparatively easy to add additional meat and vegetables as they became available. Small scraps or poor quality ingredients would be rendered more palatable in this way. Small pieces of dough cooked with the stew were known as *æpplas* 'apples', which we would call 'dumplings'. Boiling is also the only practical method of preparing meat which has been preserved by salting, or dried herbs and vegetables. The resultant broth or stew (*broþ*) was the standard Anglo-Saxon dish, well suited to providing a meal to many people at one sitting.

Another dish prepared by boiling was *briw* 'brew, porridge' made in the same manner but using cereal as a thickener. Oatmeal could be used for this purpose, and could also be used as a stuffing. Fruits and berries could be stewed in water or wine, sweetened with honey.

Baking was used in the production of bread (loaves, crumpets and pancakes) and could be applied to joints of meat, probably dipped in a damper or batter mix.

Roasting or grilling over an open fire was a prestigious method of preparing meat, requiring considerable effort to achieve an evenly-cooked end product. Not only must the meat be turned constantly, but also the fire must be regulated to ensure it neither scorches nor undercooks the food. Roasting spits were used to turn the meat on the bone, which was then cut up after cooking.

Fish was traditionally grilled, and a griddle could be used to cook flat bread and pancakes at the hearth. A dished pan could be used to take a small quantity of fat or lard for frying by this method.

Fat was also needed to make biscuits, which were apparently flat discs (*heallstan* 'hall – stone'). Flavoured with honey, they may have been similar to shortbread.

The Anglo-Saxons appreciated the uses of herbs to a great extent, and valued them both as flavourings and as medicines.[1] Sauces made from mustard, sorrel and other ingredients would have provided a welcome piquancy to a diet of mainly boiled vegetables and bread. Cooking oil was kept in an *elefæt* 'oil-vessel'; vinegar was dispensed from an *ecedfæt* 'vinegar-vessel' and pepper from a *piporhorn* 'pepper-horn', while salt was made available from a *sealtfæt* 'salt-vessel'.

It was considered impolite to eat food very quickly, or to retrieve it if it fell onto the floor.

Drink

The principal drinks available to the early English were water, milk (and by-products such as buttermilk and whey) and a variety of fermented products. Access to good, clean water was evidently a factor in siting settlements, but few people can have been confident about the purity of the contents of the local stream or well. Small wonder then that mildly alcoholic beverages – which were more trustworthy than the water supply – were favoured.

Milk was valued as a nutritious drink: ascetics on a rigorous fasting regime relied on it, and female servants (milkmaids) were allowed to take the whey in summer as a supplement to their diet.

The range of strong drinks available to the Anglo-Saxon hall-community is not dealt with in detail by any of the poets or writers from the period. In *Beowulf*, for example, the poet refers to *medu, ealu, beor* and *win* (mead, ale, beer, wine – but for *beor* see below) but the choice of word seems to have been dictated by the metre (the need for alliteration) more than by the precise reference to the kind of strong drink being consumed. In one instance a *medoful* 'cup of mead' is brought out to a drinker *æt þære beorþege* 'at the beer-drinking' (*Beowulf*, l. 624, 617) and another becomes *meodugal* 'mead-happy' *on beore* 'at beer' (*Fortunes of Men*, l.51-2).

However, wine is mentioned less than the other products in *Beowulf*, and forms only one class of compound noun: *winærn, winreced, winsele* all meaning 'wine-hall'. This may reflect the slightly prestigious and exotic nature of wine, even in a country where there were numerous vineyards. Wine seemingly did not fit in quite so well with the beer- and mead- drinking tradition of the Germanic warriors and nobles. This distinction may have been reinforced by the greater use of wine in ecclesiastical contexts. Wine was produced in England in Anglo-Saxon times, but the product would have been less sweet than its Mediterranean counterparts because ripening is less effective in cooler climes.

---

[1] Pollington, 2000 and references there.

It has been suggested[1] that of the three remaining 'native' drinks – *beor, meodu, ealu* – the highest ranking goes to *meodu* 'mead', and that the references to this drink evoke an emotional response not shared by ale or beer. This is possible, but it is not clear: for example, the situation of direst distress for a community is characterised as both *ealuscerwen* (*Beowulf*, 1.769) 'ale-deprivation'[2] and *meoduscerwen* (*Andreas*, 1.1526) 'mead-deprivation'. The implication in both cases may be that the leader and his warriors have fallen, the hall stands empty, the strong drink used at rituals and festivities is taken away: in short, all the things which affirm the community's existence have been removed.

Ale was valued for its conserving quality – properly stored it would last for a long time, and due to secondary fermentation within the cask it would grow stronger and more bitter the longer it was kept. The use of hops would have the same effect, but without making the brew quite so strong; before hops were established as the normal additive, rosemary, gale (bog myrtle) and yarrow were used. Anglo-Saxon records recognise a drink called *wylisc ealoð* 'Welsh ale' which seems to have been more expensive than the usual *hlutor ealoð* 'clear ale'.

While *beor* is glossed 'beer' here, there is some debate as to whether it really was what we now call 'beer' or perhaps a fermented fruit-based drink such as cider.[3] Although its etymology appears to lie within the same group of words as *bere* 'barley', the word glosses Latin *ydromellum*, a honey-based drink. The sources are clear that *beor* was not the same thing as *ealu*, and as pregnant women were advised to avoid it there is a probability that it was stronger than normal ale (say 4-6% alcohol), mead (10%) or wine (8-12%). Cider can reach strengths of up to 18% before the yeast stops working. Cider may also be the drink referred to as *æppelwin* 'apple-wine'; it may have been flavoured with berries or cherries.[4]

Mead is a drink made by fermenting honey; it may have been made in some households from the discarded contents of honeycombs which were taken for their wax. Flavourings such as gale could be added, to give a variety of effects. The high-status associations of mead are an indication that it was not an everyday drink, but was reserved for the rich or produced for special occasions. Bragot – a mixture of ale and honey with flavourings – may have served in households without access to genuine mead.

---

[1] C. Fell, cited in Magennis, 1996 fn.45 p. 45; see also Enright, 1996, ch.3

[2] Wrenn, 1973, s.v. *ealuscerwen* notes the possibility that originally the word stood for 'lack of luck' with *ealu* cognate with the Runic word *alu* 'good fortune' which was homonymous with *alu(þ)* 'ale, strong drink'. If so, then the first element was misunderstood, identified with 'ale' and a variant based on 'mead' was coined from it.

[3] Hagen, 1992 p.83; 1995, p.205

[4] Hagen, 1995, p.208

In *Ælfric's Colloquy on the Occupations,*[1] the teacher asks his student *7 hwæt drincst þu?* "And what do you drink?" to which he receives the answer *ealu gif ic hæbbe oþþe wæter gif ic næbbe ealu* "Ale if I have any, or water if I have no ale"; the teacher continues *ne drincst þu win?* "Do you not drink wine?" and the student replies *Ic ne eom swa spedig þæt ic mæge bicgean me win, 7 win nis drenc cilda ne dysgra, ac ealdra 7 wisra* "I am not so wealthy that I might buy wine for myself, and wine is not a drink for children nor for the foolish, but rather for the old and wise." This exchange indicates quite clearly that access to wine was restricted by age, and by accumulated wealth.

Tableware

Many pagan period Anglo-Saxon burials contained items of food for the journey to the after-life, or as presents to the deceased. Only rarely are the containers in which they were placed recordable unless these were ceramic or metal – indeed, some offerings may never have been placed in a container at all. The fugitive nature of wood, bone, horn and other organic materials makes it nearly impossible to determine what any such vessels might have looked like. Baskets and trays made from straw, withies and other vegetable matter seem to be depicted in some manuscript illustrations, but do not survive archaeologically.

It is likely that each type of container had a specific purpose or range of uses. Some must have been used for preparing food, others for carrying and serving it, and still others for consuming it. Raw foodstuffs also must have been transported and stored in some kinds of container. The close association of food containers with high-status or wealthy male burials in the pagan period is an indication of the importance placed on providing for the household and welcoming guests.

Wood

It is probable, on *a priori* grounds, that the majority of the tools, utensils and tableware available in the Anglo-Saxon period was fashioned from wood. Reliance on kindling for fuel and timber for building, as well as for domestic items, meant that woodland resources were central to the economy. It is surely no accident that the majority of the finds of small, bronze-bound wooden buckets found in pagan period graves are made from yew wood.

Woodworking was a highly developed skill in the period and early English craftsmen were able to create practical and decorative articles from the material which were felt worthy of inclusion in even the highest-status burials. A nation able to build ships capable of crossing the North Sea was undoubtedly in firm command of a range of wood-based technologies.

---

[1] Garmonsway, 1978

Food and Feasting Equipment

The pole-lathe was the principal means of creating perfectly symmetrical cylindrical or hemispherical profiles on wooden objects, although it was not limited to that purpose.[1] Bowls and platters, cups and jugs could be turned relatively quickly and cheaply from stocks of timber.

The craftsmen who made the wooden objects interred with the king at Sutton Hoo seem to have preferred maple-wood for many of the items they made, including the cups, bottles and the famous lyre. Buckets and cups often seem to have been made from yew and bound with copper alloy, or from oak staves bound with iron.[2]

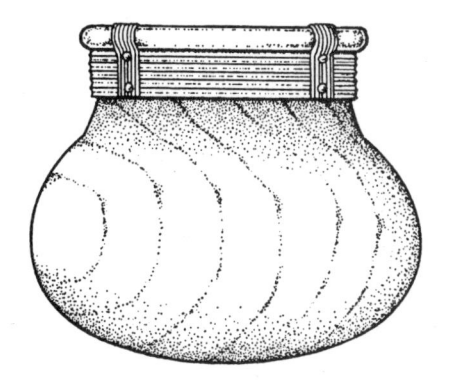

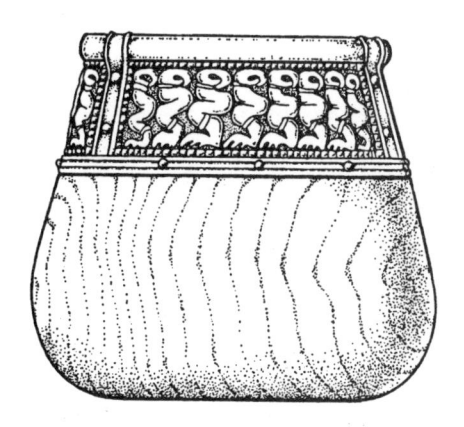

Fig.11 Two vessels from the ship burial at Sutton Hoo – Mound 1. They are of burrwood, with decorative mounts. The grave contained matched sets of cups with silver fluted collars (above) and silver-cast panels (below).

---

[1] See Dixon, 1994 for the early use of the pole-lathe, and the survival of this tradition into the mid-20th century.
[2] Watson, 1998

Horn

Small, triangular plates of horn were used to cover the metal frame of the famous Benty Grange helmet from a mound in Derbyshire. It was also used to make containers for ink; as a musical instrument; for bow-nocks and the whole article could be cleaned and used as a drinking vessel.

In chapter 104 of King Alfred's *Life,* written by his contemporary Bishop Asser, the writer describes the king's instructions for the manufacture of a horn-sided lamp in an attempt to avoid the problems of accurate time-keeping with candles in draughty halls and churches.[1]

Metal

The Anglo-Saxons' proficiency in metalworking is perhaps not so well appreciated as it deserves. Many of the fine and delicate pieces of jewellery from Anglo-Saxon graves are superbly well-made.[2] It has not yet been possible to determine all the techniques at the craftsmen's disposal, even in such straightforward matters as casting and finishing. In producing a cast item, such as a brooch, it was first necessary to make a master with some of the decoration roughed out on the surface. This was covered in clay to create a mould, a negative version of the master. If a wax master had been made, the mould could be a single piece and the wax could be melted out. If the master was bone, chalk or soft metal a two-piece mould have been needed; an example of such a mould was found at Mucking, Essex. The cavity would be filled with molten metal, and this would be allowed to cool before the mould was taken apart. The brooch would then be cleaned up, its surface decoration sharpened up and any further working – such as punch-marks – would be added. Gilding and other techniques were also available. Lugs on the reverse would be opened up for the attachment of the pin.

Aside from the raw materials needed to make the master and the mould, the metal for the castings and the materials to heat it to melting point, and to finish off the product, the craftsman would also have needed a variety of tools to handle the different stages in the production process. It is unclear whether the process was always as outlined above, or whether in some cases a mould was created to produce a blank form in soft metal which was then given more detailed surface decoration, and then a further mould was made from this. The former method requires more skill – it is a one-off process – but the latter is more risky, because there are more points at which the process can go wrong. There are known examples of plain, soft metal brooch blanks which appear to have been part of this process.

---

[1] Keynes & Lapidge, 1983
[2] Arnold, 1997

The bulk of the metal tableware recovered from Sutton Hoo, Mound 1, was of eastern Mediterranean manufacture. How it reached East Anglia is unknown although the two best guesses are either trade or a diplomatic gift from a well-wishing neighbour, such as Merovingian Francia. The exchange network for prestige goods covered all Europe and large parts of the Near East.

Ceramic

Pottery in the early Anglo-Saxon period was limited in use: loom-weights and cremation urns being the commonest finds.[1] The unexciting and often coarse finds of domestic pottery are probably to be explained by the fact that wood was easier, faster and cheaper to turn into tableware, and more durable - and a broken wooden vessel could always be used as fuel. The simple, globular forms are notoriously difficult to study due to their fragmentary preservation and the lack of any visible development.[2]

Three modes of production have been suggested for the earliest English ceramics: domestic, for use on the farm and around the home; funerary, for interring with the deceased, or to hold his ashes; imported wares. It is not clear to what extent the funerary vessels were actually different from normal cooking pots and containers: at West Stow, Suffolk, sherds were found among the domestic rubbish bearing stamps otherwise found on cremation urns. The early pottery was hand-made by coiling, and fired in simple clamps. The decorated funerary wares involved considerable labour, suggesting that simple domestic pottery was never as common as wooden equivalents; it was also fired harder than the funerary ware. Production sites have been proposed at Elsham, Lincolnshire, Cassington and Sutton Courtenay, Oxfordshire, and West Stow, Suffolk, where an area of clay was marked off with a ditch. Dies and large amounts of broken pottery were also found there. No kilns have been found from this period, suggesting that the simple clamp or bonfire was the sole means of firing. Decoration is generally in the form of incised lines and stamps (made from bone or antler, or naturally occurring shapes pressed into the clay).

The largest single such assemblage is from Mucking, Essex, where a study has determined certain regular features. Some vessels were smoothed by burnishing, others were coated with a slip to make them rougher and easier to grip. Bowls, plates, and jars were the three main categories found. Decoration was found on about 5% of the total; stamping grew in popularity through the 6th century, but decoration in general tailed off in the same century and into the 7th.

---

[1] Arnold, 1997
[2] Hurst, 1976; Evison, 1979

Chapter Four

Earthenware pots are occasionally found to have had lifting lugs at the shoulder, suggesting that they were intended for suspension over a fire.[1]

Anglo-Saxon pottery was tempered with chalk, limestone, shell, flint or other local stone, grog, sand and 'vegetable matter' – the last is sometimes called 'grass-tempered' ware, but the material may have included animal dung which would have increased the absorptive properties of the material once fired.

The earliest pottery was hand-made by the coiling method. By the mid-7th century an improved, turned[2] type came into production in East Anglia, known as 'Ipswich ware'. This fabric was fired in a true kiln, rather than a clamp, examples of which have been found in excavations at Ipswich. A similar type of thick-walled, kiln-fired pot from the north-east is known as 'Whitby ware', with wavy lines or rouletting as decoration. Its place of manufacture has not yet been identified.

'Maxey ware' is a hand-made, coil-built type of pot with shelly inclusions, roughly contemporary with Ipswich ware. Its main use seems to have been for large barrel-shaped cooking pots.

From the later Anglo-Saxon period, roughly 850 to 1150, 'Thetford ware' is a wheel-thrown, well-fired, sandy-grey fabric which is found in urban contexts across eastern England. It is taller, narrower and thinner-walled than the earlier pottery types, having been thrown on a fast-moving, powered wheel. 'Torksey ware' is similar, but rougher, with quartz inclusions, and fired black.

Another late type is 'Stamford ware', a very fine, grey-white material potted on a fast wheel and fired in a type of single-flue kiln found at Stamford, Lincolnshire. Cooking pots, bowls, cressets, crucibles, vases and pitchers are found made in this fabric.

Other regional pottery types include St. Neots ware, Otley ware, York ware, Northampton ware, Winchester ware (Fig.12) and many others. Most have a restricted distribution around the centre of manufacture. Some were heavily decorated with stamps and rouletting, while others seem to have been kept intentionally plain and utilitarian.

Glass

Anglo-Saxon glassware is not common in the archaeological record, and may never have been in widespread use during the period. Some items recovered from cemeteries appear to be superannuated Roman glassware; others are assumed to

---

[1] Hagen, 1992.

[2] It was produced on a slow-moving turntable rather than a powered wheel, giving it a characteristic profile. Welch, 1992

Food and Feasting Equipment

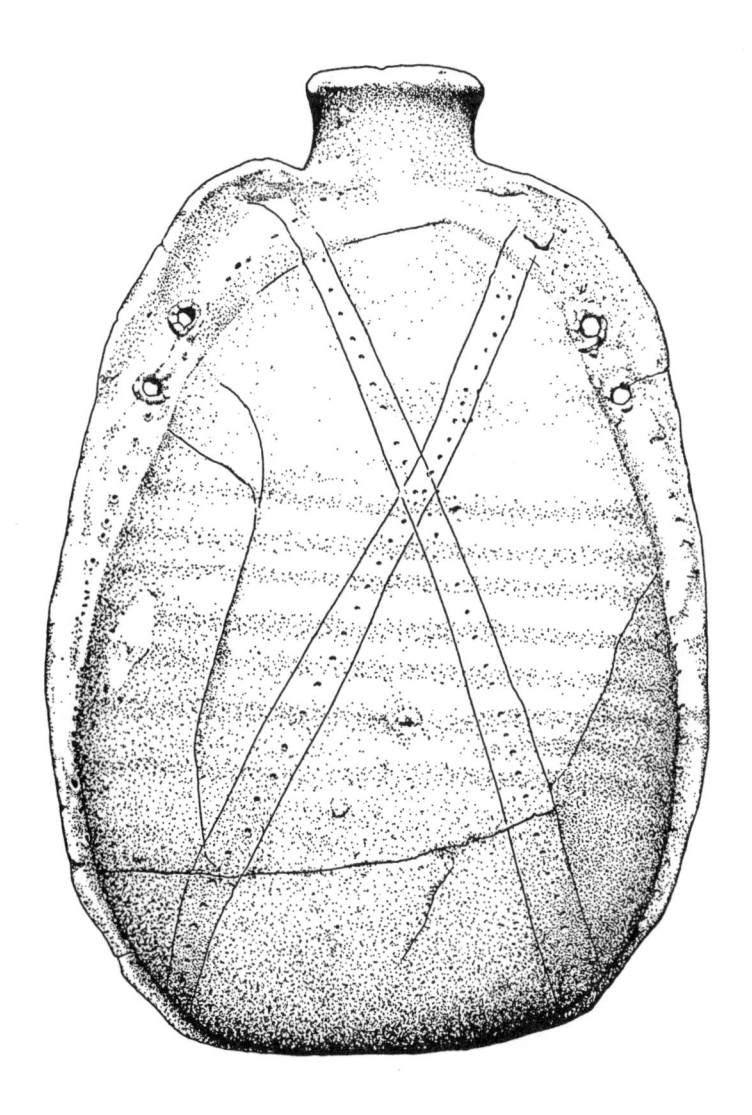

Fig.12 Ceramic bottle from Winchester, Hampshire. Vessels of this type are known as 'Winchester ware'. The simulated stitching and semi-circular extensions at the shoulders replicate the appearance of a leather flask. 10th century.

be imports from Gaul and the Rhineland,[1] and it is recognised that all the English forms of glassware have Rhenish antecedants. However, the fact that some types of glassware are more common in England than on the Continent (e.g. beakers of the Kempston type) must suggest that English manufacture is at least possible. No certain example of a glass-manufacturing site has yet been found here, but this may be due to the common practice of recycling the material as cullet; sites which may have produced glass are York, Glastonbury (Somerset),[2] Barking Abbey (Essex), Jarrow (Northumberland), Gloucester and Lincoln. The design innovations of the Kentish area and some traces of industrial production debris suggest that Kent may have been a regional glass-blowing centre in the 6th and 7th centuries.[3]

The commonest forms of glass vessel from the pagan period are claw-beakers (Fig.18 p.158), bell-beakers, cone-beakers (Fig.19 p.163), horns (Fig.3 p.49), pouch bottles, squat jars, bottles, palm-cups, bowls and - a unique find – a glass bucket from Bury St. Edmunds (Westgarth Gardens).[4] These are all known from grave contexts; how long these forms continued in use after grave-goods ceased to be deposited is unknown.

English glassware is typically coloured brown, ochre, yellow, blue or green. It has been suggested that this is largely accidental, resulting from chance variations in the firing conditions.[5] However, the range of colours is identical to those used by the Romans, and it may rather be that the conservative Anglo-Saxons continued to prefer the familiar shades rather than experimenting to produce clearer types. It should also be noted that late Roman glass production was centred on the Rhineland, where the potassium-rich ashes of trees were used in the process of manufacture, as a substitute for the marine plant (barilla) ashes used by Mediterranean glassmakers. The additional potassium content of timber would produce tints of blue, green or brown in the finished product.[6] Likewise, the presence of copper oxide would produce a blueish tint, iron a grey-black and tin a yellow.

The type of glass known to have been used in Anglo-Saxon England is known as 'soda glass', which is made from clean, finely-riddled sand often taken from river-beds, with the addition of soda. This may have continued to be imported into the Rhineland from the Mediterranean in a form known as naton, as it was in

---

[1] Arnold, 1997

[2] Wilson, 1967

[3] Wilson, 1967

[4] Arnold, 1997; West, 1988

[5] Arnold, 1997;

[6] The typical content of a greenish-yellow soda glass would be: SiO_2 66.35%, Na_2O 21.47%, CaO 6.52%, K_2O 0.65%, Al_2O_3 2.8%, MgO 1.25%, Fe_2O_3/FeO 0.45%, MnO 1.03% (M. Wilson, pers. comm.)

Roman times. In the 9th or 10th century, potash begins to be added.[1] The mixture of naton and sand was slowly heated in an oven over several days with constant stirring to allow the escape of any waste gases; the resultamt material was ground in a crucible, then melted in a furnace to a working temperature, and blown.

Open glass dishes or bowls may have served as lamps in some households. Other uses for glass include glazing, beads and enamelled decoration. Fragments of window panels survive from the monasteries at Wearmouth and Jarrow, and Bede states that the cleric Benedict Biscop imported glassworkers from Gaul for this purpose. The panels were held in H-section lead channels, were self-coloured but not further decorated.

Bone, Ivory and Antler

Bone and antler do not survive well in archaeological contexts, but from the casual nature of the occasional finds it seems they must have been common materials. One such is the bone handle of a domestic knife found in York[2] with 7th century zoomorphic decoration. However, bone combs are found on many Anglo-Saxon sites – both settlements and cemeteries[3] – and are an important diagnostic feature due to their characteristic triangular or hog-back profile.

Musical instruments in the form of whistles were made from the long bones from birds' wings; being hollow they needed only trimming, piercing and having the mouthpiece carved.[4]

Finds of 'trial pieces' are not unusual in industrial contexts, where the craftsman or designer has tried out a pattern before committing it to the final work. These are often flat bone plates, or odd off-cuts which would have been discarded afterwards.[5] These almost always occur in urban contexts,[6] suggesting that boneworking was a specialised craft, rather than a rural activity. Thetford, London, York and Southampton are the sites with good survival rates for the material. Bone objects could be manufactured by carving, sawing and turning which would mean that this craft may have been important in the Anglo-Saxon period for the production of medium- to high-status artefacts.

---

[1] Wilson, 1976. The very last known fragment of claw-beaker, found at Ipswich, was made from potash soda glass, which Evison (1988a) suggested dates to the late 9th century. (M. Wilson, pers.comm.).

[2] Webster, 1991 item 43

[3] Bone items (mostly combs, occasionally gaming pieces, etc.) can occasionally be detected among the human remains in funerary urns, e.g. in four urns out of 119 at Thurmaston (Williams, 1983) and in six urns out of 44 at Baston (Mayes & Dean, 1976).

[4] Healey, 1998

[5] Webster, 1991 items 254, 255

[6] Wilson, 1976

An antler plaque found at Southampton[1] carved with interlaced Style II animals had been thrown into a rubbish pit; the decorative style (mid-7th century) suggests that it was around 50-75 years old at the time of its disposal in 8th century *Hamwic*. It appears to have come from a storage box, and is one of a class of perishable objects[2] about which little is known. There are occasional finds of gaming pieces fashioned from antler in Scandinavian contexts.[3]

An unusual class of objects is the series of antler rings from the Anglo-Saxon cemetery at Thurmaston, Leicestershire.[4] They occurred in three separate cremation urns, so implicitly only one was used or needed by the person interred. Only one of the three bore any decoration, the standard ring-and-dot motif. They are too small for use as bag-rings – a device for holding open the mouth of a bag or pouch – or as bracelets or arm-rings. They appear to be unsuitable for use as spindle-whorls. Inevitably, amuletic purposes have been invoked but they may in fact have been nothing more romantic than suspension rings for other items hanging from a girdle or cord.

Whale's bone seems to have been prized for working fine objects, such as the Franks Casket,[5] and fragments of other, similar articles remain – for example the plaque from Larling, Norfolk.[6] Ivory was also imported for some high-status wares, and for clerical items such as pen-cases.

Leather

The extent to which leather pouches and bottles may have been used in the Anglo-Saxon period is hard to determine. The evidence is certainly not copious, but as leather is so rarely preserved – except in waterlogged conditions or as a small patch adhering to mineralised iron – this is perhaps not surprising. Technically, the Anglo-Saxons were in possession of all the necessary technology for such items to have been a part of their range of food containers: stitching and forming leather, using pitch to seal the vessel, making a stopper from turned wood.

The *scowyrhta* 'shoe-maker' in Ælfric's *Colloquy*[7] states that he also makes *higdifatu* 'hide-vessels', clearly an allusion to leather containers. It has been suggested that the pinching and surface decoration on a Winchester ware ceramic jug (Fig.12 p.135) is in direct imitation of an original made of leatherwork.[8]

---

[1] Webster, 1991, item44
[2] Webster, 1991 e.g. items 64 (a, b), 65, 69(s), 70, 100, 105, 137, 138,139, 140, 141, 142, 143, 253, 254.
[3] Healey, 1998
[4] Williams, 1983, p.17
[5] Webster, 1991, item 70
[6] Webster, 1991 item 139
[7] Text in Garmonsway, 1978
[8] Wilson, 1976

Food and Feasting Equipment

Cutlery

Old English terms for cutlery include *metseax* 'food-knife' and *sticca* 'spoon'. The word *cucler* also appears to mean a kind of spoon. A ladle was called *cruce*, *hlædel* or *turl*. The meat-hook used for taking food out of the cooking pot was called a *meteawel* 'food-hook' and this same word seems to have been used for the table-fork as well.

There are very few surviving examples of Anglo-Saxon cutlery. The table-fork was known and used in the Anglo-Saxon period, although finds are rare.[1] A remarkable survival is the combined spoon-and-fork recovered from Brandon, Suffolk.[2] This is 13.6 cm long, with a shallow spoon bowl at one end of the shaft and a three-tined fork at the other. Comparable finds have been made at Sevington, Hampshire (Fig.13) and *Hamwic* (Southampton). A large serving-fork appears in the Bayeux Tapestry.

Eating knives are hardly to be distinguished from the ubiquitous small, general purpose *handseax* of so many pagan-period graves. These unprepossessing iron tools are typically 4" to 6" (10 – 15 cm) in length, and were originally fitted with a handle of wood, antler or horn. They occur at the waists of many pagan period burials, and indeed are often the only items of burial furniture to survive as they were the sole metal articles in the grave. Although they were probably primarily tools, there is no reason to suppose that they were not also used for cutting up food before eating.

Fig.13 A double-ended spoon and combined spoon-and-fork from Sevington, Lincolnshire. An elegant solution to the problem of dealing with solid and liquid foods with one utensil. The decoration is very lightly incised. Late 9th century.

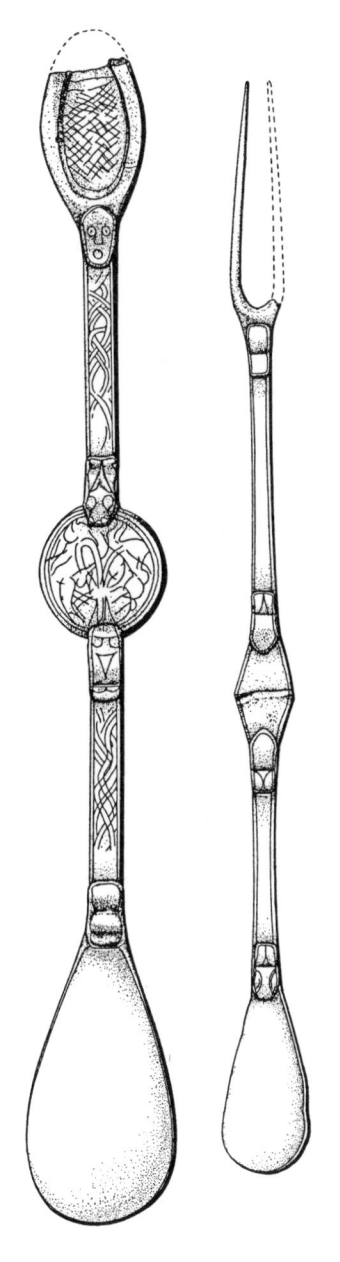

---

[1] It is sometimes asserted that one Thomas Coryate, an English visitor to Italy, brought the first forks back with him in 1608. This cannot be reconciled with the Anglo-Saxon use of the item.
[2] Webster, 1991 item 66(p)

Chapter Four

Spoons are an archaeological rarity, though not completely unknown (Figs 1, 5, 13).[1] The earliest examples are modelled closely on Roman and Byzantine types, with an elongated, shallow (spatulate) bowl and a characteristic stepped section. Many may have been imports from the Mediterranean, as is likely to be the case with the pair found at Sutton Hoo with their Christian content: one inscribed SAULOS, the other PAULOS.[2] The pair was made from the same mould and they are identical apart from the inscriptions, which are believed to be by different hands. English copies of this Mediterranean type, usually in bronze, are similarly spatulate, but commonly have a small ribbed moulding or zoomorphic head where the bowl joins the shaft. Decoration of the bowl's underside is often the ubiquitous ring-and-dot motif.

The rich barrow burial at Swallowcliffe Down, Wiltshire, featured a small iron-bound casket which contained a number of domestic items, including knives, a bone comb, a metal sprinkler and a silver spoon.[3] Its bowl is 87mm long with zoomorphic decoration at the junction with the stem, itself 62.5mm long. The whole spoon was parcel-gilt, and had been repaired in antiquity. The bowl, seen sideways-on, depicts a bird whose neck and head forms the junction with the stem, a feature also found on a similar item from Broome Park, Kent. They appear to be of 7th century Anglo-Saxon manufacture, based ultimately on Roman models.

The common Old English word for spoon *sticca* means 'stick' and denotes an item carved from wood. It is likely that carved wooden spoons were the utensil of the majority of the population, and metal spoons were a status symbol. Heated, curved horn is another material used for this purpose in later times which may have been known to the Anglo-Saxons.

A rare bone spoon was recovered from the monastic site at Flixborough, North Humberside.[4] (Fig.1 p. 38) It is 13.8cm long and 2.9cm wide at the bowl. It shows developed decoration with a pronounced central rib to the bowl, a grooved square shaft and a comma-shaped finial. Close parallels are unknown, but a spoon from Ipswich shares a similar profile.

---

[1] Mills, 2001

[2] Care Evans, 1986, 1991 (item 16). It is unclear what the significance of these spoons may have been. While the pair reading Saul / Paul would be a fitting gift to a Christian convert, there is nothing Christian about the burial from which they were taken. It may be that the occupant of the ship-burial knew nothing of the inscriptions' meaning but liked the objects themselves; they may simply have formed part of the set of feasting equipment of which the bowls, dish and other items were also parts. (The *Saulos* inscription has been regarded as a bungled attempt at *Paulos* by someone unable to read the Greek letters.)

[3] Speake, 1989, Assemblage "B"

[4] Webster, 1991 item 69(s)

By the 9th century a double-ended eating utensil was in use: a spoon at one end of the shaft, and a set of prongs at the other (Fig.13, right, p.139). These are commonly known as 'sucket' spoons, though the name is later than the Anglo-Saxon period.[1]

Plates, Bowls & Dishes

Dishes

A plate is essentially a flat surface from which to eat, while a dish has a slightly raised profile at the perimeter; both these shapes would be relatively easy to achieve using standard Anglo-Saxon woodworking methods. OE recognised a number of terms for these kinds of tableware, among them for dish: *beod, disc, læpeldre, metefæt* and *scutel*. The word *gabote* is used once for a small side-dish. A *credic* may have been a vessel for serving cream at table.

An unusual find from Sutton Hoo, Mound 1, was the famous 'Anastasius' dish, a large, flattish silver dish of Byzantine manufacture with control stamps of the Emperor Anastasius (491-518 AD) inside the foot-ring.[2] The dish has a diameter of 72.4 cm and was beaten from a single sheet of silver. Its surface is decorated with geometric, floral and figural ornament, executed in a very detailed but not entirely careful manner, suggesting that the dish was not made by the most skilled craftsmen of the Empire. It is a unique item, although there are parallels for the use of large pieces of decorated tableware from this period.

Bowls

Words for bowl in OE include: *bledu, bolla, gellet, hnæpp, læfel, mæle, orc, scealu* and *wearr*. A bowl used at table could be a *beodbolle* or *beodfæt*. Turned wooden bowls must have been a very common item of Anglo-Saxon tableware, from the highest rank to the lowest. Wood-turning may have been a Germanic introduction to Britain.[3] It is assumed that the pole-lathe was the preferred method of production. Felled timber was cut into billets, and these were halved, roughed out and left to dry. Archaeologically, these types of vessel have only been noticed till recently if they happen to have some form of metal mount or binding.[4]

An alternative form of bowl found in Scandinavia and exported into western Europe is made from steatite (soapstone).[5] This mineral is relatively easy to carve and is plentiful in Norway and Shetland. A whole range of cooking vessels seems to have been available for low-status domestic establishments.

---

[1] 'Sucket' is from the French *succade* referring to fruit preserved in sugar, according to the Oxford English Dictionary.
[2] Care Evans, 1986
[3] Arnold, 1997; Dixon, 1994
[4] e.g. the bronze mounts found in Grave 36 at Westgarth Gardens, Bury St. Edmunds (West, 1988)
[5] Healey, 1998; Hagen, 1992

Beneath the Anastasius dish was a fluted silver bowl, within which were held a set of walnut cups, three combs, four iron knives, an otter-skin cap and an iron-bound wooden box. Clothing and textiles were placed beneath the silverware. The bowl is 40cm across, is fluted, with a small foot-ring and a beaded rim. The centre bears a classical bust, positioned slightly off-centre, again suggesting that this was not the finest craftsmanship of the day. Two drop-handles had been soldered to the outer face of the bowl. Next to it was a ladle with an angular profile, carinated and decorated with gilded triangular motifs. Its handle ends in a loop through which a hoop of silver was threaded.

At the occupant's shoulder was placed a nest of ten silver bowls, each decorated with a form of equal-armed cross emerging from a central roundel; the decoration is incised, some having additional punched areas to increase the contrast with the highly-polished plain silver fields. The bowls are gently dished, have no foot-ring, and may have had some Christian significance.[1] The famous Saulos and Paulos spoons were found with these. Elsewhere in the ship-burial a large bronze hanging bowl was found, of probable Egyptian manufacture, known as a 'Coptic' bowl.[2] The bronze is zinc-rich, a feature found in some other contemporary pieces of this type. It is heavy, with a flat rim and two sturdy drop-handles. Inside, a central roundel is surrounded by a procession of four quadrupeds – a camel, donkey, lion and (probable) tiger.

Other pagan period inhumations contained comparable material. The burial mound at Taplow,[3] Buckinghamshire, revealed a fine, stemmed bowl made of bronze, standing 12" (31cm) high and with a rim diameter of 16" (41cm) (fig. 15 page 145). The rim was decorated with a series of lugs or knobs, and two large drop-handles; its base was packed with lead carbonate to ensure that its elongated stemmed profile did not tip over too easily. It is believed to be of 6th century Egyptian manufacture, like the Sutton Hoo example. At Swallowcliffe Down,[4] Wiltshire, the barrow inhumation contained fragments of an iron cooking pot or skillet. Although very badly corroded, it is estimated that the vessel would have been 33cm in diameter with an everted rim, and more than 15cm deep. There were no traces of suspension loops for a chain or handle. A similar find was made at Croydon, Surrey[5] - small bronze bowl, 7" (17cm) in diameter with a sharply everted rim, and a handle attached to two escutcheons. An enclosure

---

[1] Care Evans, 1986; the cross is not necessarily indicative of Christian symbolism at this time, but the proximity of the bowls to the inscribed spoons makes the religious interpretation more likely.

[2] Coptic bowls (Figs 14, 15 p.145) are surprisingly well-attested from pagan Anglo-Saxon England. Examples occur at a number of sites, e.g. Saltwood, Kent (*Current Archaeology* 168). They all appear to have been deposited c.600-650 AD, and they originate from a number of production centres in the eastern Mediterranean.

[3] Page, 1905

[4] Speake, 1989, Assemblage "A"

[5] Malden, 1902

known as the King's Field at Faversham, Kent,[1] produced an assemblage of pagan period items including a fine bonze bowl with an openwork foot; it is said to have still contained hazelnuts when it was discovered in 1870 when laying out the railway.

A late 8th century Anglo-Saxon bowl was discovered in the churchyard at Ormside, Cumbria.[2] It was 13.8 cm in diameter, made from silver with copper alloy fittings and gilded. The cruciform and vinescroll decoration suggest that it may have come from an ecclesiastical context, but had been buried on the site as part of a Viking interment. It had been damaged and repaired in antiquity, and could have been seized as loot by a Viking raider-cum-settler.

A squat, green glass jar was found buried before the high altar at Shaftesbury abbey. It was 2 7/8" high and 4 1/8" in diameter, decorated with a curious swirled corrugation formed by blowing it into a corrugated mould then twirling it to displace the vertical alignment, a technique known to have been in use between the 6th and 13th centuries. It was probably deposited in the 11th century – Shaftesbury was founded in 888 and received the remains of Cnut in 1035, later translated to Winchester for burial – although it would have been much more than a century old at that time and may have been a relic of some local saint or dignitary.[3]

Drinking Vessels

Old English has a good range of words for 'drinking vessel': *bune, cuppe, drencfæt, ful, scenc, wæge, wearr*. Specific types of vessel included *calic* (chalice), *drenchorn* (drinking horn), *glæsfæt* (glass vessel), *ease* (beaker), *seleful* (hall-cup). Pitchers and jugs had a variety of names: *canne, ceac, crog, stæne, wæterbuc* – the latter for holding water. Flasks and flagons were variously *ampelle, buc, bytt, cyll, flasce, steap*. Barrels and tuns were called *byden, bytt, cyf, trog, tunne* while a tub was a *tyncen*. A bucket or pail was *æscen, embren* or *stoppa*.

Cups & Bottles

A set of eight wooden cups was recovered from the Sutton Hoo ship burial, Mound 1.[4] They were turned from walnut burr-wood and each had a metal rim held on by tiny metal clips. (Fig.11) Some had an ornamental collar beneath this rim. The cups were 4-5 cm in height and 3-4 cm in external diameter at the mouth. Their small capacity suggests that they were used to serve a drink[5] which was taken in very small quantities, possibly a form of distilled spirit such as

---

[1] Page, 1908

[2] Webster, 1991 item 134

[3] Harden, 1954; the glass was found beneath a heart-shaped marble stone, which gave rise to the tradition that Cnut's heart was removed and buried at Shaftesbury.

[4] Bruce Mitford, 1983 volume 3, part1

[5] It is also possible that the cups were actually containers for medical potions or salves, and would have been sealed with an organic layer such as textile or skin.

whisky or brandy although it is not known for certain whether the distillation process was known at this early period (early 7th century). They were accompanied by a maple-wood bottle (Fig.7 p.78), decorated similarly to the cups but whereas the latter are closely similar to Scandinavian designs, the bottle's plaques have details suggesting an English provenance. At Taplow,[1] four items identified as wooden bottles were found with the drinking horns. They each had a band of ornament beneath the rim.

Because of the wide variation in size between cups and horns (10cm for the Sutton Hoo horns, but only 4.5 cm for the goat's horn from Cologne) it is not always possible to be sure what type of object is represented by a find. There are many small, metal rim-mounts and surface decorations[2] which are normally associated with drinking horns but which might in fact have been applied to wooden drinking cups, possibly of tapered stave construction. A cup of this type with bronze bands of zoomorphic interlace was excavated at Farthingdown, Surrey, in 1873. Bands which may have been fixed to similar articles come from Chartham Down and Faversham, Kent, and from Dover. Also from Kent are the two large wooden cups found in 1772 at Sibertswold with bronze rims and fluted clips; one had been repaired in antiquity with bronze strips. The barrow at Broomfield,[3] Essex, produced a pair of fragmentary cups, each with a rim diameter of 2" (5cm), of which the wood was found to belong to the genus *prunus* and is probably to be identified as cherry-wood. They were said to be similar in profile to a pair of squat blue glass jars also in the barrow, suggesting that they were very similar to the Sutton Hoo examples when in use.

A small silver cup – patched or repaired in antiquity – was among the items found inside the Sutton Hoo fluted bowl. It was only 8cm in diameter, and had a heavy foot-ring like the Anastasius dish.

Alongside the east wall of the burial chamber in Mound 1 was a small ceramic pot or bottle; this was the only earthenware item recovered from the entire ship burial. The bottle was 6" (15cm) high and 8cm at its widest, with a flat base and a conical profile rising to a long neck and rim. Three incised grooves were the only decoration. There was no trace of a stopper, and indeed it may never have had one. Being unglazed, the container would have served only for thick, heavy liquids such as honey. It is quite a crude, homely object to be found in the grave alongside the magnificent Mediterranean silverware and Germanic garnet-and-gold ceremonial wargear.

The decorative layout of the cups and bottles – a broad plain band from which ornate triangular panels depend – is very similar to the symbolism found on early Anglo-Saxon pottery where swags of stamped decoration are a common feature.

---

[1] Page, 1905
[2] East, 1983
[3] Page, 1903

Food and Feasting Equipment

Fig.14 A bronze Coptic bowl excavated from a grave at Chilton Hall, Sudbury, Suffolk and now in the Ashmolean Museum, Oxford. Height: 11.5cm, diameter: 34.5cm.

Fig.15 The remarkable bronze Coptic bowl with its pedestal, from the burial mound at Taplow, Buckinghamshire. It is unusual in having twelve knobs or lugs around the rim, and a large pair of drop-handles. The base was packed with a lead alloy to maintain a low centre of gravity, since otherwise it would have been unstable when filled with drink. Height: 20.5 cm, diameter 40.6 cm.

An 8th century silver-gilt mount from Brougham, Cumbria, may also be from a cup, and there are parallels to this from the Continent and Scandinavia. Fragments of simple rims, usually in silver or bronze and often gilded, are well recognised finds in Anglo-Saxon contexts. Two such items were found in Grave 16 at Alton, Hampshire, where they apparently formed a matching pair of beechwood drinking vessels, 10cm in height.[1]

The 7th century bed-burial at Swallowcliffe Down,[2] Wiltshire, contained many high-status finds, including two small glass palm-cups by the lady's right forearm. The first, damaged in the collapse of the barrow, is 123mm in rim diameter and 65mm tall, with a capacity of 220ml. It is made from green-blue very delicate glass, only 3mm thick in places. The second cup survived intact; made from the same material as the first, it is 59mm tall and 121mm in diameter at the rim, holding 190ml. These two fine, delicate items must have been highly prized by their owner. They are unusual in having a solid rim, unlike the majority of Anglo-Saxon examples which have an everted rim. The only English parallels were found at Cow Lowe, Derbyshire, and were so similar they could have come from the same workshop.

At Hexham abbey, Northumberland, there is a fine Anglo-Saxon portable chalice consisting of a hemispherical bowl fixed to a short, balustered shaft and foot-ring.[3] While the use of this vessel was liturgical, it indicates the kind of cup a wealthy patron might possess. Its profile is not dissimilar to articles turned from wood on a pole-lathe.

The survival of cup-types throughout the period is indicated by the 'feasting' scene of Harold Godwinesson at Bosham on the Bayeux tapestry (page 40), where the central figure – probably Harold himself – is shown sipping from a shallow bowl held balanced on his palm with the thumb and two smaller fingers, while the remaining fingers are curved elegantly away. This is clearly a palm cup of very similar design to those found from Anglo-Saxon burials of centuries earlier.

A set of six matching maple-wood bottles (Fig.7 p.78) was recovered from Sutton Hoo, Mound 1. Each had a metal rim surmounting a decorative neck, a band of gilded silver with panels of zoomorphic interlace. A series of vandykes run down to the waists of the bottles.

Drinking Horns

The horns of large bovines were valued by Germanic tribesmen, originally as a form of hunting trophy. Julius Caesar notes in his *De Bello Gallico* (Chapter VI) of the relationship of the *Germani* to the aurochs:

---

[1] Evison, 1988b
[2] Speake, 1989, Assemblage "E"
[3] Hawkes, 1996

.... qui plurimos ex his interfecerunt relatis in publicum cornibus
quae sint testimonio magnum ferunt laudem ...Haec studiose
conquista ab labris argento circumcludent atque in amplissimis epulis
proc poculis atuntur

... and those who have slain most of them [the aurochs] brings the horns to a public place in witness and earn much praise .... They collect them avidly, encase their edges with silver and at their most bountiful feasts use them as cups.

A 3rd c. or earlier Roman triumphal arch at Carpentras, Vaucluse, France, shows captured Germanic tribesmen and their equipment which includes a pair of substantial drinking horns, each of which significantly has a decorative band beneath the rim and a series of triangular pendants running down from this band.

Probably the most significant finds of drinking horns were made at Gallehus, Denmark[1] – two similar vessels found in the same field nearly a century apart (1639 and 1734). These were a pair of fine, gold horns made with incredible artistry, their surfaces covered in engraved and soldered geometric and figural decoration. One of the vessels was incomplete. Between them, they weighed nearly 7.5 kilos and the more complete vessel was 29.5 cm in diameter at the rim and 71.3 cm long on the outer edge. The curvature and rim diameter of the other suggest it was a little larger when intact. The damaged one bore a short runic inscription engraved beneath the rim:

ek hlewagastiz holtijaz horna tawido

"I, Hlewagast of Holt, made [the] horn"[2]

The inscription puts the horn into early centuries AD, but comparable finds are so rare it is not possible to say much more than that the language would have been archaic by the 5th century, which would be the upper limit for its dating. The scenes depicted appear to be mythological – a three-headed giant, an archer with his bow, warriors with sword and shield, serpents, horses, stags and a centaur are among the applied motifs with further engraved decoration infilled around them.

It is possible that the find-spot was in territory belonging to the *Anglii* at the time of the horns' manufacture, making them possibly a very early example of Anglian drinking horns. The early Anglii are believed to have been users of the

---

[1] Roesdahl, 1980

[2] The language is an example of the runic *koine* which persists into the 7th century in Denmark. The use of the ᚮ 'o' rune in *horna, holtijaz*, where the vowel must be short, shows that the inscription's spelling is inconsistent with a very early (Proto-Germanic) date. The inscription is often considered to be the earliest known example of a Germanic alliterative verse line. It retains the characteristic SOV (Subject – Object – Verb) word order of the more archaic Germanic languages.

futhark or runic script, in contrast to the Saxons who adopted it much later.[1] Sadly, the horns were stolen and melted down in 1802, and the present copies were made from contemporary illustrations.

The use of such horns as drinking vessels must be an ancient practice in Northern Europe and across the Eurasian steppe. The symbolic importance of the drinking horn in Germanic culture is indicated on a famous rune stone from Snoldelev, Denmark, where three horns are interwoven in a triskele figure. Honoured guests were always offered a horn rather than a cup in Anglo-Saxon times.[2]

Horns are not uncommon archaeological finds from the Roman and Germanic Iron Ages in Northern Europe; between the 3rd and 7th centuries they are gradually replaced by likenesses made from glass in some regions, presumably as early mediaeval trade links created a new demand for drinking vessels, based on traditional forms, from the glass-producing centres of the Rhineland and Italy.[3] High-status glassware became a fashionable accessory in those areas which traded with the Merovingian Franks and the Lombards. Their use began in the 3rd century and appears to have continued until the 6th at least.

The class of glass horns is conventionally divided into four types.[4] Type I resembles the *rhyton* of antiquity, a glass 'trumpet' with a pierced tip, produced in the Mediterranean region but occasionally found in northern Europe in Roman contexts. While the *rhyton* is not the formal predecessor of the 3rd century Germanic glass drinking horn, it may have been the ultimate inspiration for it, and derivative forms occur in the Rhineland, Sweden, Denmark and Poland. Type II is formed and decorated in a similar manner to some conical beakers, from which this Type may have evolved, with a zigzag border at the rim and criss-cross trails across the body. Suspension loops at the rim and towards the tip are characteristic of this Type. They are dated to the 4th century and occur in the Rhineland, Denmark and Norway. Type III dates from the 6th century and features successive rows of arcading on the body of the horn; the whole format is reminiscent of the tall cone beakers of the 5th – 6th centuries. A possible production centre for Type III horns has been identified at Macquenoise, Namur, Belgium. Type IV horns, which only occur in northern Italy, may also feature arcading, combined with trails of white glass on a basic deep blue hue.

Two fine examples of glass horns of Type III from Rainham, Essex, are relatively small (mouth diameters 7.2cm and 8cm, length 33.6cm for the intact vessel) but the shape mimics the natural curve and twist of a real bovine horn faithfully. They date from the 5th – 6th century and were found in a small, rich cemetery near the Thames with probably good access to the lower Rhine.

---

[1] Page, 1999
[2] Hagen, 1995
[3] Bruce Mitford, 1983 volume 3, part1
[4] Evison, 1955

The Rhenish glass horns are of relatively small capacity. The finds of drinking horns from two burials beneath Cologne cathedral show that they favoured small goat horns with tiny metal mouth fittings and no finial. One was secured by a leather shoulder-strap.

The finds of sets of paired horns seems to reflect the social uses of these items. The householder should have a fine vessel to drink from, to mark his status; another of similar worth should be available to honour special guests.[1]

The apparent reduction in large drinking horns from the 3rd century onwards may simply be the result of a fashion change which increased the prestige of imported glassware and consequently down-graded animal horn vessels. The finds from Valsgärde, Sweden, which is in many ways the closest parallel to Sutton Hoo, support this interpretation. However, the fact that the Anglo-Saxon tradition favours horn vessels over glass ones demonstrates that Sutton Hoo was no mere copy of the Swedish ship-burial tradition, but reflected an amalgamation of elements from both.

The typical early Anglo-Saxon drinking horn consists of the horn itself, hollowed and sealed, a decorative finial at the point and a metal rim at the open end (Fig.3 p.49). A median decorative band is sometimes present, and some Scandinavian examples have attachments for a carrying strap. The perishable remains do not survive well archaeologically, and the mounts occasionally occur as isolated finds.[2]

The finest and most famous English drinking horns are from Sutton Hoo, Mound 1, but four others were found in the mound at Taplow,[3] Buckinghamshire, and similar metal fittings have been found on other sites. A pair of horns without metal fittings was found at in the barrow at Broomfield,[4] Essex, while fittings without surviving organic components occurred at Little Wilbraham, Suffolk, and Loveden Hill, Norfolk (two separate vessels) and Holywell, Suffolk, where a rim and tubular median band were similar to the 5th century horn find from Nydam, Denmark. A possible further example from Strood, Kent, had repoussé decoration, groups of Christian figures; this may have been a Frankish import.

In the context of a royal burial, drinking horns symbolise the dead person's role as host and provider of strong drink. The use of such horns at the *symbel* for the

---

[1] Enright, 1996 p.138

[2] e.g. Cook, 1981, Grave 43 at Fonaby may have contained a drinking horn mount, but the poor excavation records make it impossible to be sure what the item, now lost, may have been. One of the two finds from Mound 2 at Sutton Hoo not removed by graverobbers was the metal beak from the bird finial to a drinking horn, similar to those in Mound 1.

[3] Page, 1905

[4] Page, 1903

purpose of swearing oaths is also relevant here – the horns symbolised the oaths of loyalty and mutual support between the leader and his men.[1]

Where there are rim-fittings but no finial, it is not certain that the horn was used for drinking, as it could rather have been for blowing. In many cases it is likewise not possible to determine whether the original object was a tapered drinking horn or a barrel-shaped cup. Wooden cups could taper outwards from the rim, run parallel or even taper inwards with the same profile as a horn. A series of small vandykes in *repoussé* work from Caenby, Lincolnshire, seem to be generally similar to the fittings from drinking horns (triangular outline; tiny nails holding the plates to an organic backing 3 mm thick; interlace decoration) and should probably be interpreted as such.

The Sutton Hoo ship burial contained a fine pair of drinking horns, laid on a pile of textiles at the body's feet, the ends overlapping and the curved bodies encompassing all but one of the maple-wood bottles. The horns' finials were in the form of a stylised birds' head, each cast in silver. They are similar to those found in the near-contemporary barrow grave at Taplow where four horns were decorated in two paired sets. The larger Taplow horns have a silver casing with cast ribs tapering gentling in an arc to end in a prominent avian head executed in Salin's Style II of Germanic art. The smaller ones from that site have similar heads, but attached to stubbier, plainer sockets.

At Sutton Hoo, the 4" (10cm) diameter rims (Fig.3 p.49) are metal channels held in place by decorative clips pinned into the surface of the horn. They surmount panels of stamped, gilded foil decorated with Style II animal motifs.[2] A further series of triangular pendants completes the design. The decoration closely parallels that found on the shield from the same grave, and also the Swedish grave treasures from Valsgärde. Indeed many aspects of the designs found at Sutton Hoo find their closest parallels in contemporary Eastern Scandinavia.

Whether the horn's surface was carved, painted or incised or not is unknown. It would certainly have been within the skill of the English craftsmen who produced these pieces to carefully carve panels of interlace, zoomorphic icons or geometric decoration into the soft surface of the vessels, then to pick the details out with coloured paints.

The mid-9th century Trewhiddle hoard of metalwork from near St. Austell, Cornwall,[3] gives its name to a style of Anglo-Saxon decoration which lasted for

---

[1] Neuman de Vegvar (1992) suggests that the ale-ritual was common to both Anglian (Germanic) and British (Celtic) groups, and that the rite was specifically chosen to bind together polities of both groups in the formation of the East Anglian state.

[2] Fragments of silver-gilt foil were recovered from the neighbouring Mound 2 at Sutton Hoo. They closely resemble the Mound 1 horn mounts and strongly suggest that Mound 2 once contained a similar pair of horns, among other treasures. Mound 2 was ransacked and robbed by treasure hunters, probably in the 18th century.

[3] Webster, 1991 item 246(e); Wilson & Blunt, 1961

nearly a century. Among the finds were two silver horn rims, each with a scalloped[1] lower edge dividing the rim into fields. Every second field was pierced for a rivet. Beaded frames separate the subtriangular fields, which contain animal, plant and interlace motifs. The ends of the rims display repousse animal heads, demonstrating that the rim did not extend to the full diameter of the horn's mouth. A contemporary mount from Burghead, Morayshire, is circular, with a pronounced lip and pendant triangular decoration, and much more closely related to the kinds of rim mount found at Sutton Hoo or Taplow. It has a ring for the attachment of a suspension strap.[2]

The two outer figures at table in the 'feasting' scene on the Bayeux tapestry (Fig.2 p.40) each have a drinking horn with a decorative band at the mouth end and a finial, not dissimilar to the finds of several centuries earlier.

Buckets & Tubs

Apart from the drinking vessels for personal use, ale and other drinks appear to have been served from wooden 'buckets' of barrel-type construction. These vessels are not crude pails for carrying slops, but fine, decorated containers of stave construction. It is possible that the vessels were incised, carved, varnished or painted, though very seldom does any organic material survive. Buckets are often quite small – around 4"(10cm) high and the same in diameter, giving a capacity of just over a pint (0.7 litres). At this size, they would not be practical for anything but serving one or two individuals at a time. Some are much larger – the example from Glen Parva was 54cm in diameter.[3]

The decoration of the metal fittings on these buckets is frequently similar to that on the contemporary drinking horns and cups,[4] with small triangular pendants ('vandykes') and substantial bronze or iron bands held in place by rivets. Repousse bosses at the intersection of horizontal and vertical bands are common, as on the example from Alton (Grave 2).[5] Occasionally a recognisable, bearded face forms part of the decoration of the vandykes. Frequently the mounts for attachment of the suspension loops are made in thin bronze and decorated with dots, parallel grooves, panels of interlace or stylised human masks. Iron fittings are also known. A common design feature on early examples is a vertical bronze plate which divides and curls back on itself in two zoomorphic (probably avian) heads[6] whose eyes are formed by the rivet-heads. These too bear parallel grooves

---

[1] Wilson & Blunt, 1961, suggest that the scalloping is a development of the vandykes on earlier horns such as those from Sutton Hoo and Taplow.

[2] Webster, 1991 item 247; the suspension strap has led some scholars to suggest that the horn was for musical purposes rather than for drinking.

[3] Speake, 1989 p.58

[4] East, 1983; Arnold, 1997

[5] Evison, 1988b

[6] Mills, 2001; e,g. the find from Morningthorpe Grave 35 in Green, Rogerson & White, 1987

and stamped dots. Remains of vessels of this type were found at Mucking, Essex, Long Wittenham, Berkshire, Fetcham, Surrey, Roundway Down, Wiltshire and Loveden Hill, Norfolk.

At Swallowcliffe Down, Wiltshire,[1] there were two stave-built vessels. The bronze-mounted bucket was part of the barrow burial's ornate furniture, which also included a bed. Although crushed, the bucket was reconstructed from the surviving metalwork. It was made from yew staves secured with two iron hoops and a u-shaped channel over the rim. A semi-circular handle was joined by two ring-headed projections, and eighteen triangular pendants were placed round the outside beneath the rim. The vessel was 21cm tall and 19cm in internal diameter, giving it a capacity of about 6 litres (9.5 pints). This was a prestige item and may have been filled with food or drink; it was placed near the foot of the bed. An iron-bound coopered bucket stood near the head of the bed, 30cm in diameter and 28cm high. An iron strip enclosed the rim, held in place with tinned bronze clips pinned into position. Again, the wood was identified as yew. A similar vessel from Spong Hill,[2] Norfolk, (grave 40) is unique in having been made from buckthorn (rhamnus catharticus).

A notable sub-group of buckets has arcade-and-dot decoration in repoussé work, a feature also found on the Continent; these occur in central and southern England. Continental buckets commonly have openwork triangular mounts, but this is confined to one English example from Gilton, Kent. British influence has been detected in some rare cases: a moulded bovine head on the fittings of a bucket from Twyford, Leicestershire, and a stylized human face on another from Souldern, Oxforshire.

The handles are commonly a plain bronze strip riveted through the escutcheon, or with hooked ends which engage with holes in the ends of the vertical bands. There are typically three or four surrounding, horizontal bands and two or four vertical ones. Fittings of copper-alloy could have been applied cold, while the iron ones may have been worked hot and shrunk onto the wooden components. The iron buckets tend to have few or no vertical elements, but broad bands and smaller hoops. Generally the wooden staves are carefully cut to a common width and thickness (e.g. 4cm wide and 0.5cm thick as at North Luffenham, Rutland, and Louth, Lincolnshire). The edges of the staves were cut parallel but bevelled to ensure that they would form a circle over the required distance. They must have been held in place with a former while the bronze fittings were placed over and around them. Yew is the commonest wood identified, but pine, oak and ash are also known. The base on the example from North Luffenham, was a single circular wooden plate, 0.2cm thick, slotted into a purpose-cut groove at the lower end of the staves.

---

[1] Speake, 1989, Assemblages "A" and "C"
[2] Hills, Penn & Rickett, 1984

Food and Feasting Equipment

In the burial chamber at Sutton Hoo, Mound 1, against the east wall was found a tub, made from yew-wood, which contained a smaller wooden bucket.[1] Two other buckets were identified by their metal fittings. The tub was made from wooden staves held with iron bands; its rim diameter is 51cm and its height may have been about 52cm. Three small iron feet are at its base. The iron rim-band is surmounted by a channel which is held by decorative clips riveted through the wooden staves and the iron band; escutcheons hide the riveting – flat silver ones on the tub, and small bronze ones on the buckets.

The tub had a capacity of around 100 litres. Its two heavy iron rings might have been used to pass a large wooden pole through for two people to carry it, though it would have been unstable and unwieldy if filled with liquid. It may have been the reservoir from which smaller vessels were filled.

The Sutton Hoo buckets are apparently parallel-sided, stave-built vessels with diameters of 22, 25 and 33cm respectively. It is believed that they could have been 1'1" (33cm) tall. They had bailed handles, which would make them suitable for carrying and serving useful quantities of drink at table.

There are numerous stray finds of small, circular or sub-triangular decorated metal objects which are usually interpreted as mounts of various kinds, dating up to the very end of the Anglo-Saxon period. Some may have come from books, portable shrines, horse-harnesses and the like but it is probable that some may be the continuation of the bowl-mount tradition beyond the pagan period.

At Rainham, Essex, two tiny but perfectly made vessels of bucket type, each with a rim just 2" (5cm) in diameter, may have been used as cups or for serving small quantities of liquids.[2] Similar objects were recovered from Nassington, Northamptonshire. In conjunction with the small wooden cups from Sutton Hoo, it seems that some liquids – presumably a very strong or very precious drink – was traditionally taken parsimoniously in the hall.

There were even tiny amulets in the shape of buckets, such as the ones found at Bidford-on-Avon from a 6th century female grave. Similar items are usually found in groups of seven, twelve or more. They appear to have had some magical significance, and parallels are found in Germanic cultural contexts as far afield as eastern Europe (Przevorsk culture, Chernjachov culture) where Gothic and other East Germanic groups carried the tradition with them.

---

[1] Care-Evans, 1986
[2] Bruce Mitford, 1983 volume 3, part1

Chapter Four

Strainers

Accompanying the bucket was usually a serving strainer or *situla*. A series of Anglo-Saxon female graves have yielded curious objects, like perforated spoons, which may be been used in the preparation or serving of food and drink. They are seldom very large, but they do usually have a hemispherical bowl which would make them unsuitable for eating with; they are normally pierced with a series of holes in a decorative pattern. Most have a suspension loop – or provision for one – and are found between the owner's knees, suggesting that they were worn suspended from the girdle. Since this is a very prominent position – also used to display latch-lifters, crystal balls and toilet sets – it is assumed that possession of such items distinguished the wearer as of high status.

Meaney[1] has suggested that the spoons may have been used for straining wine, and that the high-status association derives from the user belonging to a household able to afford imported luxuries. Speake,[2] however, notes that the bowls of these items are too small for that purpose, and the holes too large to exclude wine sediment. The association of these utensils with crystal spheres in many female graves he links to the folk-custom of dipping such spheres into water and then sprinkling cattle with it, which would mean that these objects are rather sprinklers than strainers. Enright,[3] however, proposes that the strainers are meant to be used with a fruit or barley beer. He notes that in Roman culture, the situla was a utensil which could be used by either sex, while in Germanic culture it is firmly associated with high-status females.

To take examples from a single cemetery, the pagan period burials from Bifrons, Kent, are worth examination. There are two examples of these strainers in the Conyngham Collection, which were recovered in unrecorded digging of the cemetery at Bifrons.[4] One (Fig.17, left) is 11.3cm long with a flat handle, its sides decorated with lines of punched dots. The top of the shaft is scrolled to take a suspension ring. Where the shaft broadens to join the bowl it is decorated with two stylised birds' heads. There are thirteen holes in the bowl, nine in a cross-shape and one in each corner. The other spoon (Fig.17, right) is slightly longer at 11.8cm, with the suspension loop still in place in the scrolled handle top. The broader end of the handle near the bowl is decorated with flanches, outlined with stamped trefoils. Nine holes pierce the bowl in a cruciform arrangement. The collection also includes a small, coopered bucket, made from staves of yew wood. It is just 10.5cm tall, with a diameter of 11cm at the base tapering to 10.5cm at the rim. Four copper alloy strips surround the vessel horizontally, and four more overlap vertically, rivetted where they intersect. The handle

---

[1] Meaney, 1981
[2] Speake, 1989
[3] Enright, 1996 p.101ff
[4] Hawkes, 2000

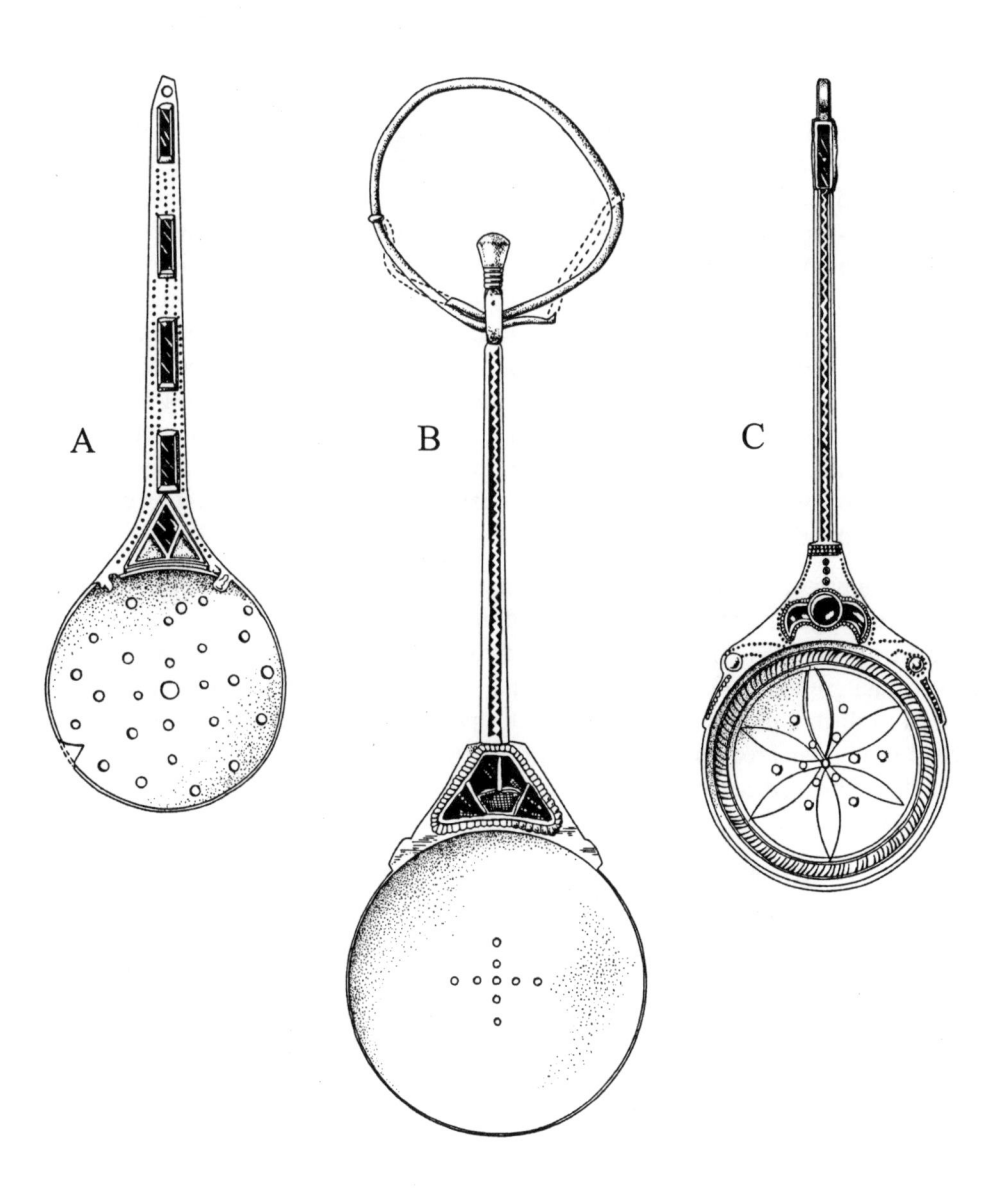

Fig.16 Three richly decorated strainers from pagan period graves in Kent. The strainers feature delicate punchwork and garnet cloisonnée.
A. Fausset Collection (from excavations at Chatham Lines) After C. Praetorius
B. Bifrons, Grave 42. After Cox & Fry-Stone
C. Bifrons, Grave 51. After Cox & Fry-Stone

escutcheon is an anchor-shaped plate of copper alloy, decorated with punched dots, as is the handle. There are sundry other, similar metal bindings, all probably from wooden cups, and a fragment of iron chain. It would be interesting to know whether the two strainers and the small bucket actually came from the same grave.

Grave 51, in the part of the Bifrons cemetery which was properly excavated, held an impressive assemblage including a fine example of a strainer (Fig.16, right). Made of gilded silver, it was 14.4cm long with an octagonal-sectioned handle decorated with nielloed triangles on the upper surface, leaving a silver-on-black zigzag down the whole handle. Its top was scrolled to take a suspension ring, and beneath this was soldered a neat, rectangular mount for a sliced garnet. At the broader end, the handle widens to a sub-triangular form and is decorated with two birds' heads with embossed eyes. Between these are three cabochon garnets in beaded settings. The circular bowl is decorated with parallel lines round the edges and a six-petal pattern in the bowl itself; two perforations lie between each pair of petals and an eleventh is in the centre of the pattern. The strainer lay between the knees of its owner and presumably was suspended by a loop of some perishable material.

No less impressive was the example from Grave 42 (Fig.16, middle), 16cm long with a rectangular-sectioned handle. The upper face had a silver-on-black zigzag formed by nielloed triagles, while the two sides had the zigzag in niello on a silver background. The handle terminates in a neat finial knob, below which it swells to form a plate which is pierced to take a metal suspension loop. Again, a broad triangular area above the bowl is flattened to take a set of five cloisonné garnets in beaded settings. The bowl is pierced by nine holes in a cruciform configuration.

A cruder, lower-status example was recovered from Grave 6 (Fig.17, middle). It was made of bronze, but tinned to give the appearance of the higher-status silver utensils. It was 13.1cm long, made from a flat bronze sheet, with the bowl worked up by hammering. The tapering, flat handle is looped over at the top to accommodate the copper-alloy suspension loop. At the broader end it joins the bowl, which is pierced by eight holes in a X configuration, each surrounded by punched dots; similar dots line the sides of the handle and form a saltire above the bowl. This spoon was also found between its owner's thighs.

It seems very likely that these were desirable objects whose possession conferred high status on their owners; whether they were really used in cooking, serving drink or exorcism is uncertain. However, brewing was a highly specialised and very important craft among the Anglo-Saxons, and it may be that a functional utensil also acquired symbolic status through this association.

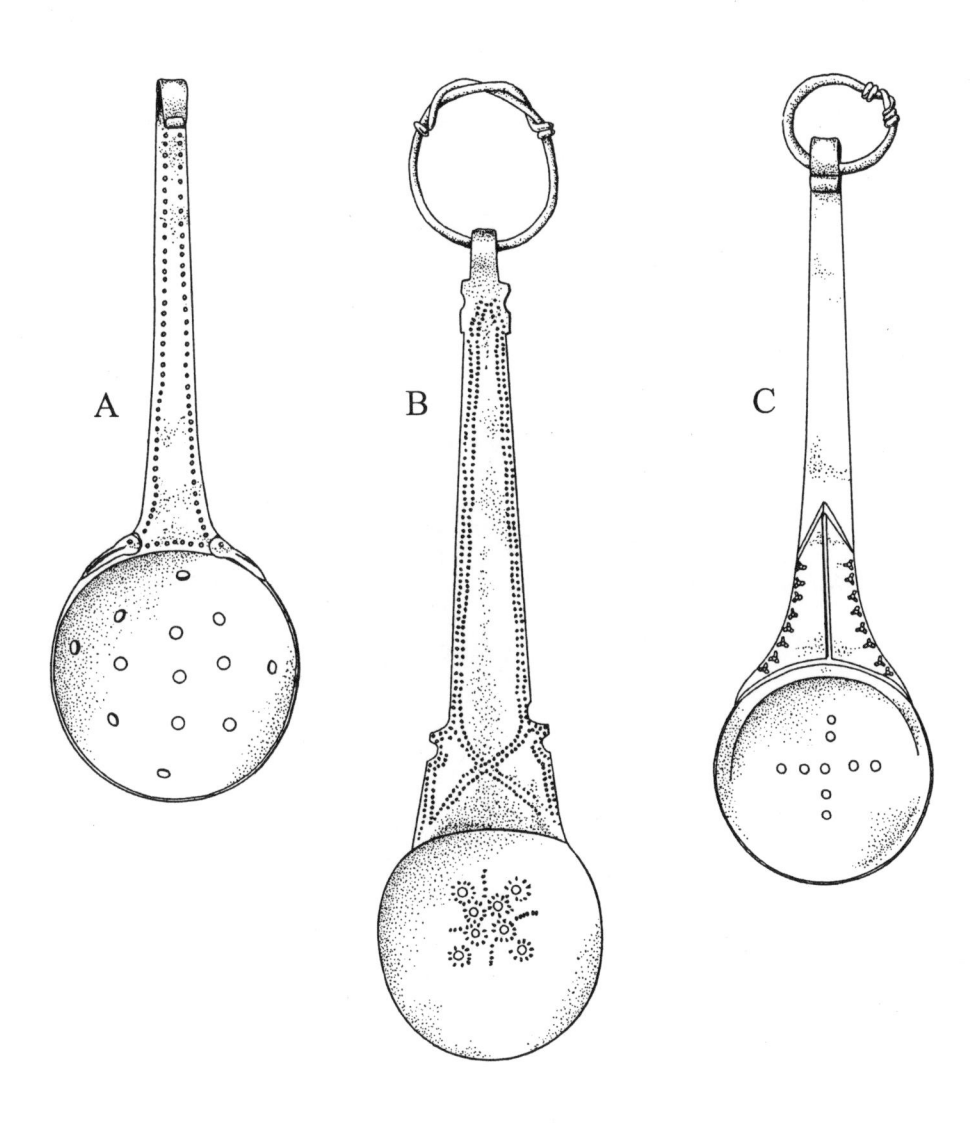

Fig.17 Three strainers from pagan period graves at Bifrons, Kent. After Cox & Fry-Stone. In contrast to the strainers in Fig.16, these examples are cruder, less carefully executed and their decoration is confined to punchwork and cast details.
A. Conyngham Collection, no.24
B. Bifrons, Grave 6
C. Conyngham Collection, no.25

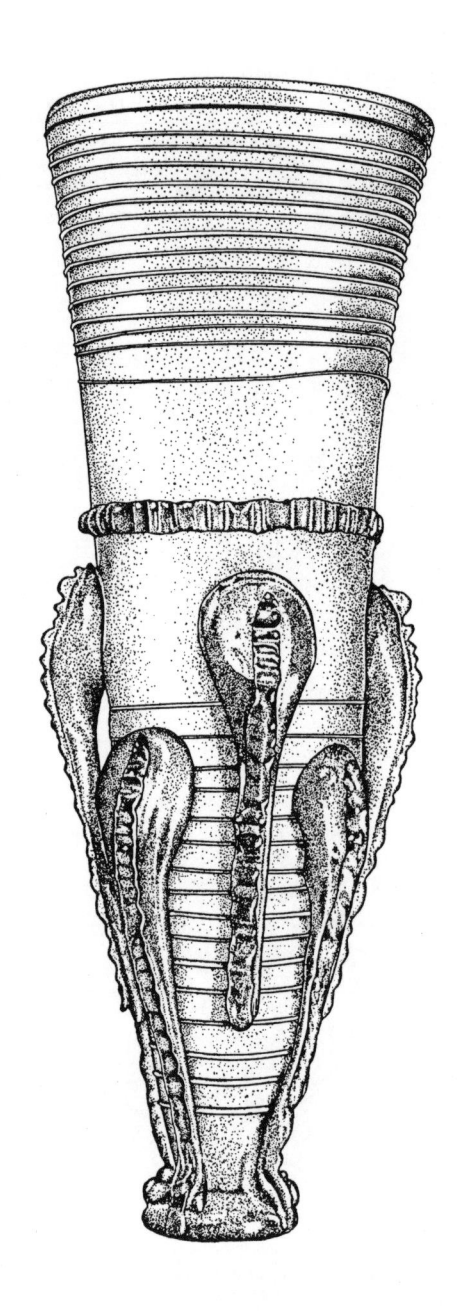

Fig.18 Clawbeaker from Taplow, Berkshire. The extruded claws with their shaped decorative trails make these vessels very distinctive. Early 7th century.

Clawbeakers

The Germanic 'clawbeaker' (Fig.18) is a curious form of glass drinking vessel which came into use in the post-Roman period. The typical clawbeaker is a conical glass jar with a small foot and an everted rim, to the which are added both a decorative horizontal trail at top and bottom, and a series of hollow 'claws'.[1] These were fashioned by affixing a blob of hot glass, blowing it and then quickly drawing it downwards and fastening at its point. The process must have been repeated for each claw. The model which gave rise to the form is a Roman vessel decorated with appliqué dolphins.

Clawbeakers are found with both male and female grave assemblages. The earliest English example, from Grave 843 at Mucking, the only certain Type 1 example from this country, was found with various female-associated items including 2 square-headed brooches. Of the three examples of Type 2a, only one has a recorded provenance – from a grave at Chatteris, Cambridgeshire, in which were also male-associated items (a shield, spear and pot). Unfortunately, the delicate nature of the items makes it very likely that grave disturbance of any kind will have destroyed them wherever they were deposited.

A typology for the clawbeaker has been developed as follows:-[2]

Type	Date	Height cm
1	early? 5th C.	20.5 cm.
	\multicolumn{2}{l}{Stemmed with wide foot, flat rim; zigzag trail below rim, vertical notched trails framing panels; two rows of claws with tails of top row resting on lower row; a notched trail across top and bottom claw}	
2a	middle 5th C.	17 – 19 cm.
	\multicolumn{2}{l}{Stemmed with foot; horizontal trail below rim (and at base); 2 or more rows of 'full' claws spaced alternately occupying 2/3 of vessel's wall; vertical notched trail from lower edge of horizontal trail zone to base, running across each claw}	
2b	middle 5th C.	17 - 19.5 cm.
	\multicolumn{2}{l}{As 2a but lacking the vertical notched trails}	
3a	early 6th C.	18 - 18.8 cm.
	\multicolumn{2}{l}{Stemmed with foot; horizontal trail below rim (and at base); taller, narrower profile than type 2, with flatter claws; vertical panel trails (some in second colour);}	

---

[1] Kämpfer & Beyer, 1966

[2] Based on Evison, 1982; the dates are based on assumptions from associated finds and are not available for all types; the heights are based on data in Evison, 1982.

3b	middle 6th C.	15 - 17.2 cm.
	As 3a but shorter, more conical profile; no stem, small foot; horizontal trail on most of wall	
3c	middle 6th C.	14 - 17.5 cm.
	As 3a but shorter, claws confined to lower half of wall; usually 2 rows of 5 claws, with vertical notched trail extending down claw's length and loop at top;	
3d		15.5 - 16.5 cm.
	As 3c but lacking the vertical notched trails	
3e		-
	As 3c but claws begin in the horizontal trail zone	
4a	late? 6th C.	29.5 cm.
	As 3a but with much taller, more conical profile; straight rim; no stem; claws flatter with notched vertical trail	
4b	7th C.	19 - 30.4 cm.
	As 4a but without notched vertical trail; often 2 rows of 3 claws	
4c	7th C.	19 - 19.7 cm.
	As 4a but with hollow, blown bosses above the top row of claws; rolled rim, no stem	
5	7th C.	18 cm.
	Similar to type 1 but without stem and foot	

There are some clear trends in the styling of the types, so that for example blue glass was not used for the decorative trails in the pagan period, except for one example found at Castle Eden, Durham. Overall, a brownish colour is the commonest among the surviving examples but this is not found on the later Types 4 and 5, where blues and greens predominate.

The following table of chronological variations in clawbeaker forms is based on evidence assembled by M. Wilson:[1]

Period	Typical Colour/s	Typical Trail Colour/s	Typical Vessel Style
Early Saxon Type 1,2	greens, olive, browns	one colour in wall, trails in same colour	claws arranged as 2x5 or less (usually 2x4)
Type 3	greens olive, browns	trails in same colour	claws arranged as 2x5 or less (usually 2x4)
Mid Saxon Type 4,5	blue with red streaks, dark olive, dark green, dark brown (with white trails)	trails in 2 colours	greater claw variety eg 2x4, 3x4, 2x3 bag beaker (no foot) some with knobs
Late Saxon		fragment of potash glass claw	

Conebeakers

Although not as visually interesting as the English claw-beakers, there is a further set of glass drinking vessels known as 'cone-beakers'.[2] These are, as the name suggests, long hollow cones made of coloured glass, often decorated with a zone of horizontal trailing beneath the everted rim. The famous Kempston beaker (Fig.19 p.163) is a good example of the type, which occurs in some high-status graves[3] of the pagan period. They are typically about 10" (25cm) high and 3.5" (9cm) in diameter at the rim, with a capacity of about half a pint (0.3 litre). The cone shape means that the vessels will not stand up by themselves. Either the feasting table was furnished with some form of (wooden?) stand to support them, or they were used in ritual contexts where the contents were served and drunk without resting the vessel – possibly standing during a solemn occasion. They would have been ideal vessels for drinking a toast to a guest, or for making a speech over, since their relatively small capacity would limit the amount of drink to be consumed.

There are no major differences between Roman and Anglo-Saxon glassware as far as the composition of the glass itself is concerned, although the English taste is certainly very different from the classical forms used in the Empire.

---

[1] M. Wilson, pers.comm..
[2] Arnold, 1997; Parfitt, 1995
[3] e.g. Westgarth Gardens, Bury St. Edmunds Grave 51 which also contained a sword, shield, spear, knife and ceramic pot (West, 1988).

Cauldrons & Hanging Bowls

The distinctive Anglo-Saxon serving vessel or 'hanging bowl' (Fig.20 p.165) is an item of household furniture which appears to come into vogue in the 6th century and continues in use some way into the 7th, when sadly the archaeological record gives out with the introduction of unaccompanied burial[1]. There is a clear distinction between the decorative – possibly ritual – hanging bowls and the practical cooking containers called 'cauldrons'. A third form of metal container is the 'pail', a cylindrical vessel with a handle; these are believed to be imports.[2]

Hanging Bowls

The tale is told of a missionary among the Suevi called Columbanus, who came into a house where a feast was in process. They were seated round a large vessel, called a *cupa,* filled with ale. The saint naturally detected Satan at work and caused the vessel to explode. The reaction of the guests is not recorded.[3] The central position of the ale-bowl at the feast in this story strongly recalls the imposing nature of the Anglo-Saxon hanging bowl.

The inclusion of a large hanging bowl in late pagan period burials was standard practice for the wealthy. Many high-status burials, whether in mounds or flat cemeteries, contain such vessels but they are never common even in the wealthiest gravefields, with only a handful of graves so furnished. The spectacular princely grave at Wollaston, Leicestershire, had all the right accoutrements for a leader of his period (c.600): a bronze hanging bowl decorated with enamelled escutcheons; a fine sword; an iron helmet (one of only four from the period known to survive).

The hanging bowl was typically a large bronze vessel with a concave 'neck' and a comparatively narrow rim. Below the rim were the three equidistant suspension points for the chain which hung them over the hearth; these suspension points were usually covered with decorative mounts made from bronze, soldered over the loop of the hanger. Many of the mounts bear Insular British (rather than specifically Anglo-Saxon) decoration: triskeles, late La Tene style trumpets and spirals executed in red enamel. (Fig.20 insert) The possible significance of this artistic exchange was discussed above (p.61).

Not all the mounts are Celtic in style, however: some are simple circular plates with running scroll motifs, similar to the decoration on contemporary Anglo-Saxon saucer brooches; others are zoomorphic, with the head and neck forming the attachment loop. The bowl from Capheaton, Northumberland, is presumed to be of Anglo-Saxon provenance, with annular mounts to which the suspension loops are attached.[4]

---

[1] Mills, 2001: Brenan, 1991
[2] Arnold, 1997
[3] Grönbeck, 1931
[4] Hawkes, 1996

Food and Feasting Equipment

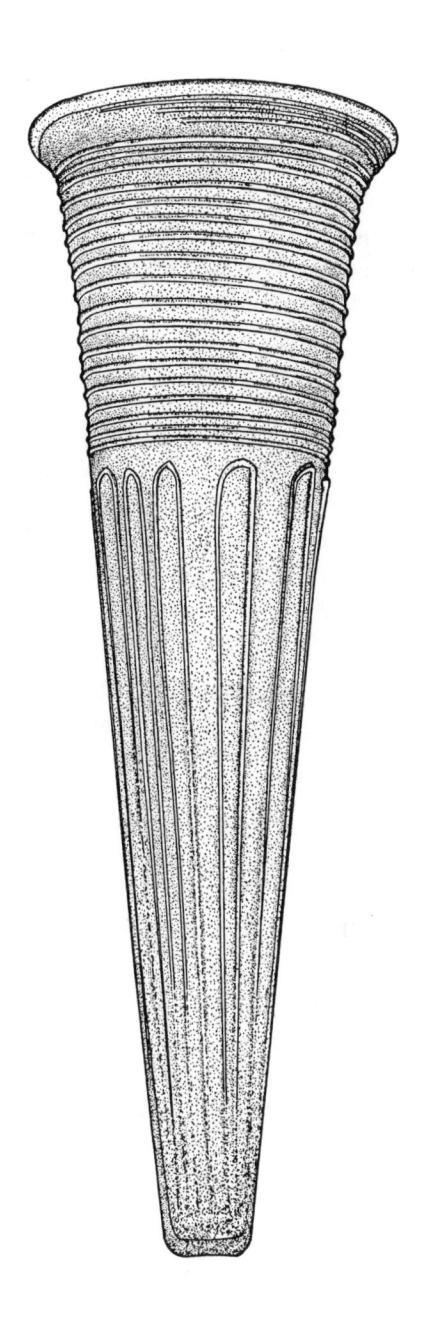

Fig.19 Conebeaker from Kempston, Bedforshire. The clean lines and gentle twist of the barrelling are typical of this kind of glassware. 6th century.

Chapter Four

The excavation of the site of Hild's famous monastic foundation at *Streoneshalh* (Whitby, Yorkshire) yielded some fragments of hanging-bowl rim and sundry mounts.[1] The bowls were made from bronze, the rims decorated with escutcheons. Sadly all the artefacts are fragmentary, but it appears that the finds represent the remains of at least ten different vessels. The escutcheons had in many cases been soldered to the rims of their bowls.

The remarkable Sutton Hoo, Mound 1, large hanging bowl was found near the east wall of the burial chamber amidships. Made of sheet bronze, it had tinned bronze and enamelled fittings decorated with Celtic scroll motifs. The bowl was delicate, only 1mm thick, with a rim diameter of 30cm and a height of 13.5cm. It had been repaired during its period of use; one of the patches bears two fine Germanic Style II avian heads. The escutcheons were surmounted by animal heads which seem to peek over the rim into the bowl's interior; at the centre, a three-dimensional enamelled bronze fish was mounted. The fish, probably a trout, had originally been tinned to give it a silvery sheen. Below each escutcheon sits a stylized boar's head; these had been re-worked by English craftsmen to give the beasts eyes of garnet backed with gold foil. Three square decorative panels sit between the escutcheons, below the waist of the container. The vessel had been hung up by one of its handles, with the rim against the wall of the chamber.

A suspension chain – an almost unique find from this period – was 3.45m long, indicating that the minimum height of the rafter from which its bowl was suspended could not have been less than 5m. It was associated with the large cauldron, but not actually attached to the vessel. Details of its construction were determined by radiography as it was badly corroded. The top consisted of a large ring with a swivel attachment, to let the bowl turn without snaring the chain. A series of seven twisted-iron hooked elements runs down to a distributor which splits into two chains, each with a sturdy pot-hook terminal.

On the west wall were the large bronze 'Coptic' bowl and two further hanging bowls of presumed Romano-British origin which had likewise been hung up from a mount on the chamber wall. One was similar in form to the large bowl, with red enamelled escutcheons and animal headed hooks. The other was provided with hooks whose escutcheons were decorated with bronze foil impressed with a zoomorphic design and a pair of mounts showing a four-headed swastika design in bronze and red enamel. Within the Coptic bowl was the maple-wood lyre (see below, p.204).

If a series of finds of sub-triangular metal items bearing 8th century interlace designs are to be interpreted as similar in function, then the use of the hanging bowl beyond the 7th century may be inferred.

---

[1] Peers & Raleigh Radford, 1943

Fig.20 Hanging bowl from the 6th century cremation cemetery at Sutton Hoo. Inset: detail of the enamelled escutcheon on the rim, with typical La Tene style ornament, and suspension ring. The vessel had been repaired before use as the container for the cremation.

Chapter Four

The use to which hanging bowls were put is not fully understood. Many would not have withstood the rigours of prolonged cooking, as they are fairly insubstantial. The decorative scheme of the large bowl from Sutton Hoo, with its tinned fish mounted centrally, suggests that it contained water or some clear liquid. If they were used at feasts, they might have been provided for the guests to wash their face and hands in warm water. Alternatively, some may have been used to serve up liquids –broth, perhaps, or ale.

It is possible that British forms of metalwork may have been given as symbolic welcoming gifts to new Germanic family members on accession to British land-holdings. If so, then the fashion must have lasted for some decades and does suggest peaceful relations between groups more often characterised as enemies (see p.60).

Cauldrons

Cauldrons differ from hanging-bowls in that the former were used for preparing food, while the latter seem to have been used exclusively for ostentatiously serving it. Old English names include *bæceling, cyll, hwer, panne, polle*. While the bowls may have hung over a fire to keep the contents warm, the lengthy cooking process had been completed in a more mundane vessel. Metal cooking pots could be made much larger than the earthenware counterparts, heated faster and were more durable. They were suspended over the fire on a pot-hanger or a long chain running up to the hall's rafters. Some may have stood on a trivet, but were lifted on or off by means of a pole through the rings on the rim.

At the east end of the Sutton Hoo burial chamber were found many fragments of bronze near the remains of the wooden tub.[1] These were from a very large, collapsed cauldron with iron fittings which appears to have been hung up on the chamber wall by one of its handles. It was 70cm in diameter and 34cm in height giving it a capacity of just less than 100 litres. The two iron rings would have engaged the hooks of a suspension chain; beneath the rings and equidistant between them are four scrolled iron strips, designed to take the strain when the pot was hung up. The cauldron was beaten out of a single sheet of bronze, and was just 1.2mm thick; a small hole in the base may have been for drainage. The nearest parallel to this find was a large vessel from Taplow, which was so similar in execution it could have come from the same workshop.

Two further fragmentary cauldrons were detected among the grave-goods, of which only the rims survived. Each was around 40cm in diameter, fitted with iron handles connected to triangular lugs. The closest parallels to these vessels are found on Gotland in the Baltic.

---

[1] Care-Evans, 1986

Textiles & Clothing

Textiles

The importance of textile production in the Anglo-Saxon period is shown by the routine finds of loom-weights, beaters and other weaving gear in domestic environments.[1] Weaving equipment in funerary contexts is as closely correlated with female graves as weapons are with males ones. Indeed, the woman's role as producer of yarn, cloth and garments was one of her more important symbolic functions. Close connections between weaving, sexuality and magic have been found in much Germanic literature.[2]

Combs are fairly well-evidenced as grave-goods in cremations, and are also found in SFBs where other weaving equipment is found. On this basis, some combs may be interpreted as having been used for finishing wool (they are believed to be too fine for carding), although they may also have been for combing the owner's hair. They are typically made from antler or bone, although even if wooden ones were common they might only rarely have survived. A flat plate of antler or bone had a central rib riveted on, and teeth cut into one or two long sides. Some elaborate examples had a purpose-made cover for the teeth, also of bone. Typical decorative schemes include incised lines (parallel or crossed), circles and ring-and-dot motifs. A recognised grave-goods assemblage of combs, shears and spindle-whorls occurs - a wool-making kit.

Weaving battens, made from bone or iron, are also known from archaeology. The metal objects tend to be found in rich women's graves of the sixth century, and some few are pattern-welded – a time-consuming and elaborate process used to produce beautiful, high-quality, durable articles.[3] Their use is to beat the weft into a tight, compacted mass before moving on to another pass of the shuttle. Pin-beaters – long, slender bone tools – are used to re-integrate single stray threads. Swindon, Wiltshire, has produced some of the best collections of weaving instruments from English contexts.

Looms are identified by loom-weights, doughnut-shaped ceramic objects which are used to add tension to the warp threads. Occasionally they occur in a row where they have dropped from the loom in the bottom of a demolished SFB, but are found more often stacked ready for use. At Grimstone End, Suffolk, the fallen rows of weights were 2.4m long and 22cm apart, suggesting that the finished cloth would be about 6'6" (2m) wide and would have needed two weavers to work the loom. A presumed loom at Bourton-on-the-Water, Gloucestershire, had postholes 2.3m apart, which would likewise give a cloth of around 6'6" (2m) in

---

[1] Arnold, 1997; Owen-Crocker, 1986

[2] Some examples in Enright, 1996, p.117ff including the OHG *First Merserburg Charm*, the reference to *wigspeda gewiofu* (weavings of war-might) in *Beowulf*, the ON *Darraðarljoð* 'Lay of Darts', and references in Bede's *HE*.

[3] It is possible that this item was only intended for display, since the effect of hard metal on wool could be damaging. (M. Wilson, pers.comm..)

width, a useful dimension when clothing adult humans of either sex. At Old Erringham, Sussex, the row was 1.5m long and consisted of 43 weights, which agrees well with the calculated 14 weights for every 0.5m. It is likely that most rural households clothed themselves by their own skills and materials, giving rise to considerable local variations in the details of costume.

Spinning[1] was the common toil of women, and must have occupied many hours of the day when other tasks could not be performed; probably, women developed the knack of spinning while watching the cooking pot, overseeing children's play and carrying out other static tasks, while also chatting and listening to stories. A fleece or plucked wool had to be combed;[2] flax, after retting, had to be beaten and combed with a hackle. The resulting mass of fibre was then attached to a drop-spindle which was released with a turning motion, twisting and pulling the fibres into a single thread; the direction of this spin determined the lay of the fibres (either Z-spun or S-spun, the former being more common). Once the spindle reached to the floor, the thread was wound onto the shaft and the process started again. The shaft of the spindle acted as a convenient bobbin for the yarn, but eventually a set length of it must have been transferred to another vehicle; a reel for winding the yarn into balls was found in the Norwegian Oseberg ship-burial.

A means of forming braids and tapes involves passing lengths of thread through holes in the corners of small, square cards ('tablets'), usually no more than 2" (5cm) square; the tablets would be turned outwards or inwards, to produce Z- or S-threaded arrangements, usually in combinations of the two to prevent the braid twisting. The single weft thread ran in the gap (the 'shed') between the upper and lower pairs of the warp threads, the tablets were turned through 90° and the weft was passed back: as any single thread reaches the upper face of the braid for two turns, then reverts to the lower, the technique lends iself to diagonal-based patterns. Continuous turning in one direction would produce too much torque, so after a given number of passes the rotation should be reversed, or the threads untwisted. By skilfully combining forward and backward motions in individual tablets, and using different colours of thread, a variety of patterns are achievable: mostly stripes, herringbones, diamonds and diagonals in the early period remains, with increasingly adventurous and complex designs emerging over time. The technique was used on its own to make braids for the cuffs and hems of garments, and also in weaving to produce a strong finished edge to a length of cloth within its own fabric. Odd finds of such textiles attached to strap-ends suggests that braids were used as belts and straps as well.[3]

The Anglo-Saxon warp-weighted loom was presumably a fixture in every domestic site, and there is clear evidence that SFBs were constructed with

---

[1] Owen-Crocker, 1986.

[2] Wool for spinning was not normally pre-washed (M. Wilson, pers.comm.)

[3] Crowfoot, 1952

Food and Feasting Equipment

Tabby weave

Tabby weave (exploded view)
The black weft goes alternately
over and under the grey warp threads.

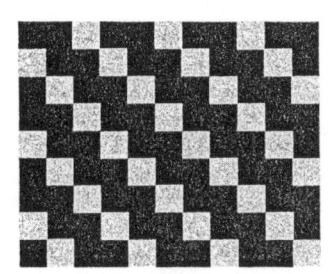

Twill 2x1

Twill 2x2

Diamond twill

Fig.21

weaving as one of their main intended uses. The uprights of the loom were inclined against a wall or roof-beam, while weighted warp threads hung over the cross-member (shed-rod) in front and behind. The gap between the two sets of threads, the shed, was where the weft passed; the back threads were attached to a movable bar (heddle rod) which could bring them forward, creating a new shed for the weft to be passed back through. For the simplest kinds of weaving ('tabby', where each thread passes under and over its neighbours) a single heddle rod can be used, but for more complex patterns ('twill', where the weft passes over or under more than one warp thread) two may be needed.

Too little fabric survives for any regional patterning to be determined, but it is nevertheless likely that districts, villages and families had their own preferred patterns and methods which would mark them out from others. Deep colours and bold patterns seem likely, on the evidence of the geometric manuscript decoration which seems to follow the same general design tradition, although the fabric colours would not have had the intensity of modern chemical dyes. There is evidence for the use of metallic thread as a high-status insert in some grave-goods, especially fine gold wire. At the Taplow barrow, traces of gold thread were discovered which were presumably part of a woven fabric.

Weaving seems to have been strongly associated with females[1] until the very end of the Anglo-Saxon period.

Archaeological traces of textiles are rare, but the mineral replacement of textile threads in corrosion contexts is quite common: many shields, spears and other iron items bear the imprint of long-decayed fabric wrappings and bindings. Elsewhere, only exceptional conditions – such as waterlogging – allow such fugitive material to survive. The details of most of the textiles placed in the Sutton Hoo Mound 1 ship-burial are lost beyond recovery.[2] There are a few areas where the textiles have been preserved in the corrosion products of adjacent metal objects, allowing archaeologists to make some deductions about the nature of the fabric which was spread over the floor of the burial chamber, or placed in neat piles alongside the other rare goods. There are also a few scraps surviving intact, where they had been carefully folded and were protected by the articles laid above them.

The most costly textiles were found to contain traces of colouring from natural dyestuffs, giving blue-black, deep red and yellow. Some items are suspected of having been wall-coverings, floor-coverings, cloaks, fringed borders, fine linen, cushion covers and various clothing-type fabrics in tabby and twill weaves. The surviving fragments of seaming show that the workmanship was exceptionally skilful.

---

[1] The surname 'Weaver' is from OE *wefere* while the alternative 'Webster' is from OE *webbestre* 'female weaver'.
[2] Care Evans, 1986

Clothing

The precise details of Anglo-Saxon dress cannot be recovered using present techniques.[1] Assumptions can be made about what some items of clothing may have looked like, based on the materials used and the places where they were fastened. While it is possible to use manuscript evidence to some extent, it is certainly the case that illustrations could be copied by successive generations of artists and the clothing depicted in any scene may therefore not be contemporary with the manuscript in which the picture is found; equally, sometimes the model illustration used was not Anglo-Saxon, and therefore the opportunities for misunderstanding are multiplied.

There are eight possible forms of female dress known from the pagan period grave material, using one to three brooches in various positions on the upper body. Some female costume included wrist-clasps, which are closely linked to the dress of the Anglian homelands in Jutland, and to southern Norway. For male costume, fastenings consisted of buckles and sleeve-fasteners. It is, however, dangerous to assume that people were invariably buried with the clothes they normally wore.[2]

The relative costliness of a piece of textile can be roughly assessed based on the density of its weave, with the following ranking:[3]

Weave	Threads per cm (warp and weft)	
very coarse	<5	
coarse	6-8	Not surface finished, typical household output
medium	9-12	
fine	13-18	Surface finished (felted) made from well-combed wool
very fine	>18	

Density is not always evenly distributed, so that it is possible to have more warp threads than weft or vice versa in a piece of very coarse or coarse cloth; a ratio of 2:1 is not uncommon.

---

[1] Arnold, 1997

[2] Many graves show no surviving fasteners of any kind: were their clothes fastened with wooden or bone buttons (which do occasionally occur), or with pins? Or were the garments simply tied off, being intended specifically for burial?

[3] Based on Tidow, 2000 whose evidence is gathered from across northern Europe.

Chapter Four

The range of colours available to Anglo-Saxon dyers was quite varied, but the majority of dyestuffs were vegetable-based; some animal-based (e.g. the murex shell) and mineral-based (e.g. crushed lapis lazuli) pigments were used in the period in the decoration of manuscripts but these are unsuitable as dyestuffs.[1] Comparatively deep, rich colours can be obtained from a variety of plants but there may have been problems with fading due to exposure to light and harsh weather; this could be partially overcome by using a mordant (fixative) such as salt, urine, tree bark, wood ash, iron rust, galls and crab apple juice;[2] these substances also affect the hue of the finished product. Club moss (diphasium complanatum), a natural source of alum, was used much as refined alum is today for this purpose.

Saffron was probably not grown in England until the very end of the Anglo-Saxon period; it gives a bright orange to yellow colour. A similar hue could be achieved using weld (dyer's rocket, reseda luteola), which can give results varying from pale lemon to dark brown.

Woad (isatis tinctoria) could give a strong blue, ranging from midnight blue to cornflower. The preparation of the dyestuff was difficult and foul-smelling, involving both fermentation and urine, but the long-lasting results made it a common crop plant in Anglo-Saxon England.

Madder (rubia tinctorum) is the source of a deep red to purple dyestuff and may be the plant called *wrætt* in Old English sources. It is not native to Britain, but may have been introduced in Roman times; grown in northern climes it is a poor dyestuff, and it is likely that well-connected Anglo-Saxons would have purchased a better quality product from the Mediterranean area. The middle of the root is used in dyeing, and the hue of the final colouring depends on the temperature of the water, with too hot a bath producing a paler result.

Black could be produced from a strong application of woad or weld over brown or black wool, or by using the bark of oak or plum, or even the fruit of the bramble, or walnut husks.

The leaves of gale were used to extract a yellow dye, while heather, ash bark and woad were all valued for their medical and colouring properties.[3]

It is also possible that plain, light woollen fabric could be dyed with a succession of different dyestuffs to produce a richer effect – for example, using a madder bath to give a red hue followed by a woad bath for a deep blue. It is known that a green hue was made by first dying with dyer's greenweed (genista tinctoria) followed by woad. The embroiderers of the Bayeux 'tapestry' used only four colours in their compositions: blue, red, yellow and green on the creamy natural

---

[1] M. Wilson, pers.comm..

[2] Messent, 1999

[3] Pollington, 2000

linen background colour. Different skeins of thread have taken the pigments with slight variation, leaving a range of final tones, and it is certain that variations in the water, temperature and number of dye-baths have also affected the colouring;[1] fading over the intervening centuries has caused the deep blue-black to lighten to a more median hue.

Linen does not take natural dyes well, and may have been left bleached but not further coloured. Silk was among the more expensive imports in Anglo-Saxon times, and could never have been common. It is not known whether the Anglo-Saxons attempted to dye lengths of silken cloth, or whether they imported made-up coloured articles.

Many people would have had clothing made from undyed fabric. They need not have been entirely plain, since variations in the natural colour of wool offer a range of shades from creamy white through to a very dark brown. Threads of different natural colours could be used in weaving to produce a pattern in the cloth.[2]

It is possible that textiles, clothing and the associated fittings may have been decorated in ways which conveyed meaning to the viewer – social status, wealth and religious affiliation would be among the most obvious. For example, people of the 'unfree' ranks may have been denied the use of certain styles of clothing, or restricted in the colours they could wear, as was the case in contemporary Irish society.[3] Wealth could be displayed through fine cloth, expensive decoration and carefully-made metal fittings. Religion could be displayed by the use of cross- and fish-based designs for Christians; that pagans might have zoomorphic designs based on totemic animals is at least a possibility, especially as such patterns do occur in the metalwork.

---

[1] Length of dye-time is only a factor if the time is very short; once the wool has completed its uptake of the dye, leaving it longer has no effect on the colour. (M. Wilson, pers.comm.)

[2] It is understood that the heavy coloration of the darker wool-types was already being selectively bred out of European sheep in the pre-Roman Iron Age. This process was intended to produce lighter coloured fleeces, which would more readily accept dyeing with vegetable-based dyestuffs. Anglo-Saxon period archaeological evidence indicates that fine and medium hairy types were desired, with a preference for fine wool at high-status sites (e.g. Sutton Hoo). Evidence from West Stow suggests that British livestock were retained by the Anglo-Saxons and imported livestock – if there ever were any – were bred out. Comparison between Anglo-Saxon yarn from England and Anglian material from Angeln shows that the Anglian material is coarser. British wool exports were noted already in the pre-Roman period, and the sheep may have been kept more for its milk and wool than for its meat in this period. (M. Wilson, pers.comm..)

[3] See Puhvel, 1987 for wider-ranging references to the three colours of ancient European societies: white for priests, red for warriors, blue/green for farmers and craftsmen.

Chapter Four

Female Dress

Typical female costume seems to have comprised: a shift or undergarment; a tubular or T-shaped dress, secured at one or both shoulders with a pin or brooch; a cloak, also secured at the shoulder or throat; a head-rail or headscarf to cover the hair. Some dresses appear to have been open-fronted as they required an additional brooch to secure them, and had split sleeves; they may have been worn over a sleeved under-dress. A girdle at the waist often carried a range of items: a pouch or bag; a set of iron keys or hangers; a small knife; accessories such as a magnifying-glass or sewing kit. Hose and shoes are depicted in manuscript illustrations.

Brooches were used as dress-fasteners, and a detailed typology has been established which is helpful in determining changing fashions and regional distribution patterns at various periods. Many of the early examples are brightly coloured (polychrome brooches) or very reflective due to gilding. Other items of jewellery included festoons of brightly-coloured beads worn on the chest between brooches, often incorporating metal pendants; this style appears to be phased out with the introduction of Christianity. Pendants could also be worn singly, most commonly Roman coins (or imitations) in the pagan period. Simple metal arm-bands or bracelets are also found, decorated with geometric punched designs. Finger rings of various designs may have been quite common, but are associated with rich burials in the pagan period. Hair- or headrail pins were worn at the temples, sometimes decorated with a small metal tag to catch the light. There is some evidence for a head-band or fillet, passing round the head from brow to nape, used to tie up the hair on the back of the head; however, a headrail was more common.

Late in the Anglo-Saxon period, women's dress was influenced by Scandinavian styles and other fashions. Large flat silver brooches became popular, often bearing decoration in Ringerike and other Scandinavian art styles, and the so-called 'nummular brooches' based on coin designs. Viking women traditionally wore an overgarment with straps at the shoulders, secured by two domed 'tortoise brooches', although this fashion died out by the 11th century. The kerchief hair-binding typical of Scandinavian women gave way to a small silk or linen cap.

Disc-headed pins flourished in the 9th century but disappeared by the 10th. A kind of short cloak or shawl appears in the manuscript art of the 11th century, as well as a hooded, sleeveless outergarment and a lower leg-binding similar to those used by men.

Male Dress

Typical basic male dress comprised a shirt or tunic, knee-length and closed at the neck; narrow trousers drawn in tight at the waist; a cloak ; socks[1] and shoes. A belt – of fabric, braid or leather – secured with a buckle of bone, copper-alloy or iron was apparently common.

In general, English males displayed wealth and status by adorning their women. Male display seems most often to have been confined to weapons and belt-sets, with the exception of the occasional high-status piece of regalia such as the garnet and gold shoulder-clasps from Sutton Hoo. Cloak-pins are illustrated in manuscript art, usually clasped at the right shoulder to leave the sword-arm free.

Belt furniture may be as simple as a copper-alloy buckle, but there are many finds from pagan graves of additional items such as decorated plates and stiffeners. Small metal objects identified as strap-ends are among the commonest metal-detector finds from the Anglo-Saxon period: being relatively heavy compared with the two-rivet fixtures, they were probably easily lost. A knife hung from the belt was part of the costume of a significant proportion of men in the pagan period, and occasional finds indicate that the leather sheaths were elaborately tooled and decorated.[2]

Hats and hoods do not figure greatly in the Anglo-Saxon tradition, with little pictorial evidence and no real archaeological remains. Apparently Anglo-Saxon men took great trouble over the appearance of their hair and beards – judging by the finds of combs, tweezers and small shears in pagan graves – which may have discouraged the use of headgear (other than helmets) for display. Large and bushy moustaches are depicted in the early metalwork, but are still a feature of the English warriors shown on the Bayeux tapestry. Pointed felt caps were certainly in use in Jutland at a time before the Anglii transferred political power out of that region; likewise, small pillar-box hats were seemingly part of the standard military dress of the late Roman Empire.

Male jewellery is almost confined to the occasional bead at the throat in grave-goods, although the literary records emphasise arm-rings as part of the warrior's reward. Finger rings are known from archaeological finds, some bearing the name of a male owner – for example, the 9th century gold ring from Lancashire bearing the inscription 'Ædred owns me, Eanred engraved me'.[3]

---

[1] Socks could be made from fabric or the knotted thread technique known as 'naalbinding'; one early pair of trousers recovered from the Thorsbjerg bog, Denmark, had 'feet' sewn to the ends of the legs.

[2] Cameron, 2000

[3] Page, 1987, p.42; Page, 1999, fig.2. The inscription is in a mixture of Roman script (represented by capitals) and runes (represented by lower case letters): + æDRED MEC AH EAnRED MEC agROf. The almost random use of these character sets suggests a community able to read both formal, ecclesiastical and informal, secular texts.

Gloves (or mittens) are mentioned in the literary sources, although there are no known illustrations of the garment or surviving examples. Leather turn-shoes are found in exceptional conditions of water-logging at Anglo-Saxon and Viking sites; an alternative was the footwear known as a *swiftlere* or *slypescoh*, a 'slipper'.

By the late Anglo-Saxon period the manuscript evidence suggests a clear distinction between clerical and secular dress. As with female costume, the influx of Vikings led to changes in fashion for men, including the introduction of large, showy penannular brooches with exaggerated pins and 'thistle' heads. Kings and dignitaries are shown wearing long gowns, probably in imitation of Byzantine imperial costume. Royalty is sometimes shown with an elaborate form of cross-gartering on the lower leg, but generally men seem to have had a length of tape or cloth strip wound tightly from below the knee to the ankle.

Remarkable fragments of presumed clerical vestments were discovered in the tomb of St. Cuthbert in Durham Cathedral.[1] Two were pieces of cream weft-patterned silk, another was a plain green tabby silk used as a seam binding. A weft-faced twill silk in purple and yellow was used as a seam binding and as a facing, while a strip of braid with Soumak brocading decorated the edges of the garment. It is likely that the garment was a dalmatic, and was presented to the saint posthumously in the 8th century (Cuthbert died in 687). It is of Anglo-Saxon manufacture, and the decoration of the Soumak braid takes the form of purple palmettes on a pale blue background alternating with a red and yellow heart shape on a tan background, with borders of dark red crossed with bars of blue, purple and yellow between dark red outlines. The basic braid was made by tablet-weaving, with blanket stitch embroidery and cording. A fragment of similar manufacture was held in the abbey of St. Peter, Salzburg, Austria.[2]

Table Linen, Tapestry & Embroidery

Tablecloths, possibly of fine linen, are referred to in 9th century sources and they may have been common in many of the better-equipped Anglo-Saxon households. Words used for this item include *beodclað* or *bordclað* 'board-cloth', *beodhrægl* 'board-covering', *beodreaf* 'board-coat', *beodscyte* 'board-sheet'. An item called a *cneorift* 'knee-cloth' was presumably similar to a modern napkin used to cover the lap while eating.[3]

Wallhangings were known as *burreaf* 'bower-cloth', *heallreaf* 'hall-cloth', *heallwahrift* 'hall-wall-garment', *pæll* 'pall, hanging', *waghrægl* 'wall-covering'. Curtains, mounted to be opened or closed, were known as *scufhrægl* 'shove-covering'.

---

[1] Webster, 1991 item 100
[2] Webster, 1991 142
[3] Hagen,1992

Food and Feasting Equipment

The full mediaeval table spread involved four seperate items: a *frontal* which covered the table-top and hung down to the floor on the side away from the diners; a long cloth which covered the table-top and reached to the floor at both sides; a covering cloth, large enough to cover the table-top with a small overhang on all four sides; a narrow draw-cloth, which was laid in front of the diners and on which stood bread, small bowls, goblets and so on. The draw-cloth was withdrawn along with all the crumbs and leftovers once the main courses had been served.[1] Manuscript illustrations of diners from the Anglo-Saxon period do not show anything quite so complex. However, the diners at Bosham in the early Bayeux Tapestry feasting scene (page 40) are shown from the waist up, suggesting that their legs were not normally visible at table (perhaps due to a cloth, similar to a frontal, having been used). In the later scene, where an *al fresco* banquet is underway at Hastings, the servants laying out food on shields have their legs clearly shown (Fig.22), while at the high-status table to their right, the waist-up convention prevails. These artistic conventions do suggest that some form of table covering extending to the floor in front of the table was the norm.

Fig.22 Norman servants preparing a meal and serving it on a makeshift sideboard formed from shields. The Normans have just landed at Pevensey Bay, Sussex, and their cooks have prepared a meal. The servant, left, is carrying spitted fowl to a trestle. The man second from right is summoning the diners with his horn. Scene from the Bayeux Tapestry, redrawn by Lindsay Kerr.

---

[1] Hartley, 1979

Chapter Four

There are a few literary references to tapestries or wall-hangings from the Anglo-Saxon period, which are brought to life by the scraps of surviving fabric and the marvellous post-Conquest embroidery known as the Bayeux Tapestry.

In *Beowulf* we read that the walls shone with textile adornments (*goldfag scinon web æfter wagum* 'gold-fair shone the weavings along the wall' 1.994-5). Weapons also may often have hung ready on pegs along the walls, since the poet envisioned, in the fight with Grendel's mother, that Beowulf could snatch a sword from its wall-hanging:

> *ac me geuðe ylda waldend*
> *þæt ic on wage geseah wlitig hangian*
> *ealdsweord eacen ...*

> but the ruler of men granted to me
> that I saw hanging on the wall a splendid
> mighty ancient sword ....
> *Beowulf*, 1.1661-3

This the hero used to despatch the demoness. Keeping their weapons to hand is something warriors must learn early on if they are to survive. For practical purposes it must have been necessary to keep the larger items of war-gear flat against the walls, thus freeing up the central area for ceremony and dining. We read in *The Ruin* (1.32-4) that

> *.... Þær iu beorn monig*
> *glædmod 7 goldbeorht gleoma gefrætwed*
> *wlonc 7 wingal wighyrstum scan*

> ...where before many a warrior
> light-hearted and gold-bright, adorned with splendour
> proud and wine-merry shone in his war-coat

with the implication that men might wear their armour to the feast. It does not seem likely that spears would be deployed at table, and indeed we have the testimony of *Beowulf* that larger weapons had to be left at the door. As the party of Geats leave the shore and approach Heorot, we read:

> *Stræt wæs stanfah stig wisode*
> *gumum ætgædere. Guðbyrne scan*
> *heard hondlocen, hringiren scir*
> *song in searwum, þa hie to sele furðum*
> *in hyra gryregeatwum gangan cwomon.*
> *Setton sæmeþe side scyldas,*
> *rondas regnhearde, wið þæs recedes weal,*

bugon þa to bence. Byrnan hringdon,
guðsearo gumena; garas stodon,
sæmanna searo, samod ætgædere,
æscholt ufan græg; wæs se irenþreat
wæpnum gewurþad.

The street was stone-fair, it showed the way
for the warriors together. The war-coat shone -
hard, hand-locked, the bright ringed-iron
sang within the armour when to hall they
came walking in their fearsome array.
The sea-weary men set down their broad shields -
mighty-hard defences – against the hall's wall,
they bent down to the bench. Their byrnies rang -
warriors' war-gear; their spears stood –
the weapons of the seamen – all together
an ash-thicket grey at the top; that iron-clad troop was
honoured with weapons.
Beowulf, l. 320-31

However, from *Egils saga* we learn that shields did form wall-decorations,[1] at least at one splendid Scandinavian feast:

Konungr hafði nærr .ccc. manna er hann kom til veizlunnar en Þórólfr hafði firi .v. hundrut manna. Þórólfr hafði látið búa kornhloðu mikla er þat var ok latið leggja becki í ok lét þar drecka þvíat þar var engi stofa svá mikil er þat fjolmenni mætti allt inni vera. Þar voro ok fester skilldir umhverfiss í húsinu.

The king had nearly three hundred men when he came to the feast, and Thorolf had a further five hundred men. Thorolf had had prepared a large corn-barn that was there, and had benches laid out, and held the drinking there because there was no hall so large that all the followers could get inside. There were shields fixed around the walls in the house.

How was the shield fixed to the wall? Two possible means are suggested, both involving pegs on the wall itself. One would involve sliding the shield's hand-grip over the peg. The other involves a loop of thong or cord secured to the grip, allowing the shield to hang freely. Both these solutions would make the shield project outwards at an angle from the wall. However, the small transverse strap

---

[1] Text from Brink1996.

Chapter Four

on the rear of the Sutton Hoo shield would have solved the problem neatly, allowing the shield to hang from near the rim rather than from the central grip.[1]

Fabric-making and embroidery were noted skills of English women in Anglo-Saxon times, for which they were famed throughout Christendom.[2] Groups of women worked at their frames on long trestle tables, where the textile base already had the design laid out in feint lines, drawn out on parchment pierced with tiny pinholes and through which lampblack was pressed onto the surface of the linen. Daylight would have been the preferred source of illumination although both tallow candles and rush lights were in use. The embroiderers used simple tools: small shears; a reel for the thread in use; needles of different lengths, thicknesses and material (antler, bone, iron, copper alloy); a heated slick-stone and board, usually a smooth pebble or glass block, for smoothing out creases.

The base fabric was linen, which was prepared by retting, beating, combing and spinning; bleached linen was produced by stretching it over tenter frames and exposing it to sunlight. The linen fabric background would be stretched onto the embroidery frame and fastened in place; the embroiderers could then work in pairs from opposite sides. The design was put in using outline stitch, then many of the internal areas filled with laidwork, with long parallel stitches held with couching and stab-stitches; chain stitch and stem stitch were also used. Blocks of colour were laid in using this technique.

Due to limitations in the size of loom that could be worked by one team, it was sometimes necessary to join together several lengths of cloth to complete the finished article – the Bayeux 'tapestry' was made up from eight separate pieces, each 18-20" inches (45-50 cm) in width, with a combined length of about 240' (73.25m). The joints were accomplished with flat or run-and-fell seams, and were so carefully executed as to be nearly invisible.

---

[1] Stephenson, 2002
[2] Messent, 1999

5 Positions of Power

The range of participants at a feast is not recorded and may never have been fixed. While we may safely assume that every household had a 'lord' (since its political existence depended on this fact), and an important, leading female (not necessarily wife to the lord), it need not have been the case that every household was structured along exactly the same lines. Some wealthy households may have had several stewards, each with specific duties, while in more modest groups these tasks may have fallen on fewer shoulders.

There are a number of job titles described as –*þegn* which are connected to the running of the household generally. Some of these, as noted below, will have had specific duties in relation to the safe and successful operation of a *symbel*.

Service in the hall was under the control of a *healþegn* 'hall-thane' or steward, whose duties could be subdivided into a range of individual jobs: *ærnþegn* 'building-thane', *bedþegn* 'bed-thane' *boldweard* 'housekeeper', *burcniht* 'bedchamber-boy' *burþegn* 'bedchamber-thane', *byrele* 'cup-bearer', *ceacbora* 'jug-bearer', *dihtnere* 'manager, arranger', *discberend* 'dish-bearer', *discþegn* 'dish-thane', *fadiend* 'arranger', *fætfyllere* 'vessel-filler', *hlafbrytta* 'bread-distributor', *hofweard* 'building-keeper', *hordestre* 'stewardess', *horsþegn* 'horse-thane', *hræglþegn* 'clothing-thane', *hundwealh* 'dog-attendant', *leohtbora* 'light-bearer', *meteþegn* 'food-thane', *rædesmann* 'adviser', *scohþen* 'shoe-thane', *seleþegn* 'hall-thane', *stiweard* 'hall-keeper'.

An estate was also expected to have a headman or *gerefa* (reeve) who was responsible for its day-to-day running, meeting its tax obligations and equipping it adequately for this purpose. A variant term *æfgerefa* glosses Latin *exactor* and refers to a tax collector; alternatives are *tungerefa* 'estate-reeve' and *feohgerefa* 'money-reeve'.

There are many words for 'servant' or 'hired man' in Old English – *ambiht, ambihtscealc, arþegn, esne, gesiþ, medwyrhta, þeningmann, þeow, þeowtling*. Some appear to have been terms of some status (*gesiþ* 'fellow traveller, companion') while others denoted grades little above the unfree (*esne* 'hireling', *þeowtling* 'little servant'). A body of men assembled to provide service was a *þeningwerod* 'service-troop'. The company of persons associated with one estate was called its *inhiwan*.

While little is known for sure of the specific duties of the feast officers, and much of our information is taken from a handful of poems, the following appear to have been the usual participants at an early English *symbel*.

Lord (Hlaford)

The 'lord' in this text means the householder who has arranged the feast, without distinction between kings, earls, ealdormenn, thanes and other ranks, all of whom may have been sufficiently wealthy and important within their own communities to decide on the expenditure of the time, energy and resources needed for such an event. In the *OE Rhyming Poem*, the lord says *secgas me segon symbel ne alegon feorgiefe gefegon* "men looked at me, the feasts did not fail, they were glad of the gift of life". Being the centre of attention at a large public gathering was part of the duty of lordship.

The word 'lord' is derived from the OE word *hlaford*, which is a compound noun based on *hlaf* + *weard* 'loaf + keeper'. The lord was responsible for conserving the food supply, ensuring that there was enough to go round. In times of hardship this duty may have meant that all had to go hungry in order that the community survive. Yet the symbolic position of *hlaford* was 'provider of food' to a hungry and grateful workforce.

One important aspect of lorship was that of constantly projecting the image of power and prestige, through regalia and ceremony. It is stated by Bede that King Edwin of Northumbria was preceded on foot wherever he went in peace and war by a standard or ensign called in Latin a *tufa* and in English a *thuuf*. It was apparently noteworthy that a king's presence should always be manifested in this way. Exactly what constituted a *thuuf* is not known. It is nevertheless possible to speculate: at Yeavering a curious wooden object was found in a 7th century grave,[1] damaged and only partially recoverable but not beyond all conjecture. It consisted of a wooden shaft with cylindrical bronze bindings, with a pointed iron spike at either end. At one end, three (of a presumed original four) short wooden arms protrude, one on each face, beneath a thick bronze feature with wires ending in spherical pellets. This may originally have been a zoomorphic decorative mount, and the wire and pellets possibly part of the figure's decoration. The whole construction resembles a Roman *vexillum* (military standard), although it could conceivably have been a form of *groma*, a surveying instrument used to lay out accurate right-angles. (Yeavering's highly accomplished design and construction must have been masterminded by a skilled and experienced overseer.)

It is an attractive possibility that the wrought iron "standard" form Sutton Hoo mound 1, surmounted by bovine heads looking outwards, might be the kind of symbolic staff Bede had in mind when he mentioned the *thuuf*. The purpose of this item has never been determined, although some form of display seems to be a recurrent theme. The object would have served quite well as a rack for the war-

---

[1] Hope-Taylor, 1977: 'A note on the possible nature and implications of the wooden object in Grave AX'

troop's spears and weapons,[1] but if this were its use it remains a mystery why the spears were placed separately in the grave.

Lady (Hlafdige)

The lady of the mead-hall is depicted in the poetry as the epitome of the hostess: gentle, loving, solicitous and wise -

> ..... medorædenne
> for gesiðmægen symle æghwær
> eodor æþelinga ærest gegretan
> forman fulle to frean hond
> ricene geræcan 7 him ræd witan
> boldagendum bæm ætsomne
>
> .... In the mead-dealing
> before the troop of fellow-travellers at every time and place
> [she must] first greet the stronghold of noblemen,[2]
> to her lord's hand the first cup
> eagerly reach out, and offer advice to him
> [being] hall-rulers both together.
> Maxims I, l. 87-92

As part of the general air of nobility and refined behaviour at the feast, the lady plays an important role in supervising the distribution of food and, especially, drink. Wealhþeow, King Hroþgar's queen, replaces the serving-thane in the *Beowulf* feasting episode referred to above (l. 491-500) and in so doing she represents the 'official' household in all her actions. Her offering of drink to the lord and his warriors follows a set ritual pattern, indicating in its order the relative ranking of all those present.

To command respect for her position she is decked out in finery: *goldhroden* 'gold-adorned', *beaghroden cwen* 'a ring-adorned queen'. The badge of her rank appears to have been the so-called girdle-hanger, a long flat copper-alloy object which was hung from the belt and was elaborately decorated with stamped motifs. It is suggested that these were intended as symbolic 'keys', and that possession of them displayed both free status and the position of 'female head of household'. They are not uncommon in pagan period female graves.[3] The symbolism is that of key-holding, specifically the keys to locked rooms and

---

[1] P. Mortimer, pers.comm..
[2] *eodor æþelinga* 'hall of princes' is a circumlocution: it refers to 'what protects noblemen' which is, naturally, their leader.
[3] Fell, 1984

Chapter Five

chests. Having control of her own property, the lady is able to make gifts on her own account. The keys also gave access to the lord's hoard, and even after her husband's death a lady might retain control of the finances[1] and the treasury.

In many ways, the descriptions of the *válkyrjar* (valkyries) of Norse tradition, and of the goddesses Frigg and Freyja give an indication of the ideal hostess, welcomer of guests, bearer of cups, source of hospitality.

The lady's public acts and speeches are supportive of her husband, without necessarily agreeing totally with his opinions – she is *wisfæst wordum* 'prudent in words'. She is at all times courteous and polite, even when she needs to argue her own case. Her valuable input to discussions of policy is important for the lord to heed.[2] Her prophetic powers are mentioned by Tacitus, and the female-dominated craft of weaving is used metaphorically for the spinning of men's fates and the magical and runic arts.[3] Women's work centred on baking, brewing and weaving – all means of production rather than resource acquisition.

In one area women were acknowledged to be especially important: prophecy. The noblewoman, mistress of the hall, was also the 'cunning woman', the person responsible for foretelling the future of the group. This aspect of her role may have been crucially important in pre-Christian times, when the results of her prophecy could mean peace or war, friendship or feud. Tacitus[4] specifically mentions that the Germanic folk of his day were accustomed to heed the prophecies of women, and he mentions two examples: Veleda, who assisted Civilis in his Batavian revolt, and Aurinia, of whom nothing else is known.[5] In Christian times, such women were often ascetics whose powers were attributed to divine grace.[6] It is suspected that entheogens (narcotic or hallucinatory substances) were often involved in freeing the seeress's spirit, and indeed the Anglo-Saxon medical tradition recognises many herbal substances with such properties.

There are only a few named female characters in *Beowulf* – the noblewomen Hygd, Wealhþeow, Freawaru and Hildeburh, and the monstrous *Grendles modor* ('Grendel's mother'). One further character is the problematic Þryþ (or Modþryþ,

---

[1] Enright cites the case of Balthild, widow of Clovis II of the Franks who continued to nourish the young men and to hand out rich gifts of gold and silver, according to the *Vita Balthildis*. Balthild was allegedly an Englishwoman who rose to the rank of Queen of Francia; a curious signet ring bearing her name was found at Norwich in 1998.

[2] Enright, 1996

[3] Tacitus, *Germania*, ch.8; Enright, 1996, p.111ff.

[4] Tacitus, *Germania*, ch.8.

[5] The name is spelt *Aurinia* in all manuscripts, but some note the variant *Albrinia*, which has led some commentators to suggest that the original may have been *Albruna* 'elf-rune'. It has to be said that, attractive though this idea may be, it is not supported by any evidence. See Rives, 1999, p.153-5

[6] Examples would include Hildegard von Bingen and Birgitta of Sweden. See Waegeman, 1998.

the manuscript is difficult to interpret at this point). Modþryþ appears as a model of ignoble and unwomanly traits: she is headstrong, vengeful, violent and irrational. Her appearance in the poem presents an opportunity to contrast these undesirable and anti-social qualities with the noble grace and good humour of the main female characters. It comes as no surprise that her behaviour is reformed when she meets the masterful Offa whom she weds: social customs and communal values are re-affirmed in the face of delinquency.

A handful of women in Old English verse do not conform to the social roles allocated to them. They stand outside – physically or emotionally – the duties and constraints of the community and its value system. One such is the outcast of *The Wife's Lament*, another the yearning, lovesick adulteress of *Wulf & Eadwacer*. However, for most women, the source of their power lies in their fertility; without them, the human societies which the males protect and promote are doomed to extinction. Women given in marriage also retain a close relationship with their blood kindred, and their children benefit from this. The closest relationship in Germanic society generally is that of maternal uncle to nephew (mother-brother : sister-son) which has important social ramifications.[1]

A young woman was to some extent in control of her future in Anglo-Saxon society, and could choose her partner (or rather, could not be forced to marry against her will). This social right may lie behind this difficult passage in *Maxims II* in the Exeter Book:

> ... ides sceal dyrne cræfte
> fæmne hire freond gesecan gif heo nelle on folce geþeon
> þæt hi man beagum bicge.....

> ... through secret craft a lady,
> a girl must seek her lover - if she does not wish to prosper so among
> the people
> that a man betrothe her with rings ...

or alternatively

> ... through secret craft a lady
> a girl must seek a lover if she cannot prosper among the people
> so that a man betrothes her with rings
> > *Maxims II, l.43-5*

The two interpretations rest on whether the phrase *gif heo nelle on folce geþeon* implies that she is of bad reputation and so is not eligible for marriage, or whether it means that she does not want to be thought eligible because she wishes

---

[1] Haymes, 1998; Pollington, 2002

to continue meeting her (unsuitable?) lover in secret. The 'secret craft' might imply some magical means to bind a man to her.

The lady has a duty to advise her husband to the best of her ability, yet he appears to have no corresponding duty to heed her advice. After the death of the lord – as in the case of Hygd in *Beowulf* – the widowed lady is suddenly in a position of power. She has a responsibility to protect the interests of her young son (as does Wealhþeow at Hroþgar's court) and to ensure continuity of leadership in the community, to which end she offers the role of leader to the warrior most likely, in her judgement, to be able to protect and preserve the status quo without endangering her own line. She expects that the warband will honour her wishes and respect her judgement: *þegnas syndon geþwære þeod ealgearo druncne dryhtguman doð swa ic bidde* (l.1230-1) "the thanes are in agreement, the folk prepared, the drink-bound warriors do as I ask". Enright[1] cites parallels from Lombard history which demonstrate quite convincingly that a respected lady was trusted by the lord's followers to choose for herself a consort, with the aim of protecting the status quo and continuing the lord's policies; in other words, the lady was herself seen as the partial architect of the policies adopted. It is unlikely, though, that she could do more than persuade and argue, since her authority in the hall rested ultimately on that of her husband (or son, if he were the lord) and she must always have had to take that into account. Only a queen able to count entirely on the loyalty of the warband to her – possibly as regent for her adolescent sons – could afford to defy her husband or act with confidence after his death. In such a situation, the lady could even be used as the warband's spokesman to make their views known to the lord whom they had sworn to obey and defend (leaving them little room for manoeuvre if they needed to bargain with the lord over some course of action).

The church did not approve of the re-marriage of noblewomen to close kinsmen of their dead husbands, and Bede criticised Eadbald, King of Kent, who married his recently deceased father's bride (not his own mother!) in 616. Likewise, King Æðelberht of Wessex (elder brother of King Ælfred) married his father's widow to the horror of Ælfred's biographer, the Welsh cleric Asser. The motives of the bereaved are not easy to determine, but among them would certainly have been preservation of the status quo – particularly in the case of a well-loved and respected lady – and the perhaps less romantic wish to keep the woman's dowry in the family. We know that noblewomen were often granted landholdings as a *morgengifu* ('morning gift' given by the groom to his bride on the first day of their marriage) and these would not necessarily be returned.[2] Likewise, many

---

[1] Enright, 1996, p.25 the ladies in question are Theudelinda of the Lombards and her daughter, Gundberga.

[2] The *morgengifu* of Byrhtnoð, a 10th century English ealdormann, consisted of many estates in the south east of England and East Anglia (Scragg, 1981). Typically, a *morgengifu* would also contain ancestral weapons of the husband's kindred, which the wife would hold in trust and would be presented to the heir on his achievement of adulthood. See Pollington, 2001.

marriages were politically motivated, and it would be folly for a folk newly weakened by the loss of its lord to insult an important ally by repudiating a member of his family.

As the key-holder accompanying the lord on his perambulations with part of the folk's treasure, it could be that the lady had access to the most worthwhile items. To secure her would then imply securing access to the *hord*, the stored wealth of the people. In all likelihood, her re-marriage to a suitable candidate would symbolise the acceptance by the warband of a new leader; her continued matriarchal role ensured the continuity of the group and the legitimacy of any succession arrangements.

The lady was apparently tasked with pursuit of family matters, especially those concerning honour and respect. Although the Anglo-Saxon evidence is thin, examples from Icelandic saga are legion of women whose nagging and constant provocation ensure that murderous feuds are perpetuated until the last man dies. Women were seemingly the 'measurers', the group who were able and expected to make comparisons between the men of the warband and the various kindred groups, who were quite able to use goading and quiet mockery to ensure that the family name was held in due respect.

Household (Hlafætan)

Enright contrasts the leader's title of 'bread-keeper' *hlafweard*, our word 'lord', with the name of the dependants *hlafætan* 'bread-eaters'.[1] Service in return for the basics of life must have been a commonplace form of social contract in Anglo-Saxon England. This is probably what lies behind the reference in Bede[2] to the luckless remnants of the Romano-British: *sume for hunger heora feondum on hand eodon 7 ecne þeowdom geheton wið ðon þe him mon andlyfne forgeafe* "some went into the hands of their enemies through hunger, and offered themselves into everlasting servitude in exchange for being given food".

It may be that when large numbers of military recruits were needed, a feast could be given at which the participants would be encouraged to bind themselves with oaths of service to the leader, as the example of Julius Civilis (below p.260) demonstrates. These 'bread-eaters' were therefore henceforth contractually dependant on the 'bread-keeper' for their sustenance.

---

[1] Hagen, 1992. The term occurs in the law-code of Ethelbert of Kent, dated 602-3, as the rank below the householder or '*ceorl*'.

[2] The OE version of Bede's *Historia Ecclesiastica Gentis Anglorum*, Book 1, Ch.15 on the arrival of the Angles, Saxons and Jutes

Þyle

The so-called "Unferþ Episode" from *Beowulf* – our best example of the usage of a *þyle* from Old English - is translated in Appendix 2.

The OE word *þyle* glosses Latin terms such as *orator* 'spokesman' and *scurra* 'satirist'. There is some confusion surrounding the proper interpretation of the word, for which our only evidence is the behaviour of Unferþ the *þyle* at Hroðgar's court in *Beowulf*. In the 'courtroom' analogy of the hall, the *þyle* appears as a kind of 'prosecutor' whose function it is to query and question the applicant's credentials and motives[1], almost as a devil's advocate. This probing of the evidence presented allows the leader to reach an informed decision about the course of action to be followed. Yet the person of Unferþ appears also to have an authority which might derive ultimately from a role in cult worship, making the spokesman the leader of group rituals.[2] Yet verbal duelling is a commonplace of heroic narrative in many cultures.[3]

The Scandinavian equivalent term *þulr* certainly denotes an association with religious tales and gnomic wisdom. A distant association with the Hittite word *talliya-* "propitiate the gods with formulaic speech" has also been suggested in this connection.[4] The basic sense seems to be the Germanic root **þul-* 'mumble, talk, sing, intone, chant'; a *þyle* could be an orator or a leader of rituals, but he might also be an entertainer or 'user of words' for specific purposes.[5]

Flyting and Verbal Duelling

Unferþ's behaviour jars a modern audience as unseemly, almost hostile towards a man who is about to risk life and limb on behalf of a community to which he has no personal ties (although there is a debt of honour through Beowulf's father). The closest analogues to "the Unferþ episode" as it is called, are in Norse literature where the tradition of *flyting*[6] is recorded, particularly the poem *Lokasenna* is the prime example, where the god Loki gatecrashes a feast of the gods, and proceeds to verbally abuse them each in turn. *Senna* – derived from *sannr* 'true' – is one such format; another is *mannjafnaðr* 'man-comparison'. Both have their origins in the Norse legal process.[7]

---

[1] Herschend, 1998; Enright, 1996

[2] Baird *Unferth the Þyle* cited in Gardner, 1975. On little more than conjecture, the office of *þyle* has been interpreted as 'priest of Woden' and thus 'troublemaker, inciter of enmity'. While stirring up warfare with his spear is an attribute of (mediaeval Icelandic) Oðinn, there is no good evidence that English Woden was viewed in this light.

[3] Parks, 1990

[4] Polome, 1982 cited in Pollington, 2001

[5] Brink, 1996

[6] Flyting is a mediaeval English term for verbal contesting between public speakers.

[7] Clover, 2000. A *senna* is an attempt to establish the truth of the accusation of guilt, while a *manjafnaðr* is an attempt to establish a murder victim's legal worth, and so his *wergield*.

A *flyting* is a verbal duel, an exchange of insults and taunts between hostile speakers. In literary contexts they are always in one of two locations: either the speakers are kept apart by a body of water, or they in a hall. In the former case, the taunts and threats are a substitute for physical violence. In hall-based contexts, the whole affair seems to be a drinking custom (ON *ölsiðr*) whereby comparisons between leading men would be drawn, deteriorating into vituperative exchanges.[1] (In the *Lokasenna* exchanges, Heimdall specifically accuses Loki of being drunk and unable to take proper care of his words.) The contenders take it in turns, and the exchanges are always directed at each other; though one man may take on a series of opponents, he must deal with each in turn.

The format of the duel is that Speaker 1 makes a claim about Speaker 2; Speaker 2 then defends the action mentioned, and issues his own counter-claim against Speaker 1. Typically, the speakers both use the other's given name in an attempt to make the claims personal and hurtful. The defence may or may not be an attempt to explain the claimed action, but more often it is a concessive 'that may be so, but ...' moving onto the counter-claim. The vocabulary and list of possible claims is rather narrow and always unheroic – cowardice, failure to fulfil a promise, failure to fulfil an honourable duty, trivial behaviour, sexual irregularities, breach of taboos. Most allegations centre on kinship in some way: incest, failure to exact vengeance for a kinsman, false dealings with kinsmen, and – for women – sexual relations with the killer of a kinsman. Defence would rely on asserting the speaker's virtuous qualities, such as strength, courage, adventurous spirit, dexterity or skill at arms; this would be followed by a jibe at the opponent's failings.

The winner of the flyting is not the most inventive or assertive, but the one who hits nearest the truth and produces a claim the opponent cannot deny or avoid. Goading an opponent into anger would guarantee victory, and this could be achieved by dragging out whatever skeletons he had in his cupboard. This was, indeed, the whole game: the speaker had to determine what Axel Olrik terms the "preliminary incident" in the opponent's life, and to put the worst possible interpretation on it. The simple truth – that the incident actually took place – is not disputed, it is in fact beyond dispute. Only the interpretation remains for the contenders to argue over.

Unferþ and The Role of the Þyle

When Unferþ decided to *onbindan beadurune* 'unbind a battle-rune' the audience of *Beowulf* knew what to expect, since they had already heard the poet leading up to a challenging exchange. This explains why Hroþgar did not intervene to stop

---

[1] A similar custom is possibly alluded to in the Old English poem *Vainglory* where bench-talk turns to spiteful arguing.

his spokesman from insulting his guest. Indeed, the guest knew in advance that the challenge would come, and was prepared for it. Unferþ decided to bring up Beowulf's youthful swimming match as an act of folly inappropriate for someone now wishing to be taken seriously as the Danes' defender. Unferþ also cast doubt on the outcome of the forthcoming fight. Beowulf's defence – that he won the contest despite being beset by sea-monsters, that it was not trivial but undertaken out of high spirits – put a different interpretation on the facts. His counter-claim was hard-hitting – while Beowulf was doing deeds of valour, Unferþ was skulking in the hall avoiding battle, but nevertheless was bold enough to kill his own brothers (a kindred-centred taunt). The clinching argument for Beowulf was that *if* Unferþ were in any way a hero, Grendel would not be able to raid Heorot. By implication, Beowulf intended to win where Unferþ had failed, making Beowulf the better man. Unferþ's silence was a concession of defeat in this game of words. For a *þyle*, a man whose function was to speak, falling silent was an act of surrender – like a warrior throwing down his weapons.

Poet (Scop)

The 'poet' or *scop* was a key figure in the cultural life of English communities. An alternative name was *gleoman* 'glee-man' which may mean a general entertainer, a singer and musician. The *scop* was not a mere 'wandering minstrel' but had a clear and crucially important function in the political and military culture of the time. The constant stream of praise for the lord from the warband's resident poet was a major part of the prestige underlying the leader's position. In a sense, the poet's position was not unlike that of the warrior:[1] both freely offer service to their lord; both receive valuables and honour at the lord's discretion; both are bound into a reciprocal relationship with the leader in which support is offered in return for honour and public praise. The *scop* could be a unifying figure for both the lower and upper hall-ends. His performance would engage all who were present, allowing praise of the leader to be delivered in an engaging and entertaining manner to the delight of the whole assembly.

The poet was not a mere entertainer, however; in pre-literate societies, it is customary for one person to act as the communal memory of the group, the custodian of their legends, myths and history, their traditions and folk-ways.[2] The poet may therefore fulfil a number of separate functions simultaneously, being:

- ❖ the semi-official voice of the people, the weathervane of public opinion;
- ❖ the ritual speaker whose job it is to offer up poems of worship to the gods, laments for the dead, mythic enactments and praise for the great and the good of the group;

---

[1] Bloomfield & Dunn, 1989
[2] Bloomfield & Dunn, 1989; Watkins, 1995

- ❖ the keeper of the tally of honour and shame for individuals within the group;
- ❖ the official entertainer and provider of diverting material when conversation flags or is inappropriate.

One theory suggests that the word *scop* is derived from the Germanic *skopon (which also gives rise to English *skip*) and refers to a priest-poet whose role including leading the company in a ritual dance. Alternatively, the term *scop* may have been generalised to incude the original 'minstrel' function, at the expense of the alternative term *woðbora* 'prophet; inspired person; poet; musician'.[1]

There appear to have been two main traditions or job opportunities for the poet: either to attach himself to a single leader and his following, or to lead the life of a traveller. Both choices could be risky: a resident court poet was only as good as his last song, and could be replaced if a more skilful contender appeared. This is the situation the poet Deor finds himself in:

þæt ic be me selfum secgan wille
þæt ic hwile wæs Heodeninga scop
dryhtne dyre – me wæs Deor noma –
ahte ic fela wintra folgað tilne
holdne hlaford oþþæt Heorrenda nu
leoðcræftig monn londryht geþah
þæt me eorla hleo ær gesealde.

I wish to say this about myself,
that for a while I was the *scop* of the Heodenings,
dear to my lord – my name was Deor –
for many winters I had a good living,
a loyal lord until now Heorrenda
the song-skilled man received the land-award
which the earls' protector gave me before.
Deor, 1.28-41

However, those poets who travelled from court to court risked their lives on the road, and their fortunes. For them, gifts of land or buildings would be less attractive and would have to be converted to *feoh*, portable wealth, which they could take with them on their journeying. In some respects poets of this kind must resemble merchants whose livelihood rests on being able to exploit the price differences for any commodity between different markets. The merchant in Ælfric's *Colloquy* stipulates that he takes trade items to foreign markets to sell

---

[1] See the discussion in Wickham-Crowley, 1992

them, and then buys articles there which he can sell more profitably at home. The peripatetic Germanic *scop* was likewise always on the move. The traffic in stories, songs, tales, riddles, gossip and news must have been two-way; at each court, the poet would hope to learn something to add to his repertoire while entertaining those present with material he had collected elsewhere. The *scop* was therefore able to bind together far-flung communities within Britain and indeed across northern Europe.[1] We know from *Widsið* that some of the events alluded to in his verse took place at a time after the initial settlement of Germanic migrants in Britain; likewise, the single known historical fact in *Beowulf* is the Scandinavian raid on the Low Countries which took place in 527 AD according to the contemporary writer, Gregory of Tours. Knowledge of such matters passed quickly round the Germanic-speaking world, and the likeliest vehicle for this information is the travelling story-tellers. Likewise the body of story, myth and legend which stands behind so much mediaeval literature – from *Beowulf* to the *Nibelungenlied* to the Icelandic sagas – is best explained through continued contact and exchange of information.

The love of poetry and legend did not die with the coming of the church, and the clergyman Alcuin was moved to ask *Quid Hinieldus cum Christo?* "What has Ingeld got to do with Christ?" in an attack on the secular tastes of his colleagues. The rhetorical question was aimed at Bishop Hygebald of Lindisfarne whose monks were not ready to turn their backs on their ancestral links.[2] Evans[3] notes Greenfield's suggestion that warbands may have deputised the position of *scop* on to one of their number. However, it seems more likely to conclude that wherever a capable military leader presented himself, a *scop* would never be far away. The transfer of political power among the leading families of the Angles from Jutland to eastern Britain would certainly have involved a court poet to record their victories and denigrate their enemies.

The similar tradition of court poets (*pencerdd, bardd teuleu*) among the British arises from the parallel nature of the warband traditions among these peoples. Gildas, the 6th century British clergyman, notably harangued the ruler Maelgwn for his refusal to listen to Christian doctrine, preferring instead to hear his bards singing his own praises.[4] The only two prominent bards of whom we know anything – Aneirin and Taliesin – were both court poets, although the latter is associated with more than one lord and may therefore have been an itinerant.

---

[1] It might be objected that no poet could possibly have command of all the necessary languages. However, there is good evidence for mutual intelligibility among the various Germanic languages until after the Anglo-Saxon period. See Moulton, 1988.

[2] Enright, 1996 suggests that Christian clergy were able to adapt heathen traditions of story-telling to their missionary ends. By the 9th century, however, the clerics were more secure in their position and maintained that all entertainments should have Christian, didactic purpose.

[3] Evans, 1997

[4] Evans, 1997, p.76

Although both the British and Germanic traditions of poethood seem to have been very similar, there is little evidence for integration among them. The influence of Old Welsh on Old English is generally negligible, outside a handful of geographical terms. Poets, it seems, stayed among their own folk and did not visit the halls of their neighbours if the inhabitants spoke a different idiom.[1]

It is a reasonable inference that *scopas* were useful to military leaders because the poets' verse praised them and supported their position. Beyond this, the verse itself carried with it a continuing tradition of virtue within the context of the *comitatus* – of bold heroes, of generous lords, of loyal retainers, of wise counsellors, of noble kings, of dignified women, of skilled poets, of fine weapons, of splendid feasts. By keeping these images continually in front of their men, the leaders were able to remind them of their part of the bargain, their duty to serve with heroic deeds. This emphasis on martial virtue was the underpinning of the lord's position as foremost man in the warband. It also gave credibility to the community's sense of identity.

The social standing of the poet was unique in his ability to manipulate reputations, yet the *scop* appears to have been a subordinate rather than a man of the highest ranks.[2] Despite the relatively large amounts of verse which survive, there is very little in the way of direct description of poets going about their work. Perhaps the clearest is the harp-player in *The Fortunes of Men* (1.80-4):

Sum sceal mid hearpan æt his hlafordes
fotum sittan feoh þicgan
7 a snellice snere wrestan
lætan scralletan sceacol se þe hleapeð
nægl neomegende biþ him nyd micel

One with his harp shall at his lord's
feet sit, receive wealth,
and ever swiftly pluck the string
let the plectrum which leaps be shrill,
the resounding nail – he shall have great delight

In *Widsið* we read of the speaker, a *scop*, who clearly enjoyed the rewards for his work:

forþon ic mæg singan 7 secgan spell
mænan fore mengo in meoduhealle
hu me cynegode cystum dohten

---

[1] It is possible that Cædmon's background may have been British (his name is Brithonic) but his life, as recorded, does not suggest that he was in any way connected to the well-developed poetic traditions of the Celtic-speaking peoples.

[2] Hagen, 1992, suggests that the guest called a 'foot-sitter' (*fotsetla*) in the Cambrtidge Thegns' Guild may have been a minstrel.

Chapter Five

> "thus I can sing and tell a tale,
> speak before the many in the mead-hall,
> how the nobles honoured me with treasures"
>
> *Widsið* 1.54-6

It is not clear to what extent the singer and the harpist could be separated in this period. Could the singer accompany himself on the harp? This is possible, and in the case of Caedmon it seems to be inevitable, but there are other indications that they worked in pairs – one singing, one playing - compare *Widsið*, 1.103-5, *ðonne wit Scilling sciran reorde for uncrum sigedryhtne song ahofan hlude bi hearpan hleoþor swinsade* "When Scilling and I with a bright voice raised a song for our victorious lord, loud with the harp the sound grew sweet."

The distinction between the formal declamation of *Widsið* in the halls of powerful kings and the rustic drinking-bout which Caedmon attended may account for the difference: a *scop* of great skill and renown would have his own harpist to accompany him.

The manner of the *scop*'s delivery is also unknown: it could have been forceful declamation, or melodic singing, or even some form of heavily rhythmic incantation. Acoustics may have played some part in the choice of style: on their return journey from Beowulf's adventure in the mere, the *scop* entertains the horse-borne travellers. In the hall we hear only of his use of harp and his address to all on the meadbench:

> *þær wæs sang ond sweg samod ætgædere*
> *fore Healfdenes hildewisan,*
> *gomenwudu greted, gid oft wrecen,*
> *ðonne healgamen Hroþgares scop*
> *æfter medobence mænan scolde*

> There was song and music both together
> Before the warleaders[1] of Healfdene,
> The play-wood was greeted, often a song was wrought
> When Hrothgar's scop along the meadbench
> Had to proclaim an entertainment in the hall.
>
> *Beowulf*, 1.1063-7

The extract from *Deor* above (p. 193) elaborates on the rewards of the poet's life, and the perennial threat of being surpassed. The poet could occupy the favoured position at the lord's feet, according to *The Fortunes of Men* (above, p.193).

---

[1] The phrase *Healfdenes hildewisan* may mean the warleaders who had fought with Healfdene, Hroðgar's father, or it may be a reference to Hroðgar himself as the champion of his father.

The presence of a court poet was an integral part of the aristocratic lifestyle. The *gleoman* of *Deor* seemingly had attached himself to a single court, and paid the price for being eclipsed by a rival, Heoden. Widsið, by contrast, seems to have enjoyed wandering the four corners of the earth with his harpist, Scilling, gaining many rewards and favours along the way.

The traditional forms of song included the *giedd*, a narrative, often sad or nostalgic in content; the *leoð*, another form of narrative song; the *folcræden*, or tribal traditions, customs and rules; the *domas*, judgements in law.[1]

A curious detail in the 12th century *Life of St Athelbert* records that the saint set off on a journey to the court of King Offa, and offered a gold bracelet to anyone who could perform *carmina regia* 'royal songs' which two of the company undertook to do, making verses about the Athelbert's royal ancestors. Such would fit in well with the subject matter of some existing verse, especially the *Battle of Brunanburh* for example.

Of humbler song-craft we know little or nothing. What were the songs which Caedmon's fellow drinkers normally sang in their hall? Did they deal with heroes and kings and battles? Or were they narrative tales from the folklore of the people? Were there stories of the world's making in English verse already, which Caedmon cleverly edited into a Christian narrative? It seems likely – the verse style is too technically well-executed to be a totally new departure. Yet nothing remains now to show for the labour of all the preceding centuries, save the highly-skilled craftsmanship of the Anglo-Saxon poetic corpus, built on the wit and invention of many generations.

Hall Attendants

Meteðegn

The *meteðegn* 'food-thane' appears to have had charge of the preparation of meals, though the serving of them was the responsibility of the *discþegn* 'dish-thane'. He was therefore in the role later known as steward or seneschal. Organising a *symbel* for a large number of people can have been no easy task – especially in an age when communication was by word of mouth, direct or through messengers – and the logistical skills needed to ensure everything was in the right place at the right time must have been uncommon. With what little we know of the food-rents of large estates, it may have been necessary to phase the supply chain so that food arrived for cooking or storage at suitable intervals. Having one man at the centre of this kind of operation would have been indispensable.

A different word *hlafbrytta* 'loaf-breaker' suggests an official in charge of distribution of bread among the household.

---

[1] Bloomfield & Dunn, 1989

Chapter Five

Discþegn

The *discþegn* apparently oversaw the kitchen staff in the serving of the meals. Food was served at table by youths and servants, who also had the duty of clearing away and cleaning the pans and utensils.[1] (Fig.4 p.58 & Fig.22 p.177) Servants are shown in manuscript illustrations kneeling before the diners, offering food on spits for the guests to take. It is possible that ranking among the servants dictated that the most proficient served the most honoured guests, and the least experienced waited on the lower end of the hall.

The privilege of sitting to eat with the lord did not extend to the *discþegn* and others who were at their busiest while the meal was in progress, ensuring the smooth running of the event and also preventing accidents.

The basic meaning of *þegn* is 'youngster, assistant' (cognate with Greek *teknos*). In early Scandinavian sources, *þegn* is contrasted with *drengr* with the respective meanings 'young man' and 'older man', both implying competence and capability. The words most often denote warriors, but the military aspect is easily overstressed when dealing with Scandinavian evidence from the Viking Age.[2] In late Anglo-Saxon England, *þegn* denoted a class of local landowners with specific privileges and responsibilities towards their workforce, not unlike the position of the knight in mediaeval times. A *þegn* was then one of a class of minor nobles and, as with so many forms of nobility, this arose from direct service in the lord's household.[3]

Byrele

The *byrele* was the cup-bearer whose function was to keep the guests supplied with drink. This was a typically female role – a facet of the 'lady with the mead-cup' theme – and King Æðelberht's law code specifies the compensation due to an *eorl* (major landowner) or *ceorl* (smallholder, yeoman, squire) if his *byrele* should be violated. Evidently the post was attached to an individual's personal circle, rather than being seen as a class of general hall-servant.

Tacitus[4] mentions that young men of noble rank were trained to act as attendants to older leaders, with a hierarchy of ranks distinguished in this form of service. The mediaeval form of apprenticeship to knighthood through the position of squire is probably similar in intent.

Male cup-bearers attached to high-status households were seemingly individuals of rank: King Alfred's mother, Osburh, was the daughter of Oslac, cupbearer to King Æðelwulf and a member of the royal clan. Harold Godwinesson – later Harold II – is known to have acted as cupbearer to King Edward the Confessor

---

[1] Hagen, 1992

[2] Herschend, 1998, p.54 discussing ideas put forward by Wimmer, Jonsson, Aakjer and others.

[3] The terms 'marshall', 'seneschal' and 'constable' were all originally positions of relative servility, which became higher-status as the court expanded and the responsibilities grew greater.

[4] *Germania*, ch. 13

while still a youth. It may be that the male 'cupbearer' fulfilled a role more like that of a personal assistant in the hall. The term *ceacbora* 'jug-bearer' occurs in Old English, denoting a male attendant, while *fætfyllere* 'vessel-filler' might be the name of the general hall-servant whose duties included ensuring that the feasters' cups were never empty.

Burþegn

There appears to be some trace – for example, in *Beowulf* where the hero is given custody of Heorot – of a guest's right to sleep in the feasting hall. This is also borne out by the story of Hnæf whose troop had to be assigned a separate hall by King Finn of the Frisians (see p.23 fn). Nevertheless, alternative sleeping arrangements seem to have been customarily available too, as we read that on the night after the Grendel-fight, Beowulf slept elsewhere, which inadvertently allowed Grendel's Mother to raid the hall:

..... Næs Beowulf ðær,	..... Beowulf was not there
ac wæs oþer in ær geteohhod	But another room had been assigned
æfter maþðumgife mærum Geate.	After the treasure-giving to the famous Geat.

Beowulf, l.1299-1301

The *in* or room Beowulf chose may have been necessary once he and his men had a quantity of treasures to take home with them. Equally, it may have been the custom that warriors slept in the hall only in times of military alert, and that in peacetime no such precautions were thought necessary. There are a number of OE words for 'visitors' quarters' including *bur* 'bower', *cumenhus* 'traveller-house', *giestærn, giesthof, giestsele* 'guest-hall'. A *tocirhus* 'turn-to house' may have been a wayfarers' hut provided in areas of danger.

The *burþegn* was the officer in charge of the *buras*, the 'bowers' or sleeping quarters; like the alternative name *burcniht*, the position of 'chamberlain' or steward of the bed-chamber is recalled. These *buras* were apparently occupied by the women,[1] while the men sometimes slept in the hall. They were seemingly homely and decorated, since the word *burreaf* means 'bower-tapestry'. We read that previously Hroðgar's men had been reluctant to sleep in the hall when Grendel's nightly onslaught began:

þa wæs eaðfynde þe him elles hwær	Then he was easily found who
gerumlicor ræste sohte,	sought a roomier resting place,
bed æfter burum	a bed among the bowers ....

Beowulf, l.138-40

---

[1] If this is so, then the poet may have meant that part of Beowulf's reward included a night with one of the women of the court; again, if this is so, then it is one of the few references to sexual favours in the poem

This would have been a clear sign to the poem's audience that the warriors were not equal to the task of safeguarding their main building, though the poet does point out that many died in the attempt.

Aside from the office of *burþegn*, there is a word for an assistant (*burcniht*) and a possible alternative title *bedþegn* 'bed-thane'. A *bur* in later Anglo-Saxon law was a kind of cottage occupied by a man of *gebur* rank, a peasant farmer.

Doorkeeper (Duruþegn)

There are a number of words in OE for 'doorkeeper' including *duruþegn* 'door-thane', *duruhaldend* 'door-keeper', *duruweard* 'door-ward' *geatweard* 'gate-ward' and *duruðinen* 'door-servant', the latter a female post. The nobleman Wulfgar was the doorkeeper at Heorot (*Beowulf*, 1.348-51):

Wulfgar maþelode - þæt wæs Wendla leod;
wæs his modsefa manegum gecyðed,
wig ond wisdom ...

Wulfgar spoke – he was a prince of the Vandals
His courage was known to many
His valour and wisdom ....

Clearly, at Heorot the care of guests and new arrivals was considered an important enough task to be entrusted to a worthy man of noble lineage.

It is believed that the guests were called to the hall by the blowing of a horn; this may have formed part of the door-keeper's duties as well as guarding access to the meal, challenging those wishing to enter, and ensuring the ritual protection of the *symbel* was respected.[1] Providing the guests with water for washing and a towel to dry their hands was a female duty, which may nevertheless have fallen to the doorkeeper to organise as part of the preliminaries to the ritual; there are two words *duruþinen* and *duruþeowen* each meaning 'female servant at the door'.

In Welsh tradition the doorkeeper could not leave his post while the feast was in progress, and drink had to be brought to him.[2]

---

[1] Hagen, 1992
[2] Hagen, 1995

6 Entertainment

The hall was important as the scene of social occasions, as well as of significant events in community's life. It was no less important as the setting for most of the entertainment and spectacle.

A period of rest or idleness (OE *æmetta, æmethwil*) was available periodically to even the busiest agricultural workforce, a period of freedom from toil (OE *rest*) when the weather prevented useful work from being carried out, beyond small repairs. At these times, various kinds of entertainment took place, whether festivities (OE *mandream, plega, gamen*) or revelry (*seledream*). A religious festival (OE *freols, freolstid*) was always a welcome opportunity to engage in sport (OE *hyhtplega, gelegergield*) and other pastimes.

Games of skill and chance were popular, and while there is no direct evidence for gambling it does seem to have formed part of the male culture of the Germanic tribes whose readiness to risk all on an enterprise was one reason for their success. Tacitus[1] notes that gambling was treated as a very serious matter among the Germanic folk of his day, at which some men with no further collateral would stake their personal freedom. The idea behind this was that of 'luck'; kings and leaders were expected to be 'lucky' men. They also used lot-casting to tell the future and to select sacrifices[2] on the same basis.

Dancing was referred to by two separate words – *hleapan* and *tumbian*, the latter perhaps associated with the acrobatic displays of professional entertainers. Juggling with knives and balls is shown in one manuscript.[3] Again, Tacitus[4] mentions a kind of dance or display of prowess performed by naked youths jumping between swords and spears.

Storytelling & Poetry

What is known of Anglo-Saxon storytelling? It seems reasonable to divide the period into two traditions – heathen and Christian. That the old stories did not die away with the advent of the new religion is manifest in Alcuin's famous remark: *Quid Hinieldo cum Christo?* "What has Ingeld got to do with Christ?"

---

[1] *Germania*, ch. 24
[2] ibid, ch.10.
[3] Cotton Tiberius C.vi. cited in Hagen, 1992
[4] *Germania*, ch. 24

Chapter Six

For the pre-Christian period, the evidence is scant and difficult to interpret. Little is known of the Old English storytelling and mythic tradition for certain. Although a great deal has been written on the subject of the beliefs and religious practices of the Anglo-Saxons, much of this is based on inference from mediaeval Icelandic material, supplemented with doses of Tacitus and Saxo Grammaticus. It may even be misleading to think of a unitary Anglo-Saxon body of belief – like a single credo and single testament – in the context of the 5th and 6th centuries when every social group had its own traditions of worship, its own legends and folklore. A number of attempts have been made to link what we think we can determine of Anglo-Saxon myth and legend to the fuller accounts of the Scandinavian cycle,[1] and to control the speculative nature of some of this work.

It seems likely enough that some aspects of Old English traditional storytelling would conform to the general, Indo-European model.[2] Typically we would expect to discover in any community's hoard of tales a 'founder' story, dealing with the coming of the first member of the group. He in turn would be succeeded by an aggressive, military leader, who in turn would be succeeded by a wealth-bringing figure. These persons would be successors to the leadership, but not necessarily blood-relations. Other elements might include a protective goddess and a pair of twin brothers who assist the folk in times of need. Are any of these figures detectable in the literature of the Anglo-Saxons?

It must be said that there are many names in the surviving king-lists and genealogies for which no known story survives, yet these names must once have been as familiar to the audience as Robin Hood or Henry VIII is to us.[3] Each one probably had a tale, legend or myth attached to it – otherwise it is unlikely that the name would survive at all. There are a handful of names in the older, more conservative verse – such as *Beowulf* - of figures who may be mythic or legendary. Among these is *Scyld Scefing*, who arrived in a boat as a child and rose to the leadership of his people before returning to the otherworld on his death. *Beow* is another name with possible associations to a fertility cult. In semi-historical times we have the brothers *Hengest* and *Horsa*, whose contract with the sub-Roman autorities in Britain led to the Germanic presence here. Hengest appears in *Beowulf* in connection with the murderous rivalry between Kings Hnæf and Finn. Aside from these human or legendary characters, there were many kinds of local hobgoblin or brownie – the *scinnan* and *scuccan* of later literature – which would have been known from folktales.

In the Christian period, biblical stories were disseminated to the general populace by churchmen, keen to drive out the old traditions and replace them with

---

[1] Stanley, 1964; North, 1997; Branston, 1974; Ellis Davidson, 1964
[2] Puhvel, 1987
[3] Hansen 1988 attempts to understand the complex area of "wisdom literature" which often conveys little to the modern mind.

approved matter. The surviving poetry suggests that the legends of famous saints were common currency – St Helena, St. Juliana, St. Guthlac are each the subject of an Old English poem. Old Testament stories of kings and miracles, and New Testament tales of the close-knit warband of disciples and their glorious leader, were all widely known. Many English locations have a local saint from the Anglo-Saxon period – Swithin, Alkmund, Aidan, Dunstan and many others are traceable even today.[1]

It is unclear whether the audience of the surviving Old English poetry was primarily clerical or secular; indeed the idea of "an Anglo-Saxon audience" has been questioned.[2] Yet the use of secular imagery focussed on the hall-based society of the Anglo-Saxon élite classes in many kinds of Old English verse indicates that even clerical or monastic communities were modelled in some way on an idealised version of human communities as they were perceived at that time. The monastic lifestyle could be presented as a more worthy and responsible version of its secular equivalent, yet still centred on communal meals, shared sleeping quarters, a web of mutual interdependence. To view the world of *Beowulf* or *The Wanderer* as a pure literary fiction is to miss the point: it was an idealised version, to be sure, but still recognisable to the poet and his audience.

The centuries-old tradition from which our existing poems spring was pre-literate, highly stylised and ornate, carefully crafted within an oral tradition with a long history. The purposes of the verse seem to have been both secular and religious. Broadly speaking, poetry may originate in liturgical utterances, formulaic speech, and be bound up with formal religious observance and ritual.[3] The secular aspect to verse lies in its use to record and commemorate memorable events, to extol the virtues of leaders and heroes, to make accessible to the society as a whole some small but important part of that society's history and place in the world. Tacitus said of the Germanic tribes of his day (1st century AD) that songs were their only form of record. Even in the 5th century, the accomplished Latin lyricist Venantius Fortunatus was composing public praise verse for his Frankish patron.[4]

Aside from didactic story-telling and verse – whether religious or practical – there does seem to have been a strong tradition of wittiness and jocular conversation. There are many OE words denoting a joker or teller of tall tales: *gliwere* 'glee-maker', *leasere* 'jester, mime, trickster, *onspillend* 'player', *sceawere* 'showman'. A female entertainer of this kind was called a *scernicge*.

---

[1] Smith, 1994; Phillips, 1994
[2] See below, Appendix 1, for more on the audience of Anglo-Saxon verse.
[3] Watkins, 1995
[4] Herschend, 1998

Chapter Six

Music

Music played a very important part in the lives of Anglo-Saxon communities. Its performance was bound up with the other 'hall-joys' and contributed to the sense of occasion, when the community gathered to celebrate and affirm its identity.

Music was probably most closely associated with the indoor world of the hall, and was used not only to entertain in the evening but also to rouse sleeping warriors in the morning:

> *... forðon sceal gar wesan*
> *monig morgenceald mundum bewunden,*
> *hæfen on handa, nalles hearpan sweg*
> *wigend weccean ac se wona hrefn*
> *fus ofer fægum ...*

> ... therefore many a spear must be
> grasped with fists, morning-cold
> taken into hands – not the harp's song
> wake the warrior, but the dark raven
> eager over doomed men ...
> Beowulf, 1.3021-5

This image of the player gently rousing his friends with a tuneful melody is rather tender, especially in a passage which foretells disaster. What the poet would have sung about and how he would have sung it are both unknown: the majority of Old English verse surviving would have been suitable for musical accompaniment – which the literature confirms was often the case – yet nothing remains of Old English music from this period. For all the battle-songs, elegies, religious and secular verse, not one note survives.

There are doubtless echoes of old songs embedded in the written records, but identifying them with certainty would seem to be impossible. The Old English charms, for example, sometimes seem to have a repetitive structure which might reflect oral performance – this is quite likely given the uses to which charms are habitually put.

The performance of music was not confined to the professional, though. The musical instrument from the Sutton Hoo burial – a *hearpe* or lyre – is not a unique find in high-status contexts (see below p.204). In *Beowulf* we learn that the old king, Hroðgar, was wont to strum his harp and sing of ancient times:

> *Hwlum hildedeor hearpan wynne,*
> *gomenwudu grette, hwilum gyd awræc*
> *soð 7 sarlic, hwilum syllic spell*
> *rehte æfter rihte rumheort cyning*

> Sometimes the battle-bold one greeted the harp with pleasure -
> the mirth-wood - sometimes recited a lay
> true and tragic, sometimes a fine tale
> he rightly related, the great-hearted king.
>
> *Beowulf*, l.2107-2110

Religious and learned works were performed musically in Anglo-Saxon times. Clerics used a form of musical notation for liturgical material, and sometimes this was extended to other worthy pieces such as the *Metres* from Boethius's *On the Consolation of Philosophy*. In the late 11th century, Latin songs were copied at St. Augustine's, Canterbury from a German original manuscript. The notation system unfortunately only records the relative raising and lowering of the melody but without specifying musical notes, so the melodies cannot be recaptured with present knowledge. It is likely that these documents were meant for use by trained clerical singers, and are far removed from the *scop* in the mead-hall.

There are occasional finds of wooden instruments from Anglo-Saxon England, which generally only survive in waterlogged archaeological conditions. Flutes of applewood and hawthorn were recovered from the Anglo-Scandinavian levels at York,[1] while others were made from the long wing bones of swans.

Illustrations of musical instruments from Anglo-Saxon manuscripts are not common. Both the *Vespasian Psalter* and the *Durham Cassiodorus* depict King David harping, in both cases using a long, straight-sided instrument with rounded ends (see below p.204). It was on the basis of such pictures that the missing parts of the Sutton Hoo lyre were inferred.

The early English church was far less intolerant of secular songs than its Continental counterparts, and it is recorded that Cuthbert, abbot of Monkwearmouth and Jarrow, sent a request to his countryman Lul, a clergyman in Mainz, in 764 asking that a player be sent to him for a kind of stringed instrument called a '*rotta*' which he had. St. Dunstan also was renowned in his day for his accomplishments in the arts, especially writing, playing the *cithara* and painting. The *cithara* is presumably what he would have called his *hearpe* and in the hagiographical *Life of St. Dunstan* it is noted that when he visited a woman's apartment to discuss the design of a stole, he took with him his harp in order to entertain the company and to lighten their spirits. Of course, being a saint's *Life*, the harp magically plays a song of warning by itself, which Dunstan correctly interprets as a presage of troubles to come.

Aside from the religious use of music, it is known that there were jugglers and other professional entertainers in the Anglo-Saxon period. Musicians

---

[1] Wilson, 1976

Chapter Six

collaborated in these spectacles, which also involved dancing.[1] There is some evidence to suggest that dancing was a mainly female activity: in one story, Dunstan entered a church and found a group of women dancing in a ring, chanting a hymn.

Old English terms for music include *gliw* and *son*, and musicianship was known variously as *dreamcræft, sangcræft, soncræft, swegcræft, swinsungcræft*.

Percussion instruments are represented by the cymbal (*cimbal*), timbrel (*hylsung*) and drum (*tunnebotm*). Wind instruments included the pipe (*hwistle, pipe*) and trumpet (*bieme, blædhorn, sarga, truþhorn*). Stringed instruments comprised the fiddle (*fiþele*), psaltery (*saltere*) and "harp" (*hearpe, citere*) with its strings (*hearpestrengas*) and plectrum (*nægel, sceacol, slegel*).

Harp or Lyre

The lyre was well-known in Anglo-Saxon England and it must have been a popular accompaniment to the recitation or composition of verse, as we can tell from the *gebeorscipe* where Caedmon felt so ashamed at his lack of skill with the instrument and the verse-form. The Old English name for the instrument was *hearpe* – our 'harp' – although the type was technically what is known as a 'lyre'.

There is a special word *salletan* meaning 'to play the harp and sing at the same time'. This would seem to be the normal practice of the typical singer and other entertainers.

Very few examples of the instrument survive. Two came from early cemeteries: Bergh Apton (Fig.23) and Morningthorpe, both in Norfolk.[2] The unremarkable nature of the graves containing these instruments suggests that the inhabitants were either professional musicians, or were at least people who were very proficient with and attached to their instruments. In both cases the lyre was positioned on top of, and close to, the body. The Bergh Apton example was fixed with mortise and tenon joints, strengthened with metal escutcheons, and the sounding board with a further metal strip. It had six tuning pegs for the strings, and a strap to support it from the wrists while it was being played. Both this and the example from Morningthorpe were made, with care and skill, from hardwood.

From Mound 1, Sutton Hoo, comes one of the earliest musical instruments found in England.[3] Inside the Coptic bowl were found the remains of lyre made from maple-wood (Fig.24 p.207), which had been kept in a beaver-skin bag. The curved upper portion of the instrument was the largest piece to survive, although it is distorted and shrunken. It held six tuning pegs – five of willow and a sixth of

---

[1] According to the *Gesta Herewardi* there was a specifically English form of dance.
[2] Arnold, 1997; Lawson, 1978, 1987
[3] Care-Evans, 1986

Entertainment

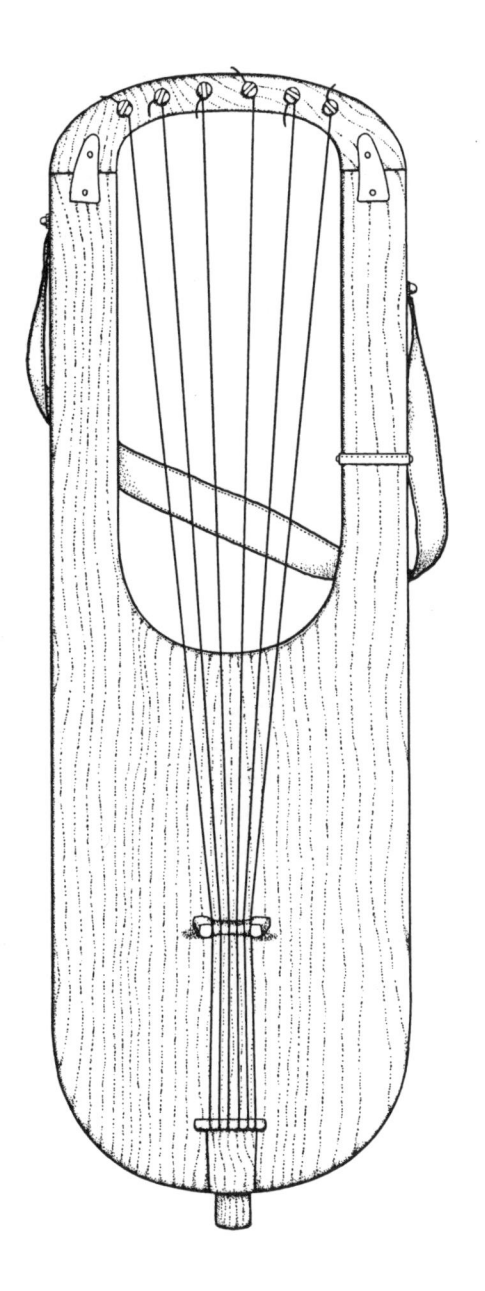

Fig.23 Lyre from Bergh Apton, Norfolk. A less regal instrument than that from Sutton Hoo, it is one of only four found in England. It is likely that an instrument such as this would have been familiar to most scopas working in the English verse tradition..

Chapter Six

alder-wood – for the horse-hair or gut strings. The upper arm was held to the body with pegs, and the joints covered with metal escutcheons or reinforcing plates, each with an upturned eagle's head. The sound-box is formed by hollowing out the centre of a block, covered with a lid held in place with bronze pins. The bridge did not survive, suggesting that it must have been made from wood, bone or ivory. (Anglo-Saxon examples made from amber and bronze are known from other sites.) The lower attachment fitting(s) did not survive.

The fourth Anglo-Saxon instrument comes from the mound at Taplow (p.18). Neither this nor the Sutton Hoo find was especially close to the body, suggesting that while harping was an accomplishment for the mighty, it was not his special area of proficiency. The standardised design of all four shows that there was a well-developed tradition of instrument-making in Anglo-Saxon England and beyond. Continental examples of similar instruments,[1] taken together with the English evidence, suggest a typical length overall of 65-70cm.

The inclusion of the instrument at both Sutton Hoo and Taplow – two very high-status burials – suggests strongly that it was a desirable accomplishment to be able to play on the instrument.

Illustrations of harps in manuscripts from around 1000 AD show a different instrument, the so-called 'pillar-harp' or 'triangular harp' which comprises a sound-box, post (fore-pillar) and peg-arm. These were apparently painted in bright, cheerful colours and, if Continental sources are to be believed, could have as many as twenty-one strings. The introduction of this instrument was complete by about 1000, although its prehistory is unknown. It may have been in use since the Roman period, although, if so, it was considered an exotic alternative to the round-headed lyre. The instrument apparently became popular only once the fore-pillar was introduced, which may have allowed it to be played in the traditional manner of Northern Europe. It has been suggested[2] that the conservatism of the traditional *scop* resisted the instrument's adoption, and only with the waning of the traditional Germanic 'wanderer-poet' tradition around 1000 AD was the way opened for the new instrument's widespread use.

English harps are shown reaching from the player's shoulder to his thigh, and are played seated with the instrument resting on the player's lap or left thigh. A strap, passed around the player's left wrist, supported the lyre during performance, allowing it to be tilted to the left. The player's hands were able to run on both sides of the instrument, unlike most traditional mediaeval harping.

The gut strings were capable of playing a major-scale sequence, which may have been an ancient trait already in the 880s according to the writings of Hucbald of

---

[1] Lawson, 1981
[2] Lawson, 1981

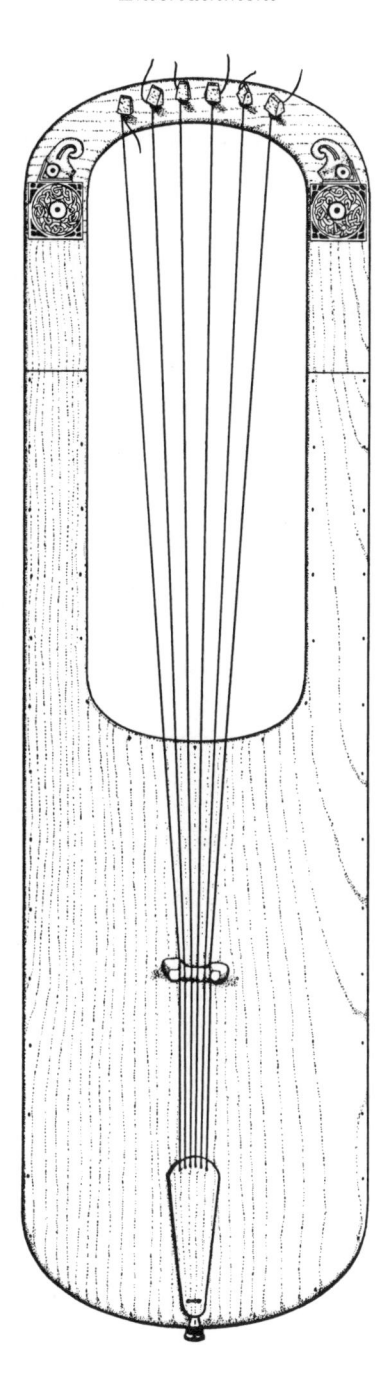

Fig.24 Reconstruction of a lyre from Sutton Hoo, Mound 1. The inclusion of the lyre in its pouch at the head end of the funerary chamber, along with the whetstone, iron stand and gaming equipment, suggests that music and song were important accomplishments for the king.

St. Amand. There have been several attempts to recapture the tuning and method of playing instruments of the Sutton Hoo type. With only six strings, the lyre's musical scale may have been very different from the modern one.

At Masham, North Yorkshire, a ninth century cross-shaft with a figural scene was shown to contain a much-weathered representation of the biblical scene of 'King David the Psalmist' in which the king is seated playing a round-headed lyre (similar to the Sutton Hoo example).[1] David the Psalmist is a rare figure in Anglo-Saxon stone sculpture, although it was a recognised motif in contemporary Ireland. Four human figures make up the scene on the cross-shaft: the king with his harp; a seated figure with a small triangular harp; a scribe with an open book on a pedestal; a crouching figure, probably a dancer or juggler. While the eroded surface makes precise identification impossible, it seems that the lyre played by David has a distinct narrowing in the middle; this feature is known from Continental manuscript art but is not otherwise represented in the English tradition. The presence of the Germanic lyre and the unusual triangular harp in the same image may indicate that the new musical instrument with the forepost was actually on its way to acceptance as early as the 9th century.

Riddles

The *scop* of Anglo-Saxon tradition was known as a *hleahtorsmið* 'laughter-smith', one who creates merriment. It is likely, judging from the small amount of OE verse handed down to us through the intervening millennium, that a lot of this laughter was occasioned by the use of riddles.

The greater part of what we know of OE riddles is based on a unique document – the magnificent book of English poetry housed in Exeter Cathedral Library[2] and known as the *Exeter Book*. It dates from the late 10th century, and its donation by Bishop Leofric, who died in 1072, is recorded in another document in the same collection.[3] There is a wide-ranging assemblage of traditional and religious verse in the book, including two sections devoted to *enigmata* or riddles rendered in verse. OE verse was traditionally written out like prose (i.e. not in individual lines) and the book follows this practice throughout. There are more than ninety riddles in the book – the exact number depends on editorial decisions as to where one ends and the next begins.

The authorship of the various poems in the book is unknown, although several attempts have been made to identify individual styles of composition. The most likely candidate for the honour is Aldhelm of Malmesbury, a 7th century cleric who is known to have composed one hundred Latin riddles and to have been a

---

[1] Lawson, 1981

[2] Crossley-Holland, 1978; Williamson, 1982; Krapp & van Kirk Dobbie, 1936; Tigges, 1991

[3] .i. mycel englisc boc be gehwilcum þingum on leoðwisan geworht "one large English book on several subjects wrought in verse" is listed among his bequests.

lover of English poetic arts. In one post-Conquest source (William of Malmesbury) he is said to have stood by a bridge singing English verse as a way of increasing curiosity among his flock. Aldhelm corresponded with King Aldfrith of Northumbria and composed a treatise on verse composition for his royal friend; the king himself had mastered Irish poetry during a period of exile in that country and was particularly well-versed in the subject.

A later monarch, King Ælfred of Wessex (Alfred the Great), was an admirer of Aldhelm's work and skilled at native verse composition; it is possible that he may have composed some riddles as well as his other literary works (for example, the *Meters of Boethius* which he rendered into Old English verse).

However, for the most part it is reasonable to suggest that the genre was traditional, and while individual poets may have re-cast the material, the subject matter and techniques were simply inherited from antiquity. There are three strands to the subject matter, which are common to virtually all aspects of Anglo-Saxon culture: the native Germanic material, the Judaeo-Christian and the Classical Græco-Roman.

Some *Exeter Book* riddles are clearly translations of Latin *enigmata* – for example, the 'one-eyed garlic seller' – and owe little to English tradition beyond their translation into the vernacular. The most influential composer of Latin riddles was Symphosius, an obscure figure of the 4th or 5th century who confined his works to a 'century' (i.e. group of 100) verses each of three lines. Aside from Aldhelm of Malmesbury (640-709, later Bishop of Sherborne), other English composers in the Latin tradition were Tatwine, archbishop of Canterbury, who composed forty pieces before his death in 734, and one 'Eusebius', identified with Hwætberht, Abbot of Wearmouth, a friend and contemporary of Bede, who wrote sixty. Even Bede himself may have composed some riddles.

The Latin texts are short, pithy, ingenious and showy: normally the title of the work is the solution, so any element of mystery is removed and the composition is a mere *tour de force*. Riddling techniques were used in the mediaeval rhetorical tradition and were raised to a high art by proponents such as the Anglo-Saxon Alcuin who provided the intellectual backbone of the Carolingian court. Something of this tradition was re-imported into (or re-surfaced in) later Anglo-Saxon England in the form of the didactic riddling dialogue, as seen in the OE texts of *Solomon and Saturn*. It is easy to overstate the importance of the classical *enigmata* tradition, and while some texts are clearly translations from Latin into Old English, there is a strong possibility that some other examples may have been English works translated into Latin.

Judaeo-Christian subject matter permeates some of the riddles, such as those which deal with the bible (no.24 and 65), Lot and his wife (44) and the chalice (57). This is hardly surprising in a society where writing was primarily a monastic achievement. Yet the subject matter of most is definitely not religious, but rather closer to the realities of the household and of secular life – the proposed solutions are mundane (plough, ox, oyster, sun, loom), martial (sword, spear, mailcoat, helmet, sheath, ballista, battering ram) or sexual. The subject matter of the tradition is varied but appears to avoid certain types, for instance there are few riddles about human beings ('Lot and his wife' and 'one-eyed garlic seller' are the main exception) yet most of the subjects are presented in human terms. Birds are riddled rather a lot, but terrestrial animals only seldom. Tools and weapons are common, means of transport rare and plants unknown (except the 'onion', which is one possible solution to a rather explicitly sexual verse).

The native tradition of riddling had a long pedigree in northern Europe, and in some Icelandic tales wily characters challenge others to a riddling-match. The tone of the *Vafþruðnismál* in the *Poetic Edda*, in which Oðinn challenges a giant, is similar to that of the Anglo-Saxon, Christian *Solomon and Saturn*: each takes the form of question and answer concerning the natural world and its history. In the Icelandic *Hervarar Saga*, a prisoner called Gestumblindi (Oðinn again) contends with King Heiðrek:[1]

> *Gestumblindi mælti: "Fjórir ganga, fjórir hanga, tveir veg visa, tveir hundum verja, einn eptir drallar ok optast óhreinn. Heiðrekr konungr, hyggðu at gátu." "Góð er gáta þín, Gestumblindi. Getit er þeirar: Þat er kýr: hon hefir fjóra foetr ok fjóra spena, tvau horn ok tvau augu en halinn drallir eptir."*

> Gestumblindi said: "Four are ganging, four are hanging, two show the way, two ward dogs off, one drags behind and is most often dirty. King Heiðrek, think on my riddle." "Good is your riddle, Gestumblindi. It is guessed: that is a cow – she has four feet and four teats, two horns and two eyes, and the tail drags after her."

This is a rather homely topic for the riddling of a king and a god, but is a good example of the technique: there is use of internal rhyme as an embellishment and elliptical number references (rather like the modern English "two legs sat on three legs while four legs ate no legs").[2]

There have been many attempts to classify riddles, based on approaches developed in cultural anthropology. Williamson[3] presents an interesting overview of the application of this work to the Old English corpus. Riddles are firstly not classified according to their subjects (the 'solution') but rather according to the presentation and characterisation they are given. The groups are:

---

[1] Text from Garmonsway, 1928.
[2] A man sat on a three-legged stool while his cat ate a fish.
[3] Williamson, 1982

Biomorphic. The subject is compared to a living creature; it may be attributed body parts (the bellows has belly and eye) and the power of intentional movement.

Zoomorphic. The subject is presented as an animal (the bagpipe has beak, hands and feet).

Anthropomorphic. The subject is presented as a person (a shield is described as a warrior). This class is very common in OE riddling.

Phytomorphic. The subject is presented as a plant. This only occurs in OE tradition when the subject is of vegetable origin (battering ram, reed pen) or a vegetable subject is a deliberately ambiguous solution (phallus/onion).

Inanimate. The subject is presented as an inanimate object. Again, this is commonest with ambiguous subjects (helmet/vagina).

Multiple. Some riddles make serial, apparently unrelated comparisons.

Selected Details. The subject is presented in a series of detailed descriptive comparisons, mostly related to form and function. These are often deliberately ambiguous and misleading.

'Neck-Riddle'. This group usually consists of something curious and known only to the riddler; Symphosius's text about the one-eyed garlic seller is an example of the *genre*. In folk-tale, riddles of this kind are used by a trickster-hero to ensure that his opponent cannot win, often in a situation where he has wagered his head to an enemy (hence the title 'neck-riddle'). Riddles of this kind need not be very well-constructed, since the puzzle lies in the unusual, unsolvable nature of the subject.

Arithmetical. The subject is described in arithmetical terms. There are no pure examples of this kind in the OE corpus, but several riddles do have a numerical element.

Family Relations. The subject is presented in terms of its relationships. This occurs in the story of Lot, whose incest means that his daughters are also his wives, their sons his sons and grandsons, etc. A native OE example presents the cuckoo as an adopted orphan.

Cryptomorphic. The solution is encoded in the text. In the *Exeter Book* this is achieved by spelling the word, usually with runestaves, within the text of the riddle; sometimes the characters are reversed, or jumbled, for additional difficulty.

Homonymic. The solution is a word with more than one meaning. In the *Exeter Book* the best example of this is number 88, *boc* which means both 'book' and 'beech (tree)'.

Chapter Six

Erotic. The subject is presented in terms of a double-entendre, with both a straightforward and a salacious solution. At least seven *Exeter Book* riddles are of this kind, and many others make some use of the device.

Non-Riddles. These are tricky questions which mimic the riddle form, but are generally light-hearted and jocular in intent ("What is black and white and re[a]d all over?" would be a modern English example).

The anthropomorphic group is by far the best attested in our small corpus, which seems to sit well with observable patterns in the literature, tending to see the inanimate in human terms (e.g. the direct address of the cross to mankind in *The Dream of the Rood*). A non-human subject given human form and motives is the classic Anglo-Saxon format. Many texts begin with the proposition "I saw a creature / wonder ..." or "I heard of a creature / wonder ...", while others put description into the 'mouth' of the thing described and end with the challenge "Say what I am called."[1]

Like the rhetorical device of metaphor, the riddle serves to both disguise and disclose the subject at the same time. By focussing on some common property – appearance, behaviour, function – the riddle-maker is able to present aspects of the subject (the 'tenor') in terms appropriate to the disguise (the 'vehicle'), often exploiting the differences between the two for paradoxical effect: the ox plunders the earth in life and binds lord and follower in death – as the draught animal for the plough, and when its hide is made into thongs. Most often it is the paradox which gives us the important clue – the insight which helps resolve the contradiction. The skilful riddler presents enough information for the riddle to be solved, and highlights the crucial data by underscoring the paradox – I am a pirate in life *but* in death I bind leaders. Of course, sometimes the paradox seems too great – the cuckoo who is an orphan before birth, thrown into a brittle lifelessness, and so on. The lack of logical entailment in these sentences is supposed to irritate our notions of cause and effect and the classificatory structures our language erects.[2]

The heart of the riddle is the principle of analogy:[3] *a is to b as c is to what?* Using the example of struts in a building and bones in a body, Williamson[4] extracts the following pattern:

---

[1] Barley, 1974

[2] The genre also makes use of 'artful ambiguities', deliberate and careful choice of words whose meanings may be interpreted in more than one way. See Robinson, 1975.

[3] The close kinship to the Norse mini-riddles called *kenningar* is evident – both types need considerable breadth of imagination and wit to resolve them; while riddles are an end in themselves, kennings are a poetic embellishment. OE examples of the type include *Godes condel* 'God's candle' = sun, or *gannotes bæð* 'gannet's bath' = sea.

[4] Williamson, 1982, p.30

```
        body              house
       ──────    : :     ──────
        bone              strut
```

From this correspondence, four kennings or riddle presentations may be derived:

bone-house	house made of bones	**body**
body-strut	strut of the body	**bone**
strut(ted)-body	body made with struts	**house**
house-bone	bone for making a house	**strut**

Taking this association further, he sees the close contextual link between the riddles and the OE poems known as *Maxims* or *Gnomic Verse* which also appear in the *Exeter Book*. In these bald statements, often not linked by any conjunction, a characteristic of a range of creatures and phenomena is noted with terse economy: *draca sceal on hlawe* "a dragon shall live in a burial mound", *cyning biþ anwealdes georn* "a king shall be keen for overlordship" *gold gerisep on guman sweorde* "gold belongs on a warrior's sword". These curt remarks summarise an attitude or customary context for their subjects, just the kind of immediate mental associations the solvers would have to use to crack the paradoxes of the riddles. In testing and circumventing the linguistic categories of the culture, riddlers provide insight into other realities – a creature abandoned by its mother before birth appears impossible, since she must have been present to give birth to it, but in the context of birds, they emerge to life from the (apparently) lifeless egg. These poems deserve a place alongside such modern *genres* as science fiction and fantasy in exploring alternative realities, other ways of being, different viewpoints from which to see the world. This verbal distortion is used in OE charms[1] to affect the material world, to render language potent over external realities, but the riddler is content merely to use this power for narrative, exploration and play.[2]

We could hardly leave the subject of riddles without offering a few short examples, in the Old English and in translation:

---

[1] See Storms, 1948; Jolly, 1996; Grattan & Singer, 1952; Cameron, 1993; Pollington, 2000.

[2] It is likely – though unprovable – that riddles formed part of the initiation process by which youths learnt the lore of their tribes; this would reinforce the link between riddle and gnomic verse. Williamson gives the example of the riddle as 'quest' i.e search for rejuvenation through confronting the unknown.

Chapter Six

Riddle 45[1]

Moððe word fræt - me þæt þuhte
wrætlicu wyrd þa ic þæt wundor gefrægn,
þæt se wyrm forswealg wera gied sumes,
þeof in þystro, þrymfæstne cwide
ond þæs strangan staþol, stælgiest ne wæs
wihte þy gleawra, þe he þam ordum swealg.

A moth ate words – to me that seemed
a strange event when I learnt of that wonder
that the worm swallowed down part of a man's song
- the thief in the darkness – his glorious saying
and its strong foundation; the stealing guest was not
any the wiser for having swallowed those words

Riddle 33[2]

Mec se wæta wong, wundrum freorig,
of his innaþe ærist cende.
Ne wat ic mec beworhtne wulle flysum,
hærum þurh heahcræft, hygeþoncum min:
wundene me ne beoð wefle, ne ic wearp hafu,
ne þurh þreata geþræcu þræd me ne hlimmeð,
ne æt me hrutende hrisil scriþeð,
ne mec ohwonan sceal am cnyssan.
Wyrmas mec ne awæfan wyrda cræftum,
þa þe geolo godwebb geatwum frætwað.
Wile mec mon hwæþre seþeah wide ofer eorþan
hatan for hæleþum hyhtlic gewæde.
Saga soðcwidum, searoþoncum gleaw,
wordum wisfæst, hwæt þis gewæde sy.

The wet earth, wondrously cold,
first gave me birth from its womb
I know I was not made with woollen fleeces
through high skill with hairs, by my wise mind
no weft shall be wound in me, nor have I a warp
nor does a thread run through me with the force of strokes
nor the creaking shuttle glide through me
nor from any side shall the weaving-slay strike me
Silkworms did not weave me with their lucky skills
who cleverly make a fine yellow fabric

---

[1] Book-worm moth
[2] Mailcoat

Yet men widely over the earth will
call me a desirable garment for heroes
Say in true speech, being wise in cunning thought
clever with words, what this clothing may be.

Riddle 23[1]

Ic eom wunderlicu wiht wifum on hyhte,
neahbuendum nyt, nængum sceþþe
burgsittendra nymþe bonan anum.
Staþol min is steapheah; stonde ic on bedde,
neoþan ruh nathwær. Neþeð hwilum
ful cyrtenu ceorles dohtor,
modwlonc meowle, þæt heo on mec gripeð,
ræseð mec on reodne, reafað min heafod,
fegeð mec on fæsten, feleþ sona
mines gemotes seo þe mec nearwað,
wif wundenlocc - wæt bið þæt eage.

I am a wonderful thing, a hope for women,
useful to those near me, none do I harm
among men except my slayer.
My standing is high and steep, I stand in a bed.
hairy beneath. Sometimes she dares -
the comely daughter of a yeoman,
the proud girl - so that she grips me,
rushes on me, ruddy, seizes my head
fixes me in a firm place, she soon feels
our meeting who comes near me
- a woman with curly hair – wet shall be her eye.

Board games

A variety of games were available to the Anglo-Saxons, although detailed evidence for how they were played is lacking. The Old English word *gamen* denotes a game or pastime, as well as more spectacular events and entertainments, while *gliw* is 'glee', happiness and the enjoyment of an activity. A gaming board was called *tæfl* which could also mean the game itself; gaming, whether playing a structured game like chess or simply dicing, was called *tæflung*. The Old English words *cyningstan* 'king-stone', *tæflstan* 'game-stone' and *teosel* 'dice' denoted different pieces used to play board games.

---

[1] Onion (or phallus)

Chapter Six

The name *tæfl* (adopted from Latin *tabula*) was used to denote the early forms of board game, which may have been acquired through exposure to Roman military institutions; Norse *tafl* and Old High German *zabel* are from the same source. Roman *tabula* was a strategy game played with counters on a grid, while *alea* was a chasing game played with dice on a board of the backgammon type; finds of dice are not uncommon from Anglo-Saxon and Viking contexts (sometimes in sets of three, as needed for the Roman *alea* game). The game of *tæfl*, developed from *tabula*, would have been a game of strategy as opposed to other types relying on luck.

Tacitus says that games of chance were treated very seriously by the Germanic tribes, and that they would gamble their entire wealth, their freedom and even their lives on a single throw of the dice. Allowing for Tacitus's tendency towards hyperbole, this suggests that the activities mentioned were no more than games of pure chance. It is possible that what the Roman reported as 'gaming' was actually a form of sortilege. There are references to lot-casting as a means of deciding on the appointee for a specific task, or the victim for sacrifice. One such occurs in the Icelandic *Gautrekssaga*[1] where a king's fleet is becalmed and the men then try to find out what must be done:

> *Þeir felldu spán til byrjar ok fell svá at Óðinn vildi þigja mann at*
> *hlutfalli at hanga ór herinum Þá var skipt liðinu til hlutfalla ok kom*
> *upp hlutr Vikars konungs*

> They threw wood-chips for a favourable wind and it fell so [as to show] that Odin[2] wanted to receive a man from among the warriors from the lot-casting to be hanged. Then a crowd drew up for the lot-casting and the lot of King Vikarr came up.

In the event, King Vikarr tried to cheat the hangman with a mock-execution but the war-god seized him nonetheless. A 5th century Roman writer, Sidonius, referring to the seamanship of the Saxon raiders of his day, mentioned that they would seize Britons to sell as slaves and would routinely cast lots to determine which among the captives - one in every ten - should be thrown overboard as a propitiatory sacrifice to the sea-gods.[3] This was their custom before sailing home, a religious act undertaken in order to have a safe journey. Games of chance may have played a similar role, allocating responsibility for the outcome to divine powers, albeit in later times the consequences of losing would have been less final.

Dice from the Roman and later periods are known archaeologically. The standard Roman *alea* was a bone cube with spots marked out on opposing surfaces 1:6,

---

[1] Text from Garmonsway, 1928.

[2] Kershaw, 2000, makes the case for the one-eyed figure of Óðinn being based ultimately on the 'one' thrown at dice in a ritual game played to determine leadership of the warband.

[3] An OE poetic name for the sea is *garsecg* 'spearman' which may conjure up images of a bloodthirsty spirit of the deep.

2:5, 3:4, as in modern dice, so that opposing sides always add up to 7. Commonly, northern European dice were similarly made but the spots are disposed 1:5, 2:3, 4:6. Examples have been found in England in the barrows at Taplow, Buckinghamshire, and Asthall, Oxfordshire.[1]

A 3rd century grave from Leuna, Saxony, contained a double-sided gaming board: one face was engraved for playing *alea* with a border of semicircles and a central rosette, the other for *latrunculi* a strategy game played on the intersections of a grid, popular on the Roman imperial frontiers. Similar board layouts occur at Vimose, Denmark (5th c.) and Gokstad, Norway (9th c.).

From Ballinderry, Ireland, comes a remarkably complete wooden gaming board with a grid of 7x7 holes into which gaming pegs could be slotted; the piece was 9.5 inches (24 cm) square, its playing surface recessed and equipped with two handles carved into the likeness of human faces; it would have served well as a travelling version of a *tæfl* board. The decoration points to its having been manufactured in the tenth century, probably on the Isle of Man.[2] Two figures are shown playing a similar type of game on one of the (now lost) golden horns from Gallehus, Denmark dating to possibly the 4th or 5th century. A Viking-period squared gaming board was found in Norway and is now in the Oslo museum. It is assumed that Anglo-Saxon boards were decorated with coloured squares or lines, as the Old English word *bleobord* 'gaming board' has as its first element *bleo* 'colour, decoration'.

The rich 7th century Anglo-Saxon barrow burial at Taplow, Buckinghamshire, was dug out in the 19th century; the best surviving excavation sketch shows a set of twenty-four disks on a rectangular structure which may represent counters on a board, or in box. Some counters from the grave survive, and are tubes of bone, lathe-turned and capped at each end by bone discs held in place by gilt-headed bronze pins. The number of surviving pins suggests a set of at least fifty-four men; one was of a different design: shorter, barrel-shaped and with a bronze band round its circumference, probably a *cyningstan*. The Taplow gaming pieces on their board were placed alongside the occupant's harp and drinking horn – a close association of the means of enjoying *seledreamas* (hall-pleasures).

The game of chess is believed to have been invented in the Middle East in the 6th century, and was known in Western Europe in the 7th where it was quickly adopted by the strategy-minded aristocracies.[3] Evidence for chess as such from Anglo-Saxon times is lacking; the earliest references are from the 11th century and the word was introduced from Old French *eschec*. It is not possible to establish for certain whether chess-like games (two sides of identical composition) were played by the Anglo-Saxons from the present evidence. The Islamic origin of the game is reflected in the early sets (and many modern ones)

---

[1] Salzman, 1939, vol.1

[2] Murray, 1952

[3] Mills, 2001; Murray, 1952.

where realistic representation of human and animal figures is prohibited: pieces from early sets are often no more than rounded cones of stone, ceramic, glass, bone, base or precious metal.

The most famous single find of gaming pieces must be the 'chessmen' found on the Isle of Lewis in 1831, consisting of some eighty two items, and therefore presumably more than one set.[1] They were carved from walrus ivory. While the pawns are simple stelae with a decorative motif, the larger pieces are carved to represent personalities. The style of armour (nasal helmet, mailcoat, teardrop shield) strongly suggests a date between the mid-11th to early 12th centuries.

One of the curious aspects of this chess set is that all the pieces are individuals: of the six pieces identified as 'kings', each with a naked sword across his knees, some are bearded and others clean-shaven, all but one have their long hair shown in strands or plaits while the other has a neat, collar-length bob. The queens have their right hands raised to their cheeks, but one nurses a drinking horn. Two bishops hold a crozier and are making a sign of blessing with the right hand; two hold a crozier and a bible in the right hand; two more are standing, with the crozier in the right hand the bible in the left. All the warriors have unique shield designs, although most are variations on the cross, saltire and lozenge. Three warriors are biting the rim of their shields in the manner of berserks. While not all the carvings are technically perfect, minor faults in carving were often remedied at the painting stage.

Less striking than the Lewis figures are the many objects identified as gaming pieces which have been found in Anglo-Saxon graves of the pagan period, and as stray finds across much of northern Europe. The grave finds are often in sets, with a number of small, plain pieces and one larger, decorated item. An important discovery was a set of thirty three plano-convex gaming pieces and thirty five roe-deer's ankle bones (astragali) found in a 5th century cremation urn at Caistor-by-Norwich, Norfolk,[2] the largest of which bears the very early runic text *raihan* (roe-deer?), possibly the oldest known such inscription in England and formally linked through the shape of the characters to southern Scandinavia. Eleven of the pieces were black and twenty two white. It has been suggested that the piece marked 'roe-deer' is the quarry in a chase game.

The renowned Anglo-Saxon royal ship burial at Sutton Hoo, Suffolk, also included some gaming pieces although they were not recognised as such during excavation.[3] A complete piece (split into three sections by decay) was found in the remains of a textile bag beneath the large silver Anastasius dish. Fragments of possibly four or five others in a poor state of preservation were found in the area

---

[1] It is speculated that the chessmen comprised four complete sets originally; they had passed through many hands before publication. They may have been the property of a dealer or merchant in antiquity. Stratford, 1997.

[2] Page, 1999.

[3] Youngs, 1983

of the shield. All had been contaminated with bronze corrosion. The complete piece was about 1.5inch (3.3 cm) high and cylindrical with a bevelled top. The material was either the tooth of a sperm whale, or elephant ivory. A beached whale would have provided enough material for a complete set of gaming pieces, with its forty to sixty teeth; on the other hand, objects of elephant ivory were included in other contemporary (early 7th century) Anglo-Saxon burials. The form of the piece suggests a possible Byzantine origin, which ties in neatly with its having been found with the Byzantine silver dish. No decoration was detectable due to the poor state of preservation, but the manufacturing process appears to have been turning on a lathe.[1]

Roman counters made from glass or ceramic occasionally occur in Anglo-Saxon (mainly Kentish) graves. The 5th and 6th century Anglian cremation cemeteries of the North Sea littoral also frequently contain items which have been identified as gaming pieces. These are mostly with apparently male burials, while female burials of the 6th and 7th centuries may be accompanied by similar articles although the fact that at least one[2] was pierced and converted to an amulet may indicate that these singletons served a different purpose. The traditional Germanic form of counter was 'plano-convex' i.e. a flat underside and a rounded or domed body; Anglo-Saxon examples are usually less than 0.75 inch (2cm) in diameter. An easy method of manufacture is presumed to be to remove the top from the ball-joint of a femur or humerus, file the bottom smooth, then polish all surfaces. Small, single-coloured pebbles were also used; many such may have been overlooked in early excavations. Glass and clay pieces may have been used for gaming, but they are rare. Wood, ivory and bone are also attested, although the rate of survival for such organic materials is understandably low. Horse molars began to be used in the late 6th century.

Decoration of bone pieces with incised lines and ring-and-dot motifs appears to have been common; twenty seven pieces recovered from a barrow at Cold Eaton, Derbyshire, featured circular drilled holes and ring-and-dot; thirteen fragments from grave 198 at Sarre, Kent, had pairs of deep holes carved into the base, a feature found on some other, early sets. This may imply that sometimes, in some games, the pieces had to be inverted.

Apart from the plain, cylindrical or domed style of figure there are a significant number of taller pieces of which the top is decorated with three to six small lugs resembling crenellation; these may represent either 'king' pieces or possibly the opposing side in a chase game of the Fox-and-Geese type.

---

[1] Youngs, 1983, p.871. Lathe-turning appears to have been common in England from the 7th century, which coincides approximately with the introduction of the pottery wheel. It was used mainly in woodworking but could equally have been adopted for the working of other organic materials such as bone. The maplewood 'bottles' from Sutton Hoo are assumed to be of local manufacture and were certainly turned, probably on a pole-lathe.

[2] Youngs, 1983 p.861 "the shaped horse-tooth piece from a female burial at Castle Bytham, Lincolnshire, was perforated for suspension"

Chapter Six

The wide range of counter types, the numbers of pieces and proportions of one kind to another within sets all suggest that considerable variety was to be found in the details of the games played; possibly this was regional, and varied over time.

The Viking period game called *hnefatafl* may be of greater antiquity than chess in northern Europe. It is a development from the standard *tafl* game; *hnefatafl* is distinguished as the *tafl* of the *hnefi*, this being the 'king' piece. It consists of a chequered board (typically a lattice of 18 x 18, 13 x 13 or 11 x 11 squares) with 'safe' squares or nodes in the centre and at each of the corners; the object is to move the *hnefi* king piece from the centre to the edge without allowing it to be taken (surrounded by opposing pieces). Many variants of the game are believed to have existed, and it continued in use into mediaeval times (e.g. Welsh *tawlbwrdd*, Lappish *tablut*).

The *Old English Rune Poem* describes a range of familiar, significant objects in order to make the names of the runes memorable. The verse dealing with the rune '⌐' with the sound value 'p'[1] runs:

⌐ *[peorð] byþ symble plega and hlehter wlancum [....] ðar wigan sittaþ on beorsele bliþe ætsomne*

[peorð] shall always be [a source of] play and laughter for proud [nobles?] where warriors sit in the beer-hall happily together.

While many solutions to this riddle-like verse have been put forward, a strong possibility is 'chessman'.[2]

Murray[3] refers to a curious English or Irish manuscript from the early tenth century in which the layout of a gaming board is assigned a scriptural significance. The *incipit* of the manuscript refers to one *Dubinsi episcopus* and to *Adalstani regis anglorum*; presumed to be the Irish Bishop Duibhinnsi who died in 953 and King Athelstan who reigned 925-40; the text implies that the cleric took the board game from England to Ireland. The layout is similar to surviving examples of actual boards, and the game itself uses two teams (48 on one side and 24 plus a *hnefi* on the other). It is called *alea evangelii* 'boardgame of the messenger/evangelist' and contains some very contrived numerological reasoning to back up its didactic purpose.

---

[1] Halsall, 1981. The manuscript actually uses a shape for this character without the upper hook, thus closer in form to ʜ. The suggested meaning 'chessman' was first proposed by Jacob Grimm and is not universally accepted; other possibilities include 'dice-box', 'apple tree' and even some sexual activities. *Peorð* does not appear to be a native Germanic word, although the name occurs frequently and persistently in association with this character e.g. Isruna tract: *perd*; Brussels Codex: *pert*; Vienna Codex: *peord* and the Gothic letter-name *pertra*.

[2] Another is 'dicing cup', see Bauschatz, 1982

[3] Murray, 1952, p.61 ff; the reference is to MS CCC Oxford, 122.

Appendices

1 Hall- and Feasting-Themes in Old English Verse

The Old English verse tradition could never entirely escape its beginnings in the early hall-culture of the Angles and their neighbours, and aspects of feasting, leadership, social obligations and rewards are all kept firmly in mind when even the most devoutly Christian poems are being composed.

It is unfortunate that modern readers face such difficulties in locating Old English poems within the landscape and chronology which scholarship provides, the history of Anglo-Saxon England. There are relatively few poems for which we can safely settle on a date or place of composition; fewer still whose author can be determined. This is partly due to the circumstances of composition and the accident of survival; the bulk of Old English verse survives in copies made in the tenth and eleventh centuries.[1] How many generations of copying were involved in creating the texts we have today is often unknowable; how many re-writings, modernisations, conversions from one dialect to another. Where we do have reasonably good evidence, as in *The Battle of Maldon*,[2] the knowledge can help us assess the issues which the poet is exploring. Putting Old English poems into their true historical and geographical contexts is essential in attempting an evaluation of the works, individually or collectively.

The fact that many of the poems were collected and copied in the tenth or early eleventh centuries may be significant, as this was a period of social upheaval due to the long and expensive wars with the Vikings, and subsequently the integration of mainly Danish settlers into English society. If issues of identity and social cohesion were foremost in the minds of men at this time – initially drawing distinctions between Englishman and Dane as defender and invader respectively, but later seeking to find common ground and a means of sharing their identities under an Anglo-Danish leadership – then the anxieties of political instability may well have found expression in the literature of the time. The reign of Cnut (1016-35), king of both Denmark and England, was a time of great artistic and religious endeavour, and many of the homiletic texts written in this period are full of vigour.

---

[1] Magennis, 1996

[2] The poem commemorates the death in battle of Ealdormann Byrhtnoð in a fight with Vikings at Maldon, Essex, which took place in August 991. Logically, the present poem cannot be older than the date of the battle. Sadly, only a fragment is left, itself a hand-written copy made in the early modern period from an original which does not survive.

Appendix 1

The intended readership of our texts must be assumed to have been mainly religious, since at the time the great books of poetry were compiled and the sermons composed, reading and writing were essentially clerical accomplishments. It may be that the increased use and recording of English should be seen against the backdrop of the Benedictine Reform and the renaissance for which that movement provided the impetus. Yet it is undeniable that much of the verse is distinctly secular in theme and origin, and the intended audience for sermonisers such as Wulfstan was presumably the powerful lay members of the community.

Features of some poems suggest composition at a significantly earlier date than the manuscripts we possess; this indicates preservation of traditional forms, with or without modernisation in language and content. Scribes did not copy such large numbers of ancient poems out of antiquarian curiosity: they had a keen interest in and knowledge of the traditional verse forms of the language and undertook the transcription of existing works with a view to continuing their performance. That very fact presupposes a readership and audience able to comprehend, appreciate and enjoy the verse, ancient or otherwise. Increasingly, the religious aspects of even originally quite secular ideas and events was emphasised and it became possible to re-cast commonplace heroic themes as complex religious symbolism.

It is therefore misleading to assume that we can know what 'an Anglo-Saxon audience' would make of any reference, theme or representation in the literature, when the term covers up to six centuries and a broad spectrum of social classes, regions and religious beliefs (Anglo-Saxon and Scandinavian pagan, pre- and post-Benedictine Christian is the most obvious of many possible splits).[1] The following is a brief summary of the uses to which the authors of various poems put the imagery of hall-life and feasting in their works. (Sections from some of the poems are given in Appendix 2.)

Beowulf is the single work which deals in greatest detail and at greatest length with the themes of heroism, social structure and the place of men within it, halls and feasting and the meaning of these for those who used them. It is the most extensive treatment, but not the only useful one by any means.

Also in the 'heroic' mould, *The Fight at Finnsburh* is a fragment of a much longer poem which tells of a peace-making visit by King Hnæf to his former rival, now brother-in-law, King Finn of Frisia, and the ensuing hostilities which lead to the death of both Hnæf and his nephew, Finn's son. The theme of warriors repaying their lord's trust is explored, as well as the tragedy of the lady who loses both son and brother in the fight. The hall here is the scene of both feasting and fighting, which is quite rare in the surviving examples of Old

---

[1] Greenfield, 1972 is a good starting point for the modern reader, although there are many others.

English verse (*Beowulf* is the only closely comparable example, and that concerns the ravages of a monster, not bad faith between men).

Later – probably datable to shortly after 937 AD when the events it describes took place - is *The Battle of Brunanburh* which has rather more to do with the exercise of power than the celebration of community. The poem – and others in the *ASC* such as *The Capture of the Five Boroughs* – are intended to promote the achievements of English armies and their leaders, to celebrate military victory and to underscore the superiority of Christian over heathen, English over Norse, defender over invader. At the time when it was written, after a century of damaging wars with the Vikings, Anglo-Saxon self-confidence was relatively weak but growing, and the triumphalism of the verse reflects the need of the English defenders to re-affirm their own character and identity. In a significant break with 'traditional' heroic verse, there is no celebration of individual deeds nor mention of individual combatants; all is centred on the figures of the English kings and their Irish Viking counterparts: *fife lægun on þam campstede cyningas giunge* 'five young kings lay dead on that field of battle' (1.28-9).

The *Battle of Maldon* exists only as a copy made shortly before the manuscript original was destroyed by fire in 1731. The poem is a fragment, having lost both beginning and end. In complete contrast to *Brunanburh*, the action centres on the loyalty of the defeated English force to its leader, Ealdormann Byrhtnoð and, after his fall, their loyalty to each other. The individual warriors are named, with brief genealogical data and occasionally an indication as to their landholdings. The 'antique' feel of the piece, with its long speeches and emphasis on personal loyalty – and lack of it – is deliberately cultivated by the poet. The intention is to evoke the traditions of the *comitatus* – devotion to one's lord, in return for public rewards. Byrhtnoð himself walks among his men with words of encouragement, more like the chief of a Germanic warband than the general of a mediaeval army. More than almost any other Old English verse, *Maldon* demonstrates the victory of a community in the face of its enemies: though they cannot win a military victory, they are not beaten because they will not surrender to their foe.

Widsið is apparently a much earlier poem, although the only surviving record is in the 10th century *Exeter Book*. It deals with and celebrates the place of the poet in the hall culture of the fictive world of Germanic antiquity (see Appendix 2 below). Although presented as the journeying of one man, the background is straight from the heroic world of the poetic tradition, and the historic time-span is several centuries. Much of the poem's content consists of a list of tribes and their rulers. Doubtless the mere mention of the people named there would call to mind some fable, legend or story; in only a few cases can we approach the necessary background knowledge to see the links between the various leaders and tribes mentioned.[1]

---

[1] Creed, 1975; for a reworking of the Offa episode in *Widsið* and a discussion of English heroic legends, see Herbert, 1993.

Appendix 1

The *Exeter Book* poem called *The Husband's Message* also deals with high-status hall-life, specifically the roles of husband and wife as hall-rulers. *The Ruin* reflects nostalgically on the brightness and pleasures enjoyed in a Roman hall, now crumbled to a ruin; the theme of transience – a common topic in Old English verse - is very well expressed in this poem. The theme of *The Wanderer* is that of exile, of having outlived one's companions and no longer having a host community. The search for a replacement is not made easier by the suspicions which the warrior's predicament arouses. The exile has only *sorg to geferan* 'sorrow as a companion'.[1] *The Seafarer* depicts the lonely life of the mariner who has only the sea-bird's cry for mirth (*to gomene*) and who laments his separation from the joys of human company. In *The Wife's Lament* an inverted image of the hall is presented, where the solitary outcast dwells in an *eorðsele* 'earth-hall' in a life of unremitting misery contrasted with the former joys of community. The poem *Christ & Satan* characterises hell as a hall, or rather a kind of anti-hall in which normal human values are inverted. Far from being the cosy indoor world of the audience, hell is *þes windiga sele* 'this windy building' an image of the exposed outdoors.

Judith – a poem from the same manuscript as *Beowulf* - shows the riotous feasting of Holofernes and his warband as a perversion of normal, restrained social values. The theme of decadence underlies this moral tale of Christian piety pitted against heathen lust and debauchery. In *Juliana* there is a full examination of the inherent transience of hall-joys. The heroine is a pious Christian paragon while the feasters are explicitly followers of Satan, seduced by the unmediated pleasures of secular life.

Genesis A presents the story of Genesis and the fall of the Angels in terms of a warband in the hall owing allegiance to God. The break with God is presented as an act of bad faith, some angels being led astray by the rise of a new leader, Satan (lines 12-18): *hæfdon gleam and dream and heora ordfruman, engla þreatas, beorhte blisse, wæs heora blæd micel, þegnas þrymfæste þeoden heredon, sægdon lustum lof, heora liffrean demdon* "they had revelry and joy, and their foremost warriors, the hosts of angels, bright happiness; their glory was great, vigorous thanes praised their lord, willingly stated their adoration, glorified their lord in life". *Daniel* recounts the biblical story of Daniel through a Germanic interpretative filter (lines 1-3) *Gefrægn ic Hebreos eadge lifgean in Hierusalem, goldhord dælan, cyningdom habban...* "I have heard of the Hebrews living in bliss in Jerusalem, sharing the hoard of gold, holding their kingdom ...".

Vainglory is the name given to an *Exeter Book* poem about the transience of earthly matters, and the consequent foolishness of pride. With such a purpose, it uses the imagery of drinking – or rather of drunkenness – to demonstrate the folly of man. The poet's contempt for feasting, feasters and the life they represent is

---

[1] Leslie, 1985

manifest in this section, unusual in Old English verse. The *Fortunes of Men* (see Appendix 2) tells the story of the various fates which may await a human being in life. Two sections deal with hall life. Lines 77-9 echoes the conviviality of hall-feasting, while lines 51-7 are much more disapproving, underscoring the dangers of drunkenness.

2 Some Old English Sources
The Poet Cædmon
From the Old English version of Bede's Historia Ecclesiastica Gentis Anglorum.

In ðeosse abbudissan mynstre wæs sum broðor syndriglice mid godcundre gife gemæred 7 geweorðad. Forþon he gewunade gerisenlice leoð wyrcan, þa ðe to æfæstnisse 7 to arfæstnisse belumpen, swa ðætte, swa hwæt swa he of godcundum stafum þurh boceras geleornode, þæt he æfter medmiclum fæce in scopgereorde mid þa mæstan swetnisse 7 inbryrdnisse geglængde 7 in Engliscgereorde wel geworht forþbrohte.

Ond for his leoþsongum monigra monna mod oft to worulde forhogdnisse 7 to geþeodnisse þæs heofonlican lifes onbærnde wæron. Ond eac swelce monige oðre æfter him in Ongelþeode ongunnon æfæste leoð wyrcan: ac nænig hwæðre him þæt gelice don meahte. Forþon he nales from monnum ne þurh mon gelæred wæs, þæt he þone leoðcræft leornade, ac he wæs godcundlice gefultumed 7 þurh Godes gife þone songcræft onfeng. Ond he forðon næfre noht leasunge, ne idles leoþes wyrcan meahte, ac efne þa an þa ðe to æfæstnesse belumpon, 7 his þa æfestan tungan gedafenode singan.

Wæs he se mon in weoruldhade geseted oð þa tide þe he wæs gelyfdre ylde, 7 næfre nænig leoð geleornade. Ond he forþon oft in gebeorscipe, þonne þær wæs blisse intinga gedemed, þæt heo ealle sceolden þurh endebyrdnesse be hearpan singan, þonne he geseah þa hearpan him nealecan, þonne aras he for scome from þæm symble 7 ham eode to his huse.

Þa he þæt þa sumre tide dyde, þæt he forlet þæt hus þæs gebeorscipes, 7 ut wæs gongende to neata scipene, þara heord him wæs þære neahte beboden þa he ða þær in gelimplicre tide his leomu on reste gesette 7 onslepte, þa stod him sum mon æt þurh swefn 7 hine halette 7 grette 7 hine be his noman nemnde:

In the minster of this abbess [Hild] a certain brother was especially made famous and honoured with a divine gift. He was wont to make fitting songs, which dealt with devotion and piety so that whatever he might learn through religious writings from scholars, after a short while he would compose into verse with the greatest sweetness, and he brought it forth into finely wrought English.

And because of his songs, the minds of many men were often inspired to contempt for the world, and to the company of the heavenly life. And likewise many others after him began to make pious songs in the English tongue, yet none but him could do so in that way. For he was not educated by a man nor about men, so that he could learn versification, but he was divinely assisted and received the skill of song-making through the gift of God. And therefore he could never make anything of falseness, nor an empty song, but only those which belonged to piousness, and it befitted his pious tongue to sing them.

That man was established in secular life until the time when he was quite old, and never learnt any verse. And for that reason often at a beer-drinking, when a cause for celebration had been determined, so that they must all sing with a harp in turn, when he saw the harp nearing him he then rose from the feasting for shame and went home to his house.

One time when he did that – he left the house of the beer-drinking and started to go out to the shed with the cattle whose care was assigned to him for that night – he laid his body into rest at the appropriate time and fell asleep, then a certain man stood by him in his dream, and hailed and greeted him and named him by his name.

Appendix 2

"Cedmon, sing me hwæthwugu."

Þa ondswarede he 7 cwæð: "Ne con ic noht singan; 7 ic forþon of þeossum gebeorscipe ut eode, 7 hider gewat, forþon ic naht singan ne cuðe."

Eft he cwæð, se ðe mid hine sprecende wæs:
"Hwæðre þu meaht singan."

Þa cwæð he: "Hwæt sceal ic singan?"

Cwæð he: "Sing me frumsceaft."

Þa he ða þas andsware onfeng, þa ongon he sona singan in herenesse Godes Scyppendes þa fers 7 þa word þe he næfre gehyrde, þara endebyrdnes þis is:

"Nu sculon herigean heofonrices Weard,
Meotodes meahte 7 his modgeþanc,
weorc Wuldorfæder, swa he wundra gehwæs,
ece Drihten, or onstealde.
He ærest sceop eorðan bearnum
heofon to hrofe halig Scyppend;
þa middangeard monncynnes Weard,
ece Drihten, æfter teode
firum foldan, Frea ælmihtig."

Þa aras he from þæm slæpe, 7 eal þa þe he slæpende song fæste in gemynde hæfde 7 þæm wordum sona monig word in þæt ilce gemet Gode wyrðes songes togeþeodde. Þa com he on morgenne to þæm tungerefan, þe his ealdormon wæs: sægde him hwylce gife he onfeng; 7 he hine sona to þære abbudissan gelædde 7 hire þa cyðde 7 sægde. Þa heht heo gesomnian ealle þa gelæredestan men 7 þa leorneras: 7 him ondweardum het secgan þæt swefn, 7 þæt leoð singan, þæt ealra heora dome gecoren wære, hwæt oððe hwonon þæt cuman wære. Þa wæs him eallum gesegen, swa swa hit wæs, þæt him wære from Drihtne sylfum heofonlic gifu forgifen. Þa rehton heo him 7 sægdon sum halig spell 7 godcundre lare word: bebudon him þa, gif he meahte, þæt he in swinsunge leoþsonges þæt gehwyrfde. Þa he ða hæfde þa wisan onfongne, þa eode he ham to his huse 7 cwom eft on morgenne 7 þy betstan leoðe geglengéd him asong 7 ageaf þæt him beboden wæs.

"Cædmon, sing something to me."

Then he answered and said "I cannot sing anything, and I went out from this beer-drinking and came here because I did not know how to sing anything."

He who spoke with him said again:
"Yet you are able to sing."

Then he said: "What must I sing?"

He said: "Sing the original creation to me."

When he received this answer, he began straightaway to sing in praise of God the Creator those verses and those words which he had never heard before, of which this is the arrangement:

"Now we must praise the Keeper of heaven,
the Measurer's might and his mind's thought,
the Glory-father's work as for each wonder he,
the everlasting Lord, set the beginning.
He first made the earth for men,
heaven as a roof – the holy shaper –
then Middle-earth mankind's keeper,
the everlasting Lord made thereafter,
the world for men – the almighty Lord."

Then he arose from that sleep and all that he had sung while asleep he held fast in his mind, and to those words he added many more words in praise of God in the same manner. In the morning he came to the town-reeve, who was his superior, and told him which gift he had received; he took him straightaway to the abbess and then told and related it to her. She then had all the most learned men and students assemble and had the dream told in their presence and the song sung, so that the judgement of them all should be established as to what it was and whence it had come. Then it was seen by them all, just as it was, that it was a heavenly gift granted to him by the Lord himself. Then they took care of him and said a holy spell and words of divine lore; they bade him, if he were able, that he should turn it into the melody of a song. When he had taken in the matter he went home to his house and came back in the morning and, set into the best verse, sang to them and gave them what was asked of him.

Appendix 2

Ða ongan seo abbudisse clyppan 7 lufigean þa Godes gife in þæm men; 7 heo hine þa monade 7 lærde þæt he woruldhad anforlete 7 munuchad onfenge: 7 he þæt wel þafode. Ond heo hine in þæt mynster onfeng mid his godum, 7 hine geþeodde to gesomnunge þara Godes þeowa; 7 heht hine læran þæt getæl þæs halgan stæres 7 spelles. Ond he eal þa he in gehyrnesse geleornian meahte mid hine gemyndgade 7 swa swa clæne neten eodorcende in þæt sweteste leoð gehwerfde; 7 his song 7 his leoð wæron swa wynsumu to gehyranne, þætte seolfan þa his lareowas æt his muðe wreoton 7 leornodon.

Song he ærest be middangeardes gesceape 7 bi fruman moncynnes 7 eal þæt stær Genesis, þæt is seo æreste Moyses booc; 7 eft bi utgonge Israhela folces of Ægypta londe 7 bi ingonge þæs gehatlandes; 7 bi oðrum monegum spellum þæs halgan gewrites canones boca; ond bi Cristes menniscnesse; 7 bi his þrowunge; 7 bi his upastignesse in heofonas; 7 bi þæs Halgan Gastes cyme, 7 þara apostola lare: 7 eft bi þæm dæge þæs toweardan domes, 7 bi fyrhtu þæs tintreglican wiites, 7 bi swetnesse þæs heofonlecan rices, he monig leoð geworhte. Ond swelce eac oðer monig be þæm godcundan fremsumnessum 7 domum he geworhte.

In eallum þæm he geornlice gemde, þæt he men atuge from synna lufan 7 mandæda, 7 to lufan 7 to geornfulnesse awehte godra dæda. Forþon he wæs se mon swiþe æfæst 7 regollecum þeodscipum eaðmodlice underþeoded. Ond wið þæm þa ðe in oðre wisan don woldon, he wæs mid welme micelre ellenwodnisse onbærned. Ond he forðon fægre ænde his lif betynde 7 geendade.

The abbess began to call out, and to love God's gift in that man, and she then urged and advised him that he should give up secular life and should receive monkhood, and he consented to that. And she took him into the minster with his goods, and joined him to the assembly of the servants of God, and bade him learn the series of the holy story and gospel. And in obedience all that he could learn he mulled over in his mind, like a pure beast chewing the cud, and turned it into the sweetest verse, and his songs and his verse were so pleasant to hear that his teachers themselves wrote them down from his mouth and learnt them.

He first sang about the creation of the world and about mankind's origin and all the Genesis story, which is the first book of Moses, and after about the departure of the people of Israel from the land of the Egyptians and about the entry into the promised land, and about many other stories of the holy text of the canonical books, and about Christ's incarnation, and about his suffering, and about his ascension into the heavens, and about the coming of the Holy Spirit, and the teachings of the apostles, and afterwards about the day of future judgement, and about fear of the torturing punishment, and about the sweetness of the heavenly kingdom, he made many songs, and likewise he made many others about divine kindnesses and judgements.

In all these he eagerly took care that drew men away from the love of sins and misdeeds, and aroused them to love and desire of good deeds. For that reason that man was very devout and humbly supported religious communities. And against those who wished to act in a different manner he was burning with the flame of a great zeal. And he therefore closed and finished his life with a fine ending.

Appendix 2

Beowulf (extract) - Heorot's Feasting
Lines 607-41

þa wæs on salum sinces brytta,
gamolfeax ond guðrof; geoce gelyfde
brego Beorhtdena, gehyrde on Beowulfe
folces hyrde fæstrædne geþoht.
ðær wæs hæleþa hleahtor, hlyn swynsode,
word wæron wynsume. Eode Wealhþeow forð,
cwen Hroðgares, cynna gemyndig,
grette goldhroden guman on healle,
ond þa freolic wif ful gesealde
ærest Eastdena eþelwearde,
bæd hine bliðne æt þære beorþege,
leodum leofne. He on lust geþeah
symbel ond seleful, sigerof kyning.
Ymbeode þa ides Helminga
duguþe ond geogoþe dæl æghwylcne,
sincfato sealde, oþþæt sæl alamp
þæt hio Beowulfe, beaghroden cwen
mode geþungen, medoful ætbær;
grette Geata leod, gode þancode
wisfæst wordum þæs ðe hire se willa gelamp
þæt heo on ænigne eorl gelyfde
fyrena frofre. He þæt ful geþeah,
wælreow wiga, æt Wealhþeon,
ond þa gyddode guþe gefysed;
Beowulf maþelode, bearn Ecgþeowes:
"Ic þæt hogode, þa ic on holm gestah,
sæbat gesæt mid minra secga gedriht,
þæt ic anunga eowra leoda
willan geworhte oþðe on wæl crunge,
feondgrapum fæst. Ic gefremman sceal
eorlic ellen, oþðe endedæg
on þisse meoduhealle minne gebidan."
ðam wife þa word wel licodon,
gilpcwide Geates; eode goldhroden
freolicu folccwen to hire frean sittan

Beowulf – Heorot's Feasting

Then it was a happy time for the dealer of rings,
hoary-head and battle-fierce, he trusted that help
the Bright-Danes' champion, he heard of Beowulf's
steadfast resolve, the people's watchman.
There was warrior's laughter, the mirth resounded,
words were joyful. Wealhþeow went forward
Hroþgar's queen – mindful of good customs,
gold-adorned she greeted the man in the hall
and then the noble woman handed a cup
first to the East-Danes' noble keeper,
bade him be merry at the beer-drinking,
dear to his folk; he willingly partook
of the feast and the hall-cup, that victory-proud king.
The Helmings' lady went around
every part of the youths and veterans,
she handed out jewelled vessels until the time came
that she, ring-adorned queen, to Beowulf
bore the mead-cup with a good heart
greeted the Geats' prince, thanked god
with words of wisdom that her wish had come about
so that she trusted in some nobleman
for comfort from the violence. He took the cup
- the slaughter-minded fighter – from Wealhþeow
and then sang out, egged on to war.
Beowulf spoke out, son of Ecgþeow:
"When I went out on the sea I believed this
as I sat in the sea-boat with my troop of warriors
that once your people's
will I would work or fall among the dead
fast in the fiend's grasp. I shall achieve
brave and noble deeds, or the end-day for me
I will await in this meadhall."
Those words pleased the woman well,
the promise of the Geat; gold-adorned went
the gracious folk-queen to sit with her lord.

Appendix 2

Beowulf (extract) – Unferþ's Flyting
Lines 500-614

Unferð maþelode, Ecglafes bearn,
þe æt fotum sæt frean Scyldinga,
onband beadurune - wæs him Beowulfes sið,
modges merefaran, micel æfþunca,
forþon þe he ne uþe þæt ænig oðer man
æfre mærða þon ma middangeardes
gehedde under heofenum þonne he sylfa:
"Eart þu se Beowulf, se þe wið Brecan wunne,
on sidne sæ ymb sund flite,
ðær git for wlence wada cunnedon
ond for dolgilpe on deop wæter
aldrum neþdon? Ne inc ænig mon,
ne leof ne lað, belean mihte
sorhfullne sið, þa git on sund reon.
Þær git eagorstream earmum þehton,
mæton merestræta, mundum brugdon,
glidon ofer garsecg; geofon yþum weol,
wintrys wylmum. Git on wæteres æht
seofon niht swuncon; he þe æt sunde oferflat,
hæfde mare mægen. Þa hine on morgentid
on Heaþoræmas holm up ætbær;
ðonon he gesohte swæsne eðel ,
leof his leodum, lond Brondinga,
freoðoburh fægere, þær he folc ahte,
burh ond beagas. Beot eal wið þe
sunu Beanstanes soðe gelæste.
ðonne wene ic to þe wyrsan geþingea,
ðeah þu heaðoræsa gehwær dohte,
grimre guðe, gif þu Grendles dearst
nihtlongne fyrst nean bidan."
Beowulf maþelode, bearn Ecgþeowes:
 "Hwæt! þu worn fela, wine min Unferð,
beore druncen ymb Brecan spræce,
sægdest from his siðe. Soð ic talige,
þæt ic merestrengo maran ahte,
earfeþo on yþum, ðonne ænig oþer man.
Wit þæt gecwædon cnihtwesende
ond gebeotedon - wæron begen þa git
on geogoðfeore - þæt wit on garsecg ut
aldrum neðdon, ond þæt geæfndon swa.

Beowulf – Unferþ's Flyting

Unferð spoke up, son of Ecglaf,
who sat at the feet of the Scyldings' lord,
He unbound a battle-rune – to him the journey of Beowulf
the proud seafarer – was a great annoyance
for he would not grant that any other man
greater fame in middle-earth
should ever receive than he himself:
"Are you that Beowulf who fought with Breca
vied in swimming on the broad sea
where you both tested the waves in your pride
and for a foolish boast in the deep water
you risked your lives? Nor could any man
- neither dear nor hateful – forbid you two
that sorrowful journey, when you swam in the water.
There with your arms you covered the water-current,
measured the sea-ways, plied your hands
glided across the sea; the water welled with waves,
winter's whelming. In the power of the water you both
toiled for seven nights; he beat you at swimming,
he had greater strength. Then in the morning
the sea cast him up among the Heaþoreamas,
from where he sought his own homeland
- dear to his people – the Brondings' land,
the fair stronghold where he had his own folk,
city and rings. Against you all his vow
Beanstan's son truly fulfilled;
then, from you I expect a worse outcome,
though everywhere you prevailed in the battle-rush
of grim warfare, if you dare await Grendel
from close by a night-long while."
Beowulf spoke up, Ecgþeow's son
"Hark! My friend Unferþ, many things you
have said about Breca, drunken with beer,
spoken of his journey. The truth I tell –
that I had greater sea-strength,
hardship in the waves, than any other man.
We both spoke of it, being just boys,
and made vows – we were both then still
in the youth of our lives – that we would both out at sea
risk our lives, and we fulfilled it thus.

Appendix 2

Hæfdon swurd nacod, þa wit on sund reon,
heard on handa; wit unc wið hronfixas
werian þohton. No he wiht fram me
flodyþum feor fleotan meahte,
hraþor on holme; no ic fram him wolde.
Ða wit ætsomne on sæ wæron
fif nihta fyrst, oþþæt unc flod todraf,
wado weallende, wedera cealdost,
nipende niht, ond norþanwind
heaðogrim ondhwearf; hreo wæron yþa.
Wæs merefixa mod onhrered;
þær me wið laðum licsyrce min,
heard, hondlocen, helpe gefremede,
beadohrægl broden on breostum læg
golde gegyrwed. Me to grunde teah
fah feondscaða, fæste hæfde
grim on grape; hwæþre me gyfeþe wearð
þæt ic aglæcan orde geræhte,
hildebille; heaþoræs fornam
mihtig meredeor þurh mine hand.
Swa mec gelome laðgeteonan
þreatedon þearle. Ic him þenode
deoran sweorde, swa hit gedefe wæs.
Næs hie ðære fylle gefean hæfdon,
manfordædlan, þæt hie me þegon,
symbel ymbsæton sægrunde neah;
ac on mergenne mecum wunde
be yðlafe uppe lægon,
sweordum aswefede, þæt syðþan na
ymb brontne ford brimliðende
lade ne letton. Leoht eastan com,
beorht beacen godes; brimu swaþredon,
þæt ic sænæssas geseon mihte,
windige weallas. Wyrd oft nereð
unfægne eorl, þonne his ellen deah.
Hwæþere me gesælde þæt ic mid sweorde ofsloh
niceras nigene. No ic on niht gefrægn
under heofones hwealf heardran feohtan,
ne on egstreamum earmran mannon;
hwaþere ic fara feng feore gedigde,
siþes werig. Ða mec sæ oþbær,
flod æfter faroðe on Finna land,
wadu weallendu. No ic wiht fram þe
swylcra searoniða secgan hyrde,

Beowulf – Unferþ's Flyting

We had naked swords when we swam in the water
hard in our hands; against whales we
thought to defend ourselves. Not at all from me
could he float far on the flood-waves,
faster on the sea; nor would I go far from him.
Then we two were together in the sea
for five nights' time until the flood drove us apart
- the welling waves, the coldest of weather,
the darkening night and the northern wind
battle-grim blew against us; the waves were rough.
A sea-beast's anger was stirred;
there against the foe my body-shirt
- hard, hand-locked – gave me help,
the braided battle-coat lay on my breast
adorned with gold. Dragged me to the sea-bed
the hateful attacker, held me fast
grim in its grip – yet it was granted to me
that I could reach the monster's front
with my battle-sword; the war-rush killed
the mighty sea-beast by my hand.
Often likewise the monsters
assailed me harshly. I served them
with my fierce sword, as it was fitting to do.
They had no joy of the slaughter
those evil killers – that they tasted me,
sat round to a feast on the sea-bed –
rather in the morning, wounded by sword-blows
they lay on the foreshore
slain by swords so that never after
in that deep ford for seamen
they could hinder their sailing. Light came from the east,
God's bright beacon, the billows lessened
so that I could see the sea-headlands,
the windy cliff-walls. Wyrd often saves
a man undoomed, if his courages is good.
However, it happened that I slew with my sword
nine nicors. At night I have never heard
of a harder fight under heaven's roof
nor of a more wretched man in the water-streams,
yet I escaped with my life the foes' clutches
weary from the journey. Then the sea bore me
onto the land of the Finns - the flood along the shore,
the welling waves. Concerning you nothing
have I heard tell of such deadly strife,

billa brogan. Breca næfre git
æt heaðolace, ne gehwæþer incer,
swa deorlice dæd gefremede
fagum sweordum - no ic þæs fela gylpe -
þeah ðu þinum broðrum to banan wurde,
heafodmægum; þæs þu in healle scealt
werhðo dreogan, þeah þin wit duge.
Secge ic þe to soðe, sunu Ecglafes,
þæt næfre Grendel swa fela gryra gefremede,
atol æglæca, ealdre þinum,
hynðo on Heorote, gif þin hige wære,
sefa swa searogrim, swa þu self talast.
Ac he hafað onfunden þæt he þa fæhðe ne þearf,
atole ecgþræce eower leode
swiðe onsittan, Sigescyldinga;
nymeð nydbade, nænegum arað
leode Deniga, ac he lust wigeð,
swefeð ond sendeþ, secce ne weneþ
to Gardenum. Ac ic him Geata sceal
eafoð ond ellen ungeara nu,
guþe gebeodan. Gæþ eft se þe mot
to medo modig, siþþan morgenleoht
ofer ylda bearn oþres dogores,
sunne sweglwered suþan scineð."
Þa wæs on salum sinces brytta,
gamolfeax ond guðrof; geoce gelyfde
brego Beorhtdena, gehyrde on Beowulfe
folces hyrde fæstrædne geþoht.
Ðær wæs hæleþa hleahtor, hlyn swynsode,
word wæron wynsume, eode Wealhþeow forð

terror of swords. Neither you nor Breca,
neither one of you at battle-play
framed such a daring deed
with deadly swords – though I do not boast much of it –
yet you became your brothers' killer,
your close kinsmen – for that you shall in the hall
undergo condemnation, though your wit is keen.
I say to you truly, son of Ecglaf
that Grendel would never hade made so many attacks
- the hateful monster – on your lord,
such shame on Heorot, if your courage,
your mind were as grim as you yourself reckon.
But he has found that he need not for that feud
- the deadly sword-attack of your people,
the Victory-Scyldings - greatly dread;
he takes his plunder, respects none
of the Danes' tribe but he raids at will,
kills and eats, expects no strife
from the Spear-Danes. But of the Geats shall
now erelong strength and courage,
fighting be offered to him. Whoever is able shall go after
proud to his mead, once morning-light
of another day over the sons of men
shines from the south, the splendid sun."
Then the treasure-giver was happy
- the grey-haired and battle-fierce; he trusted to the help.
the hero of the Bright-Danes, in Beowulf heard
the people's keeper a steadfast spirit.
There was laughter of heroes, the noise resounded,
words were merry, Wealhþeow went forth.

Appendix 2

The Fortunes Of Men (extracts)
Lines 51-7
Sum sceal on beore þurh byreles hond
meodugal mæcga; þonne he gemet ne con
gemearcian his muþe mode sine,
ac sceal ful earmlice ealdre linnan,
dreogan dryhtenbealo dreamum biscyred,
ond hine to sylfcwale secgas nemnað,
mænað mid muþe meodugales gedrinc.

Lines 77-9
Sum sceal on heape hæleþum cweman
blissian æt beore bencsittendum
þær biþ drincendra dream se micla

The Seafarer (extract)
Lines 39-47
Forþon nis þæs modwlonc mon ofer eorþan,
ne his gifena þæs god, ne in geoguþe to þæs hwæt,
ne in his dædum to þæs deor, ne him his dryhten to þæs hold,
þæt he a his sæfore sorge næbbe,
to hwon hine dryhten gedon wille.
Ne biþ him to hearpan hyge ne to hringþege,
ne to wife wyn ne to worulde hyht,
ne ymbe owiht elles, nefne ymb yða gewealc,
ac a hafað longunge se þe on lagu fundað.

Vainglory (extract)
Lines 40-4
Siteð symbelwlonc searwum læteð
wine gewæged word ut faran
þræfte þringan þrymme gebyrmed
æfestum onæled oferhygda ful
niða nearowrencum ...

Some Old English Sources

One shall be at beer by the cup-bearer's hand
a mead-proud man, when he does not know how to
mark the measure of his mouth with his mind
but rather he must sadly yield up his life
undergo loss of his lord, severed from joys
and men name him as a self-killer
declare the mead-proud man's drinking.

One, in a troop, shall please the heroes
gladden the bench-sitters at their beer,
where shall be the great joy of drinkers

Therefore there is not so mind-proud a man on earth
nor so good in his gifts, nor so brave in his youth
nor in his deeds so daring, nor so true to his lord
that he would have no sorrow at his seafaring
as to what the lord will do with him.
No thought for him of the harp or the receiving of rings
nor of woman's pleasure nor of worldly glory
nor of aught else except the rolling of the waves
for he who races on the waters shall always have longings.

Feast-proud he sits, lyingly lets
his words fly forth winged by wine
to press a quarrel swollen with anger
aflame with spite, filled with boastfulness
by cruel deceits …

Appendix 2

The Battle of Maldon (Extract)
Lines 198 – 224
Swa him Offa on dæg ær asæde
on þam meþelstede, þa he gemot hæfde,
þæt þær modiglice manega spræcon
þe eft æt þearfe þolian noldon.
Þa wearð afeallen þæs folces ealdor,
Æþelredes eorl; ealle gesawon
heorðgeneatas þæt hyra heorra læg.
Þa ðær wendon forð wlance þegenas,
unearge men efston georne;
hi woldon þa ealle oðer twega,
lif forlætan oððe leofne gewrecan.
Swa hi bylde forð bearn Ælfrices,
wiga wintrum geong, wordum mælde,
Ælfwine þa cwæð, he on ellen spræc:
"Gemunan þa mæla þe we oft æt meodo spræcon,
þonne we on bence beot ahofon,
hæleð on healle, ymbe heard gewinn;
nu mæg cunnian hwa cene sy.
Ic wylle mine æþelo eallum gecyþan,
þæt ic wæs on Myrcon miccles cynnes;
wæs min ealda fæder Ealhelm haten,
wis ealdorman, woruldgesælig.
Ne sceolon me on þære þeode þegenas ætwitan
þæt ic of ðisse fyrde feran wille,
eard gesecan, nu min ealdor ligeð
forheawen æt hilde. Me is þæt hearma mæst;
he wæs ægðer min mæg and min hlaford

The Battle of Maldon

Offa had said this to him earlier in the day
at the meeting-place, when he held a meeting
that there many spoke bravely
who later at need would not last out.
Then the army's leader was fallen.
Ethelred's earl; all could see
among the hearth-troop that their lord lay dead.
Then the proud thanes went forwards
men unafraid eagerly rushed;
they all wished for one of two things:
to give up their lives or to avenge their lord.
Thus Ælfric's son encouraged them onwards,
a warrior young in winters, he declared with words, then Ælfwine spoke,
he uttered with courage:
"Remember those words which we often spoke over mead
when we raised up a boast on the bench
about hard strife – we heroes in the hall;
now we shall test who may be bold.
I wish to declare my lineage to all,
that I was of great kindred of the Mercians;
my grandfather was called Ealhelm,
a wise ealdormann, lucky in this world.
Thanes in the nation shall not blame me,
say that I wish to quit this war-host,
seek my home now that my leader lies
cut down in war. That is the greatest of harms to me
he was both my kinsman and my lord"

Appendix 2

The Wanderer

Oft him anhaga are gebideð,
metudes miltse, þeah þe he modcearig
geond lagulade longe sceolde
hreran mid hondum hrimcealde sæ,
wadan wræclastas. Wyrd bið ful aræd!
Swa cwæð eardstapa, earfeþa gemyndig,
wraþra wælsleahta, winemæga hryre:
"Oft ic sceolde ana uhtna gehwylce
mine ceare cwiþan. Nis nu cwicra nan
þe ic him modsefan minne durre
sweotule asecgan. Ic to soþe wat
þæt biþ in eorle indryhten þeaw,
þæt he his ferðlocan fæste binde,
healde his hordcofan, hycge swa he wille.
Ne mæg werig mod wyrde wiðstondan,
ne se hreo hyge helpe gefremman.
Forðon domgeorne dreorigne oft
in hyra breostcofan bindað fæste;
swa ic modsefan minne sceolde,
oft earmcearig, eðle bidæled,
freomægum feor feterum sælan,
siþþan geara iu goldwine minne
hrusan heolstre biwrah, ond ic hean þonan
wod wintercearig ofer waþema gebind,
sohte sele dreorig sinces bryttan,
hwær ic feor oþþe neah findan meahte
þone þe in meoduhealle min mine wisse,
oþþe mec freondleasne frefran wolde,
weman mid wynnum. Wat se þe cunnað,
hu sliþen bið sorg to geferan,
þam þe him lyt hafað leofra geholena.;
warað hine wræclast, nales wunden gold,
ferðloca freorig, nalæs foldan blæd.
Gemon he selesecgas ond sincþege,
hu hine on geoguðe his goldwine
wenede to wiste. Wyn eal gedreas!
Forþon wat se þe sceal his winedryhtnes
leofes larcwidum longe forþolian,
ðonne sorg ond slæp somod ætgædre
earmne anhogan oft gebindað;
þinceð him on mode þæt he his mondryhten

The Wanderer

Often the lone-dweller awaits favour
the mercy of the Lord, though care-worn he
for a long time across the waterways had to
stir the frost-cold sea with his hands,
walk the paths of exil. Wyrd is fully determined.
Thus spoke a land-stepper mindful of troubles
of cruel slaughter, of his dear lord's fall.
"Every dawn alone I had to
speak my sorrow. There is none living now
to whom I dare my mind
to speak clearly. I know for a truth
that it is a noble custom for a hero
that he should bind up fast his heart,
hold back his feelings, whatever he may think.
A weary mind cannot withstand wyrd
nor cruel thought frame any help.
Thus fame-keen men often
bind sorrow fast in their breasts;
so too my own feelings –
often sorrow-laden, deprived of my homeland,
far from my kinsmen – I must hold in fetters
since years back my gold-friend
the earth covered with darkness and from there I
travelled winter-sad over the bound waves,
hall-sad sought a distributor of treasure
where far or near I might find
one in the meadhall who knew my wish
or would comfort me, friendless,
persuade me with pleasures. He who tries it knows
how hard a companion sorrow is
for him who has few dear supporters;
he holds the exile-path, not twisted gold
a frosty heart, not earth's richness.
He recalls hall-fellows and treasure-getting
how in his youth his gold-friend
entertained him with feasting. All joy fell away!
He knows therefore, who must his dear lord's
words of advice forgo for a long time
when sorrow and sleep both together
bind down the poor lone-dweller;
in his mind it seems to him that his lord

Appendix 2

clyppe ond cysse, ond on cneo lecge
honda ond heafod, swa he hwilum ær
in geardagum giefstolas breac.
Ðonne onwæcneð eft wineleas guma,
gesihð him biforan fealwe wegas,
baþian brimfuglas, brædan feþra,
hreosan hrim ond snaw, hagle gemenged.
Þonne beoð þy hefigran heortan benne,
sare æfter swæsne. Sorg bið geniwad,
þonne maga gemynd mod geondhweorfeð;
greteð gliwstafum, georne geondsceawað
secga geseldan. Swimmað eft on weg!
Fleotendra ferð no þær fela bringeð
cuðra cwidegiedda. Cearo bið geniwad
þam þe sendan sceal swiþe geneahhe
ofer waþema gebind werigne sefan.
Forþon ic geþencan ne mæg geond þas woruld
for hwan modsefa min ne gesweorce,
þonne ic eorla lif eal geondþence,
hu hi færlice flet ofgeafon,
modge maguþegnas. Swa þes middangeard
ealra dogra gehwam dreoseð ond fealleþ,
forþon ne mæg weorþan wis wer, ær he age
wintra dæl in woruldrice. Wita sceal geþyldig,
ne sceal no to hatheort ne to hrædwyrde,
ne to wac wiga ne to wanhydig,
ne to forht ne to fægen, ne to feohgifre
ne næfre gielpes to georn, ær he geare cunne.
Beorn sceal gebidan, þonne he beot spriceð,
oþþæt collenferð cunne gearwe
hwider hreþra gehygd hweorfan wille.
Ongietan sceal gleaw hæle hu gæstlic bið,
þonne ealre þisse worulde wela weste stondeð,
swa nu missenlice geond þisne middangeard
winde biwaune weallas stondaþ,
hrime bihrorene, hryðge þa ederas.
Woriað þa winsalo, waldend licgað
dreame bidrorene, duguþ eal gecrong,
wlonc bi wealle. Sume wig fornom,
ferede in forðwege, sumne fugel oþbær
ofer heanne holm, sumne se hara wulf
deaðe gedælde, sumne dreorighleor
in eorðscræfe eorl gehydde.

The Wanderer

he calls and kisses, and onto his knee he lays
his hands and head, as at times before
in days of old he enjoyed the treasure-seats.
Then the friendless man wakes back up
sees the dusky waves before him,
the sea-birds bathing, spreading their wings,
frost and snow falling, mixed with hail.
Then heart's wounds are the heavier,
pain for the dear one. Sorrow is renewed
when memory of kinsmen passes through the mind;
he greets them gladly, looks lovingly around
the hall-fellows. They swim back away!
The floating spirits do not bring many
well-known songs there. Care is renewed
for him who must send very often
his weary soul over the the bound waves.
Therefore I cannot recall in this world
why my mind should not grow dark
when I consider the life of heroes
how they suddenly gave up the hall,
those brave thanes. Likewise this middle-earth
every day slips and falls,
hence a man may not become wise before he has
a deal of years in the world. A wise man shall be patient,
must not be too hot-headed nor to quick to speak,
nor to weak in war nor to feint-hearted,
nor to craven nor too carefree nor to keen for wealth,
never too free with his oath before he fully understands.
A warrior must wait when he speaks his boast
until the high-spirited one truly knows
where his heart's feelings will turn.
A wise hero must understand how awesome it shall be
when all this world's wealth stands waste
as now in some places across this middle-earth
walls stand wind-blown
toppled by frost, storm-beaten the shelters.
The wine-halls totter, the rulers lie
deprived of joy, the old warriors all fell,
proud men by the wall. Some war took away,
carried them forth, one a bird bore away
over the high sea, to one the grey wolf
dealt death, one a tear-cheeked
noble hid in an earth-scrape.

Appendix 2

Yþde swa þisne eardgeard ælda scyppend
oþþæt burgwara breahtma lease
eald enta geweorc idlu stodon.
Se þonne þisne wealsteal wise geþohte
ond þis deorce lif deope geondþenceð,
frod in ferðe, feor oft gemon
wælsleahta worn, ond þas word acwið:
"Hwær cwom mearg? Hwær cwom mago? Hwær cwom maþþumgyfa?
Hwær cwom symbla gesetu? Hwær sindon seledreamas?
Eala beorht bune! Eala byrnwiga!
Eala þeodnes þrym! Hu seo þrag gewat,
genap under nihthelm, swa heo no wære.
Stondeð nu on laste leofre duguþe
weal wundrum heah, wyrmlicum fah.
Eorlas fornoman asca þryþe,
wæpen wælgifru, wyrd seo mære,
ond þas stanhleoþu stormas cnyssað,
hrið hreosende hrusan bindeð,
wintres woma, þonne won cymeð,
nipeð nihtscua, norþan onsendeð
hreo hæglfare hæleþum on andan.
Eall is earfoðlic eorþan rice,
onwendeð wyrda gesceaft weoruld under heofonum.
Her bið feoh læne, her bið freond læne,
her bið mon læne, her bið mæg læne,
eal þis eorþan gesteal idel weorþeð!"
Swa cwæð snottor on mode, gesæt him sundor æt rune.
Til biþ se þe his treowe gehealdeþ,
                                  ne sceal næfre his torn to rycene
beorn of his breostum acyþan, nemþe he ær þa bote cunne,
eorl mid elne gefremman.
                      Wel bið þam þe him are seceð,
frofre to fæder on heofonum, þær us eal seo fæstnung stondeð.

The Wanderer

The maker of men thus destroyed this dwelling
until, lacking the joyful sounds of inhabitants
the ancient work of giants stood empty.
He who has wisely thought of this wall-footing
and who thinks deeply on this dark life,
wise in his years, often remembers from afar
a deal of slaughters, and speaks these words:
"Where is the horse? Where is the warrior? Where is the treasure-giver?
Where are the seats at the feast? Where are the hall-joys?
Lo! Bright cup. Lo! Mailed warrior.
Lo! A lord's glory. How that time has passed
slid beneath the cover of night as if it had never been.
There now stands behind the dear warriors
a wondrous-high wall, adorned with serpents.
The strength of spears took away the earls
- slaughter-cruel weapons – the famed wyrd
and storms crash against the stony slopes,
the dripping storm binds the earth –
winter's tumult – then darkness comes,
night-shadow glides, sends from the north
a cruel hailstorm for men's malice.
All is troublesome in earth's kingdom
Wyrd's shaping changes the world beneath the heavens.
Here wealth is transitory, here a friend is transitory,
here a man is transitory, here a kinsman is transitory
all this set up on earth grows empty!"
Thus the wise man spoke in his heart, sat apart in thought,
It shall be good for him who keeps his trust,
                        a warrior shall never his cares too readily
reveal from his breast unless he first should know the remedy,
the noble make it with his courage.
                It shall be well for him who seeks grace,
comfort from the father in heaven, where the protection of us all stands.

Appendix 2

Widsið
Lines 1- 140[1]
Widsið maðolade, wordhord onleac,
se þe monna mæst mægþa ofer eorþan,
folca geondferde; oft he on flette geþah
mynelicne maþþum. Him from Myrgingum
æþele onwocon. He mid Ealhhilde,
fælre freoþuwebban, forman siþe
Hreðcyninges ham gesohte
eastan of Ongle, Eormanrices,
wraþes wærlogan. Ongon þa worn sprecan:
"Fela ic monna gefrægn mægþum wealdan.
Sceal þeodna gehwylc þeawum lifgan,
eorl æfter oþrum eðle rædan,
se þe his þeodenstol geþeon wile.
Þara wæs Hwala hwile selast,
ond Alexandreas ealra ricost
monna cynnes, ond he mæst geþah
þara þe ic ofer foldan gefrægen hæbbe.
Ætla weold Hunum, Eormanric Gotum,
Becca Baningum, Burgendum Gifica.
Casere weold Creacum ond Celic Finnum,
Hagena Holmrygum ond Heoden Glommum.
Witta weold Swæfum, Wada Hælsingum,
Meaca Myrgingum, Mearchealf Hundingum.
Þeodric weold Froncum, þyle Rondingum,
Breoca Brondingum, Billing Wernum.
Oswine weold Eowum ond Ytum Gefwulf,
Fin Folcwalding Fresna cynne.
Sigehere lengest Sædenum weold,
Hnæf Hocingum, Helm Wulfingum,
Wald Woingum, Wod Þyringum,
Sæferð Sycgum, Sweom Ongendþeow,
Sceafthere Ymbrum, Sceafa Longbeardum,
Hun Hætwerum ond Holen Wrosnum.

---

[1] In the translation below I have made no attempt to identify the various leaders and peoples mentioned by name. This would be a huge undertaking, outside the scope of this book. I have used more familiar English names where these are likely to be known to the general reader, e.g. "Attila" for "Ætla".

Widsiþ

Widsið spoke, unlocked his word-hoard
he who of all men the most peoples on earth,
tribes, travelled round, on a hall-floor he often got
a wished-for treasure. From the Myrgings
his noble line awoke. With Ealhhild,
the beloved peace-weaver, for the first time
he sought out the home of a glory-king
eastwards from Angeln, of Eormanric
the fearsome oathbreaker. He began to tell the tale:
"I have heard of many men ruling nations.
Each lord must live by tradition,
the earl guide his homeland after another
who wishes that his lordly seat should thrive.
For a while Hwala was the best of them
And Alexandreas the most powerful of all
of mankind, and he throve most
of those of whom I have heard on earth.
Attila ruled the Huns, Eormanric the Goths
Becca the Banings, the Burgundians Gifeca.
Ceasar ruled the Greeks and Celic the Finns
Hagena the Holmryge and Heoden the Glomms.
Witta ruled the Swabians, Wada the Halsings
Meaca the Myrgings, Mearchalf the Hundings.
Þeodric ruled the Franks, Þyle the Rondings
Breoca the Brondings, Billing the Wernas.
Oswine ruled the Eowum and Gefwulf the Yte,
Finn son of Folcwald the Frisian kin.
Sigehere ruled the Sea-Danes longest,
Hnæf the Hocings, Helm the Wulfings
Wald the Woings, Wod the Thuringians,
Seaferð the Secgas, the Swedes Ongenþeow
Sceafthere the Ymbras, Sceafa the Lombards,
Hun the Hatweras and Holen the Wrosnas

Appendix 2

Hringweald wæs haten Herefarena cyning.
Offa weold Ongle, Alewih Denum;
se wæs þara manna modgast ealra,
no hwæþre he ofer Offan eorlscype fremede,
ac Offa geslog ærest monna,
cnihtwesende, cynerica mæst.
Nænig efeneald him eorlscipe maran
on orette, ane sweorde
merce gemærde wið Myrgingum
bi Fifeldore; heoldon forð siþþan
Engle ond Swæfe, swa hit Offa geslog.
Hroþwulf ond Hroðgar heoldon lengest
sibbe ætsomne suhtorfædran,
siþþan hy forwræcon wicinga cynn
ond Ingeldes ord forbigdan,
forheowan æt Heorote Heaðobeardna þrym.
Swa ic geondferde fela fremdra londa
geond ginne grund. Godes ond yfles
þær ic cunnade cnosle bidæled,
freomægum feor folgade wide.
Forþon ic mæg singan ond secgan spell,
mænan fore mengo in meoduhealle
hu me cynegode cystum dohten.
Ic wæs mid Hunum ond mid Hreðgotum,
mid Sweom ond mid Geatum ond mid Suþdenum.
Mid Wenlum ic wæs ond mid Wærnum ond mid wicingum.
Mid Gefþum ic wæs ond mid Winedum ond mid Gefflegum.
Mid Englum ic wæs ond mid Swæfum ond mid Ænenum.
Mid Seaxum ic wæs ond Sycgum ond mid Sweordwerum.
Mid Hronum ic wæs ond mid Deanum ond mid Heaþoreamum.
Mid þyringum ic wæs ond mid Þrowendum,
ond mid Burgendum, þær ic beag geþah;
me þær Guðhere forgeaf glædlicne maþþum
songes to leane. Næs þæt sæne cyning!
 Mid Froncum ic wæs ond mid Frysum ond mid Frumtingum.
Mid Rugum ic wæs ond mid Glommum ond mid Rumwalum.
Swylce ic wæs on Eatule mid Ælfwine,
se hæfde moncynnes, mine gefræge,
leohteste hond lofes to wyrcenne,
heortan unhneaweste hringa gedales,
beorhtra beaga, bearn Eadwines.

Widsiþ

The Herefaras' king was called Hringweald.
Offa ruled the Angles, Alewih the Danes;
he was of all these men the bravest
yet he did not outdo Offa for lordship
for, the first of men, Offa won out
the greatest kingdom being yet a boy,
none of equal age to him won greater lordship
in single combat, with one sword
he fixed the border with the Myrgings
at Fifeldor, they held it ever after
as Offa won it, the Angles and Swabians.
Hroþwulf and Hroðgar held for the longest time
peace together, uncle and nephew
after they drove off the vikings' kin
and laid low Ingeld's champions
hewed down the Heaðobard's host at Heorot.
Thus I travelled round many foreign lands
throughout the wide earth. Of good and evil
I made test there, deprived of my kindred,
far from my friendly kinsmen, I wandered widely.
Therefore I can sing and tell a tale
proclaim before the gathering in the meadhall
how royalty regaled me with treasures.
I was with the Huns and the Mighty Goths
with Swedes and with Geats and with South-Danes
with Vandals I was and with Wærnas and with Vikings
with Gepids I was and with Winedas and with Gefflegas
with Angles I was and with Swabians and with Ænenas
with Saxons I was and with Secgas and with Sword-Weras
with Hronas I was and with Danes and with Battle-Reamas
with Thuringians I was and with Þrowendas
and with Burgundians where I received a ring;
there Guðhere gave me a pleasing gift
as a reward for a song – that was no negligent king!
With Franks I was and with Frisians and with Frumtingas
with Rugians I was and with Glommas and with Rome-Welsh.
Likewise I was in Italy with Ælfwine
who of all mankind, in my opinion,
had the lightest hand to earn praise
the most generous heart for giving of rings
of bright circlets, the son of Edwin.

Appendix 2

Mid Sercingum ic wæs ond mid Seringum;
mid Creacum ic wæs ond mid Finnum ond mid Casere,
se þe winburga geweald ahte,
Wiolena ond Wilna, ond Wala rices.
Mid Scottum ic wæs ond mid Peohtum ond mid Scridefinnum;
mid Lidwicingum ic wæs ond mid Leonum ond mid Longbeardum,
mid hæðnum ond mid hæleþum ond mid Hundingum.
Mid Israhelum ic wæs ond mid Exsyringum,
mid Ebreum ond mid Indeum ond mid Egyptum.
Mid Moidum ic wæs ond mid Persum ond mid Myrgingum,
ond Mofdingum ond ongend Myrgingum,
ond mid Amothingum. Mid Eastþyringum ic wæs
ond mid Eolum ond mid Istum ond Idumingum.
Ond ic wæs mid Eormanrice ealle þrage,
þær me Gotena cyning gode dohte;
se me beag forgeaf, burgwarena fruma,
on þam siex hund wæs smætes goldes,
gescyred sceatta scillingrime;
þone ic Eadgilse on æht sealde,
minum hleodryhtne, þa ic to ham bicwom,
leofum to leane, þæs þe he me lond forgeaf,
mines fæder eþel, frea Myrginga.
Ond me þa Ealhhild oþerne forgeaf,
dryhtcwen duguþe, dohtor Eadwines.
Hyre lof lengde geond londa fela,
þonne ic be songe secgan sceolde
hwær ic under swegle selast wisse
goldhrodene cwen giefe bryttian.
ðonne wit Scilling sciran reorde
for uncrum sigedryhtne song ahofan,
hlude bi hearpan hleoþor swinsade,
þonne monige men, modum wlonce,
wordum sprecan, þa þe wel cuþan,
þæt hi næfre song sellan ne hyrdon.
ðonan ic ealne geondhwearf eþel Gotena,
sohte ic a gesiþa þa selestan;
þæt wæs innweorud Earmanrices.
Heðcan sohte ic ond Beadecan ond Herelingas,
Emercan sohte ic ond Fridlan ond Eastgotan,
frodne ond godne fæder Unwenes.
Seccan sohte ic ond Beccan, Seafolan ond Þeodric,
Heaþoric ond Sifecan, Hliþe ond Incgenþeow.
Eadwine sohte ic ond Elsan, Ægelmund ond Hungar,
ond þa wloncan gedryht Wiþmyrginga.

Widsiþ

With Serkings I was and with Serings
with Greeks I was and with Finns and with Ceasar
who had control of the wine-strongholds.
The Wiolans and the Wilans and the Welsh kindom.
With Scots I was and with icts and with Scride-Finns
with Lidwicings I was and with Leonas and with Lombards
with heathens and with heroes and with Hundings.
With Israelites I was and with Exsyrings
with Hebrews and with Indians and with Egyptians
with Medes I was and with Perians and with Myrgings
and Mofdings and against the Myrgings
and with Amothings. With east Thuringians I was
and with Eolas and with Istas and with Idumingas.
And I was with Eormanric the whole time
where the king of the Goths honoured me with goods,
who gave me a ring, the foremost of the city-dwellers,
in which there were six hundred [units] of refined gold
cut up coins by number of shillings
I gave that into Eadgils's ownership
to my protecting lord when I came back home
as a reward to my dear one for granting me land
my father's homeland, the lord of the Myrgings.
And then Ealhhild gave me another
Edwin's daughter, the warriors' lady.
Her praise stretched across many lands
when in song I had to say
where the best under the sky I knew to be
a gold-adorned queen dispensing gifts
when Scilling and I with a bright voice
raised a song for our victorious lord.
Loud with the harp the sound mellowed
when many men, proud with mead,
spoke their words, who well knew
that they had never heard a better song.
From there I travelled round all the Gothic land
I always sought the best of companions
which was the household of Eormanric.
I sought the Heðcas and Beadecas and Herelingas
Emerica I sought and Fridlas and East Goths
The wise and good father of Unwene.
Secca I sought and Becca, Seafola and Þeodric,
Heaþoric and and Sifeca, Hliþe and Incgenþeow.
Edwin I sought and Elsa, Ægelmund and Hungar
and the proud troop of the Wiþmyrgings.

Wulfhere sohte ic ond Wyrmhere; ful oft þær wig ne alæg,
þonne Hræda here heardum sweordum
ymb Wistlawudu wergan sceoldon
ealdne eþelstol Ætlan leodum.
Rædhere sohte ic ond Rondhere, Rumstan ond Gislhere,
Wiþergield ond Freoþeric, Wudgan ond Haman;
ne wæran þæt gesiþa þa sæmestan,
þeah þe ic hy anihst nemnan sceolde.
Ful oft of þam heape hwinende fleag
giellende gar on grome þeode;
wræccan þær weoldan wundnan golde
werum ond wifum, Wudga ond Hama.
Swa ic þæt symle onfond on þære feringe,
þæt se biþ leofast londbuendum
se þe him god syleð gumena rice
to gehealdenne, þenden he her leofað."
 Swa scriþende gesceapum hweorfað
gleomen gumena geond grunda fela,
þearfe secgað, þoncword sprecaþ,
simle suð oþþe norð sumne gemetað
gydda gleawne, geofum unhneawne,
se þe fore duguþe wile dom aræran,
eorlscipe æfnan, oþþæt eal scæceð,
leoht ond lif somod; lof se gewyrceð,
hafað under heofonum heahfæstne dom.

Widsiþ

Wulfhere I sought and Wyrmhere; often war did not cease
when Hræda's army with hard swords
had to defend around Vistula-wood
their old tribal seat from Attila's folk.
Rædhere I sought and Rondhere, Rumstan and Gislhere,
Wiþergield and Freoþeric, Wudga and Hama
 - nor were they the least of my companions
though I have had to name them last.
Often from the troop flew a whistling,
yelling spear into an angry folk;
the adventurers there wielded the wound gold
for men and women, Wudga and Hama.
So I often found that in my wandering
that he is dearest to land-dwellers
to whom god gives the kingdom of men
to keep while he lives here."
Thus move the travellers as they must
warriors' gleemen, through many lands,
they speak their needs, say their words of thanks,
always – south or north – they meet someone
wise in songs, generous in gifts
who before his warriors wishes to raise his good name
to sustain his lordship, until all goes away –
light and life together – praise he earns,
holds a high reputation under the heavens.

3 The Structure and Origins of the Warband

In discussing the society and culture of the peoples of the ancient north, we must look to Tacitus for guidance. Speaking of the tribes of Germania[1] he remarks that kings are chosen for their nobility while war-leaders are chosen for their ability:[2] *et duces exemplo potius quam imperio si prompti, si conspicui, si ante aciem agant, admiratione praesunt* "they lead because of being admired if they are brash, if they are conspicuous, if they fight at the forefront". When they go to war they bring with them their mothers, wives and children, in order to win fame before their kinsfolk in battle; the women bind and tend their wounds, offer them food and encouragement. The tide of battle, he states, has even been turned by these women evoking the horrors to befall them if victory is not secured.

The groups represented are the 'national' armies of whole tribes, not the small single-leader warbands of the ale-ritual. The historicity of this account is partly confirmed by Tacitus's account of the leader Julius Civilis – a Germanic noble turned Roman governor turned native rebel – who in battle had the warsongs of his men mingled with the shrieks of their mothers, sisters, wives and children. In the social context of the hall, it is the females who praise the upright and shame shirkers and cowards; this duty to apportion praise and blame gives them the right to speak in the hall-assembly, to offer advice and opinion.

The Iron Age Germanic warband was not a male-only grouping but a complex structure based on interaction of leader, wife, household officers and followers. When King Masyos of the Semnones journeyed to Rome in AD 91-2, his party included Ganna, a seeress who customarily advised the ruler. Tacitus further mentions two Germanic spaewives whose fame had spread to Rome: Veleda (to whom Ganna was the successor) and Aurinia, as well as some unnamed others. A seeress called "Balouburg" or Waluburg accompanied a contingent of Germanic troops from the Semnones tribe to Egypt in Roman service. Another famous wise woman was Gambara of the Langobards, referred to by Paulus Diaconus.[3]

Scholars have been divided over the meaning of the passage in question: some have regarded it as a literary embellishment, part of the canonical tradition of

---

[1] It is not certain on what basis Tacitus included tribes among the Germani; political expediencies relevant to the contemporary state of the Empire seem often to have informed his decisions.

[2] Tacitus, *Germania*, 7 quoted in Enright, 1996

[3] The name *Ganna* appears to be cognate with the term *gand* meaning 'staff, wand' with both magical and weaving undertones, while *Gambara* may be interpreted as *gand-bara* 'wand-bearer'. *Waluburg* appears to contain the same element as Gothic *walus* 'wand, staff'. *Veleda* is formally identical with Gaulish **veleta* 'seeress' which is also found in Old Irish *filid* 'messenger, declarer of knowledge, wise man'. It has been suggested that the root **walu-* explains the first element of the name of Hroþgar's queen *Wealhþeow* (which otherwise appears to mean 'Welsh servant', not a very regal title). This same word gives the ON *volva* 'seeress'. The references point to the weaving beam as a means of divination. See above p. 184 for more on female prophetic powers.

ethnic description, emphasising the differences between barbarous Germania and Roman civilisation. Others have treated it as a slightly exaggerated statement of common opinion, and this latter approach seems to be supported by the fact that Germanic women sometimes were regarded as sibyls, they did act in the political sphere and they did have influence (if not control) over the warrior bands. Enright suggests that the Bructeri maiden, Veleda, whose clairvoyant powers were legendary in Tacitus's day, was manipulated by the rebel leader Julius Civilis, and the prophecies she delivered were based on his military and political strategies.[1] Access to the maiden was exclusively through a kinsman, which clearly offers grounds for suspicion that the messages handed down from her scrying-seat could be influenced and interpreted by the intermediary. Indeed, Germanic sacral kings were customarily deemed to be in charge of interpreting omens, as with the snorting of sacred horses [2] so the notion of restricted access to such information was not itself new.

The Germanic name for the 'warband' or group of armed followers is reconstructed as *druhtiz* giving OE *dryht, driht*, OHG *truht*, Frankish *druht* and ON *drótt*. These words are all based on the verb *dreugan* which appears in OE as *dreogan* 'suffer, undergo an experience' while its Gothic reflex *driugan* means 'perform military service'.[3] The earliest attestation of *druht* in the west is in the Frankish *Lex Salica* (c. 500 AD) where it apparently refers to the wedding procession, the passage of the bride among a group of youngsters from her paternal home to that of her groom. From this it has been argued[4] that the original meaning of *dreug-* concerned the armed escort for the bride and that, from this meaning, two sense developments took place: first, *druht* came to refer to an armed group of young men (without the notion of a festive occasion); second, a series of derivatives such as OE *dream* 'pleasure, entertainment, enjoyment' retained the festive aspect of the meaning but excluded the military dimension. A derivative of *dryht* in OE is *indrihtu* which normally means 'honour, glory' but may originally have denoted 'growth magic' based on the notion of the *dryht* as a cult group associated with fertility. Associated OE derivatives of *druht-* include *dryhtealdor* which glosses *paranymphus* 'one who brings the bride to her groom'

---

[1] Enright, op.cit.p.61ff. Enright sees the prophecying as a useful device for keeping headstrong tribesmen under control, by telling them that the omens were against a military engagement. In tribes where neither kings nor military leaders had an absolute right to command, other ways had to be found to achieve long-term aims without provoking internal challenges. The propaganda value of a prophetess was great, and her usefulness was enhanced if her prophecies could be influenced to order. There is also the morale aspect to allegedly supernatural endorsement, which is easily downplayed but must have been an important factor in early times when wars were fought hand-to-hand.

[2] Tacitus *Germania*, 10.

[3] Attempts to link the word *driht* to the same root as 'drink' have not been entirely successful; NE 'draught' is based on the root of 'draw, drag' rather than that of 'drink'.

[4] Enright, op.cit. p.72 cites Crozier's opinion that the OHG word *truhtsazzo* refers to the official responsible for seating the *druht* at the communal meal.

- yet the vast majority of these words have greater emphasis on military features e.g *dryhtguma* can mean 'best man at a wedding' but generally means 'warrior in a warband'. Likewise the honoured military 'rank' of *tacnbora* 'standard-bearer' can refer to the man who walked ahead of the group in a procession carrying a banner or emblem.[1] The likely ritual origins of this office are suggested by the association between the warband and the marriage procession.

Although Enright does not develop the point, it is perhaps pertinent to recall that the Germanic tribal army was composed of kindreds or 'clans', groups of men fighting alongside their relatives who were in many cases their neighbours.[2] Leaders of these groups were known in Gothic as *kindins* and in OE as *cyning*, both derivatives of **kuni* 'kin, family group'. The remarkable thing about the *gedriht* or 'warband' was that it cut across family structures, as we saw above (p. 24) It is possible, even likely, that when the *gedriht* transformed itself from a mainly ritual to a mainly military association, it retained the only native name for an armed group drawn from many kindreds, that of the wedding procession.

The rise of the *dux* and his *comitatus* was due to contact with the Mediterranean world. The small-scale, almost ritual warfare of the Bronze Age was transformed by the military ruthlessness of the Romans, Etruscans, Greeks and others whose purpose was to capture able-bodied slaves for their home markets. Defending themselves against these implacable foes meant that the traditional styles of fighting were transformed, and successful war-leaders could earn great respect, wealth and prestige; no doubt, in time the armed groups who had gathered to protect their folks from the Mediterranean states were able to turn their adopted techniques and technologies to new purposes and take part in settling old scores. As the *dux* grew in importance, the role of the *rex* was narrowed and eventually became marginal or merely symbolic.[3]

Similarly, with the rise of new power structures a new divinity comes to the fore: the god whose name **woðenaz* gives rise to OE *Woden* and ON *Óðinn*. The root of this name is **woþ-* which denotes 'anger', 'madness' and also 'poetry' and 'song'. In Irish the same root gives rise to the word *faith* 'poet',[4] and Latin *vates* 'seer' is also cognate. The essential idea is madness as 'ecstatic possession' by a god, giving rise to battle-fury and to soothsaying and clairvoyance.

In the context of both wedding and warband, there is a parallel structure: 'lord' / 'groom' as the leading male; 'lady' / 'bride' as the leading female and 'warband' / 'wedding party' as the gathering. The context also evokes ideas of transference

---

[1] In the *HE*, Bede states that King Edwin of Northumbria was preceded in peace and in war by his banner, called a *tufa* in Latin and *thuuf* in English.

[2] Tacitus, *Germania*, ch. 7

[3] This process is noted in respect of Central European peoples such as the Ardurni, Aedui and Helvetii where magnates felt confident enough to expel the traditional royalty. See Enright, op.cit. p.149

[4] Kershaw, 2000 p.69ff.

from one kindred to another, and of a conjoining of several groups into a temporary or fictive relationship of kinship. The ceremony celebrates and marks the transference of one party (the bride and her followers) into the kindred and social group of her husband; it is a rite of passage. The entry into the new household is marked by some ceremony – often involving the husband's weapons - and the taking of a communal drink of ale.[1]

In a further set of wedding/warband parallels, the rites attending the entry of a bride into her new, adoptive household are mirrored in those for a warrior entering into the household of his lord, his *dryht* and hall. The entrant was 'adopted' as the lord's fictive kinsman, entered his *sibbegedriht* 'band of relatives' and thenceforth stood in the same relationship to the lord as son would to father in a normal, kin-based household. Logically, his comrades are then his brothers-in-arms and they form a kind of substitute family. The bond is enacted when the leader hands weapons to the newcomer, in a rite mirroring the normal rite of passage whereby a youngster becomes a man and receives his weapons from his father or close kinsman. In a rite of closure, the members of the group drink a communal horn of strong drink together in an act of affirmation of their new relationship; the religious sanction implied by this gesture has been discussed above (p.45).

The strong and close association of free women with both drinking and binding agreements is found in English, German and Scandinavian literature from the earliest times into the Middle Ages. Typically, when a solemn or important announcement is to be made, it is rendered more potent (or sacred) by being accompanied with a drink served formally by a female. There are grounds for believing that the handfasting wedding ceremony itself may have involved the bride pouring a cup of strong drink and offering it to the groom: his acceptance and drinking of the stoup signified acceptance of the bride as his wife.[2] The cup-offering then seems to denote the completion of an agreement, whether between lord and follower or maiden and man. Furthermore, the admission of a member of the warband was parallel to the marriage ceremony in detail, because in both cases the head of the household took in a new fictive family member – the bride as fictive daughter and the warrior as fictive son. The leader's position as head of the household gave legitimacy to his authority over others, the bestower of goods over their receivers.

There is no known common ritual for the inauguration of kings (Tacitus's *reges*) among the various Germanic nations, at least until the intervention of the

---

[1] Pollington, 2002; Ellis Davidson, 1978; a modern parallel is ceremonially carrying the bride over the threshold, and drinking the 'bridal' ('bride-ale'). The use of weapons in sealing a wedding was carried forward even into Visigothic Spain where arms formed part of the *morgingeba* – the same word as OE *morgengifu* (morning-gift).

[2] The antiquity of this custom in barbarian Europe is demonstrated by a similar Celtic (Gaulish) rite enacted in the 4th century BC, cited in Enright, op.cit.p.82ff.

Christian church in bestowing full regal powers. It is likely enough that whatever local traditions had evolved within the various tribal units were maintained and adapted somewhat in isolation. Ascending to the high-seat – whether the gift-stool in the local hall or the state throne of a large nation – may have been the enabling act, when accompanied by the offering of the lord's cup by the leading lady of the group at a ritual meal.[1]

Warband leaders (Tacitus's *duces*) may possibly have been raised on a platform of their followers' shields, a practice alluded to in some later documents.

Enright shows that the theoretical 'flat' structure of the *comitatus* or warband must always have been highly stratified in reality: while group members called each other *wine* 'friend', this extended also to the leader (e.g *goldwine* 'gold-friend', etc.) and suggests that the ranking was very carefully delineated. Tacitus specifically says of the 1st century Germanic *comitatus* that it contained an array of ranks which was determined according to the leader's wishes.[2] The combination of strong drink and armed warriors doubtless led to fighting, bloodshed and deaths. It seems likely that warriors vied with each other for a position[3] close to the lord, and that the whole occasion was emotionally heavily charged, even politicised.

Looking further afield and back than the historical Germanic warband, Kershaw[4] has proposed an alternative possibility for the origins of the leader-based structure of the *druht* and the patron god, **Woðanaz*. Beginning with the close association of Norse Óðinn with the destructive military force called in OE *here* and in ON *herr*, he notes the notes the Odinic by-name *herjan* which appears to mean 'lord of the *herr*'[5] which suggests the question: what was the *herr*?

The Germanic original of *here / herr* is **harjaz* from PIE **koryos*, a word meaning 'group of young warriors' which occurs in some Celtic tribal names (*Tricorii*, *Petrucorii* with three and four such groups respectively). In Norse mythology, the special champions of Óðinn are known as the *Einherjar* 'select / singled out warriors', also based on the same root as *herr*. They traditionally ride with the god through the night sky in the Wild Hunt, a cavalcade of spectral warriors and huntsmen seen across northern Europe from France and England to Scandinavia. Details vary from place to place and time to time, but the original Ghostly Rider was the god *Woðanaz.

---

[1] The example of Julius Civilis is cited, who held a banquet at a holy site and incited his Batavians to rebellion after binding them with a customary oath after a large amount of strong drink had been consumed.

[2] Enright, op.cit.p.19 *gradus quin etiam ipse comitatus habet, indicio eius quem sectantur.*

[3] Enright, op.cit. *quibus primus apud principem suum locus*

[4] Kershaw, 2000

[5] If so, from a Proto-Germanic form **harjanaz* parallel in formation to Gothic *þiudans* 'lord of the people (*þiud*)'. In Anglo-Saxon England, thirty five armed men constituted a *here*, while among the Bavarians it took forty-two; in Denmark a *herr* was composed of five men, and in Lombardy four.

Appendix 3

It has long been recognised that these stories reflect memories of actual cult processions which once took place, connected with the worship of the god. Furthermore, the leader of the procession was a figure known as the *Erl King* or *Herlaking*, which eventually became the *Harlequin* of early modern theatre. One explanation for the name links it to **harja – kuning* 'king of the **harjaz*' and sees the **harjaz* as a religious cult grouping rather than a specifically military arrangement.

An early English reference to such a procession is found in the ASC under the year 1127:[1]

> *Ne þince man na sellice þæt we soð seggen for hit wæs ful cuð ofer eall land þæt swa radlice swa he þær com þæt wæs þes sunendaies þæt man singeð exurge quare OD þa son þær æfter þa segon 7 herdon fela men feole huntes hunten. Ða huntes wæron swearte 7 micele 7 ladlice 7 here hundes ealle swarte 7 bradegede 7 ladlice 7 hi ridone on swarte hors 7 on swarte bucces. Þis wæs segon on þe selue derfald in þa tune on Burch 7 on ealle þa wudes ða wæron fram þa selua tune to Stanforde 7 þa muneces herdon ða horn blawen þæt hi blewen on nihtes. Soðfæste men heom kepten on nihtes sæiden þes þe heom þuhte þæt þær mihte wel ben abuton twenty oðer þritti horn blaweres.*

Let no man think it strange which we truly tell, since it was well known through all the land that as soon as he [Abbot Henry] came there – that was the Sunday when one sings Exurge quare O.D. – then soon thereafter many men saw and heard many hunters hunting. The hunters were black and large and ugly, and their hounds all black and big-eyed and ugly, and they rode on black horses and on black goats. This was seen in the deer-fold itself in the estate at Peterborough and in all the woods which extended from that same estate to Stamford, and the monks heard the horns blowing which they blew at night. Truthful men who kept watch at night said this: that it seemed to them that there might well be around twenty or thirty hornblowers.

Tacitus[2] refers to a Germanic people called the *Harii*, evidently the plural of **harjaz*, who were noted for destructiveness, blackening their bodies and fighting at night. This may have been a misunderstanding on his part as regards the nature of the group. Elsewhere he notes the custom of allowing certain very fierce, dedicated warriors of the Chatti tribe a privileged lifestyle among the farming

---

[1] See Pollington, 2001
[2] *Germania* ch43.

settlements; these men owned no property except weapons and a neck-ring which marked their status. They grew their hair long as a badge of distinction whereas normally youngsters cut their hair after their first successful military encounter.[1] These warriors have been compared with the *berserkir* 'bear-shirts' of Icelandic tradition, devotees of the war-god utilising animal symbolism and probably in some kind of cult group focussed on the bear or wolf (another group called itself *ulfheðnar* 'wolf-masks').[2] These men were outside the normal rules of society, and fought in an ecstatic trance rushing wildly at the foe – much as untrained youths might do, with great enthusiasm but little caution or restraint. Furthermore, Kershaw sees the **harjaz* as identical to the foot-soldiers whom Tacitus[3] describes as fighting in a wedge formation while the mounted troops form up in their rear. Apart from the tactical value of a solid, determined infantry unit, it may be that they fought on foot because – being young and still landless – they did not have the means to buy or keep a horse. The wealthier, mounted troops were the **þiuðaz*, a word which denotes the people as a whole, the body of freemen.

Kershaw argues that the **harjaz* – or rather its predecessor the **koryos* – was a cult group in historical times but originally its purpose was quite different. He sees the group of youths as an 'age-set', a gathering of pubescent males from a single community having reached the stage of physical maturity at which they must graduate to adulthood. This process involved a period of separation from friends, family and community; a time of living rough in the woods or wilderness, accepting hospitality where it was offered, or taking supplies (especially food and strong drink) by force if necessary. Under the tutelage of an elder, they learnt to survive by hunting and foraging, and also by stealth. They adopted animal personas, wore skins and developed hunting strategies based on animal behaviour.[4] At times, they ate the hearts and drank the blood of the beasts they wished to emulate.

---

[1] The root of **harjaz* is possibly **har-* 'hair' implying that these groups were distinguished by their hair. If the length of their hair was significant, it may be that they dressed it in the famous 'Swabian knot', a top- or side-knot which has been found archaeologically (e.g. bog-body from Osterby, Denmark, see Glob, 1971) as well as in sculpture and literary references (Rives, 1999). The top-knot was kept in place by stiffening the hair with a substance called **sapo-*, Latinized and borrowed back into English as 'soap'; it was probably a mixture of tallow and ashes with a colorant added – the *Germani* were recorded to have dyed their hair red. (Green, 1998, p.188) Ptolemy groups the *Anglii* (i.e. the proto-English) among the Swabians *(Sueboi Angeiloi)*, which may indicate that the *Anglii* knew and practised this custom (Rives, 1999).

[2] Ellis Davidson, 1964; Pollington, 2001

[3] *Germania*, ch.6

[4] Ellis Davidson 1978; Pollington, 2001. Kershaw, op.cit. p.142ff, sees later, historical animal-related figures and names as a distant memory of this phase – tribal groups such as the East Anglian *Wuffingas* 'wolf-folk', and the *Glommas* of *Widsiþ* (from *glamm* 'bark') as well as many others in Germanic history and literature.

Appendix 3

In this liminal state between boyhood and manhood, the members of the *koryos* were technically (and legally) outside the family and its obligations, they lived and behaved as free individuals not subject to the traditional strictures of life within the community. In this state of being associated with their kin groups but not structurally part of them (being neither boys nor men), they took a ritual status akin to that of ancestors; they painted or blackened[1] or masked themselves and dressed in pelts to disguise their individual appearances, and so took on a ritual or symbolic role of the 'ancestors returned among the living'.[2] In this role they were accorded great honour and hospitality at religious festivals and processions involving weapon-dances and singing; the return of the ancestors brought with it blessings and prosperity for the community.

Prolonged dancing was a means of inducing the ecstatic trance state; Tacitus[3] describes Germanic youths undertaking spear-dances, and 7th century helmet-plate formers from Torslunda, Sweden, depict dancing men with spears while the Sutton Hoo helmet also features plates showing sword-and-spear-bearers in an apparently contorted pose suggestive of dancing. Sword-dances are relatively well-attested throughout northern Europe, and may reflect a vague memory of the tradition; often, the weapon is replaced by a harmless wooden wand which is used to link the dancers in an endless, undulating chain.[4]

Kershaw also sees the dedicated warrior as a 'sacred person' (*ver sacrum*) whose function it is to lead his *koryos* band away in exile from the tribal lands and to found a new settlement. As a founder, the *ver sacrum* is able to constitute a new society for his group. This is alleged to explain the many lupine, ursine, equine and canine references in the Germanic onomastic tradition – the spirit of the animal guardian is held to be responsible for the new group, and is commemorated through their group-name.

---

[1] It is suggested that soot and ash might be used to darken the appearance. Irish tradition recognises the *cu glas* 'grey dog' (= wolf), with the colour word *glas* based on the word *glasto-*, denoting woad, a plant yielding a heavy, dark pigment. It may be, then, that an infusion of woad was used for this purpose. In historical times, a *cu glas* was an exiled warrior, a lone wolf. Glastonbury, Somerset, is derived from the British plant-name.

[2] The warriors of the Chatti mentioned above were remarkable not for entering this phase, but for refusing to emerge from it. They retained the trappings of teenage excess into their adult years, and paid with their lives for their refusal to adopt full manly status within the community. Kershaw suggests that other tribes knew the same phenomenon, and that this is demonstrated by the relatively common iconography of weapon-dancers in Germanic art. The *berserkar* and other consecrated warrior groups are a historical residue of this.

[3] *Germania*, ch.24

[4] Dances of this kind form part of the English Morris tradition; some still blacken their faces, a further link with the *koryos*, rationalised as depiciton of a Moor.

Bibliography

ALLEN, J. *Metal Bowls of the Late Celtic and Anglo-Saxon Period*, in Archaeologia, 56, 1898

ANTHONY, D. *Prehistoric Migration as Social Process*, in Chapman & Hamerow, 1997

ARNOLD, C.J. *An Archaeology of the Early Anglo-Saxon Kingdoms*, London, 1997

ASTON, M. *Post-Roman Central Places in Somerset* in Grant, E. 1986

AUSENDA, G. (ed.) *After Empire: Towards an Ethnology of Europe's Barbarians*, San Marino, 1995

BAKER, P.S. *The Beowulf Reader*, London, 2000

BARFORD, P.M. *Reinterpreting Mucking: Countering the Black Legend*, in Griffiths, 1995

BARLEY, N. *Structural Aspects of the Anglo-Saxon Riddle* in Semiotica, 10, 1974

BAUSCHATZ, P. *The Well and the Tree – World and Time in Early Germanic Culture*, Amherst, 1982

BAZELMANS, J *By Weapons Made Worthy: Lords, Retainers and Their Relationship in 'Beowulf'*, Amsterdam, 1999

BETTESS, F. *The Anglo-Saxon Foot: A Computerised Assessment* in Medieval Archaeology 35, 1991

BJORK, R.E. & NILES, J.D. *A Beowulf Handbook*, Exeter, 1997

BLOOMFIELD, M.W. & DUNN, C.W. *The Role of the Poet in Early Societies*, Cambridge, 1989

BRANSTON, B .*The Lost Gods of England*, London, 1974
- *Gods of the North*, London, 1980

BRENAN, J. *Hanging Bowls and their Contexts,* BAR. 220, Oxford 1991

BRINK, S. *Political and Social Structures in Early Scandinavia – a Settlement-Historical Pre-Study of the Central Place,* Uppsala, 1996

BRUCE-MITFORD, R *The Sutton Hoo Ship Burial* Vol.3 (parts 1 & 2) London 1983

BUCKLEY, D.G. (ed) *Archaeology in Essex to 1500*, London, 1980

CALDER, D.G & CHRISTY, T.C. *Germania – Comparative Studies in the Old Germanic Languages and Literatures*, Woodbridge, 1988

CAMBRIDGE ARCHAEOLOGICAL UNIT, *A Roman and Saxon Settlement at Bloodmoor Hill, Carlton Colville, Lowestoft* published 1998
at http://www.eng-h.gov.uk/archcom/projects/summarys/html98_9/cc2313.htm

CAMERON, E.A. *Sheaths and Scabbards in England AD400-1100*, BAR British Series 301, Oxford, 2000

CAMERON, M.L. *Anglo-Saxon Medicine*, Cambridge, 1993

CAMPBELL, A. *Old English Grammar*, Oxford, 1987

CARE-EVANS, A. *The Sutton Hoo Ship Burial*, London, 1986
- *Metalwork & Sculpture*, in Webster & Backhouse, 1991

CARVER, M. (ED.) *The Age of Sutton Hoo – The Seventh Century in Northern Europe*, Woodbridge, 1992
- *Sutton Hoo – Burial Ground of Kings?* London, 1998

CESSFORD, C. *Exogamous Marriages between Anglo-Saxons and Britons in Seventh Century Northern Britain* in Griffiths, 1996

Bibliography

CHAPMAN, J & HAMEROW, H. *Migrations and Invasions in Archaeological Explanation*, Oxford, 1997

CHASE, C. (ED) *The Dating of Beowulf*, Toronto, 1981

CLARK HALL, J.R. *A Concise Anglo-Saxon Dictionary*, Toronto, 1984

CLOVER, C. *The Germanic Context of the Unferþ Episode* in Baker, 2000

COOK, A.M. *The Anglo-Saxon Cemetery at Fonaby, Lincolnshire*, Lincoln, 1981

CREED, R.P. *Widsið's Journey Through Germanic Tradition*, in Nicholson & Warwick Frese, 1975

CROSSLEY-HOLLAND, K. *The Exeter Book Riddles*, Harmondsworth, 1978

CROWFOOT, G.M. *Anglo-Saxon Tablet Weaving* in *The Antiquaries' Journal*, vol.32, 1952

CUBBIN, G.P. *The 'Anglo-Saxon Chronicle' A Collaborative Edition, Volume 6, MS D*, Cambridge, 1996

DAMICO, H. *The Valkyrie Reflex in Old English Literature* in *New Readings on Women in Old English Literature*, Bloomington, 1990

DIXON, P *Secular Architecture* in Webster & Backhouse, 1991
- *The Anglo-Saxon Settlement at Mucking: an Interpretation* in *Anglo-Saxon Studies in Archseology & History* (6), Oxford, 1993

DIXON, P.H. *The Reading Lathe – A Link with the Anglo-Saxon Migration*, Newport. 1994
- *Entrances to Sunken-floored Structures in Anglo-Saxon Times* in Griffiths, 1995

DODWELL, C.R. *Anglo-Saxon Art – A New Perspective*, Manchester, 1982

DUNNING, G. *The Anglo-Saxon Plane from Sarre* in *Arch. Cant.* 73, 1959

EARL, J.W. *Thinking About 'Beowulf'*, Stanford, 1994

EAST, K. *Review of the Evidence for Drinking Horns and Wooden Cups from Anglo-Saxon Sites* in Bruce-Mitford, 1983

ELLIS DAVIDSON, H.R. *Gods & Myths of Northern Europe*, Harmondsworth, 1964
- *Patterns of Folklore*, Ipswich, 1978

ENRIGHT, M.J. *Lady With A Mead Cup: Ritual, Prophecy and Lordship in the European Warband from La Tene to the Viking Age*, Dublin, 1996

EVANS, S.E. *The Lords of Battle: Image and Reality of the Comitatus in Dark Age Britain*, Woodbridge, 1997

EVISON, V. *Anglo-Saxon Finds near Rainham, Essex, with a Study of the Glass Drinking-horns* in *Archaeologia* (96), 1955
- *Wheel-Thrown Pottery in Anglo-Saxon Graves*, London, 1979
- *Anglo-Saxon Glass Claw Beakers* in *Archaeologia* (107), London, 1982
- *Some Vendel, Viking and Saxon Glass* in Hardh, Larsson et al, 1988a
- *An Anglo-Saxon Cemetery at Alton, Hampshire*, Hampshire, 1988b

FAITH, R. *The English Peasantry and the Growth of Lordship*, London, 1997

FARRELL, E. AND NEUMANN DE VEGVAR, C. *Sutton Hoo: Fifty Years After*, American Early Medieval Studies 2, Oxford, 1992

FELL, C. *Women in Anglo-Saxon England*, London, 1984

FERNIE, E. *Anglo-Saxon Lengths: The Northern System, the Perch and the Foot* in *Archaeological Journal*, 142, 1985
- *Anglo-Saxon Lengths and the Evidence of the Buildings*, in *Medieval Archaeology*, 35, 1991

FLETCHER, R.*Who's Who in Roman Britain and Anglo-Saxon England*, London, 1989
- *Bloodfeud – Murder and Revenge in Anglo-Saxon England*, London, 2002

Bibliography

GARDNER, J. *Guilt and the World's Complexity: The Murder of Ongentheow and the Slaying of the Dragon* in Nicholson & Warwick Frese, 1975

GARMONSWAY, G.N. *An Early Norse Reader*, Cambridge, 1928
- *Ælfric's Colloquy,* Exeter, 1978

GLOB, P.V. *The Bog People*, St. Albans, 1971

GOOLDEN, P. (ED.) *The Old English Apollonius of Tyre*, Oxford, 1958

GRANT, E. *Central Places, Archaeology and History*, Sheffield, 1986

GRATTAN, J.H.G. & SINGER, C. *Anglo-Saxon Magic and Medicine*, London, 1952

GREEN, B. & ROGERSON, A. *The Anglo-Saxon Cemetery at Bergh Apton, Norfolk*, Dereham, 1978

GREEN, B., ROGERSON, A. & WHITE, S.G. *The Anglo-Saxon Cemetery at Morningthorpe, Norfolk*, Vols. 1&2, Dereham, 1987

GREEN, D.H. *Language and History in the Early Germanic World*, Cambridge, 1998

GREENFIELD, S.B. *The Interpretation of Old English Poems*, London, 1972

GRIFFITHS, B. *The Battle of Maldon – Text and Translation*, Pinner, 1991
- *An Introduction to Early English Law*, Hockwold-cum-Wilton, 1995

GRIFFITHS, D. (ed) *Anglo-Saxon Studies in Archaeology and History*, Vol.8, Oxford, 1995
- *Anglo-Saxon Studies in Archaeology and History*, Vol.9, Oxford, 1996
- *Anglo-Saxon Studies in Archaeology and History*, Vol.11, Oxford, 2000

GRONBECH, V. *The Culture of the Tetons,* London, 1931

HAGEN. A. *A Handbook of Anglo-Saxon Food – Processing and Consumption*, Pinner, 1992
- *A Second Handbook of Anglo-Saxon Food & Drink – Production & Distribution*, Hockwold-cum-Wilton, 1995

HALSALL, M. *The Old English Rune Poem: a Critical Edition*, Toronto, 1981.

HAMEROW, H *Migration Theory and the Anglo-Saxon "Identity Crisis"* in Chapman & Hamerow, 1997
- *Early Medieval Settlements: The Archaeology of Rural Communities in North-West Europe, 400-900*, Oxford, 2002

HANSEN, E.T. *The Solomon Complex – Reading Wisdom in Old English Poetry*, Toronto, 1988

HARDEN, D. B. *A Glass Bowl of Dark Age Date and Some Medieval Grave-Finds from Shaftesbury Abbey* in *Antiquaries' Journal*, 1954

HARDH, B., LARSSON, L. et al (eds) *Trade and Exchange in Prehistory* in *Acta Archaeologia Lundensia* (16), 1988

HARTLEY, D. *The Land of England*, London, 1979

HAWKES, J. *The Golden Age of Northumbria,* Morpeth, 1996

HAWKES, S.C. *The Anglo-Saxon Cemetery of Bifrons, in the Parish of Patrixbourne, East Kent* in Griffiths, 2000

HAWKES, S.C., CAMPBELL, J. & BROWN, D. *Anglo-Saxon Studies in Archaeology and History*, vol.4, Oxford, 1985a

HAYMES, A. *Anglo-Saxon Kinship* in *Wiðowinde* 116, London, 1998

HEALEY, T. *Life in the Viking Age*, London, 1998

HEATHER, P. & MATTHEWS, J. *The Goths in the Fourth Century*, Liverpool, 1991

HEDEAGER, L. *Iron Age Societies – From Tribe to State in Northern Europe, 500 BC to AD 700*, Oxford, 1992

HENNESSY OLSEN, A. *Gender Roles* in Bjork & Niles, 1997

Bibliography

HENRY, P.A. *The Early English and Celtic Lyric*, London, 1966

HERBERT, K. *Spellcraft – Old English Heroic Legends*, Pinner, 1993

HERSCHEND, F. *The Idea of the Good in Late Iron Age Society*, Uppsala, 1998

HEWETT, C.A. *The Implications of Pre-Conquest Carpentry in Essex* in Buckley, 1980

HILL, D. *An Atlas of Anglo-Saxon England*, Oxford, 1981

HILL, J.M. *The Cultural World in Beowulf*, Toronto, 1995
- *Social Milieu* in Bjork & Niles, 1997

HILLS, C., PENN, K. & RICKETT, R. *The Anglo-Saxon Cemetery at Spong Hill, North Elmham. Part III: Catalogue of Inhumations*, Dereham, 1984

HODGES, R. *Dark Age Economics – The Origins of Towns and Trade, AD 600-1000*, London 1989

HOPE-TAYLOR, B. *Yeavering: An Anglo-British Centre of Early Northumbria*, London, 1977

HUGGINS, P. *Anglo-Saxon Timber Building Measurements: Recent Results* in *Medieval Archaeology* 35, 1991

HUME, K. *The Concept of the Hall in Old English Poetry*, in *Anglo-Saxon England*, 5

HURST, J.G. *The Pottery* in Wilson, D.M. (ed.), 1976

JOLLY, K.L. *Popular Religion in Late Saxon England: Elf Charms in Context*, Chapel Hill, 1996

JONES, M.U. *Mucking and the Early Saxon Rural Settlement in England* in Buckley, 1980

JONES, W.T. *Early Saxon Cemeteries in Essex* in Buckley, 1980

KÄMPFER, F. & BEYER, K.G. *Glass – A World History*, London, 1966

KENDRICK, T.D. *Anglo-Saxon Art*, London, 1938

KERSHAW, K. *The One-Eyed God – Odin and the (Indo-) Germanic Männerbünde*, JIES Monograph no.36, Washington D.C, 2000

KEYNES, S. & LAPIDGE, M *Alfred the Great – Asser's 'Life of Kinf Alfred' and Other Contemporary Sources*, Harmondsworth, 1983

KOOPER, E. (ED.) *This Noble Craft – Proceedings of the Xth Research Symposium of the Dutch and Belgian University Teachers of Old ande Middle English and Historical Linguistics*, Utrecht, 1991

KRAMER, E. ET AL., *Kings of the North Sea, AD250-850*, Newcastle-upon-Tyne, 2000

KRAPP, G.P. & VAN KIRK DOBBIE, E. *The Exeter Book*, New York, 1936

LAWSON, G. *The Lyre from Grave 22* in Green & Rogerson, 1978
- *An Anglo-Saxon Harp and Lyre of the Ninth Century* in Widdes, D.R. & Wolpert, R.F., 1981
- *-Report on the Lyre Remains from Grave 97* in Green, Rogerson & White, 1987

LESLIE, R. F. *The Wanderer*, Exeter, 1985

LOCHERBIE-CAMERON, M *Some Things the Maldon Poet Did Not Say* in *Parergon*, 5, 1995

MAGENNIS, H. *Images of Community in Old English Poetry*, Cambridge, 1996

MALDEN, H.E. *The Victoria History of the County of Surrey*, Vol.1, London, 1902

MALIM, T. & HINES, J. *The Anglo-Saxon Cemetry at Edix Hill (Barrington A) Cambridgeshire*, York, 1998

MAYES, P. & DEAN, M.J. *An Anglo-Saxon Cemetery at Baston, Lincolnshire*, Sleaford, 1976

MESSENT, J. *The Bayeux Tapestry Embroiderer's Story*, Thirsk, 1999

MILIS, L.J.R. (TRANS. GUEST, T.) *The Pagan Middle Ages*, Woodbridge, 1998

Bibliography

MILLS, N. *Saxon and Viking Artefacts*, Witham, 2001

MOULTON, W.G. *Mutual Intelligibility Among Speakers of Early Germanic Dialects* in Calder & Christy, 1988

MURRAY, H.J.R. *A History of Board-Games Other Than Chess*, Oxford, 1952

NEEDHAM, G.I. *Ælfric – The Lives of Three English Saints*, Exeter, 1976

NEUMANN DE VEGVAR, C. *The Sutton Hoo Horns as Regalia* in Farrell, E. and Neumann de Vegvar, C. 1992

NICOLSON, L.E. & WARWICK FRESE, D. *Anglo-Saxon Poetry: Essays in Appreciation*, Notre Dame, 1975

NORTH, R. *Heathen Gods in Old English Literature*, Cambridge, 1997

O' SULLIVAN, D. *A Group of Pagan Burials from Cumbria?* in Griffiths, 1996

OWEN, G.R. *Wynflæd's Wardrobe* in *Anglo-Saxon England*, 8, 1979

OWEN CROCKER, G.R. *Dress in Anglo-Saxon England*, Manchester, 1986
- *Hawks and Horse-Trappings: the Insignia of Rank* in Scragg, 1991

PAGE, R.I. *Reading the Past: Runes*, London, 1987
- *An Introduction to English Runes*, Woodbridge, 1999

PAGE, W. *The Victoria History of the County of Essex*, Vol.1, London, 1903
- *The Victoria History of the County of Buckinghamshire*, Vol.1, London, 1905
- *The Victorai History of the County of Kent,* Vol.1, London, 1908

PARKS, W. *Verbal Duelling in Heroic Narrative – The Homeric & Old English Traditions*, Oxford, 1990

PEERS, C. & RALEIGH RADFORD, C.A. *The Saxon Monastery of Whitby* in *Archaeologia*, vol.89, 1943

PHILLIPS, A. *The Hallowing of England – A Guide to the Saints of Old England and their Places of Pilgrimage*, Pinner, 1994

PARFITT, K. *The Buckland Saxon Cemetery* in *Current Archaeology*, Vol.XII no.12 (1995)

PLUMMER, C. & EARLE, J., *Two of the Saxon Chronicles Parallel ,* Oxford University Press, Oxford, 1892

POLLINGTON, S. *Leechcraft. Early English Charms, Plant Lore and Healing*, Hockwold-cum-Wilton, 2000
- *The English Warrior from Earliest Times to 1066*, Hockwold-cum-Wilton, 2001

POLOME, E. *Introduction* to *Homage To Georges Dumezil*, Washington,1982

PROUDFOOT, E. & ALIAGA-KELLY, C. *Anomalous Finds and Place-Names of Anglo-Saxon Origin in Scotland* in Griffiths, 1996

PUHVEL, J. *Comparative Mythology*, London, 1987

RAHTZ, P. *Buildings and Rural Settlement* in Wilson (ed.), 1976

RIVES, J.B. (TRANS.) *Tacitus – Germania*, Oxford, 1999

ROBERTS, J, KAY, C. & GRUNDY, L. *A Thesaurus of Old English*, London, 1995

ROBINSON, F.C. *Artful Ambiguitiesin the Old English 'Book-Moth' Riddle* in Nicolson & Warwick Frese, 1975

ROESDAHL, E. *The Scandinavians at Home* in Wilson, 1980

SALZMAN, L.F. *The Victoria History of the County of Oxford*, Volume 1, Oxford, 1939

SAVELLI, M. *Tastes of Anglo-SaxonEngland*, Hockwold-cum-Wilton, 2002

Bibliography

Scragg, D.G. *The Battle of Maldon*, Manchester, 1981
- *The Battle of Maldon, AD 991*, Oxford, 1991

Shippey, T.A. *Old English Verse*, London, 1972
- *Poems of Wisdom and Learning in Old English*, Cambridge, 1976

Simek, R. *A Dictionary of Northern Mythology*, Oxford, 1993

Smith. A. *Sixty Saxon Saints*, Pinner, 1994

Smith, R.A. *A Guide to the Anglo-Saxon and Foreign Teutonic Antiquities*, Oxford, 1923

Speake, G. *A Saxon Bed Burial on Swallowcliffe Down*, London, 1989

Stanley, E.G. *The Search for Anglo-Saxon Paganism*, Cambridge, 1964

Steensberg, A. *Hand-made Pottery in Jutland* in *Antiquity*, 1940

Stenton, F.M. *Anglo-SaxonEngland*, Oxford, 1971

Stephenson, I.P. *The Anglo-Saxon Shield*, Stroud, 2002

Storms, G. *Anglo-Saxon Magic*, The Hague, 1948

Stratford, N. *The Lewis Chessmen and the Enigma of the Hoard*, London, 1997

Sweet, H. *Anglo-Saxon Reader in Prose & Verse*, Oxford, 1967

Thorpe, B. *The Old English Apollonius of Tyre*, London, 1834

Thorpe, L. *The Bayeux Tapestry and the Norman Invasion*, London, 1973

Tidow, K. *Prachtmäntel, Frisian Cloth and Other Woollen Textiles* in Kramer et al., 2000

Tigges, W. *Signs and Solutions: A Semiotic Approach to the Exeter Book Riddles*, in Kooper, 1991

Todd, M. *Migrants and Invaders – The Movement of Peoples in the Ancient World*, Strood, 2001

Tolkien, J.R.R. (ed. Bliss, A.) *Finn and Hengest – the Fragment and the Episode*, London, 1982

Wade, K. *A Settlement Site at Bonhunt Farm, Wicken Bonhunt, Essex* in Buckley, 1980

Waegeman, A. *The Medieval Sybil* in Milis, 1998

Watkins, C. *How to Kill a Dragon – Aspects of Indo-European Poetics*, Oxford, 1995

Watson, J. *Organic Material Associated with Metalwork* in Malim & Hines, 1998

Webster, L. & Backhouse, J. *The Making of England – Anglo-Saxon Art and Culture 600-900*, London, 1991

Welch, C. *Anglo-Saxon England*, London, 1992

West, S. *Westgarth Gardens Anglo-Saxon Cemetery, Suffolk: Catalogue*, Bury St. Edmunds, 1988

Whitelock, D. *Sermo Lupi ad Anglos*, Exeter, 1976

Wickham-Crowley, K., *The Birds on the Sutton Hoo Instrument* in Farell, E. and Neumann de Vegvar, C., 1992

Widdes, D.R. & Wolpert, R.F. *Music and Tradition: Essays on Asian and Other Music*, Cambridge, 1981

Williams, H. *Ancient Landscapes and the Dead: The Re-use of Prehistoric and Roman Monuments as Early Anglo-Saxon Burial Sites* in *Medieval Archaeology* (41), 1997

Williams, J., Shaw, M. & Denham, V. *Middle Saxon Palaces at Northampton*, Northampton, 1985

Williams, P.W. *An Anglo-Saxon Cemetery at Thurmaston, Leicestershire*, Leicester, 1983

Williamson, C. *A Feast of Creatures – Anglo-Saxon Riddle Songs* London, 1983

Wilson, D. *A Note on OE 'hearg' and 'weoh' as Place-Name Elements Representing Different Types of Pagan Saxon Worship Types* in Hawkes, Campbell & Brown, 1985a

Bibliography

WILSON, D.M. (ed.) *The Archaeology of Anglo-Saxon England*, London, 1976
- *Craft & Industry* in *The Archaeology of Anglo-Saxon England*, London, 1976
- (ed.) *The Northern World: The History and Heritage of Northern Europe AD400-1100,* London, 1980
- *The Bayeux Tapestry*, London, 1985

WILSON, D.M. & BLUNT, C.E. *The Trewhiddle Hoard* in *Archaeologia* (98), 1961

WOOD, I. N. *Pagan Religion and Superstitions East of the Rhine from the Fifth to the Ninth Century* in Ausenda, 1995

WOOD, M. *The English Mediaeval House*, London, 1965

WOOLF, R. *The Ideal of Men Dying with their Lord in the 'Germania' and in 'The Battle of Maldon'*, in *Anglo-Saxon England*, 5, 1976

WRENN, C.L (revised by Bolton, W.F.) *Beowulf* London, 1973

WRIGHT, J. *Grammar of the Gothic Language*, Oxford, 1910

WYATT, A.J & CHAMBERS, R.W. *Beowulf with the Finnsburg Fragment*, Cambridge, 1920

YARWOOD, D. *The English Home*, London, 1979

YOUNGS, S.M. *The Gaming Pieces* in Bruce-Mitford, 1983

ZALUCKYJ, S. *Mercia: The Anglo-Saxon Kingdom of Central England*, Little Logaston, 2001

Index

(ge)driht, 12, 31, 103, 232, 260, 261

Abingdon, Oxfordshire, 37
Adam of Bremen, 45
Æðelberht, King of Wessex, 186, 196
Æðelstan, King (Athelstan), 82, 220
Æðelwulf, King, 196
Ægir, 31
Ælfhelm, Ealdormann, 28
Ælfred, King, 186, 209
Ælfred, King (Alfred), 24, 30, 79, 132, 186, 196, 209, 271
Ælfric, 59, 117, 130, 138, 191, 243, 270, 272
Æsir, 106, 108, 110
Æþelred, King (Ethelred), 95
Alcuin, 192, 199, 209
Aldfrith, King of Northumbria, 209
Aldhelm of Malmesbury, 208, 209
ale, 39, 40, 41, 43, 46, 47, 50, 60, 62, 80, 84, 85, 101, 117, 128, 129, 130, 150, 151, 162, 166, 259, 262
Alton, Hampshire, 146, 151, 269
Andreas, 30, 129
Anglo-Saxon Chronicle, 12, 24, 25, 87, 223, 264, 269
animals, 37, 50, 124, 125, 138, 173, 210
Apollonius of Tyre, 57, 270, 273
Ashingdon, Essex, 28
Asser, Bishop, 132, 186, 271
Asthall, Oxfordshire, 217
Athelney, Somerset, 69
Athelstan, King, 82, 220
Aurinia, 184, 259
Austria, 176
Balthild, Queen, 184
Bamburgh, Northumberland, 93

barrow, 12, 61, 63, 79, 119, 140, 142, 144, 146, 149, 150, 152, 170, 217, 219
Baston, Lincolnshire, 137, 271
Battle of Brunanburh, 195, 223
Bayeux Tapestry, 40, 42, 86, 87, 125, 126, 139, 177, 178, 271, 273
Bede, 6, 13, 21, 48, 57, 59, 60, 63, 80, 84, 92, 137, 167, 182, 186, 187, 209, 226, 261
beer, 30, 40, 50, 55, 56, 57, 80, 85, 105, 128, 129, 154, 220, 227, 229, 233, 235, 241
Belgium, 148
Benedict Biscop, 137
Benedictine Rule, 37
Beow, 200
Beowulf, 6, 15, 16, 19, 20, 22, 26, 27, 31, 32, 33, 34, 35, 36, 37, 38, 39, 40, 41, 42, 43, 46, 48, 51, 52, 54, 55, 56, 62, 63, 82, 84, 85, 86, 100, 101, 102, 103, 104, 105, 106, 110, 113, 115, 116, 117, 120, 121, 128, 129, 167, 178, 179, 183, 184, 186, 188, 189, 192, 194, 197, 198, 200, 201, 202, 203, 222, 223, 224, 232, 233, 234, 235, 239, 268, 269, 271, 274
Bergh Apton, Norfolk, 204, 270
Berkshire, 77, 152
Beverley Minster, Yorkshire, 81
Bidford-on-Avon, 153
Bifrons, Kent, 154, 156, 270
birch, 119
Bishopstone, Sussex, 74, 90
Blackness, 61
Blackwater, River, 127
board game, 215, 216, 220
boasts, 27, 105

Boethius, 203, 209
Book of Durrow, 60
Bosham, Sussex, 40, 87
Bourton-on-the-Water, Gloucestershire, 167
Brandon, Suffolk, 139
bread, 36, 122, 123, 124, 125, 126, 127, 128, 177, 181, 187, 195
bride, 35, 60, 104, 105, 186, 260, 261, 262
bride-ale, 60, 262
British, 4, 56, 60, 61, 68, 70, 81, 86, 88, 89, 93, 97, 98, 119, 150, 152, 162, 164, 166, 173, 187, 192, 193, 266, 268, 271
Bromeswell, Suffolk, 61
Bronze Age, 61, 115, 261
Broome Park, Kent, 140
Broomfield, Essex, 79, 119, 144, 149
Brougham, Cumbria, 146
Bructeri, 260
Brunhild, Queen, 120
Buckinghamshire, 15, 142, 145, 149, 217, 272
Bucklersbury Common, Berkshire, 77
Buiston, East Lothian, 98
Burghal Hidage, 96
Burghead, Morayshire, 151
burh, 12, 30, 113, 234
Bury St. Edmunds, Suffolk, 136, 141, 161, 273
butter, 36, 122, 124
Byrhtnoð, Ealdormann, 25, 100, 186, 221, 223

Cadwallon, King of Gwynedd, 55, 92, 98
Cædmon, 6, 56, 57, 59, 111, 115, 193, 194, 195, 204, 226, 229
Caenby, Lincolnshire, 150
Caistor-by-Norwich, Norfolk, 218
Calne, Wiltshire, 87
Cambridgeshire, 159

Canterbury, Kent, 81, 122, 203, 209
Capheaton, Northumberland, 162
Carlton Colville, Suffolk, 89, 268
carpentry, 71, 72
Castle Bytham, Lincolnshire, 219
Castle Eden, Durham, 160
Catholme, 74, 93
cauldron, 52, 61, 125, 126, 162, 164, 166
Ceolred, King of Mercia, 122
cereals, 37
chair, 80, 81
Chatteris, Cambridgeshire, 159
Chatti, 265, 266
Cheddar, Somerset, 72, 74, 93, 94, 95
cheese, 36, 37, 122, 123, 124
cherry, 119
Chilperic, King of the Franks, 120
Chilterns, 112
Christ & Satan, 23, 115, 224
Christmas, 59
cider, 129
clawbeaker, 12, 159, 161
Cnut, King, 23, 28, 143, 221
cob, 69
Cold Eaton, Derbyshire, 219
Colloquy on the Occupations, 130
Cologne, 119, 120, 144, 149
comitatus, 12, 13, 47, 84, 97, 98, 193, 223, 261, 263
community, 10, 17, 19, 20, 23, 29, 30, 31, 32, 33, 35, 36, 37, 38, 42, 46, 50, 54, 59, 60, 63, 64, 77, 98, 100, 101, 108, 114, 128, 129, 175, 182, 185, 186, 188, 190, 192, 193, 199, 200, 201, 202, 222, 223, 224, 231, 266
conebeaker, 12
consumption, 10, 32, 118, 119, 125
Coptic (bowls), 142, 145, 164, 204
Corbridge, 81
cots, 16, 69
Cotswolds, 112
County Durham, 160, 176, 203

Index

Cow Lowe, Derbyshire, 146
Croydon, Surrey, 142
Cumbria, 61, 143, 146, 272
cups, 36, 52, 98, 119, 120, 131, 136, 142, 143, 144, 146, 147, 150, 151, 153, 156, 184, 197
Cuthbert, abbot, 203
Cuthbert, St., 59, 176
cutlery, 10, 139
Cwichelm, King of Wessex, 25
cyn, 12, 106
Cynewulf, King, 24

Dal Riada, 60
dance, 191, 199, 204, 266
Danegeld, 28
Danes, 19, 23, 28, 33, 35, 36, 40, 50, 60, 85, 94, 102, 103, 105, 113, 190, 221, 233, 239, 251, 253
Daniel, 224
De Bello Gallico, 146
Deben, River, 16
Denmark, 68, 105, 111, 147, 148, 149, 175, 217, 221, 264, 265
Deor, 19, 53, 191, 194, 195
Derbyshire, 132, 146, 219
dice, 215, 216, 217, 220
Doon Hill, 98
door, 21, 71, 76, 87, 102, 103, 178, 198
door-keeper, 102, 198
doorway, 69, 91, 95, 103
Dorset, 61
dough, 124, 127
Dover, Kent, 144
dragon, 34, 36, 115, 120, 213
Dream of the Rood, 20, 35, 115, 212
drink, strong, 31, 32, 39, 54, 55, 56, 58, 60, 79, 85, 104, 110, 116, 117, 128, 129, 149, 262, 263, 266
drinking horns, 16, 40, 44, 47, 98, 116, 119, 143, 144, 147, 148, 149, 150, 151, 217, 218
drinks, 10, 17, 31, 32, 37, 39, 43, 44, 46, 47, 48, 50, 54, 55, 56, 58, 59, 60, 79, 80, 82, 85, 98, 101, 104, 110, 116, 117, 118, 121, 128, 129, 130, 143, 145, 149, 151, 152, 153, 154, 156, 161, 183, 186, 196, 198, 260, 262, 263, 266
duel, 54, 188, 189
duguð, 12, 39, 40, 41, 53, 100, 103
Dunstan, St., 203

Eadbald, King of Kent, 186
Eadgar, King, 95
Eadmund, King, 95
Eadred, King, 37, 59
Eadric Streona, 28
Eadwig, King, 95
ealdormann, 12, 21, 25, 28, 186, 221, 223, 243
Eanfrið, King of Bernicia, 60
East Anglia, 61, 89, 133, 134, 150, 186, 266
East Lothian, 98
Easter, 59
Edmund Ironside, 28
Edward the Confessor, 121, 124, 196
Edwin, King of Northumbria, 21, 25, 48, 92, 94, 182, 261
eggs, 36, 124, 213
Egils saga Skallagrímsonar, 82
Einherjar, 31, 264
embroidery, 86, 176, 178, 180
entertainers, 57, 199, 203, 204
escutcheons, 61, 142, 153, 162, 164, 204, 206
Essex, 11, 25, 28, 71, 74, 75, 76, 79, 88, 89, 96, 113, 132, 133, 136, 144, 148, 149, 152, 153, 221, 268, 269, 271, 272, 273
Ethelred the Unready, 28, 95
Exeter Book, 12, 185, 208, 209, 211, 212, 213, 223, 224, 269, 271, 273
Eyrbyggja Saga, 83

Færpingas, 112

Index

Farthingdown, Surrey, 144
Faversham, Kent, 143, 144
Fawler, Oxfordshire, 86
Feddersen Wierde, 70, 77
Fetcham, Surrey, 152
feud, 24, 36, 104, 108, 184, 187, 239
Finn, King of the Frisians, 23, 197, 200, 222, 251, 273
fish, 37, 125, 164, 166, 173, 210
Flixborough, Yorkshire, 140
floor, 17, 27, 40, 41, 69, 77, 83, 84, 86, 87, 90, 91, 94, 95, 96, 98, 105, 117, 128, 168, 170, 177, 251
flyting, 188, 189
Fonaby, Lincolnshire, 149, 269
footstool, 81
France, 68, 92, 147, 264
Franks Casket, 138
Freawaru, 41, 105, 184
Freyja, 31, 184
Frigg, 31, 184
frithstool, 4, 81
fruit, 37, 126, 127, 129, 141, 154, 172
frumstol, 12, 84
futhark, 12, 148
fyrd, 12, 29

gale, 129, 172
Gallehus, Denmark, 147, 217
Gambara, 259
Ganna, 259
Gautrekssaga, 216
Geat, 34, 40, 44, 63, 178, 197, 233, 239, 253
gebeoras, 56
gebeorscipe, 9, 32, 55, 56, 57, 58, 59, 204, 226, 228
gedriht, 12, 31, 103, 232, 260, 261
gegadorwiste, 20
Geirröðr, 31
Genesis, 34, 115, 224, 230, 231
geoguð, 12, 41, 43
Gerd, 115

Germania, 27, 50, 55, 99, 104, 108, 184, 196, 199, 259, 260, 261, 265, 266, 268, 272, 274
Germanic, 12, 17, 19, 27, 30, 34, 44, 48, 50, 51, 52, 54, 55, 60, 61, 62, 68, 69, 70, 71, 85, 88, 93, 96, 99, 104, 106, 108, 112, 113, 117, 128, 141, 144, 146, 147, 148, 150, 153, 154, 159, 164, 166, 167, 184, 185, 188, 191, 192, 193, 199, 200, 201, 206, 208, 209, 216, 219, 220, 223, 224, 259, 260, 261, 262, 263, 264, 265, 266, 267, 268, 269, 270, 271
Gesta Danorum, 105
giefstol (gift-stool), 12, 43, 46, 81, 84
gift-giving, 9, 32, 39, 51, 58, 99, 110
Gildas, 192
Glaðsheimr, 31
glassware, 52, 134, 136, 148, 149, 161
gleoman, 13, 190, 195
Gloucestershire, 167
Gnomic Verse, 213
Gododdin, 98
Goltho Manor, Leicestershire, 71, 97
Goths, 17, 32, 44, 45, 48, 54, 153, 220, 251, 253, 255, 259, 260, 261, 264, 270, 274
Gotland, 82, 166
gravemounds, 16
graves, 15, 32, 51, 52, 61, 72, 119, 120, 121, 122, 130, 132, 136, 139, 144, 145, 150, 152, 153, 154, 156, 159, 161, 162, 166, 167, 170, 171, 175, 182, 183, 204, 217, 218, 219
Greensted-juxta-Ongar, Essex, 75
Gregory of Tours, 120, 192
Gregory, Pope, 63

Index

Grendel, 22, 27, 34, 36, 43, 110, 113, 178, 184, 190, 197, 235, 238, 239
grið, 13, 108, 118
Grimstone End, Suffolk, 167
Grubenhaus *See* SFB, 13
Gudme, 70
guest, 23, 25, 27, 31, 33, 37, 42, 43, 45, 46, 48, 55, 61, 70, 82, 83, 85, 101, 102, 103, 110, 118, 120, 121, 130, 148, 149, 161, 162, 166, 184, 190, 193, 196, 197, 198, 214
guild, 48, 64
Guthlac, Saint, 29, 201

Hadstock, Essex, 76
Hákon, King of Norway, 45
hall-thane, 34, 181
Halstead, Essex, 113
Haltwistle, Northumberland, 113
Hampshire, 70, 74, 90, 92, 96, 139, 146, 269
Hamwic (Southampton), 30, 92, 138, 139
Harðacnut, King, 117
Harii, 265
Harlequin, 264
Harold, King, 40, 86, 146, 196
harp, 57, 58, 59, 111, 193, 194, 202, 203, 204, 206, 208, 217, 227, 241, 255
harrow, 113
Harrow, Middlesex, 113
Hávamál, 31, 42, 117, 118
HE (Historia Ecclesiastica Gentis Anglorum), 6, 13, 21, 57, 110, 167, 187, 226, 261
healðegn, 34
hearth, 51, 59, 63, 66, 77, 79, 82, 83, 90, 94, 96, 98, 121, 124, 125, 126, 127, 162, 243
Heiðrek, King, 210
Heimdall, 189
Hel, 31, 110

Hengest, 200, 273
Heorot, 5, 6, 33, 38, 40, 42, 59, 60, 72, 77, 101, 102, 110, 178, 190, 197, 198, 232, 239, 253
Hervarar Saga, 210
Hexham, Northumberland, 81, 146
Hicce, 112
high-seat, 54, 82, 83, 84, 103, 114, 115, 263
Hildeburh, 29, 184
hlafdige, 13
hlaford, 13, 25, 26, 53, 182, 191, 242
Hliðskjalfi, 115
hnefatafl, 220
Holywell, Suffolk, 149
horn, 38, 40, 42, 44, 46, 47, 48, 79, 111, 116, 123, 126, 128, 130, 132, 139, 140, 143, 144, 147, 148, 149, 150, 151, 177, 198, 210, 217, 218, 262, 264
hospitality, 25, 32, 37, 59, 101, 121, 184, 266

household, 12, 13, 42, 50, 71, 85, 91, 99, 100, 101, 115, 119, 126, 129, 130, 137, 154, 162, 168, 171, 176, 181, 183, 195, 196, 209, 255, 259, 262
householder, 31, 37, 83, 99, 103, 115, 118, 149, 182, 187
houses, 9, 13, 17, 21, 36, 40, 56, 57, 65, 66, 68, 69, 70, 71, 73, 77, 81, 83, 86, 88, 91, 95, 98, 108, 110, 113, 121, 162, 179, 197, 213, 227, 229
Hrafnkelssaga, 123
Hrólfr Kraki, 35
Hroþgar, King, 41, 100, 183, 186, 189, 233, 259
Hroþwulf, 35, 48, 252, 253
Hucbald, 206

Index

Hwætberht, Abbot of Wearmouth, 209
Hygd, 184, 186
Hygebald, Bishop of Lindisfarne, 192

Iceland, 31, 32, 34, 44, 48, 50, 68, 82, 83, 100, 117, 118, 123, 187, 188, 192, 200, 210, 216, 265
Ingeld, 35, 36, 38, 60, 105, 192, 199, 253
Ireland, 60, 208, 217, 220
Iron Age, 34, 50, 52, 68, 99, 148, 173, 259, 270, 271
Isle of Lewis, 218

Jarrow, 73, 80, 136, 137, 203
jewellery, 43, 71, 111, 132, 174, 175
joints, 76, 127, 180, 204, 206
Judith, 30, 224
Juliana, 201, 224
Julius Civilis, 187, 259, 260, 263

Kempston, Bedfordshire, 136, 161
Kent, 72, 122, 136, 140, 142, 143, 144, 149, 152, 154, 186, 187, 219, 270, 272
Kentish laws, 47
kinship, 22, 25, 43, 47, 77, 97, 106, 107, 108, 114, 189, 212, 251, 253, 261, 262, 266
Kvasir, 31, 111

La Tene (style), 52, 61, 162, 269
lady, 13, 29, 33, 41, 42, 43, 45, 46, 48, 50, 101, 105, 117, 146, 183, 184, 185, 186, 187, 196, 222, 233, 255, 261, 263
Larling, Norfolk, 138
Lastingham, Yorkshire, 80
laughter, 39, 208, 220, 233, 239
Laws of Alfred, 24
Leicestershire, 71, 138, 152, 162, 273
Leofric, Bishop, 208

Lex Salica, 260
Life of St Athelbert, 195
Life of St. Dunstan, 203
Life of St. Oswold, 56
lighting, 79
Lincolnshire, 97, 133, 134, 150, 152, 219, 269, 271
Lindisfarne Gospels, 60
linen, 5, 173, 176
Little Wilbraham, Suffolk, 149
loaves, 45, 122, 123, 124, 127, 182, 195
Lokasenna, 188, 189
Loki, 31, 188, 189
Lombard, 113, 148, 186, 251, 255
London, 30, 88, 137, 268, 269, 270, 271, 272, 273, 274
Long Wittenham, Berkshire, 152
lord, 12, 13, 20, 24, 25, 26, 28, 29, 33, 35, 40, 41, 42, 43, 44, 45, 46, 47, 53, 54, 63, 70, 81, 84, 85, 98, 103, 106, 112, 114, 115, 117, 181, 182, 183, 184, 186, 187, 190, 191, 192, 193, 194, 196, 212, 222, 223, 224, 233, 235, 239, 241, 243, 245, 249, 251, 255, 261, 262, 263, 264
Lord of the Rings, 9, 17
Louth, Lincolnshire, 152
Loveden Hill, Norfolk, 149, 152
lyre, 131, 164, 202, 203, 204, 206, 208

madder, 172
Maldon, Essex, 25, 26, 27, 28, 32, 55, 221, 272
manuscripts, 9, 12, 15, 86, 91, 95, 100, 112, 116, 125, 130, 170, 171, 172, 174, 175, 176, 184, 185, 196, 199, 203, 206, 208, 220, 222, 223, 224
maple, 119, 131, 144, 146, 150, 164, 204, 219
Masham, North Yorkshire, 208
Mästermyr, 72

Masyos, King of the Semnones, 259
Maxims, 17, 183, 185, 213
mead, 9, 10, 15, 26, 27, 30, 31, 32, 33, 36, 41, 42, 47, 48, 50, 55, 85, 98, 101, 111, 116, 128, 129, 183, 194, 196, 203, 233, 239, 241, 243, 255
mead-bench, 33, 85
mead-cup, 42, 48, 196, 233
mead-hall, 9, 10, 15, 26, 30, 31, 32, 33, 36, 47, 101, 116, 183, 194, 203
meals, 9, 10, 13, 36, 37, 42, 44, 45, 48, 57, 58, 59, 60, 62, 98, 120, 124, 127, 177, 196, 198, 260, 263
meat pudding, 37
meat, salted, 37
meat, stewed, 37
meats, 31, 37, 45, 48, 79, 123, 125, 126, 127, 139, 173
Mediterranean, 17, 52, 129, 133, 136, 140, 142, 144, 148, 172, 261
Meduseld, 9, 17
Mercia, 28, 55, 92, 98, 122, 274
meteðegn, 195
Meters of Boethius, 209
Middlesex, 113
Modþryþ, 184
Monkwearmouth, Northumberland, 80, 203
Morayshire, 151
Morningthorpe, Norfolk, 151, 204, 270
Mucking, Essex, 68, 71, 74, 77, 88, 92, 132, 133, 152, 159, 268, 269, 271
music, 37, 39, 40, 57, 59, 194, 202, 203, 204

Namur, Belgium, 148
Nassington, Northamptonshire, 153
Nennius, 60
noblewomen, 41, 119, 184, 186
Norfolk, 80, 138, 149, 152, 204, 218, 270

North Elmham, Norfolk, 124, 271
North Luffenham, Rutland, 152
North Sea, 17, 68, 130, 219, 271
Northampton, 74, 94, 95, 134, 273
Northamptonshire, 74, 97, 153
Northumberland, 70, 74, 80, 81, 85, 92, 93, 94, 100, 113, 136, 146, 162
Northumbria, 21, 25, 28, 60, 92, 98, 182, 209, 261, 270, 271
Norway, 45, 48, 83, 111, 119, 141, 148, 171, 217
Nydam, Denmark, 149

oath, 46, 47, 55, 60, 86, 102, 106, 107, 108, 110, 114, 150, 187, 247, 263
Óðinn (Odin), 31, 110, 113, 261, 264
Offa, 26, 185, 195, 223, 242, 243, 252, 253
Old English Rune Poem, 220, 270
Old Erringham, Sussex, 168
ombeht, 13, 43
Oseberg, 119, 168
Oswiu, King of Northumbria, 60
Oswold, King of Northumbria, 55
Oxfordshire, 37, 86, 88, 133, 217

Paulus Diaconus, 259
pear, 119, 123
Penda, King of Mercia, 55, 92
Peterborough, 265
Picts, 60
pillar-harp, 203, 206
Poetic Edda, 210
pole-lathe, 131, 141, 146, 219
poplar, 119
Portchester Castle, Hampshire, 96
pottery, 65, 80, 85, 90, 92, 98, 133, 134, 144, 219

querns, 72, 123

Rainham, Essex, 148, 153, 269

Index

Raunds, 74, 97
reeve, 121, 181, 229
Regularis Concordia, 46
Rhiainfellt, Princess of Rheged, 60
Rhineland, 136, 148
riddles, 17, 30, 192, 208, 209, 210, 211, 212, 213
ritual, 9, 10, 13, 31, 33, 35, 39, 42, 46, 47, 48, 52, 54, 58, 59, 62, 63, 77, 83, 93, 99, 100, 105, 108, 110, 113, 114, 115, 117, 129, 150, 161, 162, 183, 188, 190, 191, 198, 201, 216, 259, 261, 262, 266
Roman, 30, 50, 52, 61, 70, 71, 73, 81, 85, 86, 88, 89, 93, 94, 96, 97, 111, 115, 120, 134, 136, 137, 140, 147, 148, 154, 159, 161, 172, 173, 174, 175, 182, 200, 206, 209, 216, 217, 219, 224, 259, 260, 268, 269, 273
Roundway Down, Wiltshire, 152
Rutland, 152
Saltwood, Kent, 142
Salzburg, Austria, 176
Sarre, Kent, 72, 219, 269
sausage, 37
Saxo Grammaticus, 35, 105, 200
Saxo-Norman, 13, 76
scop, 13, 19, 20, 27, 33, 34, 39, 40, 55, 101, 190, 191, 192, 193, 194, 203, 206, 208
Scyld Scefing, 200
seating, 43, 54, 75, 80, 82, 83, 85, 115, 260
Semnones, 259
Sermo Lupi ad Anglos, 29, 273
Sevington, Hampshire, 139
SFB, 13, 65, 66, 69, 77, 88, 89, 90, 93, 108, 110, 167, 168
Shaftesbury, 143, 270
Shetland, 141
Sibertswold, Kent, 144
Skáldskaparmál, 31
Snoldelev, Denmark, 148
Snorri Sturluson, 32
Solomon and Saturn, 209, 210
Somerset, 69, 74, 93, 136, 266, 268
Sompting, Sussex, 75
song, 19, 34, 53, 59, 62, 110, 115, 116, 178, 191, 192, 194, 195, 201, 202, 203, 214, 227, 228, 229, 230, 231, 247, 253, 254, 255, 257, 261
Souldern, Oxforshire, 152
South Cadbury, Dorset, 61
Southampton, Hampshire, 30, 92, 137, 138, 139
speeches, 27, 32, 39, 58, 98, 184, 223
speech-making, 32, 39
Spong Hill, Norfolk, 80, 152, 271
Springfield Lyons, Essex, 74
St. Gall, Switzerland, 95
Staffordshire, 74, 93
Stamford, 134, 265
standard, 36, 37, 55, 71, 73, 74, 77, 79, 84, 87, 90, 96, 106, 121, 127, 138, 141, 162, 175, 182, 216, 220, 261
Starkaðr, 105
steward, 39, 126, 181, 195, 197
story-telling, 192, 201
strainer, 52, 154, 156
Strood, Kent, 149, 273
Sudbury, Suffolk, 145
Suffolk, 16, 74, 89, 133, 139, 145, 149, 167, 218, 273
Surrey, 142, 144, 152, 271
Sussex, 40, 74, 75, 87, 90, 168, 177
Sutton Courtenay, Oxfordshire, 88, 133
Sutton Hoo, 10, 15, 16, 51, 61, 72, 79, 115, 119, 125, 131, 133, 140, 141, 142, 143, 144, 146, 149, 150, 151, 153, 164, 166, 170, 173, 175, 180, 182, 202, 203, 204, 206, 208, 218, 219, 266, 268, 269, 272, 273
Suttungr, 31

Swallowcliffe, Wiltshire, 80, 140, 142, 146, 152, 273
Sweden, 72, 111, 148, 149, 184, 266
Swindon, Wiltshire, 167
symbel, 9, 13, 32, 38, 39, 42, 43, 44, 45, 46, 47, 48, 50, 53, 55, 56, 57, 58, 59, 149, 181, 182, 195, 198, 232, 236

table, 31, 35, 37, 64, 73, 80, 82, 85, 86, 125, 126, 139, 141, 151, 153, 161, 177, 178, 180, 196
table covering, 177
tableware, 10, 15, 61, 119, 120, 121, 130, 133, 141
Tacitus, 27, 50, 55, 85, 99, 104, 108, 117, 184, 196, 199, 200, 201, 216, 259, 260, 261, 262, 263, 265, 266, 272
tacnbora, 261
Talorcan, King of the Picts, 60
Taplow, 10, 15, 51, 119, 142, 144, 145, 149, 150, 151, 166, 170, 206, 217
Tatwine, archbishop of Canterbury, 209
textiles, 10, 83, 142, 143, 150, 167, 168, 170, 171, 173, 178, 180, 218
Thames, River, 16, 88, 127, 148
The Battle of Brunanburh, 195, 223
The Battle of Maldon, 6, 25, 26, 28, 32, 55, 100, 125, 221, 223, 242, 270, 272, 274
The Capture of the Five Boroughs, 223
The Dream of the Rood, 20, 35, 115, 212
The Fight at Finnsburh, 85, 222
The Fortunes of Men, 6, 128, 193, 194, 225, 240
The Husband's Message, 17, 20, 224
The Rhyming Poem, 182
The Ruin, 32, 36, 76, 178, 224
The Seafarer, 6, 19, 20, 224, 240

The Wanderer, 6, 20, 35, 54, 55, 201, 224, 244, 271
The Wife's Lament, 17, 20, 185, 224
Thetford, Norfolk, 134, 137
Thirlings, 74
threshold, 69, 262
Thurmaston, Leicestershire, 137, 138, 273
Tolkien, 9, 17, 23, 86, 273
tools, 72, 91, 111, 130, 132, 139, 167, 180
Torslunda, Sweden, 266
treachery, 23, 25, 35
trennels, 72
Tribal Hidage,, 112
Twyford, Leicestershire, 152

þegn, 13, 39, 40, 97, 104, 181, 196
Þeoderic the Ostrogoth, 23
þing, 13, 99
Þórolfr Mostrarskegg, 83
Þórr (Thor), 31, 48, 83, 113
Þrymr, 31
þyle, 13, 27, 42, 45, 188, 190, 250

Unferþ, 6, 40, 188, 189, 234, 235, 269
Uppsala, 45, 268, 271

Vafþruðnismál, 210
Vainglory, 6, 189, 224, 240
Valhalla, 31
Valhöll (Valhalla), 31, 118
válkyrjar (valkyries), 31, 184
Valsgärde, Sweden, 149, 150
Vanir, 106, 108, 110
Vaucluse, France, 147
vegetables, 37, 79, 123, 124, 125, 127, 128, 130, 134, 172, 173, 211
Veleda, 184, 259, 260
verse, 9, 12, 16, 17, 19, 20, 29, 30, 31, 32, 33, 34, 36, 55, 56, 57, 98, 104, 115, 147, 185, 192, 193, 195, 200, 201, 202, 204, 208,

Index

209, 210, 213, 220, 221, 222, 223, 224, 225, 227, 229, 231
Vespasian Psalter, 203
Vikings, 25, 28, 29, 66, 72, 76, 96, 143, 174, 176, 196, 216, 217, 220, 221, 223, 253, 269, 270, 271
Vorbasse, 68
vows, 27, 39, 235

wallhangings, 176
walls, 22, 63, 65, 69, 73, 76, 77, 80, 81, 87, 90, 91, 92, 94, 95, 96, 97, 100, 126, 144, 153, 159, 160, 161, 164, 166, 170, 176, 178, 179, 237, 247, 249
walnut, 119
Waluburg, 259
warband, 13, 19, 24, 26, 28, 36, 41, 42, 60, 84, 85, 86, 98, 103, 106, 108, 110, 186, 187, 190, 192, 193, 201, 216, 223, 224, 259, 260, 261, 262, 263
watermills, 124
Wealhþeow, 41, 48, 116, 117, 183, 184, 186, 232, 233, 238, 239, 259
wedding, 59, 60, 104, 117, 260, 261, 262
weld, 172
Welsh ale, 129
wergild, 24
werod, 13
West Stow, 74, 77, 89, 92, 133, 173
wheat, 123
wheatmeal, 124
Whitby, Yorkshire, 121, 134, 164, 272
Wicken Bonhunt, Essex, 74, 96, 273
Widsið, 14, 38, 53, 60, 192, 193, 194, 195, 223, 250, 251, 269
Wijster, 68, 70
Wild Hunt, 264
Wilfrid, St., 81
William of Malmesbury, 209
willow, 119

Wiltshire, 80, 87, 94, 97, 140, 142, 146, 152, 167
Winchester ware, 134, 138
Winchester, Hampshire, 59, 134, 138, 143
wine, 24, 34, 52, 59, 85, 98, 102, 104, 116, 117, 127, 128, 129, 130, 154, 178, 234, 240, 241, 247, 255, 263
woad, 172
Woden, 188, 261
Wollaston, Leicestershire, 115, 162
Worcester, 121
Wulf & Eadwacer, 185
Wulfgar, 102, 103, 198
Wulfstan, 29, 59, 222
Wynflæd, 119, 272

yard, 75
Yeavering, 72, 73, 74, 75, 85, 87, 92, 93, 94, 100, 122, 182, 271
York, 134, 136, 137, 203, 271
Yorkshire, 80, 81, 164, 208

Some of our titles

The English Warrior from earliest times to 1066
Stephen Pollington

This is not intended to be a bald listing of the battles and campaigns from the Anglo-Saxon Chronicle and other sources, but rather it is an attempt to get below the surface of Anglo-Saxon warriorhood and to investigate the rites, social attitudes, mentality and mythology of the warfare of those times.

> "An under-the-skin study of the role, rights, duties, psyche and rituals of the Anglo-Saxon warrior. The author combines original translations from Norse and Old English primary sources with archaeological and linguistic evidence for an in-depth look at the warrior, his weapons, tactics and logistics.
>
> A very refreshing, innovative and well-written piece of scholarship that illuminates a neglected period of English history"
>
> *Time Team Booklists* - Channel 4 Television

Revised Edition

An already highly acclaimed book has been made even better by the inclusion of additional information and illustrations.

£14.95 ISBN 1–898281–27–0   9½" x 6¾"/245 x 170mm   over 50 illustrations   288 pages

A Handbook of Anglo-Saxon Food: Processing and Consumption
Ann Hagen

For the first time information from various sources has been brought together in order to build up a picture of how food was grown, conserved, prepared and eaten during the period from the beginning of the 5th century to the 11th century. Many people will find it fascinating for the views it gives of an important aspect of Anglo-Saxon life and culture. In addition to Anglo-Saxon England the Celtic west of Britain is also covered. Now with an extensive index.

£9-95 A5 ISBN 0–9516209–8–3 192pp

A Second Handbook of Anglo-Saxon Food & Drink
Production and Distribution

Ann Hagen

Food production for home consumption was the basis of economic activity throughout the Anglo-Saxon period. This second handbook complements the first and brings together a vast amount of information on livestock, cereal and vegetable crops, fish, honey and fermented drinks. Related subjects such as hospitality, charity and drunkenness are also dealt with. Extensive index.

£14.95 A5 ISBN 1–898281–12–2 432pp

Anglo-Saxon Runes

John. M. Kemble

Kemble's essay *On Anglo-Saxon Runes* first appeared in the journal *Archaeologia* for 1840; it draws on the work of Wilhelm Grimm, but breaks new ground for Anglo-Saxon studies in his survey of the Ruthwell Cross and the Cynewulf poems. It is an expression both of his own indomitable spirit and of the fascination and mystery of the Runes themselves, making one of the most attractive introductions to the topic. For this edition new notes have been supplied, which include translations of Latin and Old English material quoted in the text, to make this key work in the study of runes more accessible to the general reader.

£4·95   A5   ISBN 0–9516209–1–6   80pp

Looking for the Lost Gods of England

Kathleen Herbert

Kathleen Herbert sifts through the royal genealogies, charms, verse and other sources to find clues to the names and attributes of the Gods and Goddesses of the early English. The earliest account of English heathen practices reveals that they worshipped the Earth Mother and called her Nerthus. The tales, beliefs and traditions of that time are still with us in, for example, Sand able to stir our minds and imaginations.

£4·95   A5   ISBN 1–898281–04–1   64pp

Rudiments of Runelore

Stephen Pollington

This book provides both a comprehensive introduction for those coming to the subject for the first time, and a handy and inexpensive reference work for those with some knowledge of the subject. The *Abecedarium Nordmannicum* and the English, Norwegian and Icelandic rune poems are included in their original and translated form. Also included is work on the three Brandon runic inscriptions and the Norfolk 'Tiw' runes.

£4.95   A5   ISBN 1–898281–16–5   Illustrations   88pp

Anglo-Saxon Riddles

Translated by John Porter

Here you will find ingenious characters who speak their names in riddles, and meet a one-eyed garlic seller, a bookworm, an iceberg, an oyster, the sun and moon and a host of others from the everyday life and imagination of the Anglo-Saxons. Their sense of the awesome power of creation goes hand in hand with a frank delight in obscenity, a fascination with disguise and with the mysterious processes by which the natural world is turned to human use.   This edition contains **all 95 riddles of the Exeter Book in both Old English and Modern English.**

£4·95   A5   ISBN 1–898281–13–0   144pp

Tastes of Anglo-Saxon England
Mary Savelli

These easy to follow recipes will enable you to enjoy a mix of ingredients and flavours that were widely known in Anglo-Saxon England but are rarely experienced today. In addition to the 46 recipes, there is background information about households and cooking techniques.

£4.95   ISBN 1-898281-28-9   A5   80 pages

Aspects of Anglo-Saxon Magic
Bill Griffiths

Magic is something special, something unauthorised; an alternative perhaps; even a deliberate cultivation of dark, evil powers. But for the Anglo-Saxon age, the neat division between mainstream and occult, rational and superstitious, Christian and pagan is not always easy to discern. To maintain its authority (or its monopoly?) the Church drew a formal line and outlawed a range of dubious practices (like divination, spells, folk healing) while at the same time conducting very similar rituals itself, and may even have adapted legends of elves to serve in a Christian explanation of disease as a battle between good and evil, between Church and demons; in other cases powerful ancestors came to serve as saints.

In pursuit of a better understanding of Anglo-Saxon magic, a wide range of topics and texts are examined in this book, challenging (constructively, it is hoped) our stereotyped images of the past and its beliefs.

Texts are printed in their original language (e.g. Old English, Icelandic, Latin) with New English translations. Contents include: – twenty charms; the English, Icelandic and Norwegian rune poems; texts on dreams, weather signs, unlucky days, the solar system; and much more.

£14· 95. ISBN 1–898281–33-5   250mm x 175mm   10" x 7"   272pp   hardback

Anglo-Saxon Books
Frithgarth, Thetford Forest Park, Hockwold-cum-Wilton, Norfolk IP26 4NQ
Tel: 01842 828430   Fax: 01842 828332   email: enq@asbooks.co.uk
Further details of titles are available on our web site at www.asbooks.co.uk

Payment may be made by Visa / Mastercard or by a cheque drawn on a UK bank in sterling.

If you are paying by cheque please make it payable to Anglo-Saxon Books and enclose it with your order. When ordering by post please write clearly.

UK deliveries add 10% up to a maximum of £2· 50

Europe – including **Republic of Ireland** – add 10% plus £1 – all orders are sent airmail

North America add 10% surface delivery, 30% airmail

Elsewhere add 10% surface delivery, 40% airmail

Overseas surface delivery 6 – 10 weeks; airmail 6 – 14 days

Most titles are available in North America from bookstores.

Organisations

Þa Engliscan Gesiðas

Þa Engliscan Gesiðas (The English Companions) is a historical and cultural society exclusively devoted to Anglo-Saxon history. Its aims are to bridge the gap between scholars and non-experts, and to bring together all those with an interest in the Anglo-Saxon period, its language, culture and traditions, so as to promote a wider interest in, and knowledge of all things Anglo-Saxon. The Fellowship publishes a journal, *Wiðowinde,* which helps members to keep in touch with current thinking on topics from art and archaeology to heathenism and Early English Christianity. The Fellowship enables like-minded people to keep in contact by publicising conferences, courses and meetings which might be of interest to its members.

For further details see www.kami.demon.co.uk/gesithas/ or write to: The Membership Secretary, Þa Engliscan Gesiðas, BM Box 4336, London, WC1N 3XX England.

Regia Anglorum

Regia Anglorum was founded to accurately re-create the life of the British people as it was around the time of the Norman Conquest. Our work has a strong educational slant. We consider authenticity to be of prime importance and prefer, where possible, to work from archaeological materials. Approximately twenty-five per cent of our members, of over 500 people, are archaeologists or historians.

The Society has a large working Living History Exhibit, teaching and exhibiting more than twenty crafts in an authentic environment. We own a forty-foot wooden ship replica of a type that would have been a common sight in Northern European waters around the turn of the first millennium AD. Battle re-enactment is another aspect of our activities, often involving 200 or more warriors.

For further information see www.regia.org or contact: K. J. Siddorn, 9 Durleigh Close, Headley Park, Bristol BS13 7NQ, England, e-mail: kim_siddorn@compuserve.com

The Sutton Hoo Society

Our aims and objectives focus on promoting research and education relating to the Anglo Saxon Royal cemetery at Sutton Hoo, Suffolk in the UK. The Society publishes a newsletter SAXON twice a year, which keeps members up to date with society activities, carries resumes of lectures and visits, and reports progress on research and publication associated with the site. If you would like to join the Society please write to:

Membership Secretary, Sutton Hoo Society,
258 The Pastures, High Wycombe, Buckinghamshire HP13 5RS England
website: www.suttonhoo.org

Wuffing Education

Wuffing Education provides those interested in the history, archaeology, literature and culture of the Anglo-Saxons with the chance to meet experts and fellow enthusiasts for a whole day of in-depth seminars and discussions. Day Schools take place at the historic Tranmer House overlooking the burial mounds of Sutton Hoo in Suffolk.

For details of programme of events contact:-
Wuffing Education, 4 Hilly Fields, Woodbridge, Suffolk IP12 4DX
email education@wuffings.co.uk   website www.wuffings.co.uk
Tel. 01394 383908 or 01728 688749

Places to visit

Bede's World at Jarrow

Bede's world tells the remarkable story of the life and times of the Venerable Bede, 673–735 AD. Visitors can explore the origins of early medieval Northumbria and Bede's life and achievements through his own writings and the excavations of the monasteries at Jarrow and other sites.

Location – 10 miles from Newcastle upon Tyne, off the A19 near the southern entrance to the River Tyne tunnel. Bus services 526 & 527

Bede's World, Church Bank, Jarrow, Tyne and Wear, NE32 3DY

Tel. 0191 489 2106; Fax: 0191 428 2361; website: www.bedesworld.co.uk

Sutton Hoo near Woodbridge, Suffolk

Sutton Hoo is a group of low burial mounds overlooking the River Deben in south-east Suffolk. Excavations in 1939 brought to light the richest burial ever discovered in Britain – an Anglo-Saxon ship containing a magnificent treasure which has become one of the principal attractions of the British Museum. The mound from which the treasure was dug is thought to be the grave of Rædwald, an early English king who died in 624/5 AD.

This National Trust site has an excellent visitor centre, which includes a reconstruction of the burial chamber and its grave goods. Some original objects as well as replicas of the treasure are on display.

2 miles east of Woodbridge on B1083   Tel. 01394 389700

West Stow Anglo-Saxon Village

An early Anglo-Saxon Settlement reconstructed on the site where it was excavated consisting of timber and thatch hall, houses and workshop. There is also a museum containing objects found during the excavation of the site. Open all year 10am–4.15pm (except Yuletide). Special provision for school parties. A teachers' resource pack is available. Costumed events are held at weekends, especially Easter Sunday and August Bank Holiday Monday. Craft courses are organised.

For further details see www.stedmunds.co.uk/west_stow.html or contact:

The Visitor Centre, West Stow Country Park, Icklingham Road, West Stow,

Bury St Edmunds, Suffolk IP28 6HG   Tel. 01284 728718